India's 'Amrit Kaal' march with
A Broken Economy

India's 'Amrit Kaal' march with
A Broken Economy

Prasanna Mohanty

BLACK EAGLE BOOKS
Dublin, USA | Bhubaneswar, India

Black Eagle Books
USA address:
7464 Wisdom Lane
Dublin, OH 43016

India address:
E/312, Trident Galaxy, Kalinga Nagar,
Bhubaneswar-751003, Odisha, India

E-mail: info@blackeaglebooks.org
Website: www.blackeaglebooks.org

First International Edition Published by
Black Eagle Books, 2024

**INDIA'S 'AMRIT KAAL' MARCH WITH
A BROKEN ECONOMY**
by **Prasanna Mohanty**

Copyright © Prasanna Mohanty

All rights reserved. No part of this publication may be reproduced, stored in a retrieval system, or transmitted, in any form or by any means, electronic, mechanical, photocopying, recording or otherwise without the prior permission of the publisher.

Cover & Interior Design: Ezy's Publication

ISBN- 978-1-64560-551-5 (Paperback)
Library of Congress Control Number: 2024938484

Printed in the United States of America

CONTENT

	Page
• Preface	9
• Introduction	11
• Electoral Bond: Mother of all Systemic Corruptions?	28
• Why India needs a 2024 poverty line	37
• Making sense of sluggish private corporate capex	46
• What will 'Viksit Bharat' in 2047 look like?	54
• Is it unfair for farmers to demand a guaranteed higher price?	62
• Can India be a 'developed nation' without quality jobs?	71
• Anything that can go wrong may have gone wrong with IBC	79
• Rethinking disinvestment or temporarily stalled?	88
• Decadal growth II: What will drive higher growth?	95
• Decadal growth I: Momentum is shifting and growth more K-shaped	103
• Short selling: What SEBI changed; who will take onus for any mishap?	112
• 2024 Ahoy! Why RBI must focus on big threats to fiscal health	118
• COP28: What India gained and lost in fight against climate crisis	125
• 2024 Ahoy! Will electoral freebies throw fiscal deficit into disarray?	135
• NBFCs add risk to slowing economy	143
• What will deliver 'strong' growth in FY24?	150
• GDP growth: Headwinds in financial assets, tax filings hurt average Indian	160
• 5 ways to resolve the unfinished agenda of freebies	169
• What is hurting India's exports engine	177
• Chandrayaan-3: 'Make in India's' moment of reckoning	184
• Data war on India lifting 135-140 million out of poverty	192
• Is India back to 'license raj'?	200

- DPDP Bill 2023: Question mark on privacy,
  more power to govt — 207
- NPAs: RBI must name and shame fraudsters, willful defaulters — 215
- 2 Chinese roadblocks to India's semiconductor ambition — 221
- Dharavi: Challenges of rebuilding economically viable cities — 228
- Paying for Russian oil in Yuan will hurt globalisation of Rupee — 235
- Are top banks getting their economics wrong? — 241
- It's time to measure the impact of PLI, DLI schemes — 249
- West is vigilant about predatory pricing, India not — 256
- The flip-side of RBI's "compromise settlement"
  formula for stressed asset — 263
- Is protectionism helping or harming India's exports? — 269
- To ban or not to ban auditors for corporate frauds — 278
- Pricing Power Behind High Inflation? — 284
- Future of Indian trade is in services exports — 291
- Credit Suisse, Yes Bank legacy: Tense future for AT1 bonds — 298
- National champions: Costs and benefits of India's new growth model — 306
- Why are Globally Systemically Important Banks
  like Credit Suisse failing? — 311
- Why Hindenburg report, short-selling are a blessing in disguise — 319
- Games shell companies and tax havens play — 327
- States' fiscal space rapidly shrinking, here's why... — 334
- Budget 2023: Why India needs a jobs policy — 341
- Why demonetisation verdict raises more questions than answers — 348
- Budget 2023: What gives China immunity from
  extreme poverty, but not India? — 354
- US, Europe lessons for gig economy law — 361
- GM mustard: Where is data on biosafety and higher yield? — 367
- COP27: Fighting climate crisis against carbon billionaires — 377
- What caused inequality to rise in India during pandemic? — 384
- Dolo-650 bribery allegation: Why pharma cos need tight monitoring — 392
- Did corporate tax cut of 2019 lead to tax, GDP boom? — 400
- The wheels-within-wheels in central govt vacancies — 408

- A house of cards that is EWS quota 415
- Global talk of taxing the rich has little appeal in India 421
- Welcome to 'stressed' PPP projects, the 2nd time round 427
- Apex court's FCRA order a big blow to NGOs, grassroot development work 433
- Fewer Rafale jets leave gaps in national security 442
- Why MGNREGS wages are below the statutory minimum 449
- Why do employed youth hanker after government jobs? 458
- Why high GST collection is bad taxation and bad economics 465
- Index 470

Preface

Before the next government takes charge in New Delhi in June 2024, this collection of articles is intended to provide the harsh ground realities of the economy with the hope that some corrective measures would be taken. The articles start *after* Prime Minister Narendra Modi declared that India had entered into "Amrit Kaal", in 2021, and was marching towards "Viksit Bharat @2047", in 2022. While nobody knows what "Amrit Kaal" stands for, the vision, goals and roadmaps for "Viksit Bharat @2047" are likely to be spelt out in the first 100 days *after* the new government takes charge, assuming as does the Modi government that its mandate would be renewed for a straight third term.

These articles pierce through the fog of incessant rhetoric of *a glorious dawn and a glorious future* – using both official statistics and other credible evidence. They seek to answer many unanswered questions and unravel mysteries behind policies and practices, covering a wide spectrum – from statistical system to growth, employment, gig economy, poverty, hunger, inequality, household finances, agriculture, industry, services, trade, private capex, corporate governance, banking, insolvency and bankruptcy code, privatisation, stock market, taxation, environmental governance, genetically modified (GM) food, freebies/welfarism, caste, data privacy etc. Some also track global economic developments.

Except for the one on the *Electoral Bond*, all other articles were published in *Fortune India* – mostly in digital and a few in print – between *December 2021 and March 2024*. Given that these are standalone articles, some repetitions are inescapable. At the end of a few, updates and contexts have been added to bring the lay readers up to speed.

This is continuation of my earlier books, "An Unkept Promise: What Derailed the Indian Economy" (SAGE Publications, December 2021) and "Attack on the Idea of India: A Decade of Social, Political and Economic Strife" (Black Eagle Books, December 2023).

April 2024   **Prasanna Mohanty**

***

Introduction

The fundamentals of Indian economy are broken. Trust in the official claims of "Amrit Kaal", "Kartavya Kaal", "Viksit Bharat @2047", "Modi's guarantee", "Ram Rajya" and "Vishnu ka Sushasan" at your peril.

That is because the headline numbers of official statistics don't provide real picture of the economy or the people. These are mostly misleading – the 2011-12 GDP series *overestimates* growth significantly; the PLFS reports show "paradoxical improvements" in employment and NITI Aayog's claims of significant reduction in poverty, hunger and income inequality are *statistical constructs* in absence of real data. Then there are critical data vacuum – no signs of the Census of 2021 even in 2024; the Economic Census, Unorganized Sector Statistics and Un-incorporated Enterprises Survey are too old and irrelevant, particularly after severe damages to informal economy constituting 50% of the GDP, which were caused by multiple economic shocks since 2016. The base years for CPI, WPI, IIP are a decade old and poverty line estimates go back to 2004-05. There isn't any sign of the Civil Registration System (CRS) data for 2021 to even know *excess deaths* during the far more devastating second wave of the pandemic in 2021 – when the WHO said India *missed 90% of the pandemic deaths*.

This appalling state of official data is not accidental, given that India *pioneered* collecting such data in the early decades of Independence. The vacuum and gaps are intended to hide reality and parade falsehood.

Yet, there are *adequate evidence* within the very official statistics and credible international reports/assessments to point to the broken state of economy – the GDP is surely growing bigger but the average Indian is not prospering. It must always be kept in mind that economy is not just about its size (GDP) but people's *quality of living*.

Here are *seven key facts* to keep in mind.

1. **Growing poverty**

Officially, "free" ration is being given to 67% of the total population. It started in April 2020 as the pandemic hit and the entire nation was locked down in a 24x7 curfew with four hours' notice – in addition to "subsidized" ration of equal amount to equal number of people that the National Food Security Act (NFSA) of 2013 mandates. It would now run till December 31, 2028 – that is for *nine straight years*. Ironically, that is a "Modi's guarantee" for his third term. But this is also the surest sign, and *official admission*, of poverty and hunger stalking India like never before. There is no guarantee where India will end up in 2029 (next five-year) or in 2047 if the current economic growth model endures.

If more evidence is needed, here is another. A Harvard study, published in the JAMA Network Open in February 2024, said India "accounted for almost half of *zero-food children*" among 92 low- and medium-income countries *during 2010-2022* (over a decade). It found India had 19.3% (or 6.7 million) children of 6-23 months who "did not consume animal milk, formula, or solid or semisolid food during the last 24 hours". India *refuted* this, as it does to every adverse finding, by saying that the study *excluded* breast-milk feeding. The study duly noted that going by the WHO's assessment, "after age 6 months, breast milk alone is insufficient to meet the growing nutritional requirements of infants and young children".

2. Growing hunger

India's progress in the Global Hunger Index (GHI) *reversed* between 2014-2022. Its rank slipped from 80 in 2015 to 111th in 2023. With a GHI score of 28.5 in 2023, India is *far worse* in hunger score than known poor countries like Rwanda, Nepal, Pakistan, Myanmar and Bangladesh. If doubts creep in, revisit point no. 1.

3. Household finances hit 50-year low

Household financial assets fell to *47-year low* of 5.1% of the GDP but household debts went up to 5.8% of the GDP in FY23. Tax filings (ITR) show those declaring *taxable income* fell by 54% in seven years between FY16 and FY23. *Paradoxically*, stock markets are booming with a sharp rise in demat accounts – crossed 150 million-mark in March 2024 – pointing to growing faith in speculative trading. Stock markets are *disconnected* from real economy everywhere in the world and have been historically likened to gambling dens or casinos.

4. Chronic job crisis intensifies

Official PLFS reports of 2017-18 to 2022-23 show progressive improvements in the headline numbers – employment rate (WPR), labour participation rate (LFPR and FLFP) and unemployment rate (UR). This happened *paradoxically* amidst intense economic shocks of the demonetisation of 2016, the GST of 2017 and the pandemic of 2020 and 2021. Nonetheless, the fine prints of these PLFS reports also show intensification of the chronic job crisis: Workers continue to flee to low-paying informal agriculture (45.8%); more than half the workforce (57.3%) are in precarious "self-employment" and 18.3% are unpaid ("household helpers"), mostly women. The ILO-IHD's March 2024 report, which uses the PLFS and other official (Indian) data, found *82.9%* of the unemployed Indians are youths in the age-group of 15-29.

While releasing this report, Chief Economic Advisor V Anantha Nageswaran said it was wrong to assume that the government could solve all social and economic problems, including unemployment, "short of hiring more itself". Truth is millions of job creation was one of the main planks of Modi and his Bharatiya Janata Party (BJP) in the run-up to the 2014 elections and later. It is also the job of elected governments – which this government has failed to do; filling only a small fraction in a decade. It doesn't even have estimates of the vacancies or how many it filled.

This decade is a *job-loss growth* one – after a *job-less growth* of the previous decade. The *unifocal* push to GDP growth, with particular incentives for manufacturing, has demonstrably *failed for decades*. This approach will continue to fail as high-tech and capital-intensive manufacturing sheds more jobs. Good quality jobs, "regular wages/salaried", continue to fall (20.9% in 2022-23 as per the PLFS), of which more than half (53.9%) have no social security cover at all. 'Real' wages consistently fell for all categories of workers, except 'causal'.

Thus, despite the "paradoxical improvement" (coinciding with the periods of economic distress) in the headline numbers, the employment rate (WPR) of India is awfully low at *38%* and labour participation rate (LFPR) at 40% in 2022-23 (PLFS). Here, the data pertains to "all ages" in "current weekly status" (CWS). The numbers are marginally better in "usual status". "All ages" is taken here because unlike developed countries India has no retirement age (at least not for 93.2% workers engaged in non-government jobs; even 6.8% jobs in the government sector are filled with retired employees on contracts with lower wages). Besides, child labour is ubiquitous. CWS is the matrix used by developed countries. In sharp contrast, the OECD average for WPR and LFPR is 70% or above (among "working age" group of 15-64 in CWS status).

Now, a WPR of 38% or LFPR of 40% point to 60% or more Indians *sitting idle* at home because there are simply no jobs! What does this mean for India's 'demographic dividend'? It has already turned into a *'demographic disaster'* because: (i) 82.9% unemployed are youths (ii) total fertility rate (TFR) dropped *below the replacement fertility rate of 2.1* in 2021 to *1.9* and expected to drop to 1.29 by 2050 (Lancet, March 2024) and (iii) working-age population will decline by 57% during 2031-41 (Economic Survey 2018-19). India's demographic dividend is over *here and now*.

Now add another factor: (iv) *unmindful* of all this (and paradoxically), Prime Minister Modi called for population control in his national address on August 15, 2019. He said: "I would like to highlight the issue of population explosion in one Country from the aegis of the Red Fort today. This rapidly increasing population poses various new challenges for us and our future generations." Finance Minister Nirmala Sitharaman went a step ahead and in her February 1, 2024 budget speech she said: "The Government will form a *high-powered committee* for an extensive consideration of the challenges arising from fast population growth and demographic changes… in relation to the goal of 'Viksit Bharat'."

Meanwhile, Franziska Ohnsorge, World Bank's chief economist for South Asia, warned in April 2024 that India and its neighbours risked "squandering" demographic dividend because not enough jobs were being created to sustain youth population, despite high GDP growth. Raghuram Rajan had warned this earlier: *Without breaking the current "mould" of economic growth model, India would continue to remain a "lower-middle income" country* – with its per capita GDP, or average income, in 2047 *below* that of China in 2022. He said, by 2047, India's 'demographic dividend' (higher youth population) would have completely disappeared.

Now consider this. In the beginning of 2024, the Modi government entered into a G2G (government-to-government) pact with war-hit Israel to supply workers like a private contractor – *without any guarantee* of their safety. Thousands lined up for these jobs in Israel knowing the risk to their lives but compelled by starvation staring at them; many have already landed in Israel. On April 12, the government issued an advisory asking Indians not to travel to Israel and Iran as the war escalated and both began pounding each other.

5. **Inequality at all-time high**

The World Inequality Lab's March 2024 report, "Income and Wealth Inequality in India, 1922-2023: The Rise of the Billionaire Raj", authored by Thomas Piketty, Lucas Chancel and their colleagues, put it in historic perspective: "Or estimates suggest that inequality *declined* post-independence till the early 1980s, after which it began rising and has skyrocketed since the early 2000s". Its estimates found this rise in inequality (K-shaped GDP growth) is sharpest in the *current decade,* reaching the "highest historical levels", thereby making India "more unequal than the British Raj" and "among the very highest in the world" in 2022-23. The income shares of the top 1% surged from 21.3% in 2014 to *22.6% in 2022* and that of their wealth surged from 33.3% in 2014 to *40.1% in 2022* and fell to 39.5% in 2023. This study also used Indian official data – "national income accounts, wealth aggregates, tax tabulations, rich lists, and surveys on income, consumption and wealth".

Long-term development in numbers: *Income shares* of the top 1% was 11.5% in 1951, which fell to 6.1% in 1982 (during the despised Nehruvian socialism era) and surged to 15.1% in 2000 (in the free-market or neoliberal era of reform and liberalizations since mid-1980s), reaching 22.6% in 2022. *Wealth shares* of the top 1% was 12.9% in 1961, which fell to 12.5 in 1981 and rose to 25.4% in 2002, reaching 39.5% in 2023.

6. **Surge in menial, below-minimum wage MGNREGS jobs**

Households and individuals availing such works in FY24 (599 million households and 834 million individuals) *surpassed* the pre-pandemic levels of FY19 and FY20. Five-year average of households availing MGNREGS work is 38.6% of all rural households (using Census 2011 data for rural households since 2021 Census is yet to begin). This type of jobs is *emergency relief* started with the MGNREG Act of 2005 to address *chronic rural distress.* Even in 2024, it gives below statutory minimum wages of states – averaging Rs 234 *after* the last revision amidst the electioneering in March 2024.

7. **Human development (HDI) reverses**

India has been languishing in the bottom half in global ranking in human development. The UNDP's HDI report of 2022-24 *ranks* India at 134th (of 193 countries) – below China (75), Sri Lanka (78), Bangladesh (129) and Bhutan (125). Its HDI *score* is 0.644 (in "medium human development country" category) – *fallen* from 0.645 in 2018, after having *consistent risen* from 0.434 in 1990. Improvement in HDI is critical to raise income levels of the masses and reduce poverty, hunger and inequality.

There are more such data but the drift is clear.

Don't forget, right now India is home to maximum poor (228.9 million MPI poor), maximum hungry (233.9 million), maximum illiterates (287 million adults), among the most unequal in the world and more unequal than it was in the British Raj (in income and wealth). Indians continue to be one of the poorest in the world – its per capita GDP (income), or average income of Indians, is lower than the average of "low-middle income" countries in which India falls and also lower than the global average. India is in the bottom 50 among 190-odd countries.

Even worse, growth in average income (per capita GDP) is not only *falling behind that of* the GDP, its decadal growth has *slowed down* compared to the previous decade of FY05-FY14! That is, average Indian is *progressively getting worse off* with higher GDP growth – a sign of *poverty trap* as income and wealth surge to the top.

India may be the *fifth largest economy* in the world but it has fallen behind Bangladesh in average income since 2018 – its average income at $2,688.3 in 2022 (current USD) is ahead of India's $2,410.9 (World Bank).

These are also the recipes bigger disasters waiting to happen – unless the drift is arrested immediately.

We do need India to grow fast and become developed, right? How can that be achieved? The answer is in *redesigning* the growth model to raise income and wealth of average Indian – 90% or more of the population. There are plenty of ideas in the inbox – repeated many times in recent years, particularly after the devastating man-made disaster called demonetisation in November 2016, by eminent economists of international repute. Some of these, and others, are evident in the articles.

Top-down, arbitrary and self-serving paradigm

The real problem is India's *top-down, arbitrary and self-serving* policies and governance since 2014. A part of these are aimed at (a) *systemically* building crony capitalism (private oligarchies or "national champions", privatisation of public assets etc.) (b) high on *capital-intensive infrastructure-led growth* and (c) giving doles ("free" ration, LPG subsidies, PM-Kisan cash etc.), along with a push for certain other essentials (electricity, toilets, banking for the unbanked) that can be easily delivered, measured and mapped ("new welfarism") and thus, *harvested for votes* but not health and education – which are critical for average Indians to prosper. The first two are the reason the chronic job crisis would continue and the third is why the masses would never prosper like those in developed nations – rather, they would remain *poor forever*.

Make no mistake, Indian economy is a strange mix of neoliberalism and socialism – which best qualifies as a 'command-and-control' regime. Public revelations post the *forced disclosure* of Electoral Bond details are just one manifestation of this twisted structural change – systemic corruption for self-aggrandizement.

It is no Nehruvian or neo-Nehruvian socialism either. The previous decade under Manmohan Singh brought rights-based laws (MGNREG Act of 2005, NFSA of 2013, Forest Rights Act of 2006, Right to Education Act of 2009 and others) and schemes (urban and rural health missions) to ensure "inclusive growth". In contrast, the "new welfarism" is building a new vote bank, called "labharthi varg" (beneficiaries) – to both soften the impact of (a) and (b) and harvest their votes. "Inclusive growth" is out.

All of (a), (b) and (c) need to be replaced with *rational and evidence-based* policies and practices.

But that alone wouldn't be sufficient, or even happen, because *much else are broken too* – which *directly flow* from the very nature of the current government.

Democratic and socio-political regression

Though not in the ambit of this collection, there are *two other factors* critical for progress and prosperity which can't be left unflagged: (a) healthy democracy and (b) inclusive social and political order.

The run-up to the general elections of 2024 has vitiated fair-play. Two important chief ministers of the Opposition-run state governments have been arrested and jailed by central agencies – *without* charge sheets, trials or reasonable ground to believe they would flee or influence investigations (controlled by central agencies). The Income Tax department, a central agency, has seized a part of the funds of main Opposition, the Congress (Rs 135 crore), and slapped multiple tax notices making humongous demands (Rs 3,567 crore or more than two-and-half times the cash and assets disclosed by the Congress by FY23) by reopening its accounts going back to 1990s. Remember, political parties are *exempt from tax*; these tax demands are *fines* for delayed filings and *interests* thereupon – howsoever ridiculous and unprecedented that is. Later, on April 1, 2024, the IT department told the apex court that it would take no coercive action until the elections are over due to public pressure. Another Opposition party, the CPI, too faces similar tax demands. But the ruling BJP, with its overflowing coffers, is *immune* from any scrutiny or tax demands.

These are over and above the *systemic targeting* of all Opposition parties since 2014. Investigating reports have found, 95% of all raids by the Enforcement Directorate and CBI (both central agencies) *after 2014* are on the Opposition leaders. Investigating reports also show, of 25 prominent Opposition leaders facing corruption probes since 2014 were *inducted into* to the BJP, of whom *23 got reprieve* as the cases were either dropped (against three) or stalled (against 20). Such brazen and partisan acts attracted censures from the UN, the US and Germany – *unheard* outside of the Emergency of 1975-77. The institutions that should step in – the Election Commission of India (ECI) and Supreme Court – are reluctant, even complicit.

There is a larger pattern here. The ruling BJP runs "Operation Lotus" to dismantle Opposition-run state governments by engineering defections, misusing the office of Governors and LGs with great deal of success. Intimidating political rivals, independents to withdraw from contests in the 2024 elections (Surat, Indore and Gandhinagar) and the blatant manipulation of the Chandigarh mayoral election in February 2024 are more reasons to fear for the survival of democracy in India.

The Modi government has also systematically weakened states fiscally, crippled civil society/NGOs, jailed dissenting voices under sedition and anti-terror laws – apparently to install *one-party-one-leader rule* like China. Sweden's V-Dem Institute *downgraded* India to "electoral autocracy" since 2018 and continued it in 20124, describing it as "one of the worst autocratizers lately". The US-based Freedom House *downgraded* India as a "partly free" country since 2020.

As for the second factor, *exclusionary* and *majoritarian* socio-political order (Public Opium Number 1 for the majority Hindu community), the latest addition is operationalization of the religion-based, discriminatory citizenship law (excludes Muslims), the CAA of 2019, in March 2024 – even as the law's constitutionality is pending before the apex court (since 2019). Apart from rights bodies, the UN and the US have slammed India for this "discriminatory" law/rules.

This is apart from the gratuitous invocation of *Pakistan, Muslims, Mughals, Muslim League* etc. by the Prime Minister and his senior colleagues while electioneering now – as *dog-whistles* for their Hindu followers. The Prime Minister is also spreading blatant lies, targeting the Congress – secured in the knowledge that neither the ECI nor the Supreme Court dare to stand up to him to uphold the rule of law.

These are also the reasons why the 2024 general election is *not free and fair* – the level-paying field having been vitiated beyond repair. No wonder one academic called it India's "Potemkin election".

Just like democracy, secularism (non-discrimination on the grounds of religion, caste, gender, race etc.) is pre-requisite for development and prosperity of the masses. The religion-based hatred and attacks on Muslims, Christians and other minorities by the ruling BJP *adds* to the historic tradition of *caste-based discrimination and exploitation* of *majority of Hindus* – the SCs, STs and OBCs constituting a whopping *78.3% of rural population (*Situation Assessment of Agricultural Households and Land Holdings of Households in Rural India of 2019).

Economists Daron Acemoglu and James A Robinson, while tracing the history of development across the world in the past 700-800 years in their book "Why Nations Fail: The Origins of Power, Prosperity and Poverty", identified "inclusive institutions" – political inclusion followed by economic inclusion – as the key driver of development. The only factor they identified for India's non-development, despite its rich civilizational and trading histories, is its "uniquely rigid hereditary caste system".

Institutional breakdowns, including judiciary and media, in the current decade are symptoms of the regressive democratic and socio-political orders.

Intrinsic to these is yet another risk. A study, "Populist Leaders and the Economy", by German economists Manuel Funke, Moritz Schularick and Christoph Trebesch, published in June 2022, concluded that "the economic cost of populism is high". It said: "After 15 years, GDP per capita is *10% lower* compared to a plausible non-populist counterfactual. *Economic disintegration, decreasing macroeconomic stability, and the erosion of institutions typically go hand in hand with populist rule.*" It examined 51 populist presidents and prime ministers between 1900 and 2020, including such episodes in India in 1966-77 and now (2014-), to arrive at these findings.

There is yet *another intrinsic risk* – which manifests

as the *rhetoric* of "Amrit Kaal", "Kartavya Kaal", "Viksit Bharat @2047", "Modi's guarantee" etc.

Propaganda: Public Opium Number 2

Such rhetoric is a cloak for multiple failures of the current regime. It began with "Achche Din" (good days) in 2013 that never came. The decade under Prime Minister Modi is more appropriate to be called *A Decade of Disasters*. Most of the disasters are *Modi-made* (including the high-handed, gross mismanagement of the pandemic in 2020 and 2021).

That should also explain why everything is now getting "amrit" and "kartavya" coat. The Rashtrapati Bhavan's famous Mughal Gardens became "Amrit Udyan", some superfast trains "Amrit Bharat Express", some railway stations "Amrit Bharat Station" and NITI Aayog's web portal on EV "e-Amrit". The majestic Rajpath is called "Kartavya Path" and 7, Race Course Road in New Delhi, the official residence and principal workplace of the Prime Minister, 7, "Lok Kalyan Marg" ('lok kalyan' is Hindi for public welfare).

Such propaganda/rhetoric are also part of *larger ecosystem* of fake news, misinformation and disinformation plaguing India in this decade. A good example is the IMF's strong rebuttal, on April 5, 2024, of its executive director and economist Krishnamurthy Subramanian's claim that India would see *sustained growth of 8% till 2047* (turning economics into astrology). Refuting this, the IMF spokesperson said: "The views conveyed by Mr Subramanian were in his role as India's representative at the IMF." Subramanian was Chief Economic Advisor (CEA) in the Modi government during 2018-21.

There is further validation of such propaganda.

Recall economists Surjit Bhalla and Sutirtho Sinha Roy, the lead authors of two reports coming out of the IMF and World Bank, respectively, in April 2022, making *absurd claims* of dramatic reduction in poverty amidst the economic shocks. Bhalla also made another *absurd claim* about (imaginary) benefits of the 2019 corporate tax cut. It is important to know Bhalla was appointed as *India's representative* at the IMF for three years (2019-21) by the Modi government; Sinha Roy worked in the office of then CEA Arvind Subramanian in the Modi government before joining the World Bank in 2017.

Meanwhile, the World Economic Forum's January 2024 Global Risk Report lists "misinformation and disinformation" as Number 1 (1st) risk for India in the election year of 2024. This is continuation of a trend that emerged a decade ago. Author Sonia Faleiro tracked and presented it her 2021 essay ("Fact-checking Modi's India"): "Misinformation is a challenge globally, but in India, it's practically *baked into* the ruling party's communications… When misinformation *first started circulating widely across the country*, it was the *run-up to the 2014.*"

Simultaneously, India tops the list of countries in *internet shutdowns* for quite some time now – shutting down public access to information.

To sum up, there are multiple reasons why India's skewed (K-shaped) and paradoxical growth (rising GDP, falling income of average Indian) would continue – unless checked. Meanwhile, India continues to slip in the World Happiness Index ranking – from 111th in 2014 to 126th in 2023, among fewer than 150 countries.

***

NB: *The BJP's high-octane public campaign for the 2024 general election is marketed as "Modi's guarantee". The guarantee includes "free" ration to 67% of population, subsidized LPG and more such does – apart from the rhetoric of Viskit Bharat@2047. Forgotten are Modi's public denouncements of welfare schemes of the Opposition-led state governments for years as "revdi" and "revdi culture". Just before the 2024 general election schedule was announced in March 2024, his government announced more "revdi": Petrol and diesel prices were cut by Rs 2 and LPG cylinder price by Rs 100 – which were then advertised also as "Modi's gift" and part of his promotion of "nari shakti" (women's power), respectively. His government actually amended the Constitution to bring 33% reservation for women in the Lok Sabha and Assemblies in a special session of the Parliament in 2023, which was sold by the Prime Minister, his government and his party as "Narishakti Vandan Adhiniyam" (Law to Worship Women Power) – but which would come to force only after the next Census, that of 2021, is held and delimitations of the Lok Sabha and Assembly constituencies are carried out thereafter. That would be possible only around 2029.*

The retail prices for petrol and diesel steadily went up since 2015 as the government kept raising taxes while the Brent prices crashed to half in FY15, of what it was in the three previous fiscals, and remained low until the Russia-Ukraine war hit in February 2022. The government reduced taxes only once in May 2022 but the retail prices remained unchanged even as India was importing substantial amount of cheap Russian oil (it still does) – ending in windfall gains for oil exporting companies. The last time LPG cylinders were cheaper was in August 2023, when the prices were slashed by Rs 200 and sold as "Modi's gift" for women, ahead of the 'Rakshya Bandhan'.

But "Modi's guarantee" can be very fickle.

The last round of elections in Madhya Pradesh, Rajasthan and Chhattisgarh in November-December 2023 saw the BJP manifestos branded as "Modi's guarantee" – which, among others, particularly promised to reduce LPG prices by more than half to Rs 450-500 per cylinder under the Centre's Ujjwala scheme. The Prime Minister himself said so. But once the BJP won all the three state elections, the BJP-run state governments passed the buck to the Modi government, which in turn, told the Parliament that it had taken no such decisions. Then, a few days ahead of the notification for 2024 general election, the prices were cut to be sold as "Modi's guarantee" for the next five years.

Just ahead of the election notification, "Modi's guarantee" got a new twist. The BJP's frontpage newspaper ads declared: "Modi ki guarantee: Vishnu ka Sushasan". What does "Vishnu ka Sushasan" (Vishnu's good governance) mean remains a mystery. Vishnu is a Hindu god. This was after the Prime Minister inaugurated incomplete Ayodhya's Ram temple on January 22, 2024, which had preceded his 11-day fasting and pilgrimage across the country. He, his government and his party have been promising to usher in "Ram Rajya" for decades.

'Amrit' is mythological nectar drinking which made gods immortal. 'Kartavya' is Hindi for duty. 'Vishnu' is one of the 'trinity' of Hindu gods known as the preserver; the others being Brahma, the creator, and Shiva, the destroyer.

April 2024

***

Electoral Bond: Mother of all Systemic Corruptions?

Prime facie, apparent connections between corporate donations and policy changes, award of government contracts and immunity from prosecution point to quid pro quo and wholesale government corruption

Political donation by businesses is not illegal, not all businesses indulge in unethical or corrupt practices and all political decisions might not have been dictated by it but the details of donations through the electoral bonds (EBs) that have emerged *after* the Supreme Court forced full disclosures in March 2024 point to widespread *systemic corruption* that was long feared – and need explanations and closure.

Many national dailies and credible news portals have dug up publicly available information and corporate balance sheets to highlight *ostensible connections* between the donations through EBs and (i) suitable changes in policies and rules (ii) award of government contracts and administrative clearances and (iii) immunity from criminal prosecution (after being raids by government agencies for financial and other irregularities). These revelations also point to (iv) bad corporate governance and (v) black money coursing through the economic and political systems.

Coming as it does *after* a series of corporate and banking frauds that has rocked India in and after 2018 – leading to the collapse of several banks and NBFCs, more than a dozen corporate loan defaulters fleeing India and Rs 14.5 lakh crore of corporate loan defaults, including those of willful defaulters, written off during FY15-FY23 – the EB revelations further strengthen the *misgivings* about systemic corruption having reached all-time high.

Black money for political donations?

About 45 corporate entities reportedly donated *more money* than their net profits (PATs) for five years during 2019-2023. The top two gave 635% and 374% and the next 22 gave 1-53% of their respective cumulative net profits (PATs); some had booked near zero-profits and some huge losses in their balance sheets in those years; some donated many times more than their total paid-up equity. Over 40 firms were found to be newly incorporated ones (in 2018 and in 2023).

Several questions arise from such public revelations: What is the source of donations (since sale of assets has not been claimed by any of the doners so far)? Were these shell companies set up specifically to make political donations through EBs – the possibility of which the ECI and RBI had warned against in 2017? Has the EB become a tool to turn black money into white (EBs are tax-free)? Are statutory auditors and regulators doing their jobs as watchdogs of corporate governance?

Shells, proxies and non-disclosures

Though the EB scheme allowed doners not to "name" political parties being donated, the Companies Act of

2013 and SEBI don't allow non-disclosure of any such donations. But many firms were found to have not disclosed donations in their balance sheets at all; some disclosed under "miscellaneous expenses" or "donations" heads without specifics or break-ups (whether political or philanthropic); a few used individuals, unlisted subsidiaries, proxies and four even used *shell companies listed with the SEBI* for such donations.

One obscure company has been found to have donated over Rs 400 crore, the three directors of which are also directors of several companies of a big business group. The group has denied this firm to be its "subsidiary" but hasn't disputed the presence of common directors. Another company, which caused a buzz as a "Pakistan firm', turned out to be a Delhi-based *fake company* (no business, unknown owners).

Even *electoral trusts* set up and run by private companies through the Electoral Trusts Scheme of 2013 (registered as Section 25 entities) for transparent and party-agnostic political funding took the EB route, apparently to hide the tracks. The biggest of such trusts, Prudent Electoral Trust, was flagged by many for channelling corporate donations from big companies through EBs, instead of dealing in cheques as it did earlier.

Several more questions arise from the above: Why did corporates use proxies, shell companies and subsidiaries when political donation is legal? Why did corporates turn the transparent mechanism of electoral trusts into opaque instruments? How did SEBI-listed shell companies bypass the SBI's rigorous KYC norms?

The SBI's claim for having institutionalized a tough KYC for EBs to prevent black money is suspect for other reasons too. Several national dailies cross-checked the unique alphanumeric EB codes to find Rs 623 crore of redemption don't carry the donors' name (unknown source). Multiple donations have been marked against "Monika" (5 lakh) in the SBI's list without making it clear whether she is an individual or company.

Quid pro quo, fear, blackmailing or something else?

Many investigating reports in national dailies and credible news portals point to apparent *connections* between political donations and changes in policies/rules, administrative clearances, award of projects and administrative clearances. A few examples:

- A big group bought EB *a month before* its mega project was *bailed out of certain bankruptcy* in 2021 – by allowing government debt to be turned into government equity.

- In December 2023, new telecom law, The Telecommunications Act of 2023, was passed by the Parliament allowing spectrum to be allotted *without auction*, *reversing* the more than a decade old Supreme Court verdict in the 2G spectrum case in 2012 in which it had mandated "auction" while "transferring or alienating the natural resources". The actual allocation, however, is yet to take place as the Supreme Court registry rejected the Centre's plea seeking endorsement of this change. One big firm, qualified for such administrative allocation, donated funds through EBs both before and after the change in law

- Another firm allegedly lobbied to get import regulations tweaked in its favour (eventually helping it to consolidate its market position) and found to be among the top doners.

- A proposed changes in rules were junked *after* huge donations by firms which were to be get affected. The changes were proposed *after* the CAG flagged irregularities in 2017. One such doner (bought EBs for over Rs 1,000 crore) had faced multiple raids by central and state agencies for financial irregularities. This doner is a *little-known company* with paid-up capital of Rs 10 crore.
- Another top doner allegedly got a number of large infrastructure projects from government departments and PSUs either just before or immediately after making donations.
- Many big companies *waiting* for green clearances and some found to have *violated* green laws bought EBs around the time.
- At least 41 companies made donations *after* being *raided* by central agencies (ED, CBI, IT etc.). These included about 20 firms in infrastructure, engineering, mining, automotive, real estate, electrical, steel and power and agri/forest-based products.
- One company flagged by the CAG for alleged rigging of an auction and helped by the Centre to win the auction also donated a huge sum though EBs.
- 35 pharmaceutical companies and hospitals donated about Rs 1,000 crore when they were facing multiple investigations for corruption and producing substandard drugs.
- One pharma company bought EB *five days after* its promoter-director was arrested by the ED in the Delhi excise policy case in 2022 – who then turned *approver* and granted immunity from prosecution (in

the same case in which Delhi Chief Minister Arvind Kejriwal, his deputy Manish Sisodia and many others have are in jail even as the 2024 general election is on. The Supreme Court had lambasted the ED and CBI in 2023 for producing no evidence but keep denying the bail nonetheless. The same pharma company later received fiscal incentive (PLI) for manufacturing and *two days later* donated even more through EBs.

- 18 of 19 companies marked 'high risk' by the Finance Ministry for money laundering (under the PMLA) bought electoral bonds and *did not* figure in the *subsequent lists*.
- One firm bought EBs worth Rs 14.9 crore in 2019 and weeks later, its property tax dues of Rs 285 crore were waived off. Until 2024, this company had donated a total of Rs 185 crore.
- Most of the biggest doners had not donated or donated only a fraction of what they did before 2018 – when EB became operational – pointing to EB's coercive power.
- Doners include owners of many large and influencing TV news networks, radio stations, newspapers, magazines, news portals and OTT – raising questions about compromised media as the fourth pillar.

These are far too serious developments and both the Centre and India Inc have plenty to explain. Given that the government had brought EB through questionable means ('Money Bill'), dismissed all objections from the RBI, Law Ministry and ECI and fought against disclosures in the apex court, it is unlikely to order a probe. Nor do the corporates who gained.

April 2024

NB: *Electoral Bond (EB), a bearer instrument introduced in 2017 and operationalized in 2018, allowed anonymous, unaccounted and unlimited flow of money from businesses and individuals in India and abroad to political parties without scrutiny – the very anti-thesis of Prime Minister Modi's promise to make India "corruption-free" and provide "transparency" in and "clean money" for political funding. Despite challenges to its legality pending before it, the Supreme Court allowed its unhindered operation for the next seven years. In the meanwhile, five Chief Justices of India retired without deciding its constitutionality.*

Finally, the court struck EB down as "unconstitutional" on February 15, 2024 and declared all the amendments in various laws which facilitated it – The Representation of People Act of 1951, The Income Tax Act of 1961, The RBI Act of 1934 and The Companies Act of 2013 – also unconstitutional. These amendments had taken EB beyond institutional scrutiny, transparency and accountability. The judgement upheld "the voters right" to know, describing it as "integral to" free and fair elections. The court forced full disclosures but didn't direct probe or return of the money collected through this "unconstitutional" tool.

By this time, 30 rounds of EBs had been sold and Rs 16,518 crore had been pocketed by political parties between March 2018 and January 2024. The Prime Minister's party, the BJP, got the lion's share, 50% or Rs 8,251.8 crore, as was feared. The next two recipients, the Congress and the TMC, got just 11.8% and 10.3%, respectively. That is not all, the SBI billed Rs 10.68 crore as "commission" to the government – a burden on public/taxpayers who were kept in dark about EB. In FY23 alone, EBs contributed 82.4% to the total political donations from "unknown sources". So much for transparency in political funding. The BJP also got 64.7% of non-EB donations, out of the Rs 7,726 crore during FY13-FY23.

The Modi government had fought hard before the court to prevent EB disclosures, arguing that citizens had "no general right to know anything and everything". Ironically, it twisted the 2017 Puttaswamy (Aadhaar) judgement, which declared citizens' privacy a fundamental right (and which the government had argued against too), to justify the privacy of doners: "Political self-expression, either through voting or donations to one's preferred party or candidate lies at the heart of the zone of privacy which the government is constitutionally obligated to respect." This is not strange since the Prime Minister has, for long, held that fundamental rights made India "weak", preferring duties over rights. Three big industry bodies – the ASSOCHAM, FICCI and CII – too jumped in to argue before the court that EB disclosures would "undermine the rule of law", harm "industry's interests" and impact "ease of doing business".

After the court rejected its arguments and ordered full disclosures by March 6, the SBI played truant, seeking four months (by June 30, by which time the general elections would be over) as the deadline of March 6, 2024 appeared. When the court threatened action, it did so within 24 hours, revealing also the secret (unique) alphanumeric code that each EB carried and through which doners and recipients could be tracked in real time by the public sector bank, the SBI, and by extension, the Centre. The Centre had earlier denied the very existence of such codes but was exposed by investigating journalist Poonam Agarwal.

Post-judgement, the Centre sought censorship of public debate on EB in social media, describing it as "witch-hunting" but the court rejected it. Post-disclosure the Prime Minister defended EB again, this time with another doublespeak: "Today Modi has created election documents; that's why you can search about it. You can find out who gave the money and who received it. Otherwise, no one knows where the money came from." In the same breath, he also said "those dancing over the issue and taking pride in it are going to regret it" and dismissed quid pro quo with corporates and misuse of official agencies to generate party funds. Home Minister Amit Shah claimed the ruling BJP received "more than 90%" donations during elections but one analysis showed the BJP got EB donations round the year, unlike others who got it during the elections. He also, quite ironically, said he "feared" black money would be back. Finance Minister Nirmala Sitharaman said the allegations of quid pro quo were "huge assumptions". But none went to the specific allegations or denied those. Not strange, Chief Election Commissioner (CEC) Rajiv Kumar too batted for protecting the "donor's privacy", while talking about transparency in political funding and voters' rights.

There were other ironies.

The EB was brought in as a Money Bill in 2017 to bypass the Rajya Sabha's scrutiny where it didn't have majority. The Prime Minister had dismissed all objections saying that "some people have issues if anything happens in the country to ensure transparency". Then Finance Minister Arun Jaitley, who piloted it, misled the nation into believing that EB would "enable clean money and substantial transparency". Their government had also dismissed all objections from the RBI, the Law Ministry, Finance Ministry and ECI.

What national dailies and other credible news portals have dug out now seem to confirm all the forebodings about the EB introducing systemic corruption in India and legalized bribery. So much for "Ram Rajya" and "Vishnu ka Sushashan".

***

Why India Needs a 2024 Poverty Line

Interpretations of data paint exaggerated picture of prosperity

The "free" ration entitlement ("@5 kg food grain per person per month") is for "67% of the population", as per the National Food Security Act (NSFA) of 2013. Going by the population estimate of 1,392.3 million in 2023 (Lok Sabha answer of July 25, 2023), 923.9 million Indians (or 67%) should get the "free" ration. But exclusion and inclusion and non-updating errors have denied 119.4 million Indians this benefit. The exclusion is so huge that on March 19, 2024, the Supreme Court directed the Centre and states to issue ration cards to 80 million migrant workers, registered on the e-Shram portal but excluded from the NFSA *within two months* – which the Centre had promised in its affidavit of April 26, 2020 (four years ago).

Going by this *fact* alone, should India's poverty estimate be 67% (923.9 million)? The basis of the claim that poverty fell to "single digit", "closer to 5% or less" and "4.5-5%", respectively, in 2022-23 is the household consumption survey (HCES or MPCE) of 2022-23. But what does this data actually tell?

Reading HCES 2022-23

The HCES of 2022-23 shows the average monthly

household expenditure (with imputation, at 2011-12 prices) is Rs 2,054 in rural and Rs 3,544 in urban areas. That is, per capita per day living expenditure of Rs 68.5 in rural ($0.8 at exchange rate of Rs 83) and Rs 118.1 ($1.4) in urban areas.

Since India's own poverty line estimate is *two-decade old*, called the Tendulkar's poverty line of 2004-05, estimating poverty on the basis of this data is a wild-goose-chase. That this grossly underestimates poverty can be gleaned from the following facts (more of it later):

(i) Harvard study, published in the JAMA Network Open in February 2024, says India "accounted for *almost half of zero-food children*" among 92 low- and medium-income countries during 2010-2022. It found India had 19.3% (6.7 million) children of 6-23 months who "did not consume animal milk, formula, or solid or semisolid food during the last 24 hours". India *refuted* this, saying that the study *excluded* breast-milk feeding. That is right, but the study cited the WHO to say why it did so: "*After age 6 months*, breast milk alone is *insufficient* to meet the growing nutritional requirements of infants and young children".

(ii) India's own (latest) national health survey, NFHS-5 of 2019-2021, says, Indian children *below 5 years* had stunting rate of 35.5%, wasting rate of 19.3% and underweight of 32.1% – due to high-level of *malnutrition* and *unhealthy* living conditions (read extreme poverty).

How poverty fell below 5%?

NITI Aayog CEO BVR Subramanyam said his estimates were based on the *fall* in household consumption of food items *below* that of non-food items for the first time since 1999-2000 – a sign of growing prosperity. He used this data to claim that the impact of *inflation* might have been overstated. Household expenditure (with imputation) on food indeed fell from 52.9% to 47.5% in rural areas and from 43% to 39% in urban areas during 2011-12 and 2022-23 (a decade).

The SBI Research report was more elaborate. It took into account (a) 2011-12 *poverty line* estimated at Rs 816 for rural and Rs 1,000 for urban areas (b) adjusts it for "decadal inflation" factor (1.89 for rural and 1.85 for urban) and (c) "imputation factor" (1.05 for rural and 1.04 for urban) to arrive at a new *poverty line for 2022-23* at Rs 1,622 per month (Rs 54 per day) for rural and Rs 1,929 per month (Rs 64 per day) for urban areas. It then estimated poverty at 7.2% in rural and 4.6% in urban areas – for which it used (d) two poverty line estimates *as the base* – (i) Tendulkar' 2011-12 poverty line and poverty estimates (25.7% poverty in rural and 13.7% in urban areas) and World Bank's 2018-19 poverty estimates (11.6% and 6.3%, respectively).

Making sense of HCES and poverty reduction

A few caveats are needed to bring clarity and perspective to the above arguments/data.

Caveat 1: HCES of 2022-23 *does not* estimate poverty line; it provides household expenditure. When poverty line is available, HCES data can be used to estimate poverty percentage or number of poor. The poverty line was estimated in 2004-05 and 2011-12 – when the earlier HCES were carried out. But not in 2022-23. The claim of fall in poverty is being *measured* from the 2011-12 poverty line – which itself is an updated version of the 2004-05 poverty line (Tendulkar's), not a new one.

Caveat 2: HCES of 2022-23 comes *a decade* after that of 2011-12 and it *lists* three "changes" in the methodology to caution against "comparability" with that of 2011-12: (i) expansion of items covered from 347 to 405 through inclusion and merger of items (ii) "three separate questionnaires" were used for food, consumables and durable goods (against a single questionnaire earlier) which were asked (iii) in "three separate monthly visits" (as against single visit).

Anyone familiar with surveys will vouch that all the three changes will change the responses (outcomes). The 2017-18 HCES, which showed *a fall* in 'real' consumption expenditure, was *junked* on the claim that an expert committee had objected to "data quality", which turned out be *false*. On the contrary, the said committee had *validated* it, stating that it was *in line* with other relevant data.

Caveat 3: The HCES 2022-23 data is *partial* – only the value data has been released, not the volume data. Hence, the role of *inflation* can't be accurately measured. SBI Research uses *only value* data, while the Tendulkar's used both *value and volume data* – for 2004-05. The 2011-12 poverty line was an *extension* of the Tendulkar's and was done by the Planning Commission as *interim* one which showed overall poverty at *21.9%* even as it waited for the Rangarajan's estimates because the Tendulkar's had come under wide-spread criticism for being "too low".

Caveat 4: Rangarajan's poverty line came in August 2014, fixing it for 2011-12 – at Rs 972 for rural and Rs 1,402 for urban areas – and estimated poverty at *29.5%* in 2011-12. This was *far higher* than the Planning Commission's 21.9% for the same year. But by then the government had changed and the new government didn't accept it. Nor has the government re-estimated it *after 2014*.

Caveat 5: SBI Research *apparently* uses (not disclosed) World Bank's *outdated* poverty line of $1.9 (at 2011 PPP) – which was changed to $2.15 (at 2017 PPP) in 2019 to account for inflation. It quoted poverty at 11.6% in rural and 6.3% in urban areas for 2018-19. But the World Bank *database* shows, India's overall poverty (at $2.15, 2017 PPP) was 12.7% in 2019, which fell to 11.9% in 2021.

The World Bank's 2022 report says, India saw "an increase of 56 million poor people" in 2020 (at $2.15) due to the pandemic. Pew Research Institute's March 2021 report (before the second wave) said the number of Indian poor ($2) increased by 75 million, its middle class shrinking by 32 million and India contributing "60% of the global retreat in the number of people in the middle-income tier" in 2020. But India never acknowledged that poverty increased due to the pandemic or due to pre-pandemic economic shocks of demonetisation of 2016 and GST of 2017 (more of it later).

Poverty estimates fail smell test

Economist Ashoka Mody analysed the HCES 2022-23 data and other indicators to write ("India's Poor Will Not Be Wished Away") that it failed the "smell test"; "in reality, poverty remains deeply entrenched in India and appears to have increased significantly". He flagged "the lack of comprehensive consumption – and inflation – data", making "it impossible to get an accurate picture". While volume data for HCES of 2022-23 is not released (hence, incomplete), about inflation he wrote, "regrettably, Indian authorities *do not provide* inflation data segmented by *household income*".

What is his own poverty estimate?

He wrote: "Adjusting the Rangarajan and Subramanian estimates using plausible current inflation rates *leads to a stark conclusion*: Urban poverty rates range between 40% and 60%, which means that 30-40% of all Indians are poor." Subramanian's reference here is to poverty expert S. Subramanian's 2012 estimates.

The gaps in HCES and other official data sets are too glaring to miss.

Here are two examples. The PLFS data from 2017-18 to 2022-23 show a *surge* in informal and low-paying *agricultural jobs* to 45.8% (sectoral distribution); a surge in *self-employment* to 57.3% due to a fall in quality jobs and *unpaid* jobs to 18.3% (category-wise distribution). Wages growth is negative for regular wages/salaried and self-employment in these five years. There is also a surge in MGNREGS's menial, below statutory minimum wages jobs, engaging (average) 64 million rural households and 93 million individuals during FY19-FY24 (up to February, 2024). They point to a surge in poverty, not reduction.

More flawed poverty estimates in 2022 and 2023

The Aayog first claimed a *dramatic fall in poverty* in 25 states/UTs during the pandemic 2020-21 – without explaining why or how – after its surge in the pre-pandemic in 22 states/UTs in 2019-20 – in its SDG reports!

More recently, on July 17, 2023, the Aayog claimed "135 million have exited multi-dimensional poverty" (MPI) during 2015-16 and 2019-21. MPI is calculated on the basis of three parameters with equal weightage – health, education and living standard (income).

But this estimate was based only on data source, health survey NHFS-5 of 2019-21. No other data source was used for education and living standard (income) – thereby excluding two-third measures of MPI. The NFHS-5 data is also questionable for using the pre-pandemic 2019 survey (70% data) and the *unusual year of the* 2021 pandemic (the rest 30% data), missing 2020 completely, and averaging 2019 data with that of 2021 – an unheard economic data collection. Its *baseline index* was "based on" the *old and outdated* NFHS-4 of 2015-16 when the NFHS-5 data for 2019-20 was already available.

Then, on January 15, 2024, the Aayog released another MPI report claiming that "24.82 crore" Indians (248.2 million) *escaped MPI poverty* during *2013-14 and 2022-23* – with MPI poor continuing "to decline from 29.17% in 2013-14 to *11.28%* in 2022-23". There was no additional survey or data to warrant this estimate. The HCES of 2022-23 data would be released in February 2024.

The Aayog's January 2024 estimate is purely *statistical* and it said so ("owing to lack of data for the years between 2005-06 and 2015-16 and after 2019-21"). The report says: "This requires *interpolation* of estimates for the year 2013-14 and *extrapolation* for the year 2022-23. Thus, 2013-14 figure was computed from the 2005-06 estimate using annual compound rate of 7.69% reduction. Similarly, 2022-23 estimate was projected by applying compound rate of reduction achieved during 2015-16 to 2019-21." The references to 2005-06 and 2019-21 are to the NFHS-4 and NFHS-5 data, respectively.

Note Aayog claimed *decline* in poverty in just *40 days* – from 11.28% on January 15, 2024 to "closer to 5% or less" on February 26, 2024. True, MPI poverty and simple poverty are different but that nuance is lost in the splashed headline numbers of 11.28% and 5%.

How to estimate poverty better?

There are certainly better ways to estimate poverty than base it on HCES.

Firstly, the HCES data are known to be widely off-the mark, these being *self-reported or voluntary disclosures*. Unlike in India, household surveys are widely studied subject in the US and *non-response and/or denial* of benefits (imputation value) by both the poor and the rich households (2015, 2017 and 2021) are well known. In India, the poor has incentives to under-report or lie about government support (imputation) to get more of it; the rich to evade exclusion and tax liability. Hence, as many have argued, India must address such issues.

Secondly, it is time to shift to collecting income data. Today's India is very different from the early decades of independence when getting income data was difficult. Like the US, India can now collect such data. Such data can be *supplemented* with income tax returns (ITRs), digital transactions, property tax, EPFO, PLFS, MGNREGS data etc. to get a better picture of income levels and hence, poverty.

The starting point, however, should be fixing a poverty line relevant to 2024 – not that of 2004-05.

Mar 28, 2024

NB: Using the HCES of 2022-23, Prime Minister Modi said poverty had fallen to "single digit", the NITI Aayog said it had fallen "closer to 5% or less" and the SBI Research said it had fallen to "4.5-5%". Recall how the Indian government went into a frenzy, erecting green walls with plastic sheets, posters *and demolishing large number of slums overnight, ahead of and during the G20 summit in September 2023 to hide abject poverty in the heart of national capital, New Delhi!*

Arvind Panagariya, the first vice chairman of NITI Aayog back as the chairman of 16th Finance Commission, wrote in a national daily on April 2, 2024 that "extreme poverty is history". His article's message was "don't lose sleep over inequality" (the headline) – days after the World Inequality Lab's "Income and Wealth Inequality in India, 1922-2023: The Rise of the Billionaire Raj" report said inequality in India had reached "highest historical levels", "among the very highest in the world" and India is "more unequal than the British Raj" in 2022-23.

***

Making Sense of Sluggish Private Corporate Capex

Measures to improve consumption demand and optimism in future growth will bring back private investment automatically

On March 6, 2024, RBI Governor Shaktikanta Das said the FY24 growth would be "close to 8%" (7.6% as per AE2) because high-frequency indicators like private investment, capacity utilisation and bank credit were showing "uptick". This is an upward revision of the RBI's earlier assessment of 7% growth (MPC of February 2024 and came after the Q3 GDP numbers showed an uptick to 8.4%. Ironically, he also projected the FY25 growth at 7% – a fall from "close to 8%" in FY24!

That none of these indicators (the Governor had listed these in December 2023 too) hold up to even 7% growth has been explained in *Fortune India* article "2024 Ahoy! Can India conjure up 7% growth for the fiscal?". Here the focus is on private corporate capex alone.

Has 'Hanuman' taken off?

The first obvious thing to notice is multiple contradictory claims.

The RBI's mid-February 2024 bulletin had said the *contrary*: (a) "*Expectations* for a fresh round of capex by the corporate sector to *take the baton* from the government and fuel the next leg of growth are *mounting*" and (b) "overall, the corporate sector *must get its act together* ready to relieve the government of capex heavy lifting…"

That was after the January 2024 bulletin said: "The government's thrust on capex is *starting to crowd in* private investment." This was in line with the RBI Governor's claim in early February 2024 (MPC) that "revival in private corporate investment is also *underway*".

The Centre's budget (speech) of February 1, 2024 for FY25 had agreed with this: "Now that the private investments are *happening at scale*, the *lower borrowings* ("small state" and "fiscal austerity") by the Central Government *will facilitate* larger availability of credit for the private sector." This claim needs to be put in perspective.

One, it is a pointer to a *new elephant* in the room: Centre's debt ballooning to *three times* in ten fiscals of FY15-FY24 (RE) – from Rs 56.7 lakh crore until FY14 (previous 63 fiscals) to Rs 170.6 lakh crore in FY24 (RE) or 58% of the GDP when the FRBM limit is 40%. This is being sought to be curtailed in FY25.

Two, there is yet another *contradiction*. Neoliberal economics India adopted since 1980s-1990s posits that high public capex *crowds-out* private capex (hence the advocacy for "small state" and "fiscal austerity"). But beginning with the budget of 2021, the Centre's public capex saw a "sharp increase" and continued in 2022 budget with the claim that it was "relying on *virtuous cycle* starting from private investment with public capital investment helping to *crowd-in* private investment.

Three, notwithstanding its 2024 budget claim on

private capex ("happening at scale"), the Centre continues its *public capex push* – apparently to *crowd-in* private capex (detailed later).

What is the actual state of private corporate capex?

Budget documents show private GFCF ("realised" private capex) has fallen steeply to 10.3% of the GDP (current prices) in FY23 (RE), up to which data is available (AE2, 2024), and remains *below 11%* since FY18 – down from a peak of 16.8% in FY08. The average private GFCF for nine fiscals of FY15-FY23 is 10.7% – down from the previous nine fiscal's 12.9%. This is the reason for continued pubic capex push.

No wonder the RBI has been *waiting* for private capex to revive for years. Its March 2019 bulletin said: "The year (FY18) marked the *seventh successive annual contraction* in the private corporate sector's capex plans." Capex plans are "envisaged investment", not "realised" investment that private GFCF shows. The hope for an "uptick" endures.

Also recall Finance Minister Nirmala Sitharaman telling the story of Hanuman's ability to fly (to Sri Lanka) in 2022 to inspire private capex to move up. She also told them her government had *acceded to* their demands for tax cut in 2019 and manufacturing incentives (PLI) in 2021.

Centre pumping capex but on infrastructure alone

Budget documents say the Centre's capex is *progressively going up* from 1.5% of GDP in FY18 (when the RBI pushed the panic button) to more than double at 3.2% in FY24 (AE2) and is set to be even higher at 3.4% for FY25 (BE).

Reading the 2024 budget speech carefully would reveal that the *entire* capex push for FY25 is on *infrastructure* alone.

The allocations touch the *magic number*, Rs 11,11,111 crore. What about agriculture (sectoral) that gives jobs to 45.8%? The budget allocation remains *below 0.5%* of the GDP – 0.47% in FY23 (actual), 0.48% in FY24 (RE) and 0.45% in FY25 (BE).

What about human capital development and social security cover?

Centre cut budget spending by 6% in 26 of 37 major 'core' and 'core of the core' social and welfare schemes – from FY24 (BE) to FY24 (RE) – impacting health, education, rural development and other areas. Besides, budget spending on these sectors as a percentage is falling in the past years. A budget analysis of 2023 shows, allocations for *five* key social security schemes (MGNREGS, PMMVY, mid-day meal, ICDS and NSAP) is back to FY07 level – falling from the peak of 0.93% of the GDP in FY10 to 0.36% in FY24 (BE).

What would be the impact of such low spending and cuts?

India would continue to languish in the *bottom half* in human development (HDI ranking at 134 among 193 countries and HDI score *going down* from the peak of 0.645 in 2018 to 0.644 in 2022, after consistently rising from 0.434 in 1990).

Remember, India is also home to *maximum poor*, both before the pandemic (World Bank 2019) and *after* (228.9 million MPI poor, UNDP-OPHI 2022 and 2023); *maximum hungry* (233.9 million, FAO *et al* 2023) and *maximum illiterates* (at 287 million adults, 37% of the global total in the world (UNESCO 2014, on the Census 2011 count, Census 2021 is yet to commence).

HDI is too critical for growth to be ignored.

China keeps pushing human development, not India

China made rapid growth for *40 years* and overtook India *after* both started from the *same level* in 1980s. In July 2023, economist Ashoka Mody wrote India can't be an economic superpower because "China grew rapidly on a strong foundation of human-capital development", India shortchanged this aspect of its growth." This was *despite* China having *advantage* of relatively higher level of education even in 1980s. Yet, China's March 2024 budget allocates *2.5 times more* on education (15%), social security and employment (15%), health and sanitation (15%) than on defence (6%)!

In sharp contrast, India's February 2024 budget did the exact opposite. Its allocations for defence (9.5%) outstripped education (2.6%), health (1.9%) and social welfare (1.2%) by miles.

Private corporates not at fault!

Make no mistake, private corporates will jack up capex *automatically* once demand and optimism in the economy are *restored*. Without such improvements, *no incentive will work* – none has for decades.

Here are the *missing perspectives*:

(i) Western major economies have grown for over 200 years (18th century industrial revolution) and can't grow at higher rate, like an underdeveloped India. Nor for that matter, China, Japan, South Korea or the Asian Tigers.

(ii) India's claim to be the fastest growing came *after* the

2011-12 GDP series – which then CEA Arvind Subramanian said *overestimated* growth by *2.5-3.7 percentage points* during 2012-2016. In September 2023, Subramanian and Mody said the GDP growth was *overestimate*d by *2.5-3 percentage points* in Q1 of FY24. In March 2024, Subramanian says the same about the FY24 GDP numbers (AE2): "I can't understand the latest GDP numbers, they are mystifying, and don't add up." He says "errors and omissions" are "actually about 4.3 percentage points".

(iii) Growth in bank credit is driven by (a) personal loans for consumption (beginning with gold loans during the pandemic distress), not for products and services and (b) debt-fuelled, not equity-fuelled, corporate business model. It may grow more because of the RBI's "compromise settlements" with corporate defaulters in June 2023, making them *eligible for fresh loans* after 12 months. Then came the *hike* in CRAR for banks and NBFCs to check "unsecured" personal loans (total rising to Rs 13.32 lakh crore by November 2023, of which banks' stressed assets ("special mention accounts") showing unsecured loans to Rs 93,240 crore or 7% of the total). Now, the Goldman Sachs says the "Goldilocks era" for banks is *ending* due to margin compression and stretched credit-deposit rate. The RBI *flagging* widening of credit-deposit gaps since 2022. NBFCs are now *panic-stricken*.

(iv) Headline employment numbers are *rosy* (unemployment rate falling to 3.1%, employment rate and LFPR zooming to 58% and 59.8%, respectively, in the PLFS for 2023 calendar year) but *scratch the surface* and the job crisis is glaring. Economists

Maitreesh Ghatak and Mrinalini Jha analysed PLFS data to *warn* "the rising spectre of a vicious cycle" to undermine demographic dividend because "a majority" of workers are in "low quality" jobs and wages have "stagnated". Raghuram Rajan too warned about *disappearance* of demographic dividend by 2047 if the current growth model continues.

Finally, a look at the state of demand and optimism in the economy.

Muted demand and optimism

- Budget documents show post-pandemic consumption is sluggish – PFCE's GDP share *falling* from 58% in FY22 to 55.6% in FY24 and PFCE growth (7.1%) *lagging* that of GDP (8.1%). During the first *three quarters* of FY24, PFCE grew at 3.7% (constant prices) – while the GDP grew more than double the rate, at 8.2%.

- Nomura analysis says the economic shocks of demonetisation of 2016, GST of 2017 and the pandemic of 2020 and 2021 *derailed* (CAGR) growth in 'real' consumption expenditure during 2012-23 (to 3.1% in rural and 2.6% in urban areas from 4% and 4.4%, respectively, during 2005-10 and 6.6% and 5.2%, respectively, during 2010-12).

- FMCG sector is seeing *decline* in volume sales and revenue to multiple year lows (volume sale hitting 14-quarter low of 2.5% in Q3 of FY24 and revenue growth lowest after Q2 of FY21).

- Manufacturing's capacity utilization (CU) is below 75% – touching or crossing 75% only *on three occasions* in the past *20 quarters*.

- RBI's enterprise surveys of Q3 of FY24 points to *rise* in business optimism in services and infrastructure for subsequent three quarters but *not for manufacturing* (significant improvement expected only in Q2 of FY25). Consumer confidence (one-year ahead) is on "recovery path" and remains below 50% – lower than pre-pandemic highs of 60% or more.

Little wonder, corporate capex is not taking off despite *all-time high profits* (touched historical high in 2020 but moderating thereafter) and robust bank balance sheets.

Even *foreign private investment* (FDI inflows) has dried (due to exogenous factors). Growth in FDI inflows hit the *second lowest* in nearly quarter century, at -16% growth in FY23, the lowest since -26% in FY13. It fell further to -31% in H1 of FY24. This has made the Centre to seek inputs to figure out the answer and frame a response.

Mar 28, 2024

NB: *In the first 11 months of FY24, personal loans accounted for "one-third" of total bank credit outflows.*

***

What will 'Viksit Bharat' in 2047 Look Like?

In short, "Amrit Kaal" culminates in "Viksit Bharat @2047" and the promise is to make India "developed nation" by 2047

As general elections loom, Centre's promise of a "Viksit Bharat" (developed nation) by 2047 is gaining prominence. But what does it mean or would mean for average Indian?

First a brief backgrounder. Its genesis can be traced to the Prime Minister's 75-week "cultural" events called "Azadi Ka Amrit Mahotsav" (India@75). It was launched on March 10, 2021 for "celebrations" of the 75 years of Independence (August 15, 2022). In his national address on August 15, 2021, the Prime Minister said this "Amrit Mahotsav of freedom" was the "start" of the "Amrit Kaal" of next 25 years (culminating on August 15, 2047). "Starting from here", he said, "the entire journey of the next 25 years, when we celebrate the centenary of Indian independence, marks the *Amrit period* of creation of a new India."

He also listed the goals: "The goal of 'Amrit Kaal' is to ascend to *new heights of prosperity* for India and the citizens of India...to create an India where the level of facilities is not dividing the village and the city...where the government does not interfere unnecessarily in the lives of citizens… where there is world's every modern infrastructure… building an AatmaNirbhar Bharat…we have to move… further. 100% villages should have roads, 100% households should have a bank account, 100% beneficiaries should have Ayushman Bharat card, 100% eligible persons should have gas connection under Ujjwala scheme and 100% beneficiaries should have Aawas…"

There were more details but the intent and the essence are very clear: In short, "Amrit Kaal" culminates in "Viksit Bharat@2047" and the promise is to make India a "developed nation" by 2047.

Thereafter, Finance Minister Nirmala Sitharaman stepped in. In the 2022 budget speech she said her budget's purpose was "to lay the foundation and give a blueprint to steer the economy over the Amrit Kaal of the next 25 years" (ending with 2047), quoted the Prime Minister and said the goals were "to ascend to new heights of prosperity for India and the citizens of India" with a focus on "macro-economic" growth, and "all-inclusive welfare". She declared her 2023 budget as "the first Budget in Amrit Kaal" and her 2024 (interim) further said: "Our vision for 'Viksit Bharat' is that of "Prosperous Bharat in harmony with nature, with modern infrastructure, and providing opportunities for all citizens and all regions to reach their potential"." These budgets had specific allocations to realise the goals too.

The question that strikes *now* is: What about all those goals and budget allocations already declared in the past two-and-half years?

Decoding 'Viksit Bharat' plan for 2047

On February 9, 2024, Bibek Debroy, chairman of the

Economic Advisory Council to the Prime Minister (EAC-PM), had pinned down the "Viksit Bharat" concept in an article, "How will we know that Bharat is Viksit?"

He concluding paragraph says it all: "Thus, here are the *options to pin down* India in 2047. (1) HDI more than 0.8. (2) A movement to the *high-income category* in constant US dollars. (3) A movement to the high-income category in current (2047) US dollars. We *usually intend* (2) or (3) and understandably. (3) is easier than (2) to reach."

Notice, Debroy *rules out* the goal of human development (HDI). What does he mean by raising India to "high-income" category?

Using the World Bank's classification of countries, the goal would be to transcend India from its lower-middle income category ("$1,086 and $4,255") to high-income one ("more than $13,205"). His numbers match the World Bank's 2023 *per capita GNI* levels (at current US dollar) for different income-group countries. The World Bank's per capita GNI is different from its current USD or PPP methods. It is also different from *per capita GDP* – India's per capita GDP for FY24 is estimated at Rs 2,10,679 while per capita GNI is lower at Rs 2,07,587 (AE2, current prices).

Since the NITI Aayog's paper on "Viksit Bharat" is not available (submitted to the Centre on February 20, 2024 but not made public) the starting point has to be Debroy's. He is not just an economist, his unique position as head of the EAC-PM gives him *rare insights.*

Side effects of unifocal push for GDP growth

Debroy's "we usually intend" sentence makes three big points about the vision/goals of "Viksit Bharat". It

- *rules out* improvement in human capital (HDI).
- *omits* income inequality.
- *exclusively focuses on* GDP growth (per capita GNI, whether at current USD or 2047 USD).

No surprises in any of it.

The Centre's economic policies of the past 10 years are exactly the same – GDP growth alone is sufficient to turn India into economic superpower. The *latest example* of this is Finance Ministry report "Re-examining narratives: A collection of essays", released in December 2023.

In that report, Chief Economic Advisor (CEA) V Anantha Nageswaran argued: "…*in contrast* to the advanced economies… the Indian experience has been that of *convergence between growth and inequality rather than of conflict*. Thus, for a developing country such as India…the *focus needs to continue* to be on growing the *size of the economic pie* rapidly, at least for the foreseeable future." He also re-emphasised *prioritising growth* over redistribution of income.

His arguments can't be dismissed merely as *contrasting reading* of the contemporary global and Indian realities, though they seem so (more of it later). Here are three instances to give a better perspective.

One, when 190-odd countries adopted the UN's SDG goals in 2015, two significant changes were made to the earlier MGD goals it replaced: (i) added the goal of "reduced inequalities" (mainly of income but also of opportunities and others) because it was realized that inequality of all kinds "deprives people of opportunity and subjects many to conditions of extreme poverty" and (ii) separated the goal of reducing poverty into two new goals, "no poverty" and "zero hunger" because despite high "growth" during the 15 years of running the MGD poverty and hunger were not eliminated to the extent it was expected.

Two, a year earlier in 2014, Thomas Piketty changed the global economic discourse forever with his magnum opus "Capital in the Twenty-First Century". It told the world about post-1980 "resurgence of inequality" in "developed countries" because of the neoliberal (free-market) *economic and political* push. This was a *reversal* of "reduction of inequality "between 1910 and 1950". Nobel laureates Stiglitz and Krugman have, before and after Piketty's 2014 book, said the same – arguing that neoliberalism is not economics or supported by evidence but a "political" doctrine/construct and has failed to deliver (eliminate poverty, hunger and inequality).

Piketty (with Lucas Chancel) also said the *same reversal* happened in India for the same reason at the same time – a sharp rise in inequality after the market-reforms of mid-1980s and liberalisation of 1991 which happened to produce *historic high* GDP growth but led to income/wealth concentrating at the top 1% and 10%, *not* the middle 40% and bottom 50%.

The pandemic *exacerbated* poverty, hunger and income inequality.

Three, in December 2023, Raghuram Rajan patiently explained how India's GDP would become *four times bigger* by 2047 (at 6% growth) – hence, *per capita* GDP (or GNI) will also rise *four times* – and yet, India would still remain a lower middle-income category with *below* China's *current* per capita income (GDP or GNI) and by which time its demographic dividend/advantage would have disappeared.

Nageswaran can't be unaware of any of the above. But he is *in sync* with the Centre's neoliberalism push which began in 1980s and 1990s – and intensified in recent years. Hence, all the focus is solely on GDP growth – as the panacea for all that ails India.

Human capital development remains neglected despite India's extremely poor record. The UNDP's HDI report of 2022-24 lists India at 134th among 193 countries, with its HDI score of 0.644 ("medium human development country") – *below* China (75), Sri Lanka (78), Bangladesh (129) and Bhutan (125). More worryingly, India's HDI score *fall* from 0.645 in 2018, after having consistent risen from 0.434 in 1990. The fall is partly because of both pre-pandemic shocks of demonetisation and GST and the pandemic shock. This report also says, "after 20 years of steady progress, *inequality between countries* at the upper and lower ends of the HDI has *reversed course*, ticking up each year since 2020". Besides, India continues to be home to *maximum poor, hungry and illiterate in the world* (both before and after the pandemic).

The World Bank and Ashoka Mody have attributed the miraculous rise of China to its relatively higher HDI before it opened its economy in 1980s, prioritized HDI growth after 1980s and continues to do so now in 2024 (allocating more on education, social security and employment, health and sanitation than defence. India did the reverse in its 2024 budget (defence outstripping the others).

Coupled with this, privatisation of health and education denies access to quality services to the masses. Jobs are rapidly *shifting* to low-productive, low-paying agriculture and self-employment as high-productive, high-income jobs disappear.

"New welfarism" and "guarantees" like "free" ration to 67% Indians for next five years and cash to farmers (PM-Kisan) and women (Ujjwala) are good to *avert* poverty and hunger but are *no replacement* for quality education, health and jobs (income) and *can't* raise average Indian to those of development countries.

Sure, without addressing human capital development and income inequality, the GDP will keep growing rapidly – as it does now. But all-round development will still remain a goal.

Mar 27, 2024

NB: *In her 2024 budget speech, Sitharaman equated "Amrit Kaal" with "Kartavya Kaal" and said: "It is our 'Kartavya Kaal'." The FinMin's White Paper of February 2024, which listed the failures of the previous decades of FY05-FY14, instead of critically examining the economic policies of the current of FY15-FY24, copy-pasted this in its concluding line: "The Amrit Kaal has just begun and our destination is "India a developed nation by 2047". It is our Kartavya Kaal."*

The penny around "Viksit Bharat @2047" dropped and the bubble burst on March 3, 2024.

That day all national dailies showcased a report (no official account, however, is available) that said the Prime Minister held a day-long meeting with his Council of Ministers to discuss "100-day agenda" for his next government (to come to power in June 2024), "action plan" for the next five years (2024-2029) and a "vision document" for the "Viksit Bharat 2047". It was also said that "more than 2,700 meetings, workshops and seminars" had been held at various levels, "suggestions of more than 20 lakh youth" had been received and NITI Aayog had been tasked with preparing a "unified vision" for "Viksit Bharat @2047" by combining 10 sectoral visions into a unified vision.

A "vision document" for Viksit Bharat 2047? What was all the fuss about it since August 2021 then? What about Debroy's pontifications of February 9, 2024? Things began to make sense with the realization that on the face of it, the Centre was claiming to set new goals but everything about it was same – the same push for GDP growth with a special focus on infrastructure investment and manufacturing – but repackaged under the rhetoric of "Viksit Bharat@2047", like the proverbial 'old wine in new bottle'.

***

Is it Unfair for Farmers to Demand a Guaranteed Higher Price?

Historic fall in farm households' income in 2022-23 points to the agrarian crisis which calls for multipronged policy responses

For the first time in Indian history, farm households' monthly expenditure (MPCE) has fallen below non-farm (and average) rural households, a national daily has reported (MoSPI released only a three-page brief). The HCS/MPCE being the proxy for income (no income survey is done in India, unlike, say the US) it points to a dramatic fall in farm households' income.

This is not unexpected. Agrarian distress is chronic and well documented, including by NITI Aayog member Ramesh Chand. As farmers' agitation on legal guarantee for higher MSP for 23 crops continues, a few other facts must be kept in mind to assess if the demand is warranted, or even sufficient.

- In 2022-23, agriculture provided maximum jobs, 45.8% (PLFS 2022-23) but earned the lowest, 15% of the GVA in FY23 (PE).
- "Agricultural labourers" (landless farmers) constituted 54.9% of total "agricultural workers" in 2011 (Census 2021 not yet initiated) – shooting up

from 28.1% in 1951. They are not covered under the PM-Kisan (6,000 per year) while even rich farmers do.

- 86% of farmers were small and marginal (less than 2 ha landholding) in 2015-16 – up from 83.3% in a decade (after 2005-06). They are engaged in subsistence farming.

Why demand for legalising Swaminathan formula?

Surely, demand for legal and higher MSP is very old.

In fact, back in 2002, the Abhijit Sen Committee had recommended "statutory" and higher MSP – "strictly on the basis of C2 cost of production (all cost including the imputed cost of family labour, owned capital and rental on land)". The 2006 Swaminathan formula of C2+50% profit is, therefore, not new. All this had to do with prolonged agrarian crisis, manifested in distress migrations from rural areas in 1990s and 2000s and massive spike in farmers' suicide in 2000s. This was followed by the reverse migration of 2020.

Why did it provoke such strong protests in 2020-21 and 2024?

There are four proximate factors (the UPA didn't accept the C2+50% formula).

One, a series of promises to implement this formula and give it legal status were made. In the run-up to the 2014 general elections (a) then prime ministerial candidate Narendra Modi promised MSP on the similar lines (Swaminathan was conferred 'Bharat Ratna' posthumously recently); (b) the BJP's 2014 manifesto promised "a minimum of 50% profits over the cost of production", without mentioning the Swaminathan formula; (c) agitating farmers' leader Jagjit Singh Dallewal says, as Gujarat Chief Minister, Modi had supported legal status for C2+50% in 2011 (so also says the Congress) and the Centre assured of it during the negotiations in 2020-21. None of these has been disputed.

Two, the Centre promised, in 2016, to double farmers' income by 2022 (more of it later).

Three, a far bigger factor was the three new farm laws of 2020 (without consultations with farmers, state governments or due diligence in the Parliament. One of those – Farmers' Produce Trade and Commerce (Promotion and Facilitation) Act, 2020 – sought to dismantle MSP through private unregulated markets without MSP, outside state-regulated APMCs and pitting farmers directly against private businesses without recourse to dispute resolution of trade through the courts of law. Before this law, multiple government reports had sought to review/restrict procurement of wheat and paddy at MSP in Punjab and Haryana.

Four, while withdrawing the farm laws in November 2021, the Centre set up a 26-member committee to look into MSP afresh (on July 18, 2022, seven months later) but nothing more has been heard of it. It was not given any deadline.

The current MSP formula is AF2+FL – "paid out" cost (A2) plus family labour (FL), excluding other "imputed" costs which C2 has, like rental value of owned land, rent paid for leased-in land, farm saved seeds, manure, owned machine labour etc.

Have farmers' income doubled?

There is no data after 2018-19 to show the status of farmers' income.

The 2018-19 Situation Assessment of Agricultural Households and Land and Livestock Holdings of Households in Rural India, released in September 2021, said "total income" of farm households was 10,218 per month. This needs to be put in perspective:

- Of 10,218 per month, 5,514 came from farming and allied activities (land lease, crop and livestock); largest component was "wages" or labour (4,063 or 39.8%) – higher than from "crop production" (3,798).

- Previous estimate was in 2012-13, when total income was 6,427 (3,844 from farming and allied activities).

- During 2012-13 and 2018-19, maximum rise was seen in "wages" (labour), which nearly doubled (from 2,071 to 4,063).

- In 2018-19, 50.2% farm households were indebted with average debt of 74,121 – more than the average annual income from agriculture and allied activities (5,514x12).

In 2016, Aayog's Ramesh Chand had lamented: "It is ironic that estimates of farmers' income are not published by the CSO, though time series and year-wise estimates of sectoral income for agriculture are available in National Accounts Statistics." Chand became Aayog member in 2015. Nine years later, neither he nor the Aayog has done so.

It must be noted that after announcing the election-eve sop, PM-Kisan, in 2019, the Centre brought new farm laws in 2020 (later withdrawn) to leave farmers to market – private market for trade, contract farming outside state-control and higher stocking limits for private business.

This wasn't a good idea because markets across the world have failed farmers.

The best evidence of this is the current farmers' protests and agitations across Europe and the US. The other is continued subsidies to agriculture/farmers by these market-driven economies. An OECD report of 2023 says, government-support to agriculture "reached record levels" of $851 billion per year during 2020-22 for 54 countries (OECD members plus 11 emerging economies like India) – a 2.5-fold rise over two decades.

Does MSP help and is it a silver bullet?

The MSP regime, brought in 1965, made India food sufficient and raised incomes of Punjab and Haryana farmers (Green revolution states) and later that of Madhya Pradesh farmers more than others. A 2020 study by the University of Pennsylvania found Punjab's completely regulated APMCs brought 30-35% higher income to farmers than Odisha's partly-regulated and Bihar's unregulated APMCs. It concluded: "…those who have access to the public procurement machinery unequivocally benefit both from a higher price and lower uncertainty in their income stream."

Evidence and logic dictate that procurement of pulses and edible oil at MSP would have made India self-sufficient in these areas too. A 2024 NITI Aayog report (formally unveiled on February 22, 2024 but not made public) warns India might fail to meet demand for pulses in edible oil even by 2047-48 – despite a 2016 report of then CEA Arvind Subramanian) – which pleaded for "higher" MSP for pulses with "effective procurement" on "war footing".

Procurement of crops other than wheat and paddy

would have forced Punjab and Haryana to diversify, prevented groundwater depletion and eliminated stubble burning/air pollution (a big factor for it being Punjab and Haryana governments' orders to delay sowing of paddy by a month to time it to monsoon, but this leaves little time to prepare the field for wheat).

But many experts and industry estimate suggest otherwise due to the following concerns:

(a) Shifting to legal C2+50% for 23 crops would cost Rs 13 lakh crore for 16 crops, although a differential payment system (gap between MSP and market price) would cost Rs 21,000 crore (for 8 of 16 crops for which market price was lower than MSP in 2022-23 (MY23).

(b) It would lead to 25-30% inflation.

(c) Sectors like horticulture, livestock, fisheries and milk have boomed without MSP.

Surely differential payment is better than MSP – but is fraught with high risks. Madhya Pradesh tried this (Bhavantar Bhugtan Yojana) in 2017 but withdrew it less than six months later as traders gamed it and market prices of supported crops (mainly pulses and oil seeds) crashed, in some cases to less than one-fourth of MSP. Haryana has a variation of it (Bhavantar Bharpai Scheme) which gives "input costs" since 2018, but farmers demand MSP instead. Karnataka has another (Price Deficiency Payment Scheme) limited to potato, onion and tomato. Any attempt to adopt this would require study and pragmatic design/implementation mechanisms.

Concerns about inflation are misplaced because procurements at MSP is meant for PDS (subsidised for consumers) and buffer stocks (emergency use). Small amounts (excess in buffer) are sold in open market but to do the reverse – tame inflation. While farmers have been dumping their produces on streets for years due to low market price, the world learnt two new phrases in 2022 and 2023 – "sellers' inflation" and "greedflation" – high inflation caused by concentrated market power. Former RBI Deputy Governor Viral Acharya even called for "dismantling" India's Big 5 (Reliance, Tata, Birla, Adani, Bharti groups) to tame inflation caused by them.

As for high-flying sectors, the HCS data of 2022-23 shows animal and horticulture products overtook cereals and pulses for the first time since 1990-2000. As against 14.9% household expenses going to cereals and pulses, 28.6% went to animal products (milk, eggs, meat and fish) and 19.6% to horticulture (vegetables and fruits) in rural areas.

These are all secular trends since 1990-2000 – cereals and pulses going down while the latter two going up (normal in growing economy). Going by the high consumption demand for animal and horticulture products, these items don't even need MSP – but the reverse is true for crops. Don't forget the 1960s' food crisis and dependence on the US brought MSP and Green Revolution to Punjab and Haryana.

Milk production has grown not due to market but farmers' cooperatives like Amul. MD of the cooperative that runs Amul RS Sodhi said in 2018 that farmers get 80-82% of market realisation. The pandemic saw private businesses dumping milk suppliers while Amul and other cooperatives came to their rescue. Horticulture is fetching high market price but for traders/companies, not farmers. Farm gate prices routinely crash (capsicum crashed to Rs 1 per kg in 2023, kinnow to 6-11 per kg in 2023-2024, apple prices down after corporate takeover of trade).

The solution lies in a mix of measures:

- MSP for bigger farmers producing surplus (only 7.2% farm households sold crops at APMCs in 2019 (NABARD 2023).
- Cash transfer for others – landless (not covered under the PM-Kisan), and small and marginal farmers. A study is needed to arrive at the right amount (Rs 6,000 was not decided on any study or evidence).
- Incentives for crop diversification outside Punjab. The Centre's offer to procure five crops at MSP (cotton, maize, arhar/tur, masur and urad) on contract for five years is meant only for Punjab (which farmers dismissed) – is off-the-cuff and illogical given that three (cotton, maize and tur) fetched higher than MSP prices in market in MY23.
- Comprehensive policies on agriculture and jobs to address chronic (and worsening) crises.

Feb 29, 2024

NB: *Despite promising to double farmers' income by 2022, the Modi government not only did the exact opposite, it dismantled all legal protections for farmers' rights by bringing three new farm laws amidst the pandemic lockdown of 2020 – first as ordinances and then ramrodded through the Parliament dismissing all objections from allies like the Shiromani Akali Dal and the Opposition. Those three farm laws brought centralized contract farming, private mandis with no MSP, freehand to hoarding food grain and other essential commodities by private traders* *and businesses and removed any role for state governments and courts of law to intervene and protect farmers rights and resolve farmer-corporate disputes. It took farmers more than a year of protests (holding siege at New Delhi's borders) and more than 700 farmers' deaths during the protests for the government to relent – and withdraw the three laws. When the protest march to New Delhi began, the government welcomed them with nails, concrete blocks, concertina wires, teargas shells and baton charges.*

When farmers marched again towards New Delhi in February 2024 to demand legalized MSP – which the Centre has been promising from time to time – they were stopped more than 200 km away at Punjab-Haryana border – with concrete barriers, tear gas shells dropped from drones and pellets fired from shotguns – first used in Jammu and Kashmir by the Modi government to devastating impact on people (more than 6,000 people, mostly teenagers, lost their eyesight fully or partially by 2018). The difference this time was the pellets were fired by the BJP-run Haryana government's police force, not central security forces. By this time, the farmers' unity had been broken and their protests ended with no gains.

***

Can India be a 'Developed Nation' without Quality Jobs?

GDP growth and manufacturing push have not produced adequate quality jobs for decades

FinMin's 'White Paper ends on a high note: "The Amrit Kaal has just begun and our destination is "India a developed nation by 2047"." But the obvious pathway to be "developed", from the current "low-middle income" status is: Access to quality jobs.

Jobs are far more critical as a channel of redistribution of wealth and income when an economy is growing rapidly but also pushing up inequality and contains the world's largest population of extremely poor and hungry – which is the case with India as multiple global reports have been saying in the past few years. But the 'white paper' doesn't mention unemployment; 'employment' and 'wages' are mentioned only as problems of the previous decade (FY05-FY14). Nor 'Demographic dividend', but 'demography' is mentioned once in the context of the current decade's social security scheme for unorganized sector workers.

The economic review and interim budget devoted to the current decades' policies and achievements, which preceded the 'white paper' also does not tackle jobs.

When jobs disappear

Nothing can be farther from the truth.

The latest manifestation is the revelations that about 100 Indians were hired as "helpers" in the Russian army in the war against Ukraine in the past one year, many of whom have ended up actually fighting the war and seeking help from the Indian government for the violation of contract – despite huge vacancies in the Indian defence forces and the 'Agniveer' scheme not even replacing those who retire every year.

This follows the desperate rush for high-risk and unprotected work in war-hit Israel (the Centre has refused to ensure their safety while facilitating such recruitments). After Haryana and Uttar Pradesh, recruitment camps would be held in Rajasthan. Four more states – Bihar, Himachal Pradesh, Telangana and Mizoram – are in the queue, having written to the Centre for such camps.

Another manifestation is the sharp rise in the number of Indians illegally entering the US (and other countries like Canada, the UK and other European countries). According to a Rajya Sabha answer of December 14, 2023, their number (as nabbed by the US authorities) went up from 8,027 in FY19 and 1,227 in FY20 to 30,662 in FY21, 63,927 in FY22 and 96,917 in FY23 (as per the US fiscal year of October to September). Undoubtedly, such illegal influx to the US poses high risks to life (some have lost theirs) and costs a bomb (Rs 60-80 lakh reportedly paid to middlemen).

This illegal influx is over and above hundreds of thousands already living illegally in the US ("unauthorised immigrants"). A Pew Research report of November 2023 said, 725,000 Indians were staying illegally in the US –

the third-largest after Mexico and El Salvador. Economist Ashoka Mody explained that while those from Mexico are rapidly falling and from El Salvador rising slowly, Indians are rising "at a brisk pace".

None of this is surprising. Every job vacancy in India attracts a disproportionately large number of aspirants, often overqualified ones (just like engineers, and postgraduates in maths and anthropology joining the Delhi Zoo as keepers).

Besides, official data confirm the crisis.

The job crisis

On the face of it, the PLFS reports of 2017-18 to 2022-23 show improvements in the headline numbers – employment rate (WPR), labour participation (LFPR) and unemployment rate (UR). But scratch the surface and the ugly reality bursts forth:

- Reverse structural transformation – a sign of lack of non-farm jobs – continues with (i) jobs shifting to informal, low-paying and low-productive farm sector, reaching 45.8% (ii) jobs in "proprietary and partnership" households in no-farm sectors (informal sector) steadily rising to 71.4% (iii) manufacturing jobs falling to 11.4% in 2022-23 and (iv) best quality jobs, "regular wages/salaried", declining to 20.9% with "no social security" cover (for these jobs) rising to 53.9%.

- WPR and LFPR numbers are (iv) abysmally low compared to the OECD averages: 38% and 40%, respectively (all ages, weekly status) against 70% and 74% (15-64 years, weekly status) in the OECD. WPR is also inflated because (iv) 18.3% of total workers are unpaid ("helpers in household enterprise", mostly women (v) very large number of people have dropped out of labour force ("more than half of the 900 million Indians of legal working age – roughly the population of the US and Russia combined – don't want a job", says a Bloomberg report after analysing the CMIE data in 2022), automatically raises LFPR and FLFP and (v) "self-employment" (underemployment, uncertain income) has risen sharply to 57.3% due to lack of jobs.

- 'Real' wages falling for "regular wages/salaried" by an annual average of -2.9% and self-employed by an annual average of -1.8%. It has risen for "casual" workers by an annual average of +0.6%.

- CMIE data shows the Indian workforce is ageing – undoing the demographic bulge/dividend – with the share of above 45 years rising sharply to 49.2% in 2022-23, from 36.9% in 2016-17; while those in 15-44 years falling to 58.2%, from 63.1%, during the same period.

- EPFO data (a proxy for the formalisation of jobs) shows, in six years of FY16-FY22, "regular contributors" increased by 8.7 million – almost the same ("more than 8 million") as annual additional jobs required to "keep employment rates constant" (World Bank, 2018).

- No official labour data says how many Indians work or are in the labour force. Hence, knowing the status of employment is almost impossible.

- MGNREGS – which provides menial jobs with below statutory minimum wages of states – provides jobs to 64 million rural households (average of FY19-FY24 up to February 16, 2024). This is 38.1% of total rural households (where 68.8% population reside, as per Census 2011). They got 49 days of work in a year at a wage rate of Rs 208.9 (average of six fiscals). If individuals are counted, their number is 93 million (average).

At least 10 "rozgar" have been held until February 12, 2024, but no data shows how many vacancies have been filled or remain vacant. About 1 million vacancies existed in June 2022 in ministries and departments – excluding CPSUs, PSBs, Central Universities, IITs, IIMs, armed police forces (CAPFs), defence forces etc., about which no comprehensive data is available.

Meanwhile, the Centre's "sanctioned" posts have declined over the years; a high proportion of jobs is either outsourced on contract (Group C and D, experts, consultants) or retired employees are rehired at low salaries (to cut down cost). The "Agniveer" scheme is also a symptom of this (cost cutting). The CMIE and a business daily estimate (based on 2024 budget data) that the number of workers in the central departments (excluding CPSUs) would decrease by about 50,000 by March 2025.

The private sector too has failed to provide adequate and secure jobs – hence the persistent agitations for quota in government jobs and a few states forcing the private sector to give jobs to locals (Punjab and Haryana High Court struck down Haryana's law mandating 75% quota for locals in private enterprises in November 2023).

Tech industries and start-ups are shedding jobs in the post-Covid recovery phase. Airlines have been in the doldrums for a long. The gig economy – hiring youngsters at abysmally low wages – is growing rapidly. The Code on Social Security of 2020 promised them social security, but not minimum wage, but there is no sign of any social security – which is unthinkable when it is secularly declining for the best quality jobs ("regular wages/salaried"). Then, a new threat is emerging: The use of Artificial Intelligence (AI). The IMF says 40% of global jobs are exposed to AI – which the FinMin quotes in its review.

Doing more of the same can't produce different results

The Centre's focus for job creation remained unchanged for a decade – reliance on growth in GDP and manufacturing ('Make in India', PLIs, DLIs and 'Skill India').

The GDP growth stopped creating proportionate jobs after 1990, more so after the 2000s when GDP growth accelerated to 7% but job growth declined to 1% due to tech revolutions and capital-intensive manufacturing (Azim Premji University, 2018). It would be more so in future (with AI coming in). Manufacturing never lived up to its promise, not even 'Make in India' (its job share falling to 11.4%) either as an income generator (GDP share) or employment (job share). A 2021 study by the Ashoka University-CMIE said manufacturing jobs halved ("declined by 46%") in five years between FY17 and FY21.

"The Indian Economy: A Review" of January 2024 says 0.7 million jobs have been created (but no evidence is available in the public domain) – as against the target of 6 million in five years. On the contrary, there is evidence that it is driving more jobs abroad than in India. In August 2023, India re-imposed "license" on laptop imports. A business daily found that 11 of the 12 winners of the PLI scheme for solar photovoltaic modules recently listed supply chain partners and service providers from China (some with more than 20 Chinese vendors). The mobile phone industry has benefited from the PLI but it is assembling phones with imported components (as Raghuram Rajan found after analysing trade data). The DLI for Micron's semiconductor (chips) plant in Gujarat is also an assembling unit.

'Skill India' was re-launched in 2015 to train 300 million youth by 2022 in industrial and services skills to raise chances of landing jobs (the Indian workforce is extremely low in education and skill levels). Its outcome is revealing: Its official 'dashboard' data (accessed on February 16, 2024) says, "as of July '21", Skill India "trained" 1,28,554, "certified" 94,852 (those informally trained) and "placed" (job placement) 48,074. That is, 0.2% of the target was achieved and 21.5% of trained ones found jobs.

A national policy on employment (NEP) – the work which started during UPA-II – is yet to materialise. A new industrial policy, the consultation paper for which was circulated in December 2022, was put on hold a year later as the focus firmly remains on the PLIs and DLIs.

None of the recent documents ('white paper', 'review' and interim budget) indicates a change in the growth model either. Without a change, Fortune India explained, using data ("2024 Ahoy! Why GDP growth must improve the livelihood of average Indian") that India would continue to remain a "lower-middle income" country in 2047, even if the GDP size jumps four times.

How would better focus on jobs help?

Good quality jobs automatically translate into better wages (income) – which improves access to better education, skills and healthcare, raising the quality of human capital (HDI). India continues to be in the bottom half of countries in UNDP's HDI ranking (132 among 191 countries in 2022); its HDI score went down from the peak of 0.645 in 2018 to 0.633 in 2022 – after consistently rising from 0.434 in 1990 (UNDP HDI).

Better HDI would automatically translate into higher productivity and hence, higher growth (than the average of 6% in current decade). On the other hand, continuation of "free" ration to 813.5 million people, Rs 6,000 cash transfer to 90.8 million farmers under the PM-Kisan (August-November 2023) or 49 days of menial low-paying MGNREGS work to 38.1% rural households (or 93 million individuals) will avert starvation – but can't make India "developed".

Feb 22, 2024

NB: *There are more distress signals. In 2023, more than 1,000 Indians risked life to cross the English Channel in inflatable small boats and reached the UK looking for jobs and asylum – up by 60% from 2022. The number of Indians applying for asylum in the UK has surged, crossing 5,000 for the first time in 2023.*

The cancelled constable recruitment exams in Uttar Pradesh (over question paper leak) in February 2024 for 60,000 vacancies attracted 48 lakh applicants – a selection ratio of just 1.25%. Both question paper leaks and abysmally low selection ratio is now common. In 2018, 62 jobs for lowly peons (class IV) in Uttar Pradesh attracted 93,000 candidates – of which 3,700 were PhD holders, 28,000 post-graduates and 50,000 graduates.

Meanwhile, more than 30% of the premier IITs continue to find no placements year after year in campus selections. As for skilling, the Skill India has been a failure and latest report suggests students are shying away from the ITI ecosystem. For more, read article "What will deliver 'strong' growth in FY24?"

***

Anything That Can Go Wrong May Have Gone Wrong With IBC

Over 90% haircut are a wakeup call to review the entire gamut of policies and governance involving stressed asset resolution

One of the existing policies and practices that needs urgent attention is stressed asset management through the Insolvency and Bankruptcy Code (IBC) of 2016. It is beset with multiple concerns best exemplified by the abysmally low "recovery". It touched a new low in December 2023 when the National Company Law Tribunal (NCLT) approved the resolution of bankrupt Reliance Communications Infrastructure Ltd (RCIL) for just Rs 455.92 crore – less than 1% of "the claimed" debt of Rs 49,668 crore and "the admitted claims" of Rs 47,251.34 crore.

This is worse than it appears at first glance because the IBC "resolution" (different from "liquidation") is not just about debt recovery but revival of a bankrupt firm. Hence, a few questions arise: What happened to the assets? What happened to the collaterals or personal guarantees the loans would have entailed?

The focus here is on a worrisome trend the causes of which need to be studied and fixed. After all, high haircut isn't new. A parliamentary panel had, in 2021, expressed serious concerns about "disproportionately large and unsustainable" haircuts going up to "as much as 95%", asked the Centre to fix a "benchmark" and sought review of "the design and the implementation" of the IBC.

That the panel's advice has not yet been heeded is bad enough. Worse, the IBC seems to enjoy wide and largely uncritical support from the power-that-be after the RCIL resolution.

Defending the indefensible?

On January 11, 2024, RBI Governor Shaktikanta Das said at an event that the IBC's performance "appears quite encouraging", arguing that the "resolution value" (recovery) should be compared with "liquidation value" or "fair value" at the time of admission since by the time a firm was admitted under the IBC "significant value destruction" would have already happened. He noted, by those yardsticks, the IBC had done well with the realization of 169% and 86%, respectively.

A few days later, on January 15, 2024, former chairman of the IBBI (IBC regulator) MS Sahoo (2016-2021) wrote (i) the recovery "is not an objective of the IBC" and "is not mentioned in the legislation", rather (ii) the objective "is resolving stress" and that it achieved this as 5,000 firms had exited, out of 7,000 that entered the IBC process. He also wrote that the IBC (iii) "penalises attempts to use the IBC for recovery" but didn't explain how or why (iv) dismissed high incidence of "liquidation" arguing that the IBC allowed "the market to make the choice" and said (v) three-fourths of the firms liquidated were "either sick or defunct".

The only issue both Das and Sahoo flagged is the long delay in the IBC process.

Chief Economic Advisor V Anantha Nageswaran followed this with "The Indian Economy: A Review", released on January 29, 2024. It had only good things to say: (a) the IBC had "rescued 808 corporate debtors" with realisations of 168.5% against "the liquidation value" and 32% against "the admitted claims" and (b) cited a study by IIM-Ahmedabad (August 2023) which had found 76% rise in average sales, 50% rise in average employee expenses and 50% rise in average total assets of the resolved ("resolution") firms. This report had also been cited by Sahoo.

The 'white paper', tabled on February 8, 2024, mentioned the IBC for Its positive Impacts on FDI inflows and bank balance sheets.

How fair is "fair value"?

All the above claims and arguments hide more than they reveal.

One, "liquidation value" is not the right yardstick in "resolution" cases – which is about reviving bankrupt firms through takeovers. It is relevant only in "liquidation" cases (the other outcome of the IBC when "resolution" fails).

Under the IBC, both "liquidation value" and "fair value" are carried out by outside agencies. This is a sound business practice but needs a closer look. For example, the cumulative IBBI data up to September 2023 shows, such valuations are abysmally low for the 808 firms which had successful "resolution": "Liquidation value" at 18.9% and "fair value" at 29.5%, respectively, of "the admitted claims" (debts) for these firms. Hence, the high recovery against these parameters. The IBBI reports are silent on the assets of those firms.

Valuation of firms has attracted attention for all the wrong reasons so far.

It came to public debate during the first privatisation of nine CPSUs during 1999-2003. The CAG's 2006 report flagged how high-value assets like land, plant and machinery, operational and reserve mines, fully developed township and power plant (in the BALCO, Modern Bread and others) were excluded from valuations. One of these, the sale of Hindustan Zinc Limited (HZL) in 2002, came back to haunt in November 2021 when the Supreme Court ordered fresh CBI investigation. The court discovered that "unknown public servant" had appointed the valuer; the valuer "didn't possess the requisite expertise", "failed to consider" various assets (including several mines and mineral reserves) and the global advisor on valuation was missing ("undergone voluntary liquidation"). The story of the privatisation of the Central Electronics Limited (CEL) and Pawan Hans Ltd (PHL) in 2022 and 2023, respectively, was no different and undervaluation was one of the reasons for termination of their sales.

Two, delays do cause "significant value destruction" but this needs to be fixed, not used as an argument to justified low recovery. "Value destruction" due to delays can happen in three ways. One is delay in approaching the IBC – which may cause to asset stripping – is counter-intuitive because the RBI mandates banks and NBFCs ("Prudential Framework for Resolution of Stressed Assets" of 2019 and also 2021) to classify and report NPAs if the interest payment is overdue by 90 days (a reversal of its 2018 directive to do so after a day's default the context is explained later).

The second way is delays in the IBC process and asset

stripping – both of which are known. The IBBI data reveals, "in 808 resolved CDs" (resolved cases), 200 applications of "avoidance transactions" worth Rs 1.13 lakh crore (another phrase for asset stripping) are pending with adjudicating authority (AA) as on September 30, 2023 – which is a reflection of systemic failure (to prevent money laundering, asset sales and timely action/decision).

The third is poor due diligence in giving loans (without verifying the assets, collaterals/personal guarantees), followed by poor monitoring of debtors (check against money laundering, assets stripping etc.).

Three, the IBC's preamble says it is meant for "time-bound" resolution "for maximisation jioBookof value of assets", "promote entrepreneurship", "availability of credit" and "balance the interests of all the stakeholders". If "recovery" is sub-optimal, none of the other IBC objectives would succeed. Hence, the argument that recovery "is not an objective" of the IBC makes no sense.

Four, the IIM-Ahmedabad study's finding is inevitable because of abysmally low valuations of firms (liquidation and fair values) and very high haircuts.

Poor outcomes of IBC

Here are the other key (cumulative) outcomes of the IBC up to H1 of FY24:

(i) 808 firms were "resolved", leading to "recovery" of 31.9% of "the admitted claims".

(ii) 2,249 cases (74% of all the IBC's 3,057 cases) ended in "liquidation" (junk sale), yielding 4.9% of "the admitted claims". 77% of liquidation cases (1,713 of 2,229 for which data is available) "were earlier with the BIFR" (pre-2016) – pointing to a massive failure of the IBC.

(iii) Total recovery (resolution plus liquidation) is 16.7% – a haircut of 83.3% against 75% haircuts under the much-maligned BIFR.

(iv) "Delay" in the IBC processes range from 414 to 867 days for "resolution" and 426 to 857 days for "liquidation" cases (against stipulated period of 180 days and maximum allowed period of 270 days).

Multiple systemic risks to IBC

There are many systemic threats to the IBC.

The Centre diluted the IBC in 2021 when it brought "Pre-Packaged Insolvency Resolution Process (PPIRP)" for MSMEs – which takes the stressed assets of MSMEs to outside the IBC mechanism. This also means moving away from the creditor-driven resolution framework of the IBC to the debtor-driven one (like in the case of BIFR) – by allowing debtors to run the business while the resolution is on. This is a reversal of the 2021 parliamentary panel's call to further strengthen the creditors' rights ("the fundamental aim of this statute (IBC) is to secure creditor rights"). Nothing is known about the PPIRP's progress.

This happened after the Centre diluted the RBI's regulatory powers in 2018. It came immediately after the RBI issued a "revised framework" asking banks to start resolution process after a day's default. Then RBI Governor Urjit Patel resigned soon thereafter and flagged it in his 2019 book "Overdraft: Saving the Indian Saver", stating that the Supreme Court had found nothing problematic with the RBI framework. He had also flagged how many Central ministers had publicly criticised the IBC. The same year, then Deputy Governor of RBI Viral Acharya wrote a book "Quest for Restoring Financial Stability in India", also accusing the Centre of diluting the IBC ("...forbearance in loss recognition crept in again for some asset classes; and the resolution of several non-performing borrowers under the Insolvency and Bankruptcy Code was stayed").

The RBI's "Prudential Framework for Resolution of Stressed Assets" of 2019 and also 2021 mentioned earlier – which mandates banks and NBFCs to classify and report NPAs after corporate entities default by 90 days.

To make matters worse, the IBC seems to have been gamed. A good example of this is a progressive fall in the "recovery" (cumulative) from "resolution": 70% in FY18, 43% in FY19, 46% in FY20, 39% in FY21, 33% in FY22, 32% in FY23 and 32% in H1 of FY24. This could be for a variety of reasons – cartelisation, official favouritism, low bidder interest or something else – which elaborate studies can establish.

Then there are related issues that need scrutiny and course corrections to make the stressed asset resolutions successful:

- Corporate structures have become increasingly complex to detect money laundering and assets stripping – multiple layers of interconnected firms with shell companies and tax havens (Panama Papers, Paradise Papers and Pandora Papers).
- Conflict of interest and poor standards of auditing by the Big 4 (recall the Satyam Computers and IL&FS cases). More recently, the National Financial Reporting Authority (NFRA) flagged deficiencies in Big 4 and their associates.

- Private bad banks, the ARCs, are under scanner. After raiding four of them at 60 places in Mumbai, Delhi and Ahmedabad in December 2021 the Income Tax Department revealed this about those: (i) "unholy nexus" with loan defaulters in which "a maze of" shell companies were involved (ii) acquired NPAs at "far less than the real value of the collateral securities" (iii) "usually" took money from defaulters to pay banks and "more often than not" stressed assets were "re-acquired" by defaulters "at a fraction of their real values" (iv) "concealed the profits on disposal", thereby "evaded" tax and "deprived" the banks their share of actual profits and (v) maintained "a parallel set of accounts" containing "cash transactions" of more than Rs 850 crore and funds were routed through "offshore structures (tax havens) to acquire the assets". More than two years later, the RBI is yet to cancel their licenses.

- Public sector bad bank NARCL (set up in 2021) is handicapped as public sector bankers are reluctant to transfer NPAs to it. Multiple newspaper reports said in January 2024 that this was because the NARCL offered lower than the liquidation value. The Rajya Sabha was told on December 12, 2023 that as against a target of Rs 2 lakh crore, only Rs 11,617 crore of NPAs had been transferred until November 30, 2023. The RBI's banking trend report of 2022-23" shows PSBs account for the least NPAs sold to ARCs and NARCL. In a meeting with PSBs on December 30, 2023, Sitharaman directed them to improve transfer of bad loans to the NARCL and also prevent banking frauds (another big concern).

- Evergreening of loans by PSBs? This became the talking point first in 2020 when the RBI-appointed KV Kamath Committee recommended this (called "Resolution Framework for Covid19-related Stress") in 26 sectors due to the pandemic stress and the RBI accepted. In May 2023, the RBI Governor revealed that PSBs had found "innovative ways to conceal the real status of stressed loans" but days later in June 2023, the RBI offered "compromised settlement" with fraudsters and willful defaulters and made them eligible for fresh loans after 12 months.

Feb 15, 2024

NB: *Add Biju's and Paytm to the long list of firms which have suffered due to bad governance, undiscovered by statutory auditors like the Satyam Computers, IL&FS and others.*

***

Rethinking Disinvestment or Temporarily Stalled?

Not only is full disclosure of disinvestment not available in public, no account exists to tell its impact, challenges and future course, let alone course corrections.

There isn't a White Paper yet on disinvestment but there is a discernible change in the Centre's approach. This year's budget speech and receipt budget skipped it altogether. So is the case with the FinMin's "White Paper on the Indian Economy" released on February 8, 2024. The FinMin's "The Indian Economy: A Review" (not the Economic Survey of 2023-24), released on the eve of the interim budget, on January 29, 2024, mentioned the word twice – both in the context of "reform" to give "space and opportunity" to private sector "to grow" as "co-partner in development" – but didn't go into the outcomes or impact on public and private sectors.

The interim budget (2024) marks a departure in the way disinvestment is being disclosed. Until 2023, budget documents listed disinvestment targets and receipts under "miscellaneous capital receipts" (non-debt), along with "others". In 2024, only a consolidated amount is mentioned under "miscellaneous capital receipts" – without explaining the change or listing the elements.

Clarity came a few days later, at the post-interim budget interactions by DIMPAM secretary Tuhin Kanta Pandey. He revealed that it consists of two items – disinvestment and asset monetisation (NMP) but *without specific targets* for either ("The fact is that we don't have a fixed number."). He acknowledged that the omission of disinvestment was due to inability to achieve targets. Only twice, in FY18 and FY19, the targets have been achieved.

His statement would mean (I) disinvestment process would continue *without targets* and (ii) receipts from the NMP, the *second channel of 'strategic' disinvestment*, is likely to make its debut in budget documents soon. The combined target for FY25 (BE) is Rs 50,000 crore. Sale of enemy property, another *disinvestment* channel (not classified as 'strategic') launched in 2018, hasn't made its debut in budget documents either.

In another interview, Pandey said there was *rethink* in the government: (iii) to move away from disinvestment as "a way to manage your fiscal deficit on a sustained basis" and (iv) look at it "in terms of how you manage enterprises" (or public wealth management).

Whither 'strategic disinvestment'?

Firstly, the Centre didn't set up the National Investment Fund (NIF), as spelt out first in 2005 and *continues* to be part of the revised Disinvestment Policy of 2016. It mandates *seven* specific capex for which the proceeds are to be used – maintain public ownership of CPSUs, recapitalise PSBs, fresh investments in RRBs/NABARD/Exim Bank and other public enterprises, capex in the Railways etc. Instead, the proceeds went into the Consolidated Fund of India (CFI). Although this was suggested by the 14th Finance Commission, the Centre never explained its position.

Secondly, the *two core objectives* ("vision") of the Disinvestment Policy of 2016 – which are (a) "promote people's ownership" of CPSUs and (b) "efficient management of public investment" in CPSUs – have been violated.

While no official assessment (FinMin, DPAM or NITI Aayog) is in public domain, the CAG has repeated flagged various issues in its reports of 2019, 2020 and 2021 (post-2014). The key findings of these reports are:

(i) CPSUs picked up the tab of 'strategic disinvestment' in *eight CPSUs* during 2014-2020 (HPCL, HSCC, DCIL, REC, Kamraj Port, NEPC, THDC India and NPCCL) – which became subsidiaries of the buyer CPSUs resulting in "transfer of resources" from one government department to another *without* "any change in the stake". Many CPSUs had to do so "by borrowing from market".

(ii) 25% public float in CPSUs was not met in a large number of cases of *listed ones*. Of 133 CPSUs eligible to be listed in stock exchanges, only two were brought to market for listing by FY20, showing "slow progress in listing".

(iii) Strategic holdings in the SUUTI (government holding of blue-chip private companies) were given up as "sweetener" *against the advice* of the Department of Economic Affairs (DEA).

(iv) "Enemy shares" (part of "enemy property" brought into the ambit of disinvestment in 2018) were sold off to generate Rs 1,881 crore in FY20 ("realised"). But the CAG report was severe for the method deployed. It said: "However, the share certificates of enemy shares in 45 listed companies and 145 unlisted companies were *not available* with the Custodian and *duplicate share* certificates were *yet to be issued*. Further, the unlisted shares in physical form were *yet to be dematerialised* for their disposal."

CPSU-to-CPSU sale was *prohibited in 2002*; it was waived off only to be *reinstated* on April 19, 2022 on the plea that this would "continue the inherent inefficiencies" and "defeat the very purpose" – but *without* explaining why it had been waived off.

The reinstatement of prohibition on CPSU-to-CPSU sale came (a) *after* repeated criticism by the CAG and also (b) *after* disinvestment policy was *tweaked* in early 202 to let go of even profit-making CPSUs (*banned* in 2005 by the UPA government, allowing only minority stake sales) and wholesale disposal of CPSUs except a few in "strategic sectors".

FinMin think tank NIPFP published a study of disinvestment during FY15-FY20. Its findings are in line with those of the CAG. On promoting public ownership, it said "minimum public float norms are yet to come into operation". On efficient management of CPSUs, it said the CPSU-to-CPSU sale made no difference (continued as "government companies"). Besides, the new "capital restructuring norms" of *compulsory* declaration of dividend, issue of bonus shares and splitting of shares might be "considered as a deviation" from promoting greater corporate autonomy envisaged under the `Ratna' system". Even the "expanded" 'strategic disinvestment' – sale of enemy shares, NMP and sale of strategic holdings in SUUTI (used as "sweetener" against the DEA advice) – attracted remarks such as these "may not reduce government's equity" in CPSUs, brought in "possibly to meet the fiscal deficit" but were "not in sync" with the government's intention to exit from the non-strategic businesses for efficient utilization of public resources.

Post-2020 saw a series of *setbacks* to strategic disinvestment: (a) awards in the case of Central Electronics Limited (CEL) and Pawan Hans Limited (PHL) were terminated *after* the allegations of under-valuation and award to ineligible firms surfaced and the processes were put on hold (b) in the case of BPCL (cleared in 2016) and IDBI due to lack of due diligence and (c) in the case of Container Corporation of India (CONCOR) and NMDC *after* the Hindenburg report hit in January 2023 and the finances of two potential buyers, the Adani and Vedanta groups, came under *intense scrutiny due to high debt*.

The only successful case was that of the chronic loss-making Air India in January 2022 – handed back to the original owner, the Tata group, nearly 70 years later (Air India was nationalised in 1953), *after writing off* Rs 61,000 crore of legacy debts and other liabilities.

The cumulative impact is: In FY22, the actual disinvest receipt was Rs 13,627 crore – against the budget target (BE) of Rs 1.75 lakh crore and revised target (RE) of Rs 78,000 crore. In FY23, the actual receipt was Rs 35,294 crore ((DPAM data, since the budget is silent) against the target of Rs 65,000 crore (BE) and revised target (RE) of Rs 50,000 crore). This means 7.8% and 54% of the budgeted targets were met in FY22 and FY23, respectively. In FY24, the disinvestment generated Rs 12,504 crore until January 23, 2023 (DIPAM) – against the budgeted target of Rs 51,000 crore.

Whither NMP and sale of 'enemy shares'?

The *second 'strategic' disinvestment channel*, the NMP, is floundering too.

It was formally launched in 2021 "to unlock the value of investments in *brownfield public sector assets*" which the Union Cabinet called "strategic disinvestment" in 2019. In 2021, a target was set to generate Rs 6 lakh crore in four fiscals of FY22-FY25. This is to be achieved by handing over *existing* public infrastructure, including those in social sector, to private businesses to run.

The NITI Aayog, which helms it (also acts as advisor on "strategic disinvestment" or privatisation), says in its 2022-23 annual report that in FY22, the NMP target of Rs 88,000 crore was achieved but in FY23, only Rs 26,000 crore of the targeted Rs 1.6 lakh crore was "completed" ("in accruals and/or investments"). This means, in the first two years (half-way mark) only *19%* of the target was achieved.

The *disinvestment channel* of sale of enemy property, was greenlighted in 2018 and made part of "disinvestment" in 2019. The CAG report of FY20 flagged how this was done (Rs 1,881 crore "realised" in FY20) even when share certificates were not available, duplicate certificates had not been issued and paper shares not dematerialised. The NIPFP study of 2022 said the sale of enemy shares may have been done to reduce fiscal deficit but it doesn't really fit into the disinvestment goal of reducing government equity in CPSUs.

How much money has been generated through the sale of "enemy shares"? That is not clear (not disclosed in budget documents). As per a Lok Sabha answer of December 5, 2023, Rs 2,709.16 crore had been generated through this. In January 2024, the Centre announced it will sell 291,000 "enemy shares" in 84 companies.

Why a review is imperative?

It is unlikely that public – to which the Centre is accountable – is even aware of all its *components*: (i) minority stake sales (including stake sales of the 'strategic' holdings in the SUUTI) (ii) strategic sales (CPSU-to-CPSU sale, sale and handover of management to private businesses and the NMP) and (iii) sale of enemy shares. They are also unlikely to be aware of all the instruments involved – like, IPOs/OFSs, sale to employees, compulsory buy backs, ETFs etc.

A comprehensive picture of the disinvestment proceeds is not in public since all of it goes to the Consolidated Fund of India (CFI). Its utilisation is not known either. And if efficient management of CPSUs means their "revival", then we're far from there.

The DIPAM secretary's indications that the Centre may pay more attention to manage CPSUs' wealth better could be misleading given that the ascent continues on handing over public assets to private businesses (CPSUs, public infrastructure (NMP) and "enemy shares").

Feb 13, 2024

***

Decadal Growth II: What will Drive Higher Growth?

By the 2011-12 GDP series data, three growth engines (PFCE, GFCE and exports) are down and by the 2004-05 GDP series, all four (including GFCF) are down

The RBI's January bulletin makes surprising claims about the state of the economy: "The Indian economy recorded stronger than expected growth in 2023-24, underpinned by a shift from consumption to investment. The government's thrust on capex is *starting to crowd in* private investment."

These claims are primarily based on the first advanced estimates (AE1) for FY24, released by the MoSPI earlier this month, which show growth in consumption (PFCE) is falling to 4.4% in FY24, from 7.5% in FY23 and its GDP share to 56.9%, from 58.5%. The RBI completely misses the point that this 4.4% PFCE growth is the lowest in 21 years (after FY03 when it was 2.9%), except the pandemic FY21 when it fell to -5.2%.

On the investment front, it is mixed. Growth in government expenditure (GFCE) is up by 4.1% from a low base of 0.1% growth in FY23, but its GDP share is down to 9.6%, from 9.9% in FY23. Growth in capex (GFCF) is down to 10.3%, from 11.4% in FY23, but its GDP share is up to 34.9%, from 34% in FY23. When GFCE and GFCF are combined (as investments) their growth is up by 8% and their GDP share is up to 44.5% – from 43.8% in FY23.

Going by the RBI's yardstick of considering GDP share as the driving power of growth (as in the January bulletin), the GDP share of PFCE is down and that of combined GFCE and GFCF is up and hence, a "shift" may be surmised. But before doing that, here are four caveats:

(i) FY24 (AE1) is a statistical extrapolation of Q1 and Q2 data.

(ii) Q1 and Q2 data are based on formal sector indicators, which largely ignore the informal sector contributing 50% to the GDP and 90% to employment.

(iii) GDP deflator (for inflation-indexing) used for FY24 (AE1) is very low at 1.6% (nominal growth of 8.9% minus real growth of 7.3%) – when headline inflation (CPI) is 5.8% during April-December 2023 and the RBI's own estimate for FY24 is 5.4% (stated on December 8, 2023).

(iv) RBI's growth estimate for FY24 is 7% while the MoSPI's is 7.3% – while both have access to the same set of formal sector indicators.

The prudent way to assess a "shift" is long or medium-term trends, not two-quarters of formal sector data.

Downward trend in both demand and investment

In a decadal comparison, the trend in PFCE remains unchanged – a slowdown in its growth and GDP share. PFCE's average growth is 5.9% in the current decade of FY15-FY24 – against 6.1% in the previous decade of FY05-FY14 – and its GDP share averages 56.8% now against 56.9% earlier (the 2011-12 series, constant prices).

But if the 2004-05 series (constant prices) data is considered for the previous decade, the PFCE's growth and GDP share were far higher at 7.4% and 63.9%, respectively. This means, the 2011-12 series data doesn't support the RBI's claim but the 2004-05 series data (which the RBI doesn't mention) does.

In the shorter time span, the PFCE's GDP share of 56.8% in the pre-pandemic FY20 is almost the same as 56.9% in FY24 (AE1) but the interim years saw a secular surge in the PFCE from 57.2% in FY21 to 58.3% in FY22 and to 58.5% in FY23. This means demand in the economy is still affected by the prolonged K-shaped growth and (post-pandemic) recovery. There is plenty of corroborative evidence of this:

- Household financial assets have fallen to a 47-year low of 5.1% of the GDP in FY23, while their debts have risen to 5.8% of the GDP in FY23 – only twice in 53 years it went above 5%, in FY06 (5.1%) and FY07 (6.6%).

- ITRs declaring taxable income have fallen 54% in seven years between FY16 and FY23.

- Tax burdens shift from the rich (corporate tax cut, manufacturing incentives like PLIs and DLIs, cut in GST on luxury items etc.) to the poor through indirect taxes (elevated oil taxes when crude price is low for years, 5% GST on food items consumed by the poor). As a result, in the past five fiscals (FY19-FY23), income tax collection has risen by 76% but corporate tax by only 24.5% and direct tax buoyancy has fallen to 1.18 in FY23 from 2.52 in FY22 (IT data released on January 23, 2024).

- "Free" ration is being given to 67% of households and

India's rank slips in the Global Hunger Index – from 80 in 2015 (of 104 countries) to 111th in 2023 (of 125 countries).

- Low-paying informal agriculture employs 45.8% of total workers and 18.3% of the total workforce are unpaid or "helper in household enterprise" (PLFS 2022-23).

- 55 million rural households were engaged in low-paying (below statutory minimum wages) menial MGNREGS jobs until January 20, 2024 (FY24). Going by the 2011 Census data of households, they constitute 33% of total rural households.

- 'Real' rural wages contracted in 21 of 23 months up to October 2023 (reflecting rural distress where 70% population reside). This contraction (negative growth) follows a deceleration since 2014.

- Loss of jobs in major IT companies (20,000 sacked from 85 firms in January 2024 alone) and start-ups.

- Thousands of youths are lining up in Uttar Pradesh, after Haryana, for construction jobs in Israel – undeterred by the war and the Indian government's refusal to provide any protection or security to those aspirants despairing for work. Meanwhile, engineers, and postgraduates in maths and anthropology have joined the Delhi Zoo as keepers.

What about investments?

Government expenditure (GFCE): Its growth averages 5.4% now, against 7.3% in the previous decade. Its GDP share averages 10%, against a higher 10.4% in the previous decade (2011-12 series). In the 2004-05 series,

GFCE grew at 7.3% (unchanged) but its GDP share was much higher at 11.8% and hence, as a driver of growth, GFCE has weakened.

Overall capex (GFCF): Average growth is 6.7% and its GDP share is 32% in the current decade – against 9% (higher) and 31% (lower), respectively, in the previous decade (2011-12 series). In the 2004-05 series, these numbers were 7.3% and 35.2% (far higher in both), respectively. Going by the 2011-12 numbers, GFCF's share has gone up but fallen by the 2004-05 numbers.

Public sector GFCF: Its GDP share averages 6.9% during eight fiscals of FY15-FY22 (up to which data is available). In the previous decade, it averaged higher at 7.6% (Economic Survey and MoSPI, at current prices).

Private corporate and household GFCFs: Private corporate GFCF's GDP share averages 10.7% in eight fiscals of FY15-FY22 (current prices) for which data is available. This is a fall from 11.9% in FY16 (to 10% in FY22). In comparison, it averaged 12.7% in the previous decade with a peak of 16.9% in FY08. So, private corporate GFCF as a driver of growth has weakened.

Households (private) contributed an average of 11% of the GDP in the current decade, against 12.9% in the previous decade (both in current prices). This has weakened. The 2004-05 series clubs private corporate with households to mark "private" GFCF, and hence, avoided.

Does the RBI's theory hold? The answer is 'no' because the GDP shares of two growth engines are down in the 2011-12 GDP series: PFCE (56.8% now against 56.9% then), GFCE (10.1% now against 10.4% then). GFCF, the third engine, is up (32% now against 31% then), taking the combined investment (GFCE plus GFCF) up (42.1% now against 41.4% then).

But in the 2004-05 series, all three are own (PFCE, GFCE, GFCF and even GFCE+GFCF).

In a shorter-time span, the post-pandemic fiscals of FY22-FY24 (2011-12 series) saw mixed trends – the GDP share of PFCE maintains a secular rise and then suddenly falls in FY24 (AE1); GFCEs keep falling, GFCFs keep rising and that of combined GFCE and GFCF also keep rising.

Interestingly, the RBI assumes growth in investment from (a) "anecdotal evidence" pointing to "home renters becoming owners of bigger homes" and (b) "the rate of real fixed investment is at a historic high in 2023-24" due to "high corporate profitability quarter after quarter".

RBI's own data for Q1 of FY24 (August 2023 bulletin) on private "envisaged" investments (intentions, not actual) also reflects a declining momentum. The Bank of Baroda/CMIE data shows Private "envisaged" investment continued to decline in Q2 and Q3 of FY24. Besides, corporate profit is no indicator of capex – which, ironically is moderating in FY23 and FY24. As for house sales, the Knight Frank India data shows the sale of luxury houses overtook that of affordable houses in Q2 of FY24 – pointing to K-shaped growth (as is the case with vehicles, smartphones and many FMCG items).

Outside the GDP data, three other investment indicators can be considered.

FDI inflows: The DPIIT data show, it grew at an average of 8.4% during the nine fiscals of FY15-FY23 and by H1 of FY24 it declined by -31% (y-on-y). The previous decade saw FDI growth averaging 31%. So, FDI also has slowed down considerably.

VC funding for start-ups: It has fallen to the lowest in 2023 since 2019 as start-ups go through a prolonged "funding winter".

Bank credit outflow: The RBI bulletin talks of high growth in bank credit – ignoring its own clampdown on banks and NBFCs due to an alarming rise in "unsecured" personal loans for the past two years. It raised the capital adequacy ratio (CAR) for banks and NBFCs on November 16 by 25 percentage points to prevent a meltdown, having ignored the fact that personal loans were driving credit growth and overtaking credit to industry, services and agriculture. Meanwhile, the RBI Governor warns against "exuberance in lending" for three months of November, December and January.

These facts and evidence don't point to a "shift" to investment-driven growth. Further, the decadal GDP growth is down – from 5.9%, from 6.8%.

What is driving growth in the decadal comparison – if not consumption and investment?

Significant changes in the GDP share come from three components: (i) net exports are down to -2.4% of the GDP, from -3.7% in the previous decade (ii) inventories (change in stocks) and valuables are down to 2.7% of the GDP, from 4.9% and (iii) discrepancies have doubled to 0.8%, from 0.4%.

A fall in net exports is mainly due to a significant drop in imports, down to 23.6% of the GDP in the current decade, against 25.4% in the previous decade (difference of -1.8 percentage points). But this is bad news because exports – the only remaining growth engine – are down to 21.1% of the GDP from 21.7% in the previous decade.

The questions that beg answer are: If all the four growth engines – consumption (PFCE, GFCE, GFCF and net exports) are down what really is driving growth? What will drive higher growth going forward? These questions bring back another question: When will the 2011-12 GDP series will be replaced for the most significant statistical data? These are the points to ponder for economists and policymakers.

Jan 31, 2024

NB: *India uses single GDP deflator, not double deflators separately for input and output, and its deflator has questioned by former CEA (2014-2018) for underestimating inflation.*

The GST rates are far too long and tedious for even tax experts and its structures are so devious that gold attracts 3% tax, diamonds 0.25% or less while non-branded food items for poor 5%, biscuits and educational instruments 18%. Read article "Why high GST collection is bad taxation and bad economics" for more.

***

Decadal Growth I: Momentum is Shifting and Growth More K-shaped

During FY15-FY24, growths in GDP and average income have gone down compared to the previous decade FY05-FY14, this calls for course correction.

India has undoubtedly made rapid economic progress in the last ten years. The IMF database shows, it is the fifth largest economy in GDP size (current USD) – significantly up from the 10th position it occupied in 2014. It is also the fastest growing major economy. Given that the first advance estimates (AE1) for FY24 is available, released on January 5, 2024, it is possible to do a decadal comparison – between FY15-FY24 and FY05-FY14.

The picture that emerges Is as follows:

Decadal growth significantly down

The average GDP growth in the current decade (FY15-FY24) stands at 5.9% (taking 7.3% growth for FY24 as per the AE1). In comparison, growth averaged 6.8% during the previous decade of FY05-FY14 (2011-12 series, constant prices) – that is, 0.9 percentage points higher. It was on a smaller size of GDP though. While FY14 GDP was $1.7 trillion, by FY23, India's GDP had already crossed $3.3 trillion (at current USD). But the actual gap is much bigger. Here is why.

Under the 2004-05 GDP series (constant prices), the previous decade's growth averaged 7.6% – that is, 1.7 percentage point *higher*. Even this doesn't give an accurate picture for the following reasons.

One, former CEA Arvind Subramanian believes the 2011-12 GDP series released on January 30, 2015 *overestimates* growth. This made India surpass China in 2015 to become the fastest growing major economy.

Subramanian (CEA for the period 2014-2018) was the first to red-flag this in 2019, after quitting the office. He used 17 high frequency indicators to demonstrate that the 2011-12 series overestimated growth by *2.5 to 3.7 percent* during 2012-2016. He also pointed out that since the underlying GDP data were *not available in public* (a first in post-independent history) nobody outside the government, not even then CEA, could estimate GDP using the official data.

More recently, in September 2023, Subramanian and Ashoka Mody, another Indian-American economist, argued that the GDP growth was overestimated by 2.5 to 3 percentage points in Q1 of FY24. The AE1 numbers for FY24 say: (a) *discrepancies* in the GDP estimate is Rs 2.6 lakh crore or 1.5% of the GDP and (b) the GDP inflation at 1.6% (nominal growth of 8.9% minus real growth of 7.3%) is abysmally low compared to the headline CPI inflation estimated at 5.4% (RBI's projection on December 8, 2023) and actual of 5.8% during April-December 2023 (MoSPI). These two factors (discrepancies and inflation numbers) had provoked Subramanian and Mody to raise the stink in September 2023.

Overestimated growth in the 2011-12 GDP series means the decadal growth during FY15-FY24 is much less than 5.9% – at least by 2.5 percentage points – bringing it down to 3.4%. This would mean the previous decade's growth was higher by *4.2 percentage points*.

Two, the 2011-12 back series data was released almost *four years* later on November 28, 2018 (not on January 30, 2015 when the rebasing happened) – also an unusual event. In 2015, then chairman of National Statistical Commission (NSC) Pronab Sen revealed (on December 10, 2018) that NITI Aayog vice chairman of the time Arvind Panagariya *dismissed* the back series data prepared by the Central Statistical Office (CSO).

The second back series data was prepared by a sub-committee of finance ministry think tank NIPFP, which released it on July 15, 2018. This too was *dismissed* by the NITI Ayog (then under Rajiv Kumar) and the MoSPI for showing two double-digit growths in the previous decade – 10.2% in FY08 and 10.8% in FY11.

The appropriate authority for economic data is the NSC – apex, autonomous body for standard setting, quality control and regulation of all official data. The CSO was the autonomous agency tasked to prepare the GDP numbers. In 2019, the CSO was made "integral part of the main ministry (MoSPI)"; the NSC remains autonomous on paper as the real power has passed on to the MoSPI since 2019.

When the back series was finally released on November 28, 2018, the MoSPI *showcased a graph* to let the world know that it had *lowered* the growth of FY06-FY12 by 1.34 percentage points – from average of 8.24% under the 2004-05 series to 6.9% under the 2011-12 series. For the entire decade (FY05-FY14), the growth was lowered by 1.7 percentage points (as noted earlier).

But Subramanian's desire to independently assess the 2011-12 GDP series was for a different reason.

There were significant changes in the methodology adopted for the 2011-12 GDP series. Most important was the first-time use of MCA-21 database of the Ministry of Corporate Affairs (MCA) to estimate *manufacturing and services* GVAs (constituting 82% to the total GVA in FY12). The MCA-21 database is *self-populated* by registered companies and is *unaudited* and *secret* (not in public domain); it was *untested* then. In 2019, the NSSO *tested* only services industries and found 45% data defective ("out-of-survey/casualty" or inappropriately listed). As of now, this MCA-21 remains unaudited, untested, secret and also beset with *technical glitches* (as on January 19, 2024) despite a year-long efforts.

It was this flawed MCA-21, which came into existence in 2006 (as revealed by the NIPFP sub-committee), that the back series data couldn't be tracked back to 1950-51 (the usual practice) by the CSO and the NIPFP sub-committee. But the MoSPI quietly did this (without public announcement) and published the back series data extending from 1950-51 (first noticed in 2021) *without revealing* how it did this (MCA-21 didn't exist before 2006).

Three, multiple and routine *retrospective revisions* in GDP numbers in 2011-12 series have made the numbers unreal, provoking former RBI Governor YV Reddy to comment in 2017: "In India not only the future is uncertain, even the past is uncertain. So, they keep revising the data."

Nevertheless, another way to map the decadal growth is the decadal *jump* (from first to tenth fiscal).

Growth *jumped* by 75.3% from FY14 (inherited

growth) to FY24. This was much higher at 93% – from FY04 (inherited growth) to FY14. Both are in the 2011-12 GDP series. If the 2004-05 series is considered, the jump during the previous decade was higher, at 107%.

It may be argued that the current decade saw once-in-100-year pandemic crisis. True, but the GDP growth had sunk to 3.9% in FY20, before the pandemic hit (FY21) – from the peak of 8.3% three years earlier in FY17. Ironically, this *high growth* of 8.3% came in the fiscal which saw the first of *twin shocks, demonetisation* of November 2016, which began the derailment as millions of jobs and businesses were lost overnight. The previous decade had also seen the 2007-09 Great Recession, plunging growth to 3.1% in FY09 but bounced back to 6.4% in FY14 (both in 2011-12 series, constant prices). The bounce back from the pandemic is good on paper, at 7.3% in FY24 but lacks credibility (as explained earlier).

Average income going down

There is yet another cause of big concern.

Notwithstanding growth in GDP, average Indian remains *one of the poorest* in the world – lower than those of "low middle income" countries and also the global average. IMF data shows, average Indian income (per capita GDP at current USD) was in the *last quarter* among 190-odd countries – both in 2014 and 2022.

During the current decade, per capita income (GDP) has grown by average of 4.7% (less than the GDP growth), while it was much higher at 5.2% in the previous decade (2011-12 series, constant prices) and 5.7% (2004-05 series, constant prices). In terms of *decadal jump,* it is 57.2% now (from FY14 to FY24), while it was 65.4% in the previous decade (from FY04 to FY14) in the 2011-12 series and 73.6% in the 2004-05 series (both at constant prices).

This slowdown in average income is reflected in slowing down consumption (PFCE) or demand in the economy.

The decadal growth in PFCE during FY15-FY24 is 5.9% and falling to 4.4% in FY24 (AE1) – lowest in the past 21 years after FY03 (2.9%), except for the pandemic FY21 (-5.2%). The previous decade saw higher PFCE growth, at 6.1% (2011-12 series) or 7.4% (2004-05 series). That poverty is rising is also reflected in the "free" ration to 67% *households* or over 813.5 million Indians left out due to non-updating of data) since April 2020, which continues till December 2029.

So, who actually benefiting from GDP growth?

Quite clearly, those at the top of the economic pyramid (the top 10%, particularly the top 1%) – as Lucas Chancel and Thomas Piketty first flagged in 2017 and 2019 and the ICE360 report of 2021, 2023 and World Inequality Report of 2022. The same is also reflected in the rise in sale of luxury items (houses, SUVs, smart phones etc. catering to 'affluent India' (FMCG) – *above* those that are affordable for the larger population.

There are other tangible indicators of the skewed growth which needs attention.

(a) Haryana youths are lining up for Israeli jobs, very much like 'indentured' labour during the colonial period – despite *high risks*. Newspapers report their compulsion variously as "better to die while working (in Israel) than to die of hunger without a job" and "if we sit back scared, what will we eat?". These job camps are organised by the

Indian (National Skills Development Corporation) and Israel governments with the Haryana Kaushal Rozgar Nigam Ltd (HKRNL) pitching in. More camps will be set up in Uttar Pradesh and Rajasthan.

A national daily flagged the risks of Israeli jobs: (I) workers are *not required to register* on the Indian government portals ('e-migrate' of the MEA and other such portals of other ministries and agencies and (ii) all the Indian government agencies have *disclaimed any responsibility* for the welfare, safety and rights of these workers.

(b) Job crisis continues. CMIE data shows in October-December 2023 quarter, *joblessness* in the age group of 20-24 grew to *44.5%* and for 25-29 years at 14.3%.

The official PLFS 2022-23 data shows, 38% of people are working (employment rate or WPR in CWS for all ages) – which means, 72% are sitting idle. In sharp contrast, average employment rate or WPR (CWS, 15-64 years) of OECD countries (mix of developed and developing countries) is 71%. But India's 38% workers include a significant chunk of *unpaid workers* ("helper in household enterprise") which increased from 13.6% of the total workforce in 2017-18 to *18.3% in 2022-23*.

This PLFS report also shows that more workers are *moving back* to *low-paying informal* agricultural work (45.8% of total workforce), as per the PLFS report. Demand for *below-minimum wage menial work* under thew MGNREGS galloped to *55 million rural households* – or *33% rural households,* going by the 2011 Census since there is no sign of 2021 Census yet – in by January 20, 2024 in FY24.

Jobs being the best source of income redistribution, such a state of workers amounts to *regressive or reverse* of the Lewisian transformation of the economy – which is going *backward* in quality of jobs and sectors.

Such a skewed growth makes growth unsustainable and hence, the need to redesign the growth model.

NITI Aayog estimate of poverty reduction

In July 2023, the Ayog claimed "135 million have exited multi-dimensional poverty" during 2015-16 and 2019-21. It was based on the health survey data (NFHS-4 of 2015-16 and NHFS-5 of 2019-21), *without accounted for two-thirds of MPI parameters* – income level and educational deprivation. The NHFS-5 is *defective* because it averaged data of pre-pandemic 2019 with partly pandemic-impacted 2021.

On top of it, the Aayog released fresh report on January 15, 2024 (Multidimensional Poverty in India since 2005-06: A Discussion Paper) – without fresh data or survey – saying the MPI "found to decline from 29.17% in 2013-14 to 11.28% in 2022-23 with about 24.82 crore (248.2 million) people escaping poverty during this period". It says: "*Owing to lack of data* for the years between 2005-06 and 2015-16 and after 2019-21 concerning the *incidence of poverty levels*, headcount poverty ratios for 2013-14 and 2022-23 have been estimated based *on compound growth rate of the reduction in the incidence of poverty levels* between 2005-06 and 2015-16 and 2015-16 and 2019-21 respectively."

Incidentally, there is no poverty estimate after 2004-05 (Tendulkar line) or MPCE after 2011-12. *So, there is no way of knowing the level of poverty after 2011-12.*

Jan 31, 2024

NB: *The Q1 of FY24 data was released ahead of the G20 summit in New Delhi in September 2023.*

India became the fifth largest in GDP size (current USD) in 2022 by overtaking the UK. It may become the third largest in GDP size, next to the US and China, by 2029, the SBI Research tells us. Few know that the World Bank ranked India as "the world's third largest economy, moving ahead of Japan" in PPP terms in 2011. About 150 million are left out of the "free" ration coverage due to inclusion and exclusion errors – going by the UN's 2024 projected Indian population of 1441.7 million.

Short Selling: What SEBI Changed; Who will Take Onus for Any Mishap?

SEBI tightens short selling. SC seeks "probe" and "suitable action" if it violates the law and causes loss to investors, together putting a virtual ban on it

Market regulator SEBI's January 5, 2024 circular brought back two rules in its "framework" for short-selling which have far-reaching consequences: (a) "the institutional investors shall disclose upfront at the time of placement of order whether the transaction is a short sale" and (b) "the brokers shall be mandated to collect the details on scrip-wise short sell positions, collate the data and upload it to the stock exchanges before the commencement of trading on the following trading day".

Before explaining the implications, it must be noted that these changes came two days after the Supreme Court directed, on January 3, 2024, that "SEBI and the investigative agencies of the Union Government shall probe whether the loss suffered by Indian investors due to the conduct of Hindenburg Research and any other entities in taking short positions involved any infraction of the law and if so, suitable action shall be taken".

The last word on the Adani-Hindenburg saga, which

prompted the court's directive, has not been heard yet because (i) although the court said the SEBI's investigations into 22 of 24 cases have been "completed" it is not yet in public domain ("SEBI submitted a status report dated 25 August 2023 providing comprehensive details about all the investigations") and (ii) the court gave SEBI more time ("preferably within three months") to complete investigations in the remaining two.

The significance of both, the directive and SEBI's tighter rules on short selling, would be clear soon.

First, what changed?

The relevant elements in SEBI's January 2024 "framework" circular are:

(i) Short selling is allowed for institutional and retail investors but "naked" short selling is not.

(ii) No day trading for institutional investors but allowed for retail investors.

(iii) Institutional investors need to "disclose upfront" if they are short selling (at the time of placement of order); for retail investors, disclosure by end of the transaction day.

(iv) Brokers "mandated" to collect, collate, and upload data on short selling before commencement of trading the next trading day.

(v) No restriction on short selling in F&O segment.

It also added: "In this regard, it is mentioned that the contents of 'Annexure 3' of Chapter 1 of the Master Circular dated October 16, 2023 shall be read as under (which are in line with the provisions of rescinded SEBI Circular No. MRD/DoP/SE/Dep/Cir-14/2007 dated December 20,

2007)..." Then the points listed above follows, along with others.

In effect, the "rescinded" SEBI circular of 2007 (when short selling was first allowed) stands restored. So is also the July 5, 2021 framework (before the Hindenburg report of 2023) – which was identical to the 2007 circular mandated. But the "master circular" of October 16, 2023 had removed the two rules (iii) and (iv) – which were quoted in full at the beginning. Hence, the January 2024 framework was brought "in line" with the 2007 framework.

Virtual ban on short-selling

Why did the SEBI liberalise or remove rules (iii) and (iv) from the framework on October 16, 2023?

The SEBI did not explain and hence, the suspense would continue but the timing needs to be noted. It came after the Hindenburg report hit in January 2023; the tightened checks of January 5, 2024, came after the Supreme Court backed SEBI's investigations (and ruled out handing it over to the CBI or a SIT) on January 3, 2024.

A tightened regulation was expected and understandable when short selling was first introduced in India in 2007 (initial hesitation). During the 2007-09 Great Recession, India did not ban short selling but the US and European countries did (the US regrated later, vowing never to do it again). During the pandemic crisis of 2020, India and some European countries banned it but the US did not. The World Federation of Exchanges (WFE), of which India's NSE is a member, reacted strongly to the ban in April 2020, presenting a host of global studies to assert that a ban on short selling did the opposite of what is intended by market regulators (to stop further market crash) – and that a ban harms market by reducing liquidity, increasing price inefficiency, and hampering price discovery.

It must also be noted that corporate entities all over the world vigorously demand ban on short selling when markets are going down (to prevent further fall). The Hindenburg report did cause a crash in the Adani group's stocks but by January 6, 2024, those stocks had recovered or bettered the pre-Hindenburg price levels.

A tighter regulation of the kind the SEBI reintroduced on January 5, 2024 (for institutional investors to make upfront declarations and brokers to upload such information before the next day's trading) is a signal to investors and stock markets that (a) the Hindenburg-type short selling is being viewed with suspicion and will be watched closely. The Supreme Court's directives (b) to the SEBI and the Centre to "probe" into "any infraction of the law" in short selling causing "loss" to investors, and take "suitable action" will have further chilling impact on institutional investors thinking of short selling.

The combined impact of the two amounts to a virtual ban on short selling by institutional investors – a situation the WEF strongly opposed in April 2020 and which also goes against the SEBI's very arguments supporting short selling in its discussion paper of 2005 that eventual allowed its introduction in 2007.

Short-selling is a legitimate and logical investment practice. It is an efficient tool to (i) accelerate price corrections (ii) check price anomalies and (iii) facilitate liquidity. By virtue of such characteristics, short selling (iv) prevents stock market bubbles (v) checks stock manipulations (vi) promotes good corporate governance and (vii) helps in regulatory oversight.

A virtual ban on it would mean stock investment is a one-way traffic – betting only for upward movement, notwithstanding weak fundamentals, financial frauds and stock manipulations. Recall the Satyam Computers' collapse in 2009 or more recently, the National Financial Reporting Authority (NFRA) pointing out deficiencies in auditing by the Big 4 – KPMG, Deloitte, PwC and EY and their associates. These are evidence of true betrayal of investors. It would be patently wrong to presume that a tighter regulation on short selling will protect investors or stock markets by bringing a misdirected transparency in short selling.

The world has repeatedly paid a heavy price because of stock price manipulations and/or stock market bubbles which eventually burst, hurting 'real' economy. The 2007-09 Great Recession caused big multinational banks and other financial institutions to collapse overnight, wiping out immense wealth and millions of jobs – thereby causing global recession and forced the US and other countries to spend huge sums in bailing out many "too big to fail" corporations. This has happened many times since the 1929 Great Depression.

Overvalued Indian stock markets

It is no secret that Indian stocks and stock markets are highly overvalued. Stock market booms are known to be disconnected from 'real' economy. The RBI used to repeatedly warn against the stock market booms after the initial collapse in early part of 2020 (warned also in 2021) but stopped thereafter as a secular boom continued.

Here is another historical prospective.

The Economic Survey of 2022-23 said Indian stock

markets were way too "expensive". It pointed out that the Nifty50 with a PE multiple (price to earnings ratio) of 21.8x in 2022 was overpriced compared to its global peers – the PE of MSCI World (large and midcaps of 23 developed economies) was 17.3x and that of MSCI EM (24 emerging economies) was 14.6x (in 2022). In the previous five years between 2017-2021, the PE of Nifty50 averaged 27.4x – against MSCI World's 19.4x and MSCI EM's 14.6x (Economic Survey of 2022-23).

What is the status now? Not different at all

As on December 29, 2023 (the latest data easily available), the Pes of MSCI World and MSCI EM were 20.7x and 14.5x, respectively – when the Nifty50 was far higher at 23.17x.

What happens if the galloping stock markets panic due to the virtual ban on short selling? Would SEBI and the Supreme Court take responsibility for any mishap in the markets?

Jan 26, 2024

PS: *The SEBI has been probing the US short-seller Hindenburg's January 2023 allegations of stock manipulations and accounting frauds against the Adani group remains incomplete in April 2024. The case is pending before the Supreme Court for closure since its probe panel came to no definitive conclusions.*

***

2024 Ahoy! Why RBI Must Focus on Big Threats to Fiscal Health

The central bank's focus on states with good fiscal management records while giving more than a free pass to delinquent industries and the Centre is counter-productive.

In the past few years, the RBI has exclusively focused its attention on fiscal management of states, often pointing at all transgressions, while giving a free pass to delinquent industries as well as the Centre. To serve the economy better, it must change course. The list of omissions is long. Here are a few significant ones.

State governments on target, free pass to industry and Centre

Its latest report on states' finances, released on December 11, 2023, is relatively mild – having dented its own reputation in 2022 (explained later). In this report, it concludes that state finances *continue* to be robust "with adequate fiscal space for undertaking higher capex." Here is what it shows about states' fiscal performance (all in percentage of GDP):

- **Fiscal deficit**: 2.8% in FY23 (RE) which is "below the budget estimate for the second consecutive year" and also below "the Centre's limit of 4%." This was "primarily (achieved) through a reduction in revenue deficit." For FY24, fiscal deficits are budgeted at 3.1%. Average fiscal deficit for seven fiscals of FY18-FY24 is 2.9% (less than the FRBM limit of 3%, the Centre has allowed an additional 1%).

- **Revenue deficit**: "Near elimination of the revenue deficit" with 0.3% in FY23 (RE) and 0.1% in FY24 (BE). Average of seven fiscals of FY18-FY24 is 0.5%.

- **Revenue surplus**: 14 states/UTs in FY22 (actual), 18 in FY23 (RE) and 20 in FY24 (BE) – of the 31 states/UTs it covered.

- **Capex**: Budgeted to "increase by 42.6% to 2.9%" in FY24 (BE). Average of *six* fiscal of *FY19-FY24* is 2.6%. The Economic Survey of 2022-23, however, shows the average far higher at 3.7% for six fiscals of FY18-FY23).

- **Outstanding liabilities/debt**: Budgeted to fall to 27.5%, from the peak of 31% in FY21 (pandemic fiscal). Average of FY18-FY24 is 27.5% (FRBM limit is 20%).

Nonetheless, RBI flagged "many states" have outstanding liabilities of over 30%; "primary deficit remained sizeable" (although merely 1.2% of the GDP); "19 States and UTs have budgeted a GFD-GSDP ratio exceeding the FRL limit of 3%"; a few states returning to the old pension system (OPS) and others moving in that direction "would exert a huge burden on State finances" with "additional burden reaching 0.9% of GDP annually by 2060" (ignoring revenue surplus in 20 states/UTs) and "restrict their capacity to undertake growth enhancing capital expenditures etc."

In sharp contrast, the RBI hasn't critically examined the Centre's fiscal performance. Here is what the data of Economic Survey of 2022-23 and 2023 budget reveal about the Centre's fiscal performance:

- Fiscal deficit was 6.4% in FY23 (RE) and budgeted at 5.9% in FY24 (BE); average of seven fiscals of FY8-FY24 is 5.7% of the GDP – far above the FRBM limit of 3% (as against states' less than the limit).
- Revenue deficit was 4.1% in FY23 and is budgeted at 2.9% in FY24; average for FY18-FY24 is 3.9% (far higher than states).
- Centre's capex was 2.7% in FY23 and budgeted at 3.3% in FY24; average for FY18-FY24 is 2.2% (far less than states' 2.6-3.7%).
- Outstanding liabilities (debts) were 57% in FY23 and budgeted at 57.2% in FY24; average of FY18-FY24 is 54.3%, which is far higher than the FRBM limit of 40% (far higher to states' 27.5% too as against their FRBM limit of 20%).

Both the trends (of states and Centre's) are *historical*, more so in the entire 2011-12 GDP series. Hence, there is a need to focus on the Centre.

Its criticism of states' finances is relentless and harsh.

In June and July 2022, its June 2022 bulletin first warned of a Sri Lanka-like "financial risks" developing in India because of states' rising "non-merit freebies" (ranging from 0.1% to 2.7% of GSDP), "off-budget" borrowing (going up to "4.5% of the GDP") when their "own tax revenue" was on "slowdown" and said states' fiscal conditions were "showing warning signs of building stress". Its July 2022 bulletin asked: "Are financial risks moving sub-national?"

Finally, it corrected itself months later in January 2023; *commended* states for their fiscal prudence; freebies, off-budget borrowing and rising debt were conspicuous by absence and instead it noted that *19 states/UTs were revenue surplus*. This report came months after finance ministry think tank NIPFP ran counter to RBI's findings ("Beware of Lanka-like crisis with 'non-merit freebies'" and "States' fiscal space rapidly shrinking, here's why...").

The RBI's 2022 reports coincided with the Centre's campaign against 'revdi' and 'revdi culture' of state governments – ahead of the state elections in Himachal Pradesh and Gujarat (and after the Punjab elections which the Aam Admi Party won).

In 2019, in response to the Centre's offensive against *farm loan waivers* by states, RBI said in "Report of the Internal Working Group to Review Agricultural Credit" (September 2019) that there was "an unprecedented increase" in farm loan waivers during 2014-2019 by 10 states, blaming this for increasing agriculture NPAs "sharply" to 8.44% in FY19. It called the loan waivers "not the panacea" and condemned saying, "they destroy the credit culture", "harm the farmers' interest" and "squeeze the fiscal space".

The fact is: (i) loan waivers are paid by states and hence, no burden on banks (ii) at that time, agriculture's share of NPAs in SCBs (RBI data) was mere 8.5% (industry accounting for the rest 94.5%) (iii) Centre's farm loan waiver of Rs 60,000 crore had an impact in 2008 budget (by UPA-I) (iv) Centre had introduced a cash transfer of Rs 6,000 (PM-Kisan) to *all farmers* (including big farmers owning 10 hectare and above) announced earlier in the year and (v) write-off of corporate loan defaults, including those of declared fraudsters and willful defaulters since FY15 (rising to Rs 14.6 lakh crore by FY23).

Besides, the RBI guards identities of declared (by banks) fraudsters and willful defaulters, who keep multiplying by the year and also flee the country with bank loans as their loans are written off, except once in February 2021 which was in response to a RTI query. The RBI guards their identity on the plea of protecting *business interests*. Rather, in June 2023, RBI offered "compromise settlement" with them and made them eligible for fresh loans after 12 months! This was weeks after the RBI Governor flagged (on May 29) that banks were indulging in "innovative ways to conceal the real status of stressed loans".

Nothing can create more macro-financial risks for the economy than such practices and policies.

There is more.

Centre's fiscal performance

The CAG has been flagging GST Compensation Cess, disinvestment proceeds and many other cesses and surcharges which are meant for specific and exclusive use but ploughed into the Consolidated Fund of India (CFI). After examining the CAG audit reports from 2020 to 2022, the Centre for Social and Economic Progress (CSEP) said (in 2023) that the Centre's off-budget borrowing disclosures (Statement 27") had "deficiency in the format," was "incomplete" and suffered from "non-disclosure of certain entities' debt." *Fortune India* ("5 ways to resolve the unfinished agenda of freebies") noted how Centre's Statement 27 does not disclose off-budget borrowings – disclosing only Rs 1.39 lakh crore during FY17-FY22 while the revised FY21 budget alone showed food and fertiliser subsidy skyrocketing from the budgeted Rs 1.9 lakh crore to Rs 5.6 lakh crore (excess of Rs 3.7 lakh crore).

Ironically, on the off-budget borrowing disclosed in the FY22 budget, the RBI said in its analysis of the Centre's budget that it brought "greater fiscal transparency," describing it as "another positive aspect" of the budget and that this "has been well received by the markets as well."

Perusal of its analysis of the Centre's budget for FY21, FY20, FY19 and FY18 shows the RBI did not flag 'off-budget' borrowing.

Its analysis of FY23 budget, titled "Union Budget 2022-23: Some Pleasant Fiscal Arithmetic," hailed Centre's fiscal performance saying it, "calibrates a thrust to growth with feasible rectitude," "moderation in the cyclically adjusted fiscal deficit," "going forward, debt reduction needs to assume prominence in the fiscal policy strategy" etc.

Its budget analysis of 2023-24 calls provision of "capital expenditure as a key lever of growth", commitments to "credible fiscal consolidation for strengthening macro-stability", "public debt levels have moderated" as the Centre "resorted to prudent fiscal management notwithstanding the challenges induced by the pandemic" etc.

Centre's debt has since grown from Rs 56.7 lakh crore in FY14 to Rs 152.2 lakh crore in FY23. It has missed fiscal deficit targets every fiscal since FY12, its tax-to-GDP remains stuck at 10-11% since FY12.

Even with the industry, the RBI must note routine misreporting of trade invoices (India-China trade data mismatch has increased to $15 billion in Jan-Oct), private investment is stuck despite corporate tax cut and a series of tax incentives, the insolvency and bankruptcy processes leading to huge loss of bank loans (17.6% recovery, 75% firms ending in scrap sale during FY18-FY23). NCLT recently approved sale of Reliance Communications for just 0.96% (Rs 455.9 crore) of the 'admitted claims' (Rs 47,251 crore).

Does such approach improve fiscal management? That's to ponder over!

Jan 4, 2024

NB: *Fertilizer subsidy given directly to corporates, not farmers, despite Aadhaar-enabled ecosystem being used for direct cash transfers to more than 90 million farmers under the PM-Kisan since 2019, "free" ration to 813.5 million people since April 2020 and subsidized LPG to more than 102 million women.*

***

COP28: What India Gained and Lost in Fight Against Climate Crisis

Given that India is already committed to tripling renewable and nuclear energy by 2030 and energy surplus since FY11, it doesn't need to hung up on coal

COP28 would be remembered as the one in which India lost the *moral high ground* in fighting climate crisis – in spite of winning (along with other *developing* countries) the fight to (a) *dilute* exclusive focus on coal and (b) *inclusion* of oil and gas (in the fossil fuel mix) for "transition away".

It had a head-start in 2018, when Prime Minister Narendra Modi received the UNEP Champion of the Earth award in recognition "for his bold environmental leadership on the *global stage*. Under Modi's leadership, India pledged to eliminate all single-use plastics in the country by 2022. Prime Minister Modi also supports and champions the International Solar Alliance, a global partnership to scale up solar energy".

This was a first for India (the award was instituted in 2005). The Prime Minister put a firm (policy) foot forward at COP26 (Glasgow) in 2021 by presenting his "Panchamrit" (five nectar elements) philosophy for India: (i) "reach" non-fossil energy capacity to 500 GW by 2030 (ii) "meet" 50%

energy needs from renewable energy by 2030 (iii) "reduce" carbon emissions by one billion ton by 2030 (iv) "reduce" carbon intensity by less than 45% and (v) "achieve" net-zero emission by 2070. These became India's "Long-Term Low-Carbon Development Strategy" or India's Nationally Determined Contribution (NDC) in 2022.

The moral high ground came in 2023, when the Prime Minister declared "Vasudhaiva Kutumbakam" or "One Earth, One Family, One Future" as the theme of G20 presidentship – advocating, among others, "living in harmony" with nature "in a sustainable, holistic, responsible, and inclusive manner". The G20 declaration sought to "urgently accelerate" climate actions "by strengthening the full and effective implementation of the Paris Agreement" (COP21 of 2015 that brought in equity and Common but differentiated responsibilities (CBDR) which is what the NDC is all about but India had played a *passive role* at COP21).

These gains *dissipated* at COP28 in Dubai.

At COP28, India skipped four key commitments:

- 118 countries pledged to decarbonise the energy sector (which contributes the most to greenhouse gas emissions) by *tripling green energy* capacity by 2030.
- More than 150 countries, including the two major methane emitters Turkmenistan and Kazakhstan, pledged to *cut methane emissions* by 30% by 2030.
- 22 countries pledged to *tripling nuclear energy* by 2050 (from 2020 level).
- 63 countries pledged to *cut down cooling-related emissions* (which includes refrigeration for food, medicine and air conditioning etc).

Instead, India's focus *shifted* to pushing (a) "green credit initiative" which the Prime Minister co-hosted (b) *equity and CBDR* (of COP21) which India's chief negotiator Naresh Pal Gangwar (MoEFCC official) disclosed and (c) better clarity on "climate finance" which Environment Minister Bhupender Yadav flagged.

The big win came on December 13, 2023 when the final declaration was announced. It *diluted* the COP26 commitment to "*phase-down* of coal power" (to which India was a party by replacing it with "accelerating efforts towards the *phase-down* of *unabated* coal power" and "drive the *transition away* from *fossil fuels* in energy systems" (notice the changed terminology and missing "phase-down" or "phase-out" for oil and gas).

India, along with China and other *developing* countries, had fought for this *change* at COP26 and COP27 also and finally won. The fight was legitimate because COP26 had *singled out* coal. The changes are two: (a) "coal" was replaced with "unabated coal" (burning coal *without carbon capture and storage* technology) and (b) "fossil fuels" (not just coal, but oil and gas) was included for the first time in three decades of climate negotiations for action.

What did India gain at COP28?

India's problem (and that of China and many developing ones) is its overdependence on coal, which provided 49% of *installed energy* capacity and lignite another 1.6% as on December 13, 2023 (Ministry of Power), although coal-based thermal power accounts for 74.6% of the *electricity generated* in 2021-22 (P) as per the Energy Statistics of 2023). *Developed* countries (the US and Europe) have already *shifted* away from coal to oil and gas and the OPEC countries (oil producers) are on their side. Their clout was evident at COP28: (i) «a record» and «unprecedented» number of lobbyists/delegates for oil and gas companies ("at least 2,456") were in attendance and (ii) "leaked letters" showed the OPEC asked its members to "proactively reject any text or formula that targets energy, i.e., fossil fuels, rather than emissions".

The three fossil fuels together account for about 80% global energy and 66% electrical generation, contributing nearly 60% of greenhouse gas (GHG) emissions responsible for climate change (as per the UNEP). Hence, including oil and gas is critical in fighting climate crisis.

At COP26, India had agreed to "phase-down" coal (not "phase-out" to which it had strongly opposed). "Phase-down" coal meant India *not* commissioning *new* coal mines and coal-based projects (power, steel, cement etc.) – not abandoning coal altogether. "Phase-out" coal was meant for "unabated coal".

India should have committed to both – for the following *six reasons*.

One, going by India's NDC commitment of 2022, its goal for 2030 is to raise renewable energy (RES) production to *500 GW*. Since its current installed RES capacity (including hydro but excluding nuclear energy), as on December 12, 2023, is *173.6 GW* – achieving 500 GW would mean *tripling* it. The NDC has already declared to *triple* nuclear power by 2030.

So, why did India skip these pledges at COP28 is not clear.

Two, not many know that India is *energy surplus* at least since FY11 – that is, India generates far more "net" electricity ("available" from all sources) than its "net" sale to consumers (domestic as well foreign) – and the surplus is growing by the day.

The Energy Statistics of 2011 and 2023 show, the "net" surplus went up *consistently* from 1,94,537 GWHr in FY11 to 2,99,006 GWHr in FY22 (P) – up to which data is available – *without* accounting for T&D losses. If T&D losses are added – "net" surplus is mostly zero, except for -1 GWHr in FY18 and +7,596 GWHr in FY22 (P). The T&D losses are declining but at a slow pace – from 24% of "net" available in FY11 to 20% in FY22 (P).

The two above points raise a question: Does India really need coal?

Three, India faces severe air pollution and deaths caused by it. Here are three sobering data:

- India has 39 of world's 50 most polluted cities in the world – as per the fifth World Air Quality Report – with both New Delhi and Delhi-NCR figuring at the top 10.
- A 2022 *Lancet* report said, 93% of India had higher air pollution level than the WHO's 2021 norms for safe air.
- A 2020 *Lancet's* report had said air pollution killed *1.67 million in India in 2019*, accounting for 17·8% of the country's total deaths.

Four, the Global Carbon Project's 2023 study (presented at COP28) says India was *one of the top four* polluters of CO2 (from fossil fuel) in 2022: China (31%), the US (14%), India (8%) and the EU27 (7%) – together contributing 59%. In 2023, it said, India would see *8.2% rise in fossil emission* over 2022 – *maximum growth* in the world and twice that of China's

4%, while both the U.S. and EU would *decrease* theirs by 3% and 7%, respectively. These are in line with long-term trends.

Five, the Yale Center for Environmental Law & Policy's Environmental Performance Index of 2022 (EPI) placed India the last – 180th among 180 countries – as the "least sustainable" country from environment view.

Six, the RBI's "Report on currency and finance: Towards a greener cleaner India" of May 2023 says: "India ranked high (seventh) in the list of most affected countries in terms of exposure and vulnerability to *climate risk events* as per the Global Climate Risk Index 2021" It listed a sharp rise in "extreme weather events" in 2022 "on 314 of 365 days…which claimed 3,026 lives, affected 1.96 million hectares of crop area and 4,23,249 houses, and killed over 69,899 animals"); it estimates that "up to 4.5 per cent of India's GDP could be at risk by 2030 owing to lost labour hours from extreme heat and humidity conditions".

Both the recent *cyclone* hitting Tamil Nadu and Andhra Pradesh and the *air pollution* hitting Delhi NCR and other parts of north India in October-November 20203 ("new normal") have been attributed to *climate change* by experts (including Prof Gufran Beig, founder director of SAFAR-India).

All the six reasons call for India to take urgent steps to fight climate crisis – including "phasing-out" *unabated coal*.

Instead, India is doing the exact opposite.

India pushing coal

India *stepped up* coal use in the past few years – before and after its COP26 commitment:

Coal Minister Prahlad Joshi has repeatedly said (in 2023) that India plans to *export coal* by 2025-26.

Union Cabinet extended contract period for coal mining up to *30 years* in April 2022 to ramp up coal production (which will run to 2052 – beyond *2030*).

Coal was opened for "commercial mining" *in a big way in 2020*; Coal India auctioned *91 new coal mines* (with 221 MT per annum capacity) until 2023 and announced further auctioning of *39 new mines* for FY25 on November 13, 2023 – raising the numbers from *23* mines decided in May 2023.

Coal India is *re-opening* old mines ("discontinued/ abandoned mines") to raise coal production on revenue-sharing basis or outsourcing; *30 mines* have been identified so far and are in various stages of being outsourced – as per the Coal Ministry's annual report of 2022-23.

On June 7, 2023, the CCEA cleared outlay of Rs 2,980 crore for coal exploration, which involves private sector participation.

The RBI's November 2023 bulletin says, India has lined up "sanctioned" coal-fired power projects of *28.2 GW* (which are under various phases of construction).

States like Karnataka, Tamil Nadu and Uttar Pradesh are *riding on coal wave* to set up new coal-based power plants – while private players are shifting to green – says a news report of November 2023.

India is now considering easing the lending norms for *new coal-fired power plants* to meet demand.

In fact, Washington Post flagged many of these in February 2023 to say, "in India, 'phase down' of coal actually means rapid expansion of mining". The COP28 merely provides a convenient excuse now. The big question that arises is: Is India pushing coal to serve private interests?

India harming environment and forests

India hasn't pledged to protect forests (carbon sinks) or reduce deforestation and *skirted* it in its NDC stating that (a) India has "24.62%" forest cover and (b) "among the lowest rates of gross deforestation in the world". But this undermines the National Forest Policy of 1988 which set the target of forest cover at "minimum of one-third of the total land area" – 33.3% of land.

Like coal, India has *stepped on* diverting forest land in the name of faster growth.

The Forest Conservation (Amendment) Act of 2023, passed in August 2023, *significantly dilutes* (i) definition of forests and (ii) gives *wholesale exemptions* from forest clearances – up to *100 km* in international borders, up to *10 hectare* for security-related infrastructure, up to *5 hectare* in naxal-affected areas, land *not notified* as forest in government records on or after 1980 (which is substantial, forcing the Supreme Court to assign "dictionary meaning" to forests and ask states to notify additional areas as forests in the Godavarman case) and declaring "forestry" to include zoos and wildlife safaris etc.

Similarly, India has withdrawn legal protects against environment.

The Jan Vishwas (Amendment) Act of 2023 passed in August 2023 *significantly weakens* protections provided under three laws – the Environment Protection Act of 1986, Air (Prevention and Control of Pollution) Act of 1986 and Water (Prevention and Control of Pollution) Act of 1974.

These amendments *de-criminalised* pollution and handed over adjudicating powers to government servants (away from independent authorities and courts).

There is more.

Methane is 'no-go' area

India has been coy about methane, second only to fossil fuel in causing climate crisis. From COP26 to COP28 and its NDC, it refuses to commit to reduce methane without explaining why. It is commonly understood that agriculture and livestock – the main producers of methane – are politically sensitive areas and would call for *overhauling* existing policies for which the necessary bandwidth may be missing.

No time to waste

Climate negotiations began with the first Earth Summit in Rio in 1992 (when the UNFCCC holding COP negotiations was adopted). Conflicts of interests – developed economies primarily responsible for global warming and now developing ones like India and China are doing the same as they grow – has dogged the negotiations then.

The victory for India (and China and other developing countries) at COP28 is, however, a double whammy. The climate crisis is here and now.

The UNEP's Emissions Gap Report 2023, released on November 20, 2023, said the world *breached* the 1.5°C threshold (above pre-industrial levels) on *86 days* (more than one-fourth days) this year. Washington Post reported that July 4, 2023 was the hottest day on Earth since at least 1979, with the global average temperature reaching 62.9 degree Fahrenheit (17.18 degree Celsius), quoting the data of US National Centers for Environmental Prediction; it added, some scientists believed July 4, 2023 might have been one of the hottest days on Earth in about *125,000 years*.

Dec 21, 2023

PS: *London-based think tank InfluenceMap listed government-owned Coal India as the third most polluter (CO_2 emitter) in the world in 2024.*

The RBI's MPC statement of April 2024 flagged extreme weather events adversely impacting its monetary policy by directly stoking "inflation" and lowering output. In April 2024, the Supreme Court flagged that India had "no single umbrella legislation" to address climate change and attendant concerns.

***

2024 Ahoy! Will Electoral Freebies Throw Fiscal Deficit into Disarray?

A large number of welfare schemes (subsidies) were announced in 2023 in view of elections in heartland states. More may be expected ahead of the 2024 general elections

Until the halfway mark of FY24 (H1), the Centre did well to keep its fiscal deficit under control. The Controller General of Accounts (CGA) data shows, that the "actual" fiscal deficit stood at 39.3% of the budgeted Rs 17.86 lakh crore (5.9% of the GDP) by the end of September 2023. This was "marginally" higher than 37.3% during the corresponding period of FY23 (H1). The RBI's November bulletin commanded this and attributed the "marginally higher" figure to a "marked improvement in the quality of spending".

However, the RBI also warned against "complacency" given the "current uncertain environment", pointing to global growth slowing down (the FinMin's monthly report for October 2023 also warned of this) but omitted the obvious domestic risks from (i) November-round of elections in heartland states of Madhya Pradesh, Rajasthan and Chhattisgarh and others, Telangana and Mizoram, and (ii) forthcoming general election of 2024 (April-May 2024). Big elections tend to bring higher fiscal outgo due to populist (welfare) schemes.

To put the Centre's fiscal deficit in perspective, it was 6.4% of the GDP in FY23 (RE) and the target for FY24 (BE) was 5.9% – both higher than the FRBM limit of 3% but given the post-pandemic reconstruction this was to be expected.

The fiscal deficit target for FY24 is headed for a big breach. Here is why.

LPG subsidy goes up

Post-February 1, 2023 budget presentation, a series of additional LPG subsidies under the Ujjwala scheme were announced. It started in March 2023.

On March 24, 2023, the Cabinet Committee on Economic Affairs (CCEA) approved "a subsidy of Rs 200 per 14.2 kg cylinder for up to 12 refills per year" to raise the average annual refill from 3.68 in FY22 (it was 3.01 in FY20). For this, expenditure of Rs 6,100 crore for FY23 and Rs 7,680 crore for FY24 was approved.

This was followed by more such announcements.

- On August 29, 2023, the Ministry of Petroleum & Natural Gas said the Prime Minister had announced a subsidy of Rs 200 as "a gift" for 'Raksha Bandhan'.
- On September 13, 2023, the Union Cabinet approved "75 lakh additional Ujjwala connections" to take the total Ujjwala beneficiaries from 9.6 crore to 10.35 crore over three fiscals of FY24-FY26. Union Minister Anurag Thakur said these would put an additional fiscal burden of Rs 7,680 crore.
- On October 4, 2023, Thakur announced the government had decided to give an additional Rs 100 subsidy "for every refill".
- On October 5, 2023, PMO said the Prime Minister

declared in Jabalpur: "…in the last few weeks alone, the cylinder has become cheaper by Rs 500 for the beneficiary sisters of Ujjwala. Now my poor mothers, sisters and daughters who are beneficiaries of Ujjwala will get gas cylinders for only Rs 600."

The average price of LPG cylinders in four metros stood at Rs 1,113.25 on March 1, 2023 – as per the Indian Oil. Hence, the subsidy had increased by Rs 500 as the Prime Minister said.

Then came the November round of elections, announced on October 9, 2023.

- In November 2023, the ruling BJP presented its manifestos in the heartland states as "Modi ki Guarantee 2023" with a promise to give LPG cylinders under the same Ujjwala scheme (a) at Rs 500 each in Chhattisgarh, Madhya Pradesh and Telangana and (b) Rs 450 in Rajasthan. This was a further subsidy of Rs 100-Rs 150 (down from Rs 1,100 in March 2023).

Now that the BJP has won in Madhya Pradesh, Rajasthan and Chhattisgarh, it is time to fulfil the "guarantee" for the January-March quarter (Q4) of FY24 before the next Central budget is presented. The total cost of the LPG subsidy outgo is not known.

Then, there are other post-budget fiscal burdens.

'Free' ration for Q4 of FY24 and 'Bharat Atta'

- On November 5, 2023, the Prime Minister announced extending the "free" ration to 67% of households in the country for five more years – which could come into effect from January 1, 2024. On November 29, 2023, the Union Cabinet approved it. This means a substantial fiscal outgo – over and above the food subsidy of Rs 1.97 lakh crore marked for FY24 (BE). The current "free" ration scheme ends on December 31, 2023.

- On November 5, 2023, the Prime Minister also launched a new tribal welfare scheme, "PM Janjati Adivasi Nyaya Maha Abhiyan (PM- JANMAN)" with a budget of Rs 24,000 crore.

- On November 6, 2023, the Ministry of Consumer Affairs, Food & Public Distribution flagged off a new welfare scheme called "Bharat Atta" – subsidised 'atta' (wheat flour) at 27.5 per kg. This will be "available at all physical and mobile outlets of Kendriya Bhandar, NAFED and NCCF from today and will be expanded to other co-op/retail outlets"– through 800 mobile vans and 2,000 outlets. The cost of the scheme is not known yet.

Additional Fertiliser and G20 summit expenses

- On May 17, 2023 (post-budget), the Union Cabinet approved a proposal of the Department of Fertiliser to upwardly revise non-urea fertilisers (phosphatic and potassic (P&K) fertilisers), by Rs 38,000 crore. On that occasion, Chemical and Fertilisers Minister Mansukh Mandaviya said the total fertilizer subsidy bill for FY24 was set to overshoot by Rs 46,000-50,000 crore (including urea) to Rs 2.25 lakh crore due to the rise in imported fertilisers (caused by the Russia-Ukraine war).

- On June 30, 2023, the Union Cabinet also approved "a special package of innovative schemes with a total outlay of Rs 3,68,676.7 crore" (urea subsidy) for three

Do electoral freebies matter?

Since 2019, the Prime Minister has repeatedly denounced electoral freebies ("revdi" and "revdi culture"). Days before the elections were announced, the Prime Minister warned, on September 3, 2023, that "financially irresponsible policies and populism may give political results in the short term but will extract a great social and economic price in the long term" and that "those who suffer those consequences the most are often the poorest and the most vulnerable".

But soon, the Centre and the BJP offered a series of freebies to the voters, billed as welfare schemes, not "revdi". What changed? The elections were on in the backward heartland states collectively called 'BIMARU'. Until a few years ago, south India was more famous for electoral freebies (free TVs and grinders etc.) but not anymore.

A recent study by the Centre for New Economics Studies (CNES), of the OP Jindal Global University provides a new insight into this.

The CNES created the "Access (In)Equality Index" to measure access to human development opportunities for people (five "pillars") – basic amenities (water, sanitation, housing, nutrition, clean energy, digital access), healthcare, education, socio-economic security and justice. It classified states into (i) aspirants (ii) achievers and (iii) front-runners depending on their overall performances.

- Best performing states (more than 0.42), called "front-runners", are 12: Goa, Sikkim, Tamil Nadu, Kerala, Himachal Pradesh, Telangana, Punjab, Mizoram, Karnataka, Andhra Pradesh, Nagaland, Haryana.
- Worst performing ones (less than 0.33), called

years to promote sustainable agriculture. This meant, an additional outgo of Rs 1.22 lakh crore (one-third) in FY24. The budget for FY24 earmarked fertilizer subsidy at Rs 1.75 lakh crore.

- Meanwhile, the G20 summit held in New Delhi overshot the budgeted Rs 990 crore spending to reach Rs 4,100 crore (excess of Rs 3,110 crore).

The next general election is due in March-April 2024. More welfare schemes may be launched before and at the next interim or vote-on-account budget of February 1, 2024.

There is a precedence for this. On February 1, 2019, an interim or vote-on-account budget was presented – because the general elections were due in March-April 2019 and this budget was meant to provide for the expenses for the first quarter (Q1) of the next fiscal year of FY20 to allow the new government to present full budget for FY20. Instead, it contained an unusual item: the PM-Kisan scheme with a retrospective effect. The budget said "around 12 crore small and marginal farmer families" would be given annual cash transfer of 6,000 in three instalments, at an estimated cost of 75,000 crore, which was to be applicable from "1st December 2018". It further said "the first instalment for the period up to 31st March 2019 would be paid during this year itself" – that is, a fiscal burden on FY19. On March 7, 2019, the Ministry of Agriculture & Farmers Welfare announced that "more than 2 crore small/marginal farmers have benefitted so far" with cash transfers of 2,000 each – that is over Rs 4,000 crore of fiscal outgo in FY19, adding to the fiscal deficit.

If such a thing were to happen on the next budget of February 1, 2024, the fiscal deficit for FY24 would go up further by Rs 4,000 crore.

"aspirants", are six: Madhya Pradesh, Odisha, Assam, Bihar, Uttar Pradesh and Jharkhand.

- Average performers (0.33-0.42), called "achievers", are 10: Maharashtra, Arunachal Pradesh, Gujarat, Uttarakhand, Chhattisgarh, Rajasthan, Tripura, West Bengal, Manipur and Meghalaya.

Note, the Hindi heartland states that went to polls are either average or worst performers – not front-runners. That should tell its tale and the relevance of electoral freebies.

The Prime Minister validated the role of electoral freebies by calling his party's victory the victory of the poor, deprived, farmers and the tribals. The BJP won 52 of the 81 assembly seats falling in the "aspirational districts" of Madhya Pradesh, Rajasthan, Chhattisgarh and Telangana – doubling its win from 23 seas in 2018.

"Aspirational districts" are the "most under-developed districts" and 112 of them were identified for special attention and in January 2018 "Aspirational Districts Programme" (ADP) was launched for their quick and effective transformation.

Dec 10, 2023

PS: "Modi's guarantee" of subsidized LPG would be denied after the BJP won the elections – the state government passed the buck to the Centre and the Centre denied any such move even though the Prime Minister had declared the additional subsidy under his Ujjwala scheme. The price would be lowered by Rs 100 ahead of the 2024 general election. Subsidies by Modi was called anything but "revdi" by his government and party.

The 2019 interim budget had violated the budget norms

by not only (i) brining in the PM-Kisan with retrospective effect but also (ii) introduced pension for unorganized sector and (iii) declared that individuals with income up to 5 lakh per annum would receive full tax rebate of Rs 12,500. Vajpayee's 2004 interim budget had also changed many tax structures.

***

NBFCs Add Risk to Slowing Economy

Banks are significantly upping lending to risky NBFCs, forcing RBI to sound an alarm

Month after month, finance ministry and Reserve Bank of India (RBI) have been citing improved asset quality of banks, robust credit off-take and strong earnings growth as evidence that the economy is on the right trajectory. On the face of it, this may be true, but disaggregated data paints a different picture. Before getting into that, here is a brief backgrounder.

Recall how three big NBFCs, IL&FS, DHFL and HDIL, collapsed one after the other beginning 2018. This also led to collapse of Punjab And Maharashtra Cooperative Bank (in 2019) and Yes Bank (in 2020). The chain of events created panic in the economy as credit dried up and a fresh NPA crisis emerged. Central government asked SBI and LIC to pump in money to save IL&FS and Yes Bank. DHFL, HDIL and PMC went into bankruptcy.

What caused the collapse of NBFCs and banks together? Their finances were interlinked and all of them were done in by massive fraudulent activities involving mala fide loans and money laundering. Hundreds of shell companies, supposedly rooted out by government, also tumbled out, further demonstrating lax regulations. Since

NBFCs source a big chunk of their funds from banks, lax regulation meant financial risks travelled to banks and the rest of the economy. RBI's Financial Stability Report (FSR) of July 2020 pointed out that NBFCs' bank borrowings went up from 23.1% in March 2017 to 28.9% in December 2019.

Since then, RBI has taken several measures to tighten oversight of NBFCs, but its ineffectiveness is all too evident.

Quantum Jump In Bank Credit To NBFCs

RBI's October 2023 bulletin says NBFCs' bank borrowings went up to 41% (of their total borrowings) at the end of March 2023 (FY23), a massive jump from 35.5% at end of March 2022 and 33% at end of March 2021. This data also confirms rise in credit to NBFCs as proportion of total credit to non-food sector from 8.3% in FY21 to 8.6% in FY22 and 9.7% in FY23. In September 2023, it stood at 9.4%. NBFCs are part of the services sector.

Recognising the financial risks, RBI Governor Shaktikanta Das warned in the bulletin: "Banks and NBFCs would be well advised to strengthen their internal surveillance mechanisms, address build-up of risks, if any, and institute suitable safeguards in their own interest. The need of the hour is robust risk management and stronger underwriting standards."

However, it is RBI's Centre for Advance Financial Research and Learning (CAFRAL) which has spelt out in detail how rise in bank lending to NBFCs is creating financial risks. Its November 2023 report, "India Finance Report 2023: Connecting the Last Mile," takes into consideration data up to H1 of FY23, when bank lending to NBFCs had risen to 36% (as against 41% in full FY23). The report flags four points about financial health of NBFCs:

(i) Rise in bank borrowings by NBFCs raises concerns about "systemic contagion" and underscores the need for tighter preventive measures to mitigate potential systemic fallout; public sector banks are the largest lenders and most of it is "direct" lending (lending through debentures and commercial papers is a much smaller component).

(ii) On assets side, there is "a large fall in secured borrowings" and "a marginal increase in unsecured borrowings," showing "increased exposure to riskier finance"; there is also a "significant fall in reserves and surplus," indicating "buffers grow thinner."

(iii) Capital market exposures, led by equity share ownership, increasing risk; this "risk-taking behaviour" is prompted by interest rate tightening.

(iv) There are concerns about "spillover of losses" from online lending to traditional banking; the stronger the linkages between traditional lending and online lending, the larger the spillover; hence, digitalization needs to be "accompanied by quick and nimble regulation."

The question that must strike is: Why are banks lending more to NBFCs despite knowing the risks? The answer is that banks are either developing risk aversion (for lending directly) or not finding enough takers as it happened during 2017-19. Banks had cut down lending drastically after the collapse of NBFCs. Finance ministry and RBI know the reality but robust growth in overall credit outflow to non-food sector from 5.5% in FY21 (pandemic fiscal) to 15.4% in FY23 has provided a convenient cover for ignoring it. There is enough evidence of banks' aversion or no takers for their loans because the economy is slowing down.

Risk Aversion Or No Takers?

RBI recently recast its data system, removing details of credit outflows in pre-January 2019 period. Even then, the disaggregated data between January 2019 and September 2023 show that within the credit outflow to non-food sector, share of personal loans went from 24% (of non-food off-take) in January 2019 to 31.9% in September 2023.

Of this, gold loans went up from 0.3% to 0.6%. Credit to NBFCs went up from 7.2% to 9.4%. Credit to large industry went down from 24.2% to 17%, to 'industry' as a whole from 29.3% to 22.9%. Credit to MSMEs rose from 5.1% to 5.9%. Credit to services went up from 23.7% to 26.6% and to agriculture from 11.7% to 12%. The rise in credit to services is driven by NBFCs.

The above points reflect double inversion in credit outflow — personal loans and services overtaking 'industry' and 'large industry' in quantum. It must be kept in mind that loans to industry and services reflect the need for working capital and investment to produce more goods and services. Personal loans, on the other hand, are meant only for consumption expenditure in which NBFCs provide the last-mile connectivity. Hence, rise of credit to services should count as rise in personal or consumption loans.

That there are fewer takers for bank loans in industry is also evident in (a) eight-month fall in PMI in October 2023, and (b) three-month fall in growth of industrial production.

Balance sheets of banks and NBFCs are surely better now than during 2017-19 but it shouldn't be forgotten that this happened more because of (a) massive NPA write-offs (Rs 14.5 lakh crore since FY15) and recapitalisation (Rs 3.12 lakh crore) of banks (b) recapitalisation of NBFCs by SBI and LIC (mentioned earlier) and (c) removal of collapsed NBFCs and banks (those that went into bankruptcy).

Days after RBI's October bulletin and CAFRAL report, RBI realised the gravity of the situation and raised capital to risk-weighted asset ratio of banks and NBFCs on November 16 by 25 percentage points to 125%, back to the 2019 level, to cover unsecured loans (personal loans, excluding housing loans, education loans, vehicle loans and loans secured by gold and gold jewellery, but including credit to NBFCs) which, industry estimate shows, will cost banks Rs 84,000 crore in excess capital, raising borrowing costs for consumer loans.

That the improvement is not because of better governance, regulatory oversight or credit culture of corporations is also evident.

Willful Defaults and Bank Frauds Grow

As per the RBI-registered Transunion CIBIL database, willful defaults (of over Rs 25 lakh) jumped from Rs 3.04 lakh crore in FY22 to Rs 3.55 lakh crore in FY23, a rise of Rs 50,000 crore. Number of willful defaulters went up by 2,002 during the period. Perhaps that is what prompted RBI to issue "Framework For Compromise Settlements and Technical Write-offs" on June 8, 2023, handing over power to bank boards (i) to go for 'compromise settlements' with willful defaulters and (ii) give fresh loans to willful defaulters after 12 months of such settlements. The earlier 2019 framework didn't allow such "restructuring" or "evergreening" of loans.

Fortune India had then pointed out that this was an invitation to more willful defaults and banking frauds. As per RBI, willful defaulters are ones who have the ability to pay but don't and divert loans for other purposes. A compromise settlement involves a sharp haircut. The number of willful defaulters (CIBIL) was rising even before RBI's 2023 framework for compromise settlement. Giving willful defaulters access to fresh loans points to the probability of further spike in such cases.

Along with willful defaults, banking frauds have also risen in recent years, both in and after 2018. Their number jumped 17 times during FY15-23 to 5,88,744 from 34,198 during FY04-14. The amount involved nearly doubled (1.9 times) to Rs 65,812 crore during FY15-23 as against Rs 34,904 crore during FY06-14, as per the RBI data. That is not all.

Credit Culture, Respect For Governance

On November 9, 2023, Supreme Court upheld the constitutionality of the IBC provision (introduced in 2019) expanding insolvency proceedings against personal guarantors. This judgement shows two bad corporate governance practices: (i) it wasn't part of the IBC of 2016 but inserted three years later in 2019 and (ii) more than 200 petitions were filed before the court to challenge it. Isn't personal guarantee meant to recover the outstanding if the one taking the loan defaults or fails altogether?

Also, on May 3, the Supreme Court upheld a provision in the Companies Act of 2013 which allowed a five-year ban on auditors found guilty of indulging in corporate frauds. It was challenged by auditors of IL&FS Financial Services Ltd — BSR & Associate, a KPMG affiliate and Deloitte — in the same case mentioned at the beginning. The auditors took the plea that since they had resigned from the firm — even though it was post facto and their collusion in the banking fraud had been proved by then — they shouldn't be prosecuted or banned.

The last two Instances show scant respect by corporations for both good corporate governance practices and law of the land.

Dec 5, 2023

***

What will Deliver 'Strong' Growth in FY24?

Debt-fuelled consumption marked by growing "unsecured" loans, high-frequency indicators limited to formal sector and government capex which is feeble don't really add up.

The FinMin is gung-ho about "strong growth" in FY24 "as projected" by the RBI (6.5%) "amid a global slowdown" in its latest monthly report (MER) released on November 21, 2023. It argues that "solid" domestic demand, which is "the strongest driver of India's growth so far in FY24"; "declining" unemployment; "sustained investment push" by the government "imparting an impetus to private investment"; "healthy" corporate profits; "accumulated savings"; "reduction" in non-performing loans; "strong" services exports, etc. would lead to 6.5% growth.

To begin with, what is left unsaid is that even at 6.5%, the FY24 growth would be significantly less than 9.1% in FY22 and 7.2% in FY23 – indicating loss of growth momentum. Secondly, the MER comes days ahead the Q2 data for FY24 is to be released (November 30) – and hence, a bit premature when global growth is slowing down (which the MER acknowledges). But more significantly, it comes *two days after* Union Ministers Gajendra Singh Shekhawat and G Kishan Reddy, Maharashtra Deputy

Chief Minister Devendra Fernandes and business tycoon Gautam Adani *hailed* the Indian economy and the Prime Minister, on November 19, 2023, for breaking into *$4 trillion mark.*

Interestingly, the budget's (nominal) GDP projection for FY24 is $3.6 trillion (@ Rs 83 per dollar) and in Q1 of FY24, it was mere $0.85 trillion. The claim of $4 trillion economy, as on November 19, 2023, was *attributed to the IMF*. But the MER is silent on it.

More importantly, the growth seems to be slipping.

Flight of capital, capitalists and labour/citizens

Investment is critical to growth. What does the latest FDI inflows data show?

It shows a sharp fall in both *total* FDI (-16%) and *equity* FDI (-20%) inflows (in USD) in FY23. It also shows a sharp fall in *equity* FDI inflows (-31%) in H1 of FY24 vis-à-vis the corresponding period of FY23 (no comparative data available for total FDI inflows in H1 of FY24). This is an indication that global funds are *going elsewhere* since FY23 – either due to higher interest rates in the US and Europe and/or better investment environment elsewhere, like Canada, Australia, Brazil, Mexico, Vietnam etc.

The *FDI outflows* are falling in FY24 – by $20 billion during April-October 2023 (FY24) I the corresponding period of FY23. How does this matter? Since about *85%* of India's FDI inflows and outflows are through opaque tax havens and shell companies – indicating high probability of round-tripping of funds – a fall in FDI outflows may mean a further fall in FDI inflows.

Hot money (FII) or *FII inflows* have increased in FY24

(up to November 21, 2023) – after two years of *net pullout*. This money goes to stock markets, which are booming, but since stock market boom is *disconnected with the real economy* and FIIs may leave overnight, without warning (hence called 'hot money'), this rise is not a good indicator of long-term investment or growth. FDI inflows, in contrast, are long-term investments.

Outward remittances (LRS) are consistently going up too – from $12.7 billion in FY21 to $19.6 billion in FY22, $27 billion in FY23 and $18 billion in H1 of FY24. This spike can't be attributed to 20% tax on such remittances (beyond Rs 7 lakh) – which was to come into effect from October 1, 2023. Though the remittances are mainly on account of travel, education and maintenance of relatives settled abroad, a significant amount also goes into *foreign deposits, gifts, equity investments and buying properties* – 21.5% of the entire outward remittances in H1 of FY24.

LRS outflows should worry and could be counted as the flight of capital (along with capitalists and labour) because more and more Indians are also *fleeing* to foreign shores for (a) studies (25% of all students landing in the US in the 2022-23 academic year) and (b) in search of better life.

The latter category includes (i) those seeking *citizenship* abroad – their numbers rising from 1,22,819 in 2011 to 1,31,405 in 2015 to 2,25,620 in 2022 and 87,026 till June 2023 (halfway mark for the calendar year), as the Lok Sabha was told in July 2023. Such citizenships often involve investment in and flight of assets to those countries ("citizenship-by-investment" programmes). Besides, some of them are fugitives, like Mehul Chokshi and Sandesara brothers, who have decamped with bank loans. There is a sharp spike in *banking frauds and willful defaults* in and after 2018.

Those leaving India for better life also include (ii) thousands of Indians *illegally migrating*, despite facing death and hardships. In less than a year between November 2022 and September 2023, *97,917 Indians were arrested* by the US authorities alone for illegally entry, a five-fold rise since 2019 – of which about 45,000 said this was due to the "fear in their own country" and the 730 arrested were *unaccompanied minors*.

The effect of this flight of capital, capitalists and labour points to loss of faith in growth and better economic prospects in India.

Meanwhile, *inward remittances* grew by 24% in 2022 to reach $111 billion but as the World Bank report of June 2023 says, this growth is expected to fall to *0.2% in 2023* "due to slowing economic growth in major source countries". This means, less funds for domestic economy in FY24.

The net effect of all the above is a pessimistic outlook for FY24.

Feeble growth drivers and worsening household finances

Those familiar with GDP data know that India is a *single engine-driven* economy for several years. It is the government investment/expenditure (PFCE) which is providing the real impetus. Other three engines – demand (PFCE), private capex (private GFCF) and net exports – are merely pulling along.

Government expenditure (GFCE) has grown but consider four facts: (i) GFCE averages just *10%* of the GDP (FY12-FY23) with a *declining trend* – from 11.1% in FY12 to 9.9% in FY23 and 10.1% in Q1 of FY24 (ii) during FY13-FY23 its growth averages 4.6% – *lower* than the GDP growth rate of

5.7% during the same period (iii) in Q1 of FY24, its growth fell to minus (-) 0.7% and (iv) government capex (*public* GFCF) is stagnant at about 7% of the GDP for the past 11 *fiscals up to FY22* (up to which data is available). The Controller General of Accounts (CGA) data shows, the Centre's expenditure is 49% of the budgeted expenditure in H1 of FY24.

How much impetus can such a GFCE provide?

Second engine (not in any particular order) is private capex (*private* GFCF) which collapsed during the Great Recession of 2007-09 and is yet to rev up – falling from 16.8% of the GDP in FY08 to 10% in FY22, the last fiscal for which data is available. Considering the RBI data on "envisaged" private investment as proxy for private GFCF in FY23 and Q1 of FY24, the trend remains downward – as *Fortune India* article 'Is private investment in the economy on revival path?' had demonstrated.

Further, the latest RBI data shows, net *financial assets* of households touched 47-year low of 5.1% of the GDP in FY23. The MoSPI's data on *net household savings* (financial and physical assets) shows a fall from 23.6% of the GDP in FY12 to 19.7% in FY22 (last fiscal for which data is available) and *household savings* as percentage of GFCF (capex) has fallen from 45.9% (constant prices) to 40% during the same period.

Sure, unemployment rate is declining but the same PLFS reports also show this is accompanied with a *fall* in good quality jobs (regular wage/salaried), *shift* of work from high-productive and high-income manufacturing to low-productive, low-income agriculture and *unpaid* self-employment, a fall in social security cover and negative wage growth (except for 'casual' category). Inflation has also been high in the past two years.

All this means, household incomes would worsen and going forward, *availability* of household savings for capex (GFCF) would *fall further*. It is probably this distressing development that led the FinMin to talk of "accumulated savings" – meaning bank deposits – but unbeknown to it, banks and NBFCs are facing (a) fresh financial risks due to rise in "unsecured" consumption loans and (b) a large amount of bank deposits have been wiped out (i) in writing-off NPAs, recapitalising banks since FY15 (ii) rescuing and recapitalising collapsed bank (Yes Bank) and NBFC (IL&FS) and (iii) massive loss of credits as collapsed banks and NBFCs (PMC, HDIL and DHFL) went into bankruptcy after 2018.

Third engine, consumption or demand (PFCE), about which the FinMin says it is "solid" and "the strongest driver of India's growth so far in FY24", needs a detailed scrutiny.

Debt-fuelled consumption, fall in good jobs and wages

The FinMin's reliance on high demand is based on high-frequency data, like sale of passenger vehicles (PVs) and houses, bank credit outflows, air travel, credit card transactions etc. and "a surge in consumer spending during the ongoing festive season". These data hide more than they reveal:

- High-frequency data is limited to *formal* economy, *not informal* economy which constitutes about 50% of the total economy and which has received shocks other than the pandemic –demonetisation of 2016 (informal economy is cash-driven) and GST of 2017 (its input tax credit shifting business from informal to formal). No data/survey has been carried out to measure the impact and so apportioning of formal sector data to informal sector would *overestimate* GDP growth.

- Rise in sales of PVs and housing are due to sharp rise in high-end luxury products but *fall* in low-end products (affordable to larger population) – pointing to sharp income inequality which makes growth *unsustainable*. The SIAM data shows, sale of entry-level cars (PCs) began falling behind high-end cars (UVs) in FY22 and continues until now – the April-October 2023 (FY24) sales of UVs at 13.85 lakh units outstripped that of 9.4 lakh units of PCs. Knight Frank report shows, *sale* of luxury houses of Rs 50 lakh-1 crore and above Rs 1 crore accounted for 36% and 35%, respectively, in Q2 of FY24 – far higher than affordable houses of below Rs 50 lakh at 29% of FY24 – across big cities.

- Air travel (relatively better offs) is up but it is well known since 2021 that only 1% Indians account for 45% of flights (frequent fliers). Meanwhile, rail travel (relatively poor) in FY23 (4,183.6 million) is less than 50% of the pandemic FY19.

- Number of passengers travelling by rail (poorer segment) in FY23 (up to February 2023) at 5,864.39 million was substantially less *than* 8,439 million in the pre-pandemic FY19 (it was 3,519 million in FY22). This points to K-shaped economy and economic *distress* of the masses – not a good sign for sustaining high growth.

- Income of most Indians remains precarious is also reflected in "free" ration to 67% households – started in April 2020 and would continue till the end of 2029.

Bank credit outflow data reveals distressing news:

Growth in bank credit is led by *personal loans for*

consumption and *NBFCs* – up at 31.9% and 9.4% of the nonfood offtakes, respectively, at the end of September 2023. NBFCs are giving more *personal loans* – up at 31.2% by the end of March 2023. Both banks and NBFCs are giving large amounts of "unsecured" loans too, forcing the RBI to raise capital to risk-weighted asset ratio (CRAR) of both banks and NBFCs to 125% (back to 2019 level) on November 16, 2023. Even after that, the RBI Governor is warning banks and NBFCs against "all forms of exuberance" and ensuring that lending to all categories is "sustainable". The Finance Minister is advising NBFCs to rein in their enthusiasm in disbursing unsecured loans.

Meanwhile, in Q1 of FY24, PFCE fell to 57.3% of the GDP – from 58.8% in FY23 and 58.3% in FY22. Its *growth* is not very inspiring. During FY13-FY23, it averaged 6.1% growth – barely above the GDP growth of 5.7% – and fell to 6% in Q1 of FY24. Other indicators of demand – growth in industrial production (IIP), PMI and FMCG sale – are sluggish, particularly in Q2 of FY24.

The fourth engine, net exports (trade balance), has always been in the negative territory – except only twice in post-independent history, in 1972-73 and 1976-77. During FY12-FY23, it ranged between -1.1% and -6.5%; in Q1 of FY24, it was -6.4%. So, this is actually a drag on growth. That leaves "strong" services exports – which has helped in reducing trade deficit but as yet not good enough to reverse the trend, particularly when merchandise imports keep rising.

Ironically, the Centre has played little role in boosting services exports, the Foreign Trade Policy (FTP) of 2023) is silent on how to push it and tax incentives are concentrated on manufacturing and merchandise exports. Worse, it is even hurting future services exports by tilting the balance away from English education (key to IT development and IT services exports) to vernacular languages in universities and undermining primacy of English in senior level employments (UPSC exams) – as *Fortune India* article 'Future of trade in services exports' explained earlier.

Now, the sudden *ban and crackdown* on production, storage and sale of 'halal' products – which go beyond meat to include edible oil, mint, rice and bakery items – by the Uttar Pradesh government is bound to impact (merchandise) exports of these items – until at least the state government sets its own standards, opens and operationalises its certification centres for these products. Going by the contemporary history, the ban and crackdown may also travel to other states to the detriment of merchandise exports.

Are demand and corporate profits pushing growth?

The FinMin's argument of "healthy" corporate profits for "strong" growth is misplaced too.

In the pandemic fiscals of FY21, corporate profits touched historic high but (a) the GDP growth collapsed (b) corporate tax hit a historic low (below income tax collection) and (c) there was massive loss of jobs and wage cut in the corporate world. A 2022 analysis showed, the "stellar rise" in corporate profits in FY21 and FY22 didn't lead to corresponding boom in capex, with listed companies' investment in fixed assets rising by only 2.3% (year-on-year) in FY22 – the slowest in the previous six years! Even the corporate tax cut of 2019 didn't lead to fresh investments – as the RBI had pointed out.

Another analysis of November 2023 shows a

slowdown in corporate *revenue (sales) growth* in the past one year has *slowed down their capex* (combined fixed assets of listed companies) in H1 of FY24 – while profits went up by 12% (H1 of FY24). This fall-in-revenue (sales)-but-rise-in-profit is a widespread phenomenon – in India and in the US and Europe – and goes by the sobriquets "sellers' inflation" or "greedflation". Yet another analysis shows, the profits of Adani group (nine listed companies) profits doubled (107.7%) in H1 of FY24 even as its sales dipped by 14% during the same period.

Thus, to argue that "healthy" corporate profit will lead to "strong" economic growth is unconvincing. So is the case with the argument that "reduction" in non-performing loans would lead to strong growth.

To sum up, what will drive "strong" growth in FY24 remains unclear.

Nov 30, 2023

***

GDP Growth: Headwinds in Financial Assets, Tax Filings Hurt Average Indian

Household financial assets are at 47-year low pointing to headwinds against growth

A year ago, there was a sense of déjà vu when India overtook the UK as the fifth largest economy (in Q1 of FY23). Centre has promised to make India the third largest economy in the world in the next few years. A couple of months ago, both the NITI Aayog and the Centre claimed that 135 million had been lifted out of multidimensional poverty in six fiscals between FY16 and FY21. The first quarter of GDP numbers in the current fiscal (Q1 of FY24) show India grew at 7.8%.

The economy is surely growing, even if the GDP data is being questioned, but the average Indian is poorer, not prosperous. There are two official data pointing to this: Household financial assets and tax returns.

Household financial assets at 47-year low

On September 18, 2023, the RBI released data on financial health of households. It shows, net financial assets of households dropped sharply from 11.5% of the GDP in

FY21 to 7.2% in FY22 and 5.1% in FY23. Going by the RBI's database (since 1970-71), this fall to 5.1% in FY23 is a 47-year low. The last time it went below 5.1% was in 1975-76 when it was 4.7%; the next low was 5.2% in 1977-78.

This is a big fall. In 16 out of 18 fiscals between 1993-94 and 2010-11, net financial assets averaged 10.8%, peaking at 12% in FY10. After FY11, the only fiscal it touched double-digit was in FY21 (11.5%) – the pandemic fiscal in which the GDP growth plunged to -5.8% – and then dropped to 5.1% in FY23 when the GDP growth was 7.2%.

The fall in net financial assets is due to a sharp rise in financial liabilities. The latest RBI data shows, financial liabilities fell from 3.9% of the GDP in FY21 to 3.8% in FY22 and went up to 5.8% in FY23. In the past 53 fiscals for which the RBI provides data (since 1970-71) only twice financial liabilities crossed 5% – 5.1% in FY06 and 6.6% in FY07.

It isn't as if this is not known. Here are four more official data to demonstrate this.

(a) The NSSO's 2017-18 household consumption expenditure survey (MPCE) showed a fall in 'real' expenditure – but it was junked on claims (that an experts committee questioned the data quality). No MPCE survey has been taken up thereafter.

(b) The MoSPI data shows, net household savings (financial and physical assets) have fallen from 23.6% of the GDP in FY12 to 19.7% in FY22 (up to which data is available) and

(c) Net physical assets have fallen from 16.3% to 12% during the same period.

(d) The RBI data shows bank credit outflow inverted in

FY20 – "personal loans" for consumption overtaking that to industry, large industry and services and continues to do so in FY24.

Tax base shrinks by 54% in seven years

Tax data too points to impoverishment of people in the lowest income group and a 54% fall in the taxbase in seven years between FY16 and FY23.

The Lok Sabha answer of July 24, 2023 (for FY20 to FY23) showed, the ITRs declaring taxable income (total ITRs filed 74 million minus 51.6 million ITRs showing zero tax liability) were 22.4 million (1.6% of population) in FY23. This is a sharp fall from 35.8 million in FY20 (pre-pandemic), 18.7 million in FY21 (pandemic) and 18.9 million in FY22 (partly impacted by the second wave). The impact of the pandemic and K-shaped recovery are obvious.

Going back to previous fiscals, the IT department's annual data shows ITRs declaring taxable income (total ITRs of 49.5 million minus 0.91 million ITRs with zero tax liability) were 48.6 million (3.8% of population) in FY16 (pre-demonetisation) and 48.9 million (3.8% of population) in FY17 (demonetisation fiscal). The impacts of the twin-shocks of demonetisation and GST are obvious.

In all, the above tax data shows, there is a massive fall in ITRs declaring taxable income from FY16-FY17 to FY17 – by 53.9% or more than half!

Why did this happen? The obvious factors are the twin shocks, the pandemic and the K-shaped recovery. There is yet another factor. A sharp rise in ITRs declaring zero-tax liability – up from 29 million in FY20 to 51.6 million in FY23 (Lok Sabha answer). These numbers were 0.9 million in FY16 and FY17. The sharp rise in zero-tax is also due to the rise in taxable limits since 2019 (overall rise by Rs 2 lakh over the previous UPA regime and would further rise to Rs 2.5 lakh from FY24).

True, during the same period (FY16-FY23), the total number of ITRs including zero tax liability or taxpayers without taxable income has gone up from 49.5 million in FY16 to 74 million in FY23 – growth of 42%.

But this 74 million ITRs of FY23 also include 51.6 million ITRs with zero tax liability (taking the total ITRs declaring taxable income to 22.4 million). The net value of this 51.6 million from the view of tax payment is 'zero'.

An analysis of total ITRs without zero tax liability but income group wise data (e-ITR), provide another aspect to the financial health of taxpayers.

The data for the past six fiscals of FY18-FY23 shows:

(i) Number of ITRs by the lowest income category (0-5 lakh) fell from 52.55 million in FY18 to 49.78 million in FY23. Average growth in their number is -0.4%.

(ii) In contrast, average growth for all higher income categories is positive: 5.4% for 5-10 lakh and 10.3-13.5% for over Rs 10 lakh-over 1 crore.

(iii) As for percentage of population, ITR filed is stagnant – 5% in FY18, 4.9% each in FY19 and FY20, 5.3% in FY21, 4.6% in FY22 and 5.0% in FY23 (population data taken from the budget documents).

SBI's 4 contrarian claims

However, SBI Research which analysed the total number of ITRs filed (from FY13 to FY22), has made four contrarian claims: (a) rise in "weighted mean income" (b) rise in tax efficiency (c) rise in tax buoyancy because of

(a) and (d) transition "from lower income group to upper income group" because of (a).

About the rise in income, the SBI says: "Weighted mean income of Rs 4.4 lakh in AY14 has increased to Rs 13 lakh in AY23." That is, the "weighted income" went up by 195.5% between FY13 and FY22 – a fantastic development to be proud of.

What is 'weighted mean income"? The SBI uses three elements to calculate it: (i) income tax brackets (ii) number of ITRs filed in each bracket and (iii) 'weight' for each bracket is the "mid-point" of each bracket, except for the topmost bracket, for which it is Rs 2 crore.

What it doesn't consider though are the most critical for any such calculations:

The humongous number of ITRs with zero tax liability (zero tax paid). In FY23 alone (as per the LS reply of July 2023), such ITRs constitutes 51.6% of the total ITR. That is, 51.6% tax filers for FY23 paid no tax and declared they didn't have the income to pay tax.

ITRs in the lowest income bracket (up to Rs 5 lakh) constitute about 80% of the total ITRs (76.6% in FY23, for example). As mentioned earlier, the numbers of the ITRs in the lowest income bracket fell from 52.55 million in FY18 to 49.78 million in FY23 and average growth in their number was – (minus) 0.4%.

So, essentially, what the SBI report is telling is this: Sale of SUVs has witnessed quantum jump. What it isn't telling: Sale of passenger cars (PVs) and two-wheelers has crashed at the same time! In other words, the income of the rich (fewer in number) is rising fast and that of the poor (masses) is going down equally fast or faster.

Regarding SBI's other three claims. It doesn't support with evidence other than the rising number of total ITRs and an estimate of "weighted" income.

However, tax efficiency and buoyancy have fallen – as per official data.

(a) Percentage of ITRs declaring taxable income has fallen from 3.8% of population in FY16 and FY17 to 1.6% in FY22. This means a sharp fall in tax efficiency.

(b) Budget documents show direct tax-to GDP is stagnant for 11 fiscals – from 5.6% in FY12 and FY13 to 6% each in FY21, FY22 and FY23 – another measure of tax efficiency.

(c) Tax buoyancy factor (ratio of growth in tax and growth in GDP) for direct tax was 2.52 in FY22 – a sudden jump from "nil" in FY21 (when growth in both tax and GDP was negative). It was less than 2 between FY09 to FY19 and negative (-1.2 in FY20) – having peaked at 2.59 in FY03. All these are from the IT data and doesn't show tax buoyancy going up.

SBI's fourth claim points to transition from low income to middle income. Had that been the case the taxbase would have expanded, not declined (ITRs declaring taxable income) or stagnated (ITRs with zero tax liabilities)

(i) Direct tax-to-GDP and direct tax buoyancy would have gone up, not stagnated or fallen and

(ii) Gross tax-to-GDP would have gone up, not fallen from 11.2% each in FY17 and FY18 to 11.1% in FY23 and FY24 (BE) – as budget documents show.

As for lifting 135 million people out of

multidimensional poverty during FY16-FY21, it is based on a single source health survey data of NFHS-5 of 2019-21 – without any data to measure two other components of multidimensional poverty – education and standard of living (due to data vacuum).

Both the fall in household assets and fall in people declaring taxable income mean less savings and less consumption demand and funds for future investment – which would adversely impact the growth potential. They need to be addressed.

High GDP growth giving misleading picture

High GDP growth and worsening household income are not incompatible or contradictory. It can be explained by the sharp rise in income inequality in India.

The latest slugfest is over 7.8% growth in Q1 of FY24. Economists like Arun Kumar and Ashoka Mody questioned it by drawing attention to unacceptably high discrepancy of 2.8% of GDP on the expenditure side. Arvind Subramanian and Josh Felman questioned the wide gap between headline inflation CPI and GDP deflator (India uses single deflation rather than international standard technique of double deflation) on the production/income side – pointing out that GDP deflator peaked at 11.6% in H1 of FY23 and then collapsed to 0.2% in Q1 of FY24 and asked "does this really correspond to our sense of inflation trends in the economy? The CPI was 4.6% in Q1 of FY24.

They all arrived at the same conclusion after taking into consideration various growth drivers like investment, exports and also imports (consumption demand): The GDP number for Q1 of FY24 (7.8%) is overestimated by about 3 percentage points. In the meanwhile, the government has said its crop yield is overestimated – leading to poor planning for imports and exports of agri commodities and sudden announcements of trade bans or restrictions.

This is something Subramanian had also found in 2019. Subramanian, who was the CEA during 2014-18 and during whose time the 2011-12 GDP series was introduced (in January 2015), compared the new GDP numbers with 17 high frequency indicators (because he said the underlying GDP data were not available publicly and hence, nobody outside the CSO could "estimate GDP") to assert that the GDP growth was overestimated by 2.5-3.7 percentage points every year during 2011-12 and 2016-17.

The problem with the GDP data hasn't gone away. The back series data was released only in November 2018 (nearly four years late). There have been repeated retrospective revisions in the numbers. Besides, the current GDP numbers are based on too old data:

(a) Informal economy contributes "about 50%" to the GDP but this was said in a 2012 report without specifying the year of assessment.

(b) Population data is 12 years old, economic census 9 years, MPCE, CPI, WPI and IIP data are 12 years and so on.

Prudence demands that existing data (tax, household assets) are studied, more data are collected or updated (Census, MPCE, CPI, WPI, IIP, informal sector survey etc.) to develop better understanding of ground realities and then devise appropriate plans and strategies to improving the living standards of people.

Oct 18, 2023

PS: *Arvind Subramanian would raise the same question about inflation-indexing and other "errors and omissions" in FY24 GDP numbers (AE2), in March 2024, pointing out that such "errors and omissions…are actually about 4.3 percentage points".*

***

5 Ways to Resolve the Unfinished Agenda of Freebies

India needs to go beyond FRBM Act of 2003, set up a 'fiscal council' to redefine, expand the scope and monitor all fiscal practices

Now that five state elections are scheduled for November 2023, state governments' 'revdi' (freebies) and 'revdi culture', their rising debt and off-budget expenditures are back in focus. On October 6, 2023, the Supreme Court issued fresh notices to the chief ministers of Rajasthan and Madhya Pradesh over their announcement of election freebies. The Centre has already warned that "financially irresponsible policies and populism may give political results in the short term but will extract a great social and economic price in the long term" and that "those who suffer those consequences the most are often the poorest and the most vulnerable".

These are legitimate issues about fiscal management (freebies, off-budget borrowing and debt) and hence, must be debated and fixed.

But the chances are that this round of debate would end up, like the one in 2019 and 2022 – seasonal, political, partisan and inconclusive. On the previous two occasions, the debate began immediately after the BJP lost elections in important states – which were fought on competitive promises of welfare and populist schemes – and ahead of the next round of elections. Once the next round of elections was over, the issues were forgotten. This time too it seems no different.

Recall January 2019 when the farm loan waivers announced by Congress-ruled states (Rajasthan, Madhya Pradesh and Chhattisgarh) were described as "lollipops" and "political stunts". The BJP had lost the election in all those three states, the 2019 general election was looming and then Congress president Rahul Gandhi was proposing a minimum income guarantee scheme 'NYAY' – to transfer Rs 6,000 per month (Rs 72,000 a year) to 50 million poor families. The two questions raised then were: Will India's fiscal condition allow this and how the beneficiaries would be selected. This was *after six BJP-ruled states had announced farm loan waivers* – Uttar Pradesh (2017), Maharashtra (2017), J&K (2017), Chhattisgarh (2015), Rajasthan (2018), Madhya Pradesh (2018) – and two more BJP-ruled states, Assam (2018) had declared 25% farm loan waiver and Gujarat had waived off power bills of farmers (2018).

The debate ended with the Centre declaring Rs 6,000 per year to farmers in the 'vote-on-account' budget on February 1, 2019.

In 2022, the RBI made the beginning, in its June 2022 bulletin. It sparked off the debate by warning of a Sri Lanka-like fiscal crisis by cautioning against fiscal profligacy of state governments but was silent on the Centre's fiscal performance. It corrected itself seven months later in January 2023 and commended state governments for their fiscal prudence. This came five months after the finance ministry think tank National Institute of Public Finance and Policy (NIPFP) had already contradicted the RBI's June 2022 findings. The RBI had done a rushed job – which was unwarranted, given the long history of states outperforming the Centre in every single fiscal parameter in the entire 2011-12 GDP period.

But by then, 'revdi' and 'revdi culture' had been introduced in public debate in July 2022. The Supreme Court conducted daily hearings in August 2022 – to which the Election Commission of India (ECI) and Finance Commission (FC) were dragged in.

The debate remained inconclusive. The court referred the matter to a three-judge bench to take it forward – which is yet to be constituted. The ECI asked political parties to disclose the cost of freebies they announce – which is not feasible because none has defined what is a freebie and which are 'rational' or 'irrational' (used by the court), 'merit' or 'non-merit' (used by the RBI), 'populist' or otherwise (used by the FC), 'unwarranted' or 'wasteful' (used by others). Budget documents and Economic Surveys use different terms altogether – 'subsidies' for the poor and 'stimulus', 'tax incentive' or 'revenue foregone' for the rich (HNIs) and businesses and trusts.

The existence of these terms underlines the fact that freebies per se are a necessity in India because it is home to the maximum poor (228.9 million) and maximum hungry (224.3 million) in the world. Nonetheless, good fiscal management calls for eternal vigilance.

For a closure to the debate, the following five measures are necessary.

What is a freebie?

First, 'freebie' needs to be defined – for both the Centre and states.

The Centre runs many welfare schemes that can be called freebies: Subsidised LPG cylinders to poor families in which a Rs 200 cut was announced recently; "free" PDS to 67% households (Rs 2.87 lakh crore given for this in FY23 (RE); fertilizer subsidy to industry (Rs 22.5 lakh crore given in FY23 (RE); the PLIs and DLIs to industry (allocated Rs 2.82 lakh crore); Rs 1.45 lakh crore corporate tax cut in 2019; annual average NPA write-off of Rs 1.62 lakh crore during FY15-FY23 (total of Rs 14.56 lakh crore); annual cash transfers of Rs 6,000 to farmers (Rs 60,000 crore given in FY23) etc.

So is the case for states: 200 units of free electricity and 20 KL of free water by the NCT of Delhi, free bus travel for women by Delhi and Karnataka governments, 10 kg free rice for BPL families by Karnataka government etc.

Second, limits to freebies. The limit could be a percentage of revenue or fiscal deficit of states/Centre.

How much freebies states give is known – the RBI said (June 2022) said it was 0.1% to 2.7% of respective GSDPs in FY23 (BE), with only two of nine states it tracked recorded over 2%. The RBI (January 2023) also found 19 of 31 states/UTs were revenue surplus in FY23 (BE). Their total revenue deficit was 0.3% of the GDP and fiscal deficit 3.4% of the GDP in FY23 (BE).

No such exercise has been undertaken by the RBI for the Centre. In FY23 (RE), the Centre's revenue deficit was 4.1% and fiscal deficit 6.4% of the GDP – far higher than those of states.

Off-budget accounting and disclosures

Third, accounting standards and disclosure norms for off-budget borrowings.

Off-budget borrowings are not easy to detect; the very nomenclature makes that clear. Only the CAG can do the job because it has the power to seek documents and ask questions and clarifications from governments. But even then, it isn't quite possible to monitor off-budget borrowings – which will become clear soon.

Recall the Centre's budget for FY22. It showed, for FY21 (RE) fertilizer subsidy was Rs 1.34 lakh crore – 1.9 times the budgeted Rs 71,309 crore and food subsidy was Rs 4.2 lakh crore – 3.5 times the budgeted Rs 1.2 lakh crore. This couldn't have been possible without hidden off-budget borrowings (totalling Rs 3.69 lakh crore) – even if it was a pandemic fiscal. There is little logic to support 1.9 times rise in fertilizer subsidy in a pandemic year; food subsidy would have gone up by a maximum of 2 times, given the additional "free" ration, but not by 3.5 times.

Few know that this extraordinary spending (RE) happened despite the introduction of "statement of extra budgetary resources (EBRs)" – or "statement 27" in the "expenditure profile" – in FY20.

This statement is supposed to disclose all off-budget borrowings. The "statement 27" of FY24 (BE) shows, between FY17-FY22 (six fiscals), off-budget borrowings amounted to a mere Rs 1.39 lakh crore – a lot less than Rs 3.69 crore of extra subsidy outgo in FY21 (RE) alone! How did that happen?

The "statement 27" for FY24 (BE) also shows "nil" off-budget borrowings in FY23 (BE and RE) and FY24 (BE).

Watch out for the next "statement 27" to see, for example, how the additional spending of over Rs 3,110 crore for the G20 summit in New Delhi is accounted for. The budget allocation for the G20 summit was a mere Rs 990 crore – against which the actual spending is over Rs 4,100 crore.

Here is more evidence of bad off-budget disclosures.

Delhi-based think tank, Centre for Social and Economic Progress (CSEP), published a study on off-budget borrowings in June 2023, "An Analysis of Off-Budget Borrowings by Indian Governments and their Legal Context". For this study, the CSEP relied on CAG audit reports because it said budget documents didn't give proper accounts (due to "non-standard accounting").

About the Centre's disclosures, it said: "The CAG audits from 2020-2022 of the union government point out the inadequacies of Statement 27, which include deficiency in the format, and incomplete and non-disclosure of certain entities' debt." About states, it said, their disclosures are (i) "highly understated" and suffer from additional deficiencies like (ii) for states like Madhya Pradesh, Uttarakhand and Gujarat "no data is available at all" and (iii) for many other states, data is "not consistently available for the last few years".

Sharp rise in Centre's debts

Fourth, a 'fiscal council' to redefine standards and monitor fiscal management. This is essential as the CAG is not good enough a watchdog.

Several older Finance Commission reports had recommended a 'fiscal council' for better fiscal management; the 15th one sought a "high-powered inter-governmental group". Such a mechanism is essential. Besides, the Interstate Council (ISC) and National Development Council (NDC) – both are non-functional after 2015 – also need to be revived to get a better handle on fiscal management.

Fifth, empowering 'fiscal council' to set new standards on fiscal deficit and debt.

The logic is simple: (i) higher debts are needed to boost growth, particularly when private investment is muted for long and also (ii) because the IMF, which put the limits that the FRBM Act of 2003 adopted, has argued for upward revision in both fiscal deficit and debt limits in view of the changed financial realities in both in the pre-pandemic low interest rate regime and the post-pandemic needs for higher fiscal supports to people and businesses which went through hardships.

Incidentally, states outperform the Centre in government capex too.

During the past 12 fiscals of FY12-FY23, the share of government capex for the Centre and state are in the ratio of 36:64 – exactly the reverse of their tax collections – 62:38. Which means, the Centre collects more tax but spends comparatively less on capex than states.

'Fiscal council' needs to keep in mind that the Centre has (i) more tax rights like monopoly over direct taxes (on individual income and corporate profits), while states gave up several indirect tax rights by adopting the GST. It collects more revenues through tools unavailable to states, like (ii) cess and surcharges (risen in recent years) and (iii) disinvestments and privatisations (risen in recent years) – which are not shared with states – and (iv) dividend and surplus transfers from the RBI and CPSUs (risen too). It was, in fact, the demand for additional Rs 2-3 lakh crore transfers from the RBI ahead of the 2019 general elections that caused a clash between the two – former RBI Deputy Governor Viral Acharya disclosed recently. Besides, (v) devolution of Finance Commission award to states is falling in recent years.

To sum up, the 'revdi' debate must lead to new standards and better monitoring of fiscal management by both the Centre and states, equity and 'cooperative federalism' between them.

Oct 17, 2023

***

What is Hurting India's Exports Engine

Exports as % of GDP have remained rangebound in recent years.

Where India's interests are being hurt need to be flagged for several proximate developments, but before that a fact for better perspective. Exports, the fourth engine of growth, remain rangebound since FY15. From 23.9% of the GDP in FY15, they have slid a bit to 23.5% in FY23 – averaging 21% during this period (nine fiscals). After the 1991 trade liberalisation, exports had zoomed from 6-7% of the GDP in early 1990s to 21% in FY07 and averaged 22.7% during FY07-FY14 (eight fiscals).

First India went back to 'import substitution' to promote 'local for global' products, added incentives like the PLIs and DLIs to a long list of tax incentives to promote exports of local products and now it is back to 'licensing' to make the PLIs and DLIs work for local laptops, PCs and tablets.

Setback for trade liberalisation

Take the latest case. On August 3, 2023, the government announced a ban on imports of laptops, PCs and tablets "with immediate effect" and mandated "valid licence" for "restricted imports" of these items. The next day, on August

4, 2023, the ban was put on hold for three months. More than a month-and-half later, on September 26, 2023, IT minister (MoS) Rajeev Chandrasekhar declared "no license" would be needed for such imports as it would be replaced, shortly, with "import management system"; the new system would have a "built-in" mechanism to allow "certain amounts" of imports on the basis of a company's local manufacturing of these items.

Interestingly, the "import management system" already exists under the Ministry of Commerce and Industry to regulate "imports". Under this, "licence or registration" is required in case of any "restrictions or quota" on import of goods; the "modules" (for applications for imports) require importers "to apply for import licences, quotas and other registrations which are issued by DGFT". Some of the "modules" listed include "Import License for Restricted Items", "Import License for Tariff Rate Quota (TRQ)", "Registration Certificates". In short, there is no escape from "license".

Licenses/registrations are now routine part of trade because of frequent bans and "restrictions" not just on laptops or other electronic items but also a host of agriculture produces like wheat, rice, sugar and pulses.

There are three contradictory claims in the statements: (i) the government "never" believed, "doesn't believe" and "will certainly not believe" in a license regime (ii) the ("immediate") ban was "not taken in haste" and was "not abrupt" but came after consulting industry on the PLI for hardware and (iii) the government wants a «trusted supply chain».

The contradictions would be apparent by the fact that (a) importers cried foul at the sudden ban, pointing out that

90% of laptops, PCs and tablets sold in India are imported – forcing the government to immediately defer the ban and (b) global suppliers like Apple, Samsung, HP immediately stopped supply, on August 4, due to the ban and warned of supply disruptions and price rise.

However, the key to the puzzle lies in another parallel development. Four days before the "immediate" ban, the Reliance launched JioBook, about which the Amazon›s listing said it was being "manufactured" in China (not India).

Bumper harvests but exports not allowed

Frequent ban on export of agriculture produce like wheat, rice, sugar and pulses, point to yet another policy impulse – data dissonance.

On September 19, 2023, Finance Minister Nirmala Sitharaman called for "real-time estimation" of yields of rice, wheat, pulses etc., stressing that the "country suffers for want of" reliable estimates, unable to "plan" imports or exports of these produces.

On September 25, 2023, food and public distribution secretary Sanjeev Chopra said: "there has been a mismatch between the agriculture and trade figures" on wheat production. He pointed out that while the government was "reporting 112 million ton" of wheat in 2023-24 (October-March), the trade reported "102-103 million ton" – a difference of 10 million ton. He assured that "in the next one or two years" the government would ensure that the estimates are "driven by the ground reality".

To say that India can't estimate its crop yield correctly ("ground reality") despite being the pioneer of statistical standards and systems since 1970s, much ahead of the developed world is difficult to digest. What has gone wrong?

The obvious answer is data dissonance. Particularly since 2018, the GDP numbers are questioned by all independent economists every time fresh data is released. September 2023 saw Ashoka Mody and Arvind Subramanian do it once again. They point to the GDP growth being overestimated by about 2.5 to 3 percentage points.

FTAs with EU, UK, Canada stuck

There is a third policy impulse to worry: stalled multilateral FTAs and diplomatic row stalling bilateral FTAs.

The negotiations with the UK are stuck just as ahead of Prime Minister Rishi Sunak's visit to India to attend the G20 summit, his spokesman said, on September 7, 2023, that his government won't change its immigration policy to secure trade deal with India. In June, their trade minister Kemi Badenoch was categorical that "there are no plans to change our immigration policy" to allow Indian workers free access to UK's labour market.

Now, the diplomatic chill over the killing of Canadian citizen and alleged terrorist Hardeep Singh Nijjar in its soil has stalled the bilateral FTA. After Canada said it, India has confirmed that trade talks are on "pause" until the situation improves.

India's trade talks with the European Union (EU) are stuck for quite some time. The latest hurdle is the EU's proposed Carbon Border Adjustment Mechanism (CBAM) principles for imposing carbon tax on all imports. In response, India is mulling imposing and collecting its own carbon tax on goods coming from the EU. This is over and above the tussle over the WTO ruling of May 2023 which censured India. The EU, Japan and Taiwan had complained about tariff barriers of 7.5-20% on ICT products India imposed while the WTO mandates 0% tax on these items. This remains a stumbling block and at stake is trade ties with not just the EU but Japan and Taiwan also.

India's diplomatic and trade ties with China remains strained since 2020 – over the latter's intrusion in Ladakh. Though trade negotiations have progressed with Australia, a "comprehensive" deal is expected by the end of 2023.

Now, look at India's top 10 trade partners. All these countries figure in that list.

India also "unilaterally" cancelled 68 bilateral investment treaties (BITs) – which are linked to bilateral FTAs. It has to renegotiate each of the bilateral FTAs to yield intended benefits. Besides, India has avoided all big multilateral FTAs – like the RCEP, IPEF and CPTPP – which are groupings of all big economies controlling most of the global GDP and trade and having overlapping memberships. Instead, India has opted to renegotiate only bilateral FTPs but not one of the three reports (Economic Survey of 2021-22, NITI Aayog of 2018 and Exim Bank of 2022) cited by Indian officials to justify such approach to trade treaties recommends this.

The above moves are linked to two developments:

- Growth in FDI inflows is slowing down from 25% in FY15 to 3% in FY23 and (-)16% in FY24 (up to June 2023) – the latest DPIIT report shows. A Nikkei Asia report explains this slowdown to MNCs finding Vietnam and other competitors more attractive – an indicator that the China+1 strategy of MNCs is not working for India.

- Indian exports share of GDP are lower in FY24. Monthly trade data for FY24 shows, during April-August 223, merchandise exports fell by $23.4 billion from the corresponding FY23 level. Imports fell even more – by $37.4 billion – taking the deficit to -$37.5 billion, which would have been bigger had it not been for the surplus of $61.4 billion generated by services trade.

Injury to services exports

There is a fourth policy impulse to worry: injury to services trade.

Indian trade has generated surplus only twice in post-independent history (since 1949-50) – in 1972-73 and 1976-77 (Economic Survey of 2022-23). The UNCTAD data for 2005-2021 shows, services exports are delivering a surplus since 2010 to cut down trade deficits. As against less than 2% share in merchandise goods, Indian services exports has a global share of is 3-4% (2015-2020).

Yet, the Foreign Trade Policy (FTP) of 2023 is silent on services exports. It exclusively focuses on process improvements and not product improvements; it is silent on global geo-economic fragmentations that the US President Trump-led de-globalisation caused after 2016, further aggravated by the Russia-Ukraine war of 2022.

New Indian education (NEP 2020) and recruitment (UPSC exams) policies will also have a bearing on services exports because they may affect Indians' English skills that led to growth of IT sector and exports of IT services. The emphasis in both is on developing Indian language skills at the cost of English by cutting down English classes in colleges and universities and ending primacy of English in civil services exams.

Sept 30, 2023

NB: In March 2024, the US trade officials would reveal that the 'license raj' for laptop/PC was replacing with "import management system" due to the US pressure. Trade data would reveal that laptop/PC imports from China zoomed from 70% of total imports in August-October quarter of 2023 to 87.5% in the subsequent quarter of November-January.

***

Chandrayaan-3: 'Make in India's' Moment of Reckoning

'Make in India' falls short on two counts: (i) well-defined policies, and strategies and (ii) post facto studies and reviews to assess the impact

India achieved a rare technological breakthrough in space science with the Chandrayaan-3 successfully landing near moon's south pole on the August 23, 2023 – a culmination of exploration that, in a way, began with the Chandrayaan-1 (which orbited the moon in 2008) and Chandrayaan-2 (which crash landed on the moon's surface in 2019).

The ISRO scientists may indeed "have taken Make in India to the Moon" but this is not an outcome of the flagship mission-mode programme launched in September 2014. The ISRO belongs to another era when the focus was on developing scientific temper and building institutions of excellence (along with IITs, IIMs and AIIMS and many others). The delink would be clear soon.

Has 'Make in India' achieved goals?

Such linkage is not surprising because many myths are associated with 'Make in India' – which need to be unravelled to make it achieve its stated goals. The first *myth* is that 'Make in India' is a programme with clear goals.

When it was launched on September 25, 2014, 'Make in India' was an idea with no goals, no policy frameworks and no planning or strategy. Revisit the statement issued on the occasion, "PM launches 'Make in India' global initiative". It talks of pushing investment (particularly FDI), skilling and creating jobs but no roadmap, goal or strategy. Several months later, on March 18, 2015, the Ministry of Commerce and Ministry spelt out its twin goals: (i) "enhancing the share of manufacturing in GDP to 25%" and (ii) "creating 100 million jobs over a decade or so".

It was this statement which said that (a) the twin goals and (b) the "specific policy instruments" to achieve these goals were "conceptualised" under the National Manufacturing Policy "notified» on November 4, 2011 – nearly five years earlier. Those "specific policy instruments" were in "areas such as rationalisation and simplification of business regulations, financial and institutional mechanisms for technology development, incentives for SMEs, Special Focus Sectors, etc."

Revisit the 2011 National Manufacturing Policy – prepared and notified by the same Ministry of Commerce and Industry – to know why it said what. It said: "The share of manufacturing in India's GDP has stagnated at 15-16% (of the GDP) since 1980 while the share in comparable economies in Asia is much higher at 25 to 34%." It didn't give the manufacturing's job share but the Planning Commission regularly did– average of 10.5% during 2004-05 and 2009-10. This was down from 11.1% during 1999-2000 to 2004-05. The Planning Commission also said (for better comparison) the manufacturing's GVA share was 15.3% during 2004-05 and 2009-10 (down from 15.5% during 1999-2000 and 2004-05).

A Broken Economy | 185

What is manufacturing share in GVA and employment now?

During the subsequent period covered by the 2011-12 GDP series, from FY12 to FY23, the manufacturing's GVA share is (average) 17.8% (MoSPI). In FY23, it was 17.7%.

But wait, before assuming that this is a marked improvement (over 15.3% seen between 2004-05 and 2009-10), here is a caveat.

When the 2011-12 GDP series was introduced in January 2015, it *statistically raised* the manufacturing's GVA share by an average of *3.86%* for FY12, FY13 and FY14 – from (av) 13.9% under the 2004-05 series to (av) 17.76% under the 2011-12 series.

This happened because, for the first time, an MCA-21 database (self-populated by industry) of the Ministry of Corporate Affairs (MCA) was used for the manufacturing's GVA share (and also that of services). This MCA-21 data base was exposed for *45% data flaw* in 2019 by the NSSO and it remains *flawed* even in 2023.

Now consider manufacturing's job share.

The annual PLFS reports show its job share is (average) 11.6% during 2017-18 and 2021-22. Manufacturing jobs have been falling from 12.1% in 2017-18 to 11.6% in 2021-22 (much lower in 2019-20 and 2020-21). Since it was 10.5% during 2004-5 and 2009-10, there is a marginal improvement (to 11.6%) more than a decade later. But here too, there is a caveat.

The PLFS data shows there was no job loss due to the GST of 2017 and the pandemic lockdowns of 2020 and 2021 – as all the relevant headline indicators, the WPR, LFPR and

UR (unemployment rate), *progressively improved* during the period of 2017-18 to 2021-22. How is that even possible? Given this, the marginal improvement in manufacturing's job share is questionable.

Besides, do you know the PLFS reports don't tell the total number of jobs in the economy or how many new jobs are created every year and in which sector? The Planning Commission used to do that by analysing the PLFS's unit level data and other surveys and datasets. Its replacement, the NITI Aayog, doesn't.

The other measure of job creation is the payroll data, EPFO numbers.

The government cites this data. For example, Union Minister Ashwini Vaishnaw said on August 15, 2023 that 1.4 million new jobs were being created every *month*. A few months earlier, in December 2022, he said 1.5-1.6 million jobs were being created every month. On both occasions, he cited *monthly* EPFO data.

Since monthly EPFO data undergoes corrections every month (due to non-elimination of duplications and other reasons), it is better to look at the *annual* data.

The EPFO's annual reports provide that data and show:

- In FY16 (from when it was tracked), the number of "regular contributors" to the EPFO was 37.6 million.
- It went up to 46.3 million in FY22. The FY23 report is not available.

That is, 8.7 million jobs were added in six years or *8.7% of the 100 million jobs that 'Make in India' promised in March 2015 – nowhere closer to Vaishnaw's two claims.

Arbitrary drivers of 'Make in India'

'Make in India' falls short on two counts: (i) well-defined policies, strategies and planning to push 'Make in India' and (ii) *post facto* studies and reviews to assess the impacts and lack of course corrections to 'Make in India' mission.

This would become clear from the *five* major discernible drivers of 'Make in India': (a) liberalisation of FDI to attract investment (b) ease of doing business, of which decriminalization of Companies Act of 2013 is one part (c) manufacturing incentives like the PLIs and DLIs (d) import substitution to promote domestic manufacturing and now (e) license to import manufacturing products.

Here is a brief sketch of how these drivers have played out.

FDI inflows: The DPIIT's FDI inflow factsheet up to June 2023 shows, *growth* in FDI inflows is consistently slowing down from 25% in FY5 to 3% in FY23 and (-) 16% in FY24 (up to June 2023). Three questions arise: Why this slowdown? What is the FDI inflow doing to manufacturing? Is FDI achieving its goals of technology transfer, marketing expertise, modern managerial techniques and export boost?

None of these questions can be answered because there are no official studies or assessments. Private studies have shown, for a long time, that more than 85% FDI inflows and outflows are through shell companies and tax havens (involving round-tripping).

Ease of Doing Business 1.0 and 2.0: India did achieve remarkable success in improving in the World Bank's Ease of Doing Business ranking – it jumped from 142 in 2014 to 63 in 2019. Thereafter, the World Bank's DBI shut it down due to data manipulation allegations. Here is how this success was achieved.

In October 2017 – immediately after the twin shocks of demonetisation and GST that derailed the economy and after India's rank jumped 130 to 100 – the World Bank's Country Director in India Junaid Ahmad was questioned about this improvement. He told a national daily that its data didn't capture demonetisation and GST. He said these impacts would be reflected in next year's ranking. But the next year, in 2018, India's rank jumped 23 places to 77 and in 2019 to 63 – while India's growth slipped to 3.4% in FY20 (corresponding fiscal of 2019). What was the impact of Ease of Doing Business 1.0? Not known because there is no official study. Yet, India ventured into Ease of Doing Business 2.0 (budget 2023) – through more decriminalisation of Companies Act of 2013 and the Jan Vishwas Act of 2023 which amended 42 laws at one go a few days ago.

PLIs and DLIs: The impact of these incentives to push 'Make in India' are not known either. Many economists have questioned their efficacy and sought impact assessments before going further. But there is no sign of that happening – even when it is known that such incentives are ending up promoting assembling units (in the mobile phone sector, for example), and leading to higher imports and higher trade deficits (in the mobile phones case). The Micron's chips project in Gujarat is also an assembling project, not 'Make in India.'

Import substitution policy: This was the first step to promote 'Make in India' and is in force since 2014 but its impact has not been studied. Trade data shows, it has led to fall in exports – disabling one of the four main growth drivers.

License to import: About a month ago, the DGFT imposed ban on import of laptops, PCs and tablets and proposed a licensing regime – even when *90% of all domestic sales* are imported. It could inconvenience millions of Indians to pursue education, business, leisure, travel and virtually everything else. It has been put on hold for three months.

Since the Chandrayaan-3 has already been branded as 'Make in India' here are two inevitable comparisons – to make the delink obvious.

A recent CAG revealed that 'Make in India' roads cost a bomb. It flagged two arbitrariness: "Selection of ineligible bidders, award of works without approved detailed project reports or based on faulty detailed project reports." Such arbitrariness, it said, led to the Dwarka Expressway, being built under the Bharatmala Pariyojana (a PPP project), cost Rs *250.77 crore per km* – as against the CCEA approved cost of R 18.2 crore per km – *13.8 times more*. No probe has been announced. And the CAG's findings have been *dismissed*.

The Micron's chips assembling unit in Gujarat, mentioned earlier, comes with Rs 16,000 crore of *public money* (70% of the total project cost of $2.75 billion) by way of the DLI.

Contrast these with the Chandrayaan-3 which landed on the moon (located at a distance of 3,84,400 km). It cost the ISRO, set up in a different era of ‹Make in India›, Rs 615 crore.

Here is a larger perspective to all this.

India's post-colonial re-industrialisation and manufacturing push began with the *First Industrial Policy of*

1948 (72 years ago) – assisted by the five-year plans and the Planning Commission. This was *after* then business tycoons expressed *inability* to invest and lead the re-industrialise drive through a document called "Bombay Plan of 1944" – which was authored by JRD Tata, GD Birla, Sir Ardeshir Dalal, Sri Ram, Kasturbhai Lalbhai, AD Shroff and John Mathai. India's mid-1980s› reforms and 1991's liberalisation – which pulled India out of the 'Hindu rate of growth' – were also assisted by the five-year plans and the Planning Commission.

The point of all this perspective is: It needs sound policies, strategies, planning, reviews and course corrections to achieve goals, not arbitrariness.

Aug 31, 2023

NB: It was Prime Minister Modi who linked the success of the Chandrayaan-3 to his 'Make in India' scheme while addressing the ISRO scientists in Bengaluru on August 26, 2023.

***

Data War on India Lifting 135-140 Million Out Of Poverty

Both NITI Aayog and UNDP-OPHDI estimates are based only on health survey, NFHS-5 of 2019-21 -- 71% of its data was collected before the pandemic hit

On July 17, 2023, the NITI Aayog claimed that "135 million have exited multi-dimensional poverty" during 2015-16 and 2019-21, in its report "National Multidimensional Poverty Index: A Progress Review 2023". How accurate is this assessment? Not very. Here is how.

To understand its claim, one must look at the source of its data.

The report says its estimate is "based on" National Family Health Survey-5 (NFHS-5) of 2019-2021 – which was released in two phases in 2020 and 2021. The Aayog's baseline MPI of 2021 – on which the MPI of 2023 is built – was released on November 24, 2021 – and was "based on" NFHS-4 of 2015-16.

The first question that arises is: Why was the baseline MPI of 2021 prepared on the old NFHS-4 of 2015-16 data when the new NFHS-5 of 2019-21 data was already known?

Note, the day (November 24, 2021) the MPI of 2021 was published also saw the publication of phase II NFHS-

5 of 2019-21 data – covering 11 states and 3 UTs.[3] The phase I data had been published long ago, in December 2020 – covering 17 states and 5 UTs. Also note, when the NFHS-5 data was released in phases, all data on a particular state/UT was released together. This means the Aayog had the NFHS-5 data on the majority of states/UTs by December 2020. All the rest became available in 2021 but going by the fact that the foreword of the phase II report was signed by Health Secretary Rajesh Bhushan on September 22, 2021, the Aayog could have had this data at least for three months (September to November 2021) in advance to work on.

Why did the Aayog rely on the old 2015-16 data is not known but it certainly is a very unusual practice for an economist.

The second question is about the NFHS-5 data of 2019-21: Why were the years 2019-2021 selected? Why not a single year of 2019-20 or 2020-21 – which is a standard practice in India and abroad? Remember, 2019-20 was a pre-pandemic year and 2020-21 was the first pandemic year (unusual year). Why mix the data of a normal year data with that of an abnormal year? The only logical explanation could be that the Aayog wanted to lessen the true impact of the pandemic on health, education, and living standard -- all three parameters on which MPI is built and all of these were severely hit in the pandemic year.

The third question arises out of the Aayog report (page 4) which reads: "It is important to note that the poverty estimates presented in this report may not fully assess the effects of the COVID-19 pandemic on poverty, since more than 70% of the data (NFHS-5) was collected before the pandemic. At the same time, this report does not capture the economic and social progress the country has made in the last two years."

This statement is corroborated by the UNDP-OPHDI's MPI report of 2022 (page 19[5]), released in October 2022, but missing from its abridged version released on July 11, 2023) which reads: "The effects of the COVID-19 pandemic on poverty India cannot be fully assessed because 71 percent of the data from 2019/2021 Demographic and Health Survey for the country were collected before the pandemic."

The question then arises: Since most of the NFHS-5 data ("more than 70%" or "71%") is on the pre-pandemic 2019-20, how could this represent the data for 2019-20 and 2020-21? It would only mean, the impact of the pandemic was captured to the extent of 29%. This would mean a highly skewed number for 2019-21.

The fourth question is: Why did the Aayog use only the NFHS data – which is about health – but not on education and standard of living (income/expenditure) – the other two components of the MPI? Another question relating to it is: How reliable then is Aayog's MPI report of 2023? Or for that matter, its MPI of 2021 report?

Fifth question: Why didn't the Aayog use the two standard parameters to measure poverty – poverty line and household consumer expenditure (MPCE) which acts as a proxy for household income?

The answers are known: (a) the poverty line was last fixed in 2004-05, called the Tendulkar poverty line – about two decades old and (b) the MPCE was last carried out in 2011-12 – a decade old; the one of 2017-18 was junked in the name of bad data quality but it was actually for showing that poverty went up between 2011-12 and 2017-18 for the first time in 40 years. Another related question arises: Why hasn't the poverty line been updated and fresh MPCE data collected?

Sixth question: Isn't this data vacuum giving rise to speculative and flawed estimates on poverty?

UNDP-OPHDI: 140 million lifted out of MPI poverty

While the Aayog claimed 135 million were lifted out of MPI poverty during 2015-16 and 2019-21, the UNDP-OPHDI reports of 2022 and 2023 (abridged version of 2022) said 140 million did so during the same period. (The UNDP-PHDI report said 275 million were lifted out of MPI poverty during 2005-06 (NFHS-3) and 2015/2016 (NFHS-4) also, taking the total to 415 million during 2005-06 and 2019-21).

Both use the same NFHS-5 data. Why does the UNDP-OPHDI use no other data? The answer is data vacuum.

The only difference between these reports is the rate of MPI reduction. The Aayog said it fell from 24.95% in 2015-16 to 14.96% in 2019-21, while the UNDP-OPHDI said it fell from 27.7% to 16.4% during the same period (it was 55.1% in 2005-06, which is NFHS-3). The percentage points matter because India's population is estimated at 1.425 billion in 2023 (as per UN DESA). Apparently, the two reports used different population bases.

Seventh question: Why is this difference in fall percentage (9.99 percentage for the Aayog and 11.3 percentage for the UNDP-PHDI) when the data source is the same?

The answer: (a) different methodology and (b) two additional indicators (taking the total to 12) used by the

Aayog: maternal health and bank account. Two eminent economists with extensive working knowledge of the Indian economy have objected to the Aayog's methods and indicators. Pronab Sen, who heads the new Standing Committee on Statistics, said: "The way the MPI is structured, it is almost impossible to show a decrease in these indicators over a period of time". C Rangarajan said: "The MPI takes into account bank accounts, which does not indicate welfare. Bank accounts will keep increasing over a period. Therefore, it needs to be discussed how relevant some of these indicators are."

One must remind here that the Aayog has a questionable reputation in such matters. Its pandemic year report "SDG India-Index & Dashboard 2020-21" showed a dramatic fall in poverty, hunger, and inequality – of 28 states/UTs it mapped, poverty fell in 25, hunger in 23, and income inequality in 13. This was a dramatic reversal of pre-pandemic 2019-20 when poverty had gone up in 22, hunger in 24, and income inequality in 25 of those states/UTs.

It never explained how did poverty, hunger, and inequality went down during the two devastating pandemic waves, national lockdowns, and the economic collapse.

Data vacuum

The latest round of poverty debate, however, didn't start in July 2023. It started in April 2022.

In April 2022, the IMF's "Pandemic, Poverty, and Inequality: Evidence from India" and the World Bank's, "Poverty in India Has Declined over the Last Decade But Not As Much As Previously Thought" provided fresh estimates of "extreme poverty" in India (per capita per day expenditure of $1.9).

The IMF report covered 2011-2020 and said: extreme poverty in 2019 (pre-pandemic FY20) was 1.4% – declining by 10.8 percentage points since FY12 – and in 2020 (pandemic fiscal of FY21) it declined to 0.8% due to food "transfers" ("free" over and above "subsidised" ration to 62.5% households), without which it would have been 2.48%.

The World Bank report covered 2011-2019 and said: poverty (at $1.9) declined from 22.5% in 2011 (FY12) to 10.2% in 2019 (FY20) – a drop of 12.3 percentage points but it didn't explain why this happened.

The lead authors of these reports were Indian economists: Surjit Bhalla for the IMF and Sutirtha Sinha Roy for the WB. What data did they use? Both took the MPCE of 2011-12 as a base for their statistical projections into FY21 (IMF) and FY20 (WB). That is, these were statistical constructs – not based on actual data.

There are several problems with the IMF estimates:

- IMF justifies junking of MPCE of 2017-18 on the ground that an expert committee had questioned its data quality (but unbeknownst to it, the said committee had refuted this and upheld the data quality). At the same time, it used the very same NSSO's MPCE of 2011-12 as its base.

- It's the consumption data for post-2011-12 years taken from the 2011-12 GDP series (PFCE) which maps the consumption of all Indians, rich or poor, except government consumption (GFCE) and doesn't tell which income segment group consumes how much. Besides, if then Chief Economic Advisor (CEA) Arvind Subramanian didn't trust the 2011-12 GDP series (introduced in 2015), stating that it overestimated the GDP growth by 2.5 percentage points during 2012-2016, it is tough for others to trust it either (add to that frequent retrospective revisions).

- It assumes that all 67% of households received the full quota of PDS supply (money value was used for the calculations). This is wrong and the repeated tongue-lashing by the Supreme Court for not providing ration to millions of migrants in both 2020 and 2021 is a testament to that. The Global Hunger Index report of 2022 shows India is not only home to the maximum undernourished population (224.3 million or 27% of the world) but its progress reversed during 2014-2022 (hunger score went up from 28.2 to 29.1) – unlike others like Rwanda, Nepal, Pakistan, Myanmar, Bangladesh who continued to reduce hunger and all of them have a lower level of hunger in 2022 than India. The UNDP-OPHDI of 2022 (its 2023 is an abridged version, not a new estimate) said: "India still has the highest number of poor children in the world (97 million, or 21.8 percent of children ages 0–17 in India)."

- Free and/or subsidised ration can avert hunger – not poverty. Poverty gets reduced only by raising income. So, using PDS supply underestimates poverty.

The World Bank report is also questionable: It uses the MPCE of 2011-12 as a base and then uses private sector CMIE's CPHS data to estimate poverty in FY20, even while admitting that it is not comparable with the NSSO's MPCE (and hence, tweaks it). The CPHS data is known to underestimate poverty vis-à-vis other surveys and is also known for its bias for the well-off (urban population)

– which the CMIE admitted and promised to look into in 2021.

How reliable then are the IMF and WB estimates on poverty?

But why do the IMF and WB estimate poverty statistically? The answer is the same: data vacuum.

The lesson in all this?

Indian government must collect relevant data – to rebase the poverty line and update MPCE. Better if it starts collecting (household) income data – as the US, for example, does periodically. The MPCE is for India in which the economic structure didn't allow collecting income data directly and hence, MPCE was used as a proxy.

Aug 16, 2023

NB: *Bhalla was appointed as India's representative at the IMF for three years (2019-21) by the Modi government. Sinha Roy had worked in the office of then CEA Arvind Subramanian in the Modi government before joining the World Bank in 2017.*

***

Is India Back to 'License Raj'?

India is a true command-and-control economy. Only a few policies can be attributed to 'Make in India' initiative and 'National Champions' growth model.

Many seem to think India is back to 'license raj', after the DGFT "restricted" imports of laptops, personal computers, tablets and other items (in HSN 8741 category) "with immediate effect" on August 3, 2023 – requiring "a valid Licence for Restricted Imports". This is both right and wrong.

Right because MoS for MeiTY Rajeev Chandrasekhar met panicked industry representatives five days later on August 8, 2023 (*post facto* announcement and a freeze for three months) to assure that the licensing procedures, in the works, would be "simple and easy". This means, there is no escaping the 'license raj' now – which had been supposedly dismantled in the reforms and liberalisation era starting with the mid-1980s'.

Wrong because, this isn't the first time.

On July 30, 2020, the DGFT had "restricted" imports of 10 categories of TV sets with a declaration that the procedure for "license" would be notified separately. In fact, the DGFT says whenever it notifies "restrictions or quota or conditions on import of goods" it "may require a licence or registration". Going by bans and restrictions on both *imports* and *exports* in the past few years, the DGFT is certain to have opened a full-fledged licensing unit now.

Wrong also because India is running a *command-and-control economy*. And no, India didn't follow the de-globalisation march U.S. President Donald Trump is credited to have started (after 2016). India pioneered it (although it matters little to global trade) by re-adopting the import substitution policy of 1960s and 1970s in 2014.

Here is how.

Command-and-control economy

The import substitution *practice* began immediately after the new government took over in 2014. But it was so *subtle* that it took then Chief Economic Advisor (CEA) Arvind Subramanian (along with fellow economist Shoumitro Chatterjee) to *decipher* it in 2020 – two years after he quit the job.

In the paper, "India's Inward (Re)Turn: Is it Warranted? Will it Work?" the economists wrote: "Between 1991 and 2014, average MFN tariffs declined from 125% to 13%. *Since 2014, there have been about 3,200 tariff increases* at the HS-6 digit level (on most-favored-nation imports), a strikingly large increase. As a result, the average tariff has increased from 13% to nearly 18%. The largest increases occurred in 2018 when there were nearly 2,500 tariff increases amounting to nearly 4 percentage points. We estimate that the tariff increases affected import categories that amount to about $300 billion or about 70% of total imports." The tariff rise continues.

This (unofficial) import substitution policy coincided

with the launch of 'Make in India' initiative in September 2014 and became 'official' as part of the "AatmaNirbhar Bharat" mission launched *four years later* – amidst the pandemic lockdown of 2020. This too was a *smart move* as even those who don't support import substitution couldn't quibble over India's desire to become 'AatmaNirbharar Bharat' – self-reliant or self-sufficient in manufacturing ('holy grail' of being developed) – even though this journey had begun 72 *years earlier* with the *First Industrial Policy of 1948*, which adopted a government-led manufacturing push. The previous UPA government too pushed it through the National Manufacturing Policy of 2011. In September 2014, the new government launched 'Make in India' to manufacture in India or make India self-reliant.

The import restrictions on laptops and TV sets are mere *extensions* of that import substitution practice and policy of post-2014. The manner in which the latest restriction (on laptops, PCs and tablets) has been announced reflects new cues on running the economy.

That it was *put on hold* for three months within the next 24 hours (as imports got stuck in ports and spread panic in the industry) reflects (i) policymaking which doesn't take into account ground realities, consult stakeholders, study or gather evidence and make preparations before taking a policy leap. This isn't the first such instance though. Recall, in May 2022, India suddenly announced a *ban* on export of wheat and then relaxed it for some (to allow consignments handed over and registered with the Customs on or prior to the date of ban). Recall also how this was weeks after India promised to "feed" the world following the global food shortage the Russia-Ukraine war had sparked.

Ironically, the laptop restriction was announced *four*

days after Reliance launched JioBook and the Amazon's listing of it showed that the JioBooks are "manufactured" in China, not India. Such practices (ii) undermine *competition and* distort *level-playing field* – something to be expected in a 'National Champions' model (explained in *Fortune India* article "National champions: Costs and benefits of India's new growth model).

A sudden ban (iii) jeopardises not just 'Digital India' initiative but hits education, business, employment and day-to-day functioning of millions of Indians.

The DGFT's notification didn't give any reason for the import restriction on laptops, PCs and tablets. Official sources were quoted as saying that this was due to (a) "genuine apprehension of a future security risk" even while admitting that *not a single such case had come to notice* and/or (b) to promote domestic manufacturing of these products under the PLI scheme.

The command-and-control regime continued through the demonetisation and GST. The demonetisation of 2016 was to eliminate black money, counterfeit currency and terror funding - but none of it was achieved. The GST was launched with a mid-night session of the Parliament in 2017 to end multiplicity of indirect taxes. Both ended up derailing the economic growth (the 'twin shocks').

Beyond 'Make in India' and 'National Champions' model

The 'Make in India' initiative and the 'National Champions' model can't fully explain the economic policy *intransigencies*. Nor are numerous other economic policies. Here are a few more examples for illustration:

- Demonetisation of 2016 had nothing to do with either

– the stated goals of ending black money, counterfeit currencies and terror funding.

- The oil sector was "partially" decontrolled in 2010 by the previous UPA government but "fully" by the new government in 2014 and the phrase "under-recovery" disappeared from the economic lexicon. The goal was to free the sector (predominantly PSUs) from government control. But when the Brent crude prices fell to half in 2015 (of over $100 per barrel in FY12-FY14), the retail prices didn't go down but went up – as more and more taxes (Excise, Customs, IGST, CGST, Service Tax, Cess, Royalty, Surcharge) were imposed. In 2022 and 2023, India has received a bulk of cheap oil from Russia but the fuel prices have either stagnated (petrol and diesel) or steadily gone up (LPG and CNG).

- Trade has become wholly *unpredictable* in the past few years, marked by– sudden bans and restrictions on trade in wheat, rice, sugar, iron ore, steel, gold, coking coal, ferronickel etc. It continued after the Foreign Trade Policy (FTP) of 2023 was announced on March 31.

- A *quantum jump* in writing-off NPAs – Rs 14.5 lakh crore during FY15-FY23) to improve bank balance sheets. It involves many corporate loan defaulters. It involves banking frauds by banking and non-banking operators along with others (the PMC Bank, Punjab National Bank, ICICI Bank, Yes Bank, Lakshmi Vilas Bank, IL&FS, HDIL, DHFL etc.).

- In fact, RBI's June 8, 2023 policy of "Framework for Compromise Settlements and Technical Write-offs" allows fraudsters and willful defaulters to get

- away and eligible for more loans after a lapse of 12 months – thus, incentivising banking frauds and willful defaults.
- RBI's irrational withdrawal of Rs 2,000 notes on May 19, 2023 – while declaring such notes to *continue* as "legal tender" is another such step.
- Continuous expansion of the PLIs and DLI *without studying* their impacts on the economy and without trying to decipher why the manufacturing's share is *stuck at 17-18% of GDP for 16 years.*
- "Big ticket" IBC reform of 2016 has failed to achieve its objective – free stuck-up capital and promote entrepreneurship – with a total yield of *17.6%* of the "admitted claims" during FY18-FY23 and *75% of the firms* ending in scrap sale (far worse than the previous FRBM yield of 25%). Yet, there is no attempt to study what ails it (lack of political will, poor regulatory culture and gaming of the system) or redraft it.
- Corporate tax cut of September 2019 led to revenue loss of Rs 2.28 lakh crore in two fiscals of FY20 (Rs 1.28 lakh crore) and FY21 (Rs 1 lakh crore) – as the Parliament has been told. There is no evidence of direct benefits of it to the economy since corporates used it for "debt servicing, build-up of cash balances and other current assets rather than restarting the capex cycle" as per the RBI's annual report of 2019-20.

The surest signs of a command-and-control economy is when economic logic, planning, preparations, evidence *don't matter* to policymaking, nor do adverse consequences lead to disbanding of the policy. The above instances demonstrate just that.

Aug 15, 2023

PS: *In March 2024, the US trade officials would reveal that India had rolled back its licensing regime for laptop/PC imports, replacing it with a "import management system" in September 2023 (see article "What is hurting India's exports engine") after their representatives met Commerce Minister Piyush Goyal and expressed concerns about the compliance with the WTO rules. Trade data would reveal that laptop imports from China surged subsequent to these developments – China's share zoomed from 70% of total imports in August-October quarter of 2023 to 87.5% in the subsequent quarter of November-January.*

Meanwhile, arbitrariness in decision making continues – bringing more unpredictability to policies. In December 2023, the Centre went against the Supreme Court-mandated auction for all natural resources to usher in executive allocation of spectrum. In January 2024, it brought non-urea fertilizers under the price control regime (urea has always been price controlled) to go back to the era before nutrient-based subsidy (NBS) system was introduced in 2010.

***

DPDP Bill 2023: Question Mark on Privacy, More Power To Govt

Four iterations of privacy bill since 2018 show regression in privacy protections and progression in empowerment of govt

Do you know there are ten agencies that are authorised to breach your privacy through "interception, monitoring and decryption of any information generated, transmitted, received or stored in any computer" – without any oversight (of Parliament, independent authority or judiciary)?

This authority was given by the Ministry of Home Affairs (MHA) on December 20, 2018, under the Information Technology (IT) Act of 2000 and the IT Rules of 2009. These agencies are: Intelligence Bureau (IB), Narcotics Control Bureau (NCB), ED, CBDT, DRI, CBI, NIA, Cabinet Secretariat (RAW), Directorate of Signal Intelligence (for areas in Jammu & Kashmir, Northeast and Assam) and Delhi's Commissioner of Police.

Do you know there are many other central agencies, which don't need such authorisation; they have been created to run mass surveillance projects?

Here are some examples: National Technical Research Organisation (NTRO) of the DoPT (under PMO); National

Intelligence Grid (NatGrid) of the MHA itself; Crime and Criminal Tracking Network and Systems (CCTNS), a joint venture of Centre and states; Central Monitoring System (CMS) of the Ministry of Communications etc. Then there are many others under the MHA and Defence Ministry about which very little is known. Some are set up to collect and share (private) information (NatGrid, CCTN) with all other intelligence, security, and police agencies.

True, such surveillance is needed to protect national security, friendly relations, public order etc., but (a) how do you know their action is lawful and (b) for the specific purposes their action is meant to be? It would be naïve to think that an act is lawful (and fair) just because a law allows it; even a lawful act is not meant to be abused or carried out with mala fide intent or violate the due processes or without accountability, transparency, and oversight.

Recall the Pegasus investigating reports of 2021 which pointed to extensive use of the Israeli military-grade spyware – allegedly targeting hundreds of academics, human rights activists, journalists, opposition leaders, even MeiTY Minister Ashwini Vaishnaw who introduced The Digital Personal Data Protection (DPDP) Bill of 2023 to protect privacy, senior CBI officers, a Supreme Court judge and an Election Commissioner. What legal recourse is then left for the breach of their privacy? The IB and RAW are not even legal entities; created as they are under executive orders and "at least one" of these is known to have bought the Pegasus in the past.

What is the point in all the above?

It is that (i) the DPDP Bill of 2023, introduced in the Lok Sabha on August 3, 2023, doesn't mention or cover any of these government agencies and their activities, and hence, it can't protect your privacy from the government. A government is the biggest and most powerful entity to intrude into privacy in India and elsewhere in the world. That is why all developed countries like the US, the UK, Australia, Canada, New Zealand have multiple layers of oversight (accountability) mechanisms: parliamentary accountability, judicial accountability, expert accountability, and complaint mechanisms. India has none.

The onus is on the DPDP Bill of 2023 because (a) privacy is a fundamental right since 2017 (didn't exist earlier) and (b) it would be the first legislative attempt to protect it.

On the contrary, the DPDP Bill of 2023 (ii) gives additional and unrestraint power to the Centre and its "any instrumentality" to breach privacy with no accountability and transparency. Additional because the power under the DPDP Bill of 2023 is in addition to such powers which exist in the IT Act of 2000 and the IT Rules of 2009, IT Rules of 2021, and IT Rules of 2023. Why it is unrestrained power (to the government) will become clear soon. The DPDP Bill of 2023 does promise to protect individual privacy from breaches by a data fiduciary (a company) collecting and using personal data but (iii) allows the government to exempt certain data fiduciaries from their legal "obligations" to follow under the law.

Before explaining these points in detail, here is one critical point about the MHA's 2018 order mentioned earlier. The order says it is issued "in exercise of the powers conferred" by the IT Act (Section 69) and its 2009 Rules (Rule 4). But Section 69 also says (a) the "reasons" need "to be recorded in writing" and also subject to (b) "the procedure and safeguards…shall be such as may be "prescribed". The

MHA's 2018 order is silent on both. Section 69 and the Rule 4 of the IT Rules 2009 don't prescribe any procedure or safeguard, merely repeat each other – and hence, the onus was on the MHA order to do so.

So, the first principle of the DPDP Bill of 2023 – which is "lawful usage" of personal data, "protection from the breach" and "transparent access", as spelled out by MoS for MeiTY Rajeev Chandrasekhar the day (August 3, 2023) the DPDP Bill 2023 was introduced in the Lok Sabha – stands violated by the MHA's 2018 order.

The other five principles the minister listed are: purpose and storage limitation, data minimisation, protection and accountability, safe storage, and mandatory reporting of breach by data platforms. Note, not one of these principles talks about protecting privacy from the government – the biggest and perennial threat to individual privacy.

Progressively regressive privacy legislation

In fact, successive drafts of the bill (iv) progressively diluted privacy right by giving more and more powers to government, its "instrumentality" and data fiduciary (businesses) to breach it through exemptions and legal immunity – as it progressed from the first privacy bill of 2018 to the fourth in 2023. Note, the bill originates from the Supreme Court's declaration of privacy is a fundamental right in 2017. Except for the 2018 iteration, none other privacy bill recognises this "fundamental right". The third and fourth iterations actually shifted the primacy from protection of privacy to the "need to process" personal data and put the "right of individuals" (note, the word "fundamental" is missing) at par with the need.

The DPDP Bill of 2023 (v) makes the fundamental right to privacy so vulnerable as to virtually extinct it. Here is how.

- A new insertion (Clause 7) allows "access" to personal data to the Centre and any of its "instrumentality" for "legitimate purpose" – a new coinage – which is defined to include "any function" under "any law", in the interest of sovereignty and integrity of India, security and public order. This is in addition to a wide range of "exemptions" given in national security, friendly relations, public order etc. (Clause 17 (2a)). Both powers are without checks and balances, without prescribed processes and guidelines to be followed.

- Another new insertion (Clause 17(3)) is exemptions from compliances (checks and balances) to certain data fiduciaries "including start-ups". These exemptions include "obligations" (a) to inform individuals about the nature of personal data to be collected and the "purpose" of its processing (b) to comply with the law (including not to share and erase data when need is over) (c) to audit and study impact assessments (d) to provide summary of personal data (recognised as an individual's "right"), processing activities and identities of other data fiduciaries with which the data is shared.

- New power (Clause 27) to the Centre for "blocking" access by the public to "any information generated, transmitted, received, stored or hosted, in any computer resource" – which didn't exist in the earlier iterations. This is also in addition to the existing powers to regulate online content under the IT Act of 2000 and IT Rules of 2009, 2021, and 2023.

- New immunity (Clause 35) to the Centre, the Board,

Board members, officers, and employees as it provides that "no suit, prosecution or other legal proceedings shall lie against" them for acting "in good faith".

- Civil courts are out of the adjudication process – continuation of earlier iterations – but far more reprehensible because of two new provisions: (a) immunity to the Centre against legal proceedings and (b) Centre's total control over the appellate tribunal – the TDSAT (specified this time) – as the Centre alone appoints the TDSAT's chairman and members.

Count *four more major vulnerabilities* of the privacy continued through all iterations.

- Data Protection Board, which is the adjudicating authority, remains unformed and executive-controlled – its composition, manner of appointments, salaries and service conditions and the processes it would follow are not specified (Centre "may notify"). Appointments of employees too will be with prior Centre's approval. All this amounts to handing over legislative powers to the executive. For the bill to then state (Clause 28) that the Board "shall function as an independent body" is not just ironic but farcical.

- No compensation for victims of data breach is provided; worse, the right to compensation provided under the IT Act of 2000 (Sections 43A, 81 and 87) is extinguished (Clause 44).

- The RTI Act of 2005 (Section 8) has been diluted (by Clause 44) by taking away the powers of information officers (IC) and appellate authority for RTI Act to decide disclosure of personal information on merit (test of public interest).

- "Consent" remains "free, specific, informed, unconditional and unambiguous" but undermined by (a) "deemed" consent (without consent) which gets a new coat or "legitimate use" (Clause 7) – for the purpose of national security, friendly relations, public order etc. and (b) a wide range of "exemptions" to the government, data fiduciary and the Board and its members/staff.

Count another one which protected privacy in the 2018 and 2019 iterations but deleted subsequently:

- Classification of personal data as "sensitive" (financial, health data etc.) and "critical" (were to be defined by the Centre) restricting domestic "processing" and banning from sharing outside India.

Given all this, the six principles behind the DPDP Bill of 2023 are a mere lip service and a far cry from the six principles behind the European Union's GDPR (General Data Protection Regulation)– considered to be the best in the world in protecting privacy.

The last point about the DPDP Bill of 2023 is (vi) it has gone straight to the Lok Sabha after the Union Cabinet's approval on July 5, 2023. It has neither been put in public domain for debate nor examined by a parliamentary standing committee – and may or may not go to it either, going by the MeiTY Minister Vaishnaw's statement of August 4, 2023 (that the government will answer all concerns about it in the Parliament).

As for businesses, the privacy iterations have been progressively more friendly (after 2018 and 2019). Unlike the restrictions put earlier, personal data transfer to outside India for "processing" is allowed – unless restricted (2023).

Its 2022 iteration had allowed such data transfers only to notified countries. Since the classification of personal data as "sensitive" and "critical" (existed in 2018 and 2019) no longer exists, it is now a free flow of personal data. Domestic companies are allowed to process personal data of people residing outside India too (restricted in the 2018 and 2019 iterations).

Aug 10, 2023

***PS**: DPDP Bill was passed by the Parliament in August 2023 – without parliamentary scrutiny, parliamentary debate and without any change. The Parliament's nod was obtained amidst the turmoil and Opposition's boycott over the Manipur violence. Protection of data privacy is a bad joke. It was already selling private data to make money. At least on one occasion, in February 2021, Transport Minister Nitin Gadkari had told the Parliament that his ministry had made over Rs 100 crore by sharing the Vahan and Sarathi databases (of vehicle registration and driving license, respectively) to private entities.*

In the Pegasus snooping case, even the Supreme Court failed to act, keeping the report of its panel a secret – which reached no conclusion in any case – admitting that the Centre didn't cooperate or respond to the panel's summons but initiated no contempt action, not even a rebuke/rhetoric about accountability to the Centre. The case remains pending. The Pegasus is arguably the worst instance of snooping by the Centre on civilians by using Israel-made military grade spyware. Its targets were journalists (more than 40), academics, human rights activists, opposition leaders and governments, a scientist, businessmen, two cabinet ministers (including IT Minister Ashwini Vaishnaw, who defended the Centre in the Parliament), senior CBI officers, a Supreme Court judge and other court officials and an Election Commissioner.

NPAs: RBI Must Name and Shame Fraudsters, Willful Defaulters

RBI must make public the debtors who are marked 'fraud' and 'willful defaulter' to stop money laundering, fleeing the country and also to prevent negligence of banks, law enforcement agencies, if any

On July 24, 2023, a report quoted the RBI's RTI reply saying scheduled commercial banks (SCBs) had written off Rs 2,09,144 crore in FY23, giving rise to the question whether the NPA crisis is still simmering in the banking system.

With this, the total write-offs since FY15 – when it spiked following a concerted drive to actively identify and recognise non-performing assets – NPAs have gone up to Rs 14.6 lakh crore, of which 68% is by public sector banks (PSBs). That is, an average of Rs 1.6 lakh crore is being written off every year for the past nine years. This is 24 times more than the write-offs in the previous nine years of FY06-FY14 – Rs 61,039 crore!

Former RBI Governor Raghuram Rajan pushed the banking system through his 2015 Asset Quality Review (AQR). He gave a list of high-profile banking fraud cases to the PMO for investigation and also sounded alarm to a parliamentary panel, headed by then BJP member Murli Manohar.

The Economic Survey of 2020-21 said the AQR "led to a second round of lending distortions", by arguing that it "could not bring out all the hidden bad assets in the bank books and led to an under-estimation of capital requirements". On June 9, 2023, Union Minister Rajeev Chandrasekhar said Rajan "wrecked the entire banking system and the financial sector".

More recently, on July 22, 2023, the Prime Minister said the previous UPA government's "phone banking scam" ("powerful leaders close to a family would call the banks to get loan…those loans were never repaid") which, he said, "broke the banking system of the country". He also said his government "nursed it (banking system) back through various measures".

RBI Governor Shaktikanta Das says the banking system is now robust. In his foreword to the RBI's Financial Stability Report (FSR), released on June 28, 2023, he wrote "both banking and corporate sector balance sheets have been strengthened", NPAs are at "low levels" and there are "adequate capital and liquidity buffers".

Before getting into the details of these claims, it is more important to know who are these loan defaulters and why their identities are not disclosed.

Who are the big loan defaulters?

The first thing to note is that NPA write-offs involve big individuals and businesses. The RBI's Central Repository of Information on Large Credits (CRILC), set up in 2014 during the previous UPA government, requires banks to regularly report all debts of Rs 5 crore and more –

for the purpose of early recognition of financial distress or detecting signs of incipient stress.

But their identities are not revealed because Section 45E of the RBI Act of 1934 prohibits it, saying that "credit information" shall be treated as "confidential" and "shall not" be published or otherwise disclosed – outside the banking system. Apparently, this is to protect genuine businesses and the fact that business failures can happen for genuine reasons.

But why should RBI not make public the debtors classified as "fraud" and "willful defaulter" (those who can pay but don't)? These are the ones who divert bank loans, launder bank loans using shell companies and tax havens and at times, also flee the country. Only once has the RBI made public a list of 38 "willful defaulters" who fled the country during 2015-2020. It needs to disclose such lists more often and before they flee – not after. Timely public disclosure of their names could have prevented them from fleeing and made it tougher for banks and law enforcement agencies to allow it through negligence or complicity.

Such public disclosures are all the more necessary after the RBI issued a circular on June 8, 2023, "Framework for Compromise Settlements and Technical Write-offs" – allowing and empowering all financial institutions to offer "compromise settlements" with fraudsters and willful defaulters. Even more shocking, it permits such debtors to avail fresh loans after 12 months – which could cause more fraud and willful default.

Here is how serious the problem is:

- The number of banking frauds jumped 17 times during the nine fiscals of FY15-FY23 to 5,88,744 – from 34,198 in the previous nine years of FY04-FY14. The amount involved nearly doubled (1.9 times) to Rs 65,812 crore during the nine years of FY15-FY23 – as against Rs 34,904 in the previous nine years of FY06-FY14 (RBI data).

- As for willful defaults, by December 2022, 15,778 of them had accumulated debts of Rs 3.4 lakh crore (as per the RBI registered Transunion Cibil).

An additional problem with "compromised settlements" is no "recovery" after the high haircuts – a double whammy. In any case, the "recovery" by SCBs is not much – 16.6% during the five years of FY18-FY22 (as per a Rajya Sabha reply of March 28, 2023).

In such a situation, the following claims of the FSR seem highly exaggerated:

- "SCBs' gross non-performing assets (GNPA) ratio continued its downtrend and fell to a 10-year low of 3.9% in March 2023 and the net non-performing assets (NNPA) ratio declined to 1.0%" and

- "Macro stress tests for credit risk reveal that SCBs would be able to comply with the minimum capital requirements even under severe stress scenarios".

Remember, the "compromise settlements" came on June 8, 2023, less than a month after the RBI withdrew Rs 2,000 notes (May 19, 2023) even while declaring these notes will remain legal tender. The SBI Research then said (on June 19, 2023) this withdrawal would give a net deposit boost of Rs 1.5 lakh crore (after partial withdrawal) to banks. Has this really happened? That is not known.

Now recall two precedents.

Following Centre's drive to identify and recognise NPAs, write-offs (corporate loan defaults) recorded a quantum jump after the demonetisation of November 2016 (FY127) – from Rs 59,445 crore in FY16 to Rs 1,07,823 crore in FY17, Rs 1,62,733 crore in FY18, Rs 2,36,725 crore in FY19 and Rs 2,37,876 crore in FY20 (all pre-pandemic).

Then, on August 26, 2019, the RBI declared a transfer of 1.76 lakh crore to the Centre from its reserves and surpluses. Less than a month later, on September 20, 2019, the corporate tax cuts of 1.45 lakh crore was announced. For the next two fiscals of FY20 and FY21, therefore, the Centre borrowed (from the RBI) and gave loans to states – Rs 1.1 lakh crore in FY21 and Rs 1.58 lakh crore in FY22 – in lieu of the GST Compensation.

How bank and corporate balance sheets improved?

Besides, the corporate tax cut caused a loss of Rs 1.84 lakh crore in FY20 and FY21 – as a parliamentary panel report said – and for the first time in recent memory, corporate tax collections fell below that of personal income tax. What did corporates do with the tax cut? The RBI said, it was utilised in debt servicing, build-up of cash balances and other current assets – rather than restarting the capex cycle.

So, a part of the improved balance sheet of corporates is due to the tax cut for them.

The bank balance sheets have improved primarily because of four factors: (a) NPA write-off of Rs 14.6 lakh crore during the past nine fiscals (b) bank recapitalisation of Rs 3.12 lakh crore (c) bailouts of collapsed private banks and NBFCs (like Yes Bank and IL&FS) by public sector banks and (d) the corporate tax cuts of Rs 1.45 lakh crore.

All these involve costs to public. There is little role of (i) improvements in banking governance or banking oversight.

The genesis of the NPA crisis was surely in the banking exuberance (high disbursal of loans) witnessed during the previous UPA government. But a few factors should not be ignored.

The UPA years recorded high growth rate since independence – the GDP growth averaged 7.6% (2004-05 GDP series) and 6.8% (2011-12 GDP series). The twin shocks of demonetisation of 2016 and GST of 2017 derailed the economy and the GDP growth plunged from 8.3% in FY17 to 3.9% in FY20 (pre-pandemic).

FY18 saw a dramatic rise in banking frauds, contributing to the collapse of banks and NBFCs (Yes Bank, IL&FS, HDIL, DHFL etc.).

On May 31, 2023, the RBI Governor expressed serious concerns at "innovative" ways banks have found to evergreen stressed loans (through restructuring, hiding and changing methods when caught). RBI advised banks to follow the existing banking norms and guidelines. This was followed by its "compromise settlements" circular.

The RBI's other claim about "new credit and investment cycle" brightening the prospects of the Indian economy in its FSR is flawed too. Credit flows inverted in FY20. "Personal loans" overtook credit to 'large industry' in FY20 and 'industry' and services in FY22 – and the trend has continued in FY23. It had overtaken agriculture years earlier. A credit growth driven by consumption loans is not the same as one driven by "real" sectors of economy – industry, services and agriculture – which leads to higher investment, higher productivity and more jobs.

Jul 31, 2023

2 Chinese Roadblocks to India's Semiconductor Ambition

Semiconductor mission: Mere fiscal incentives aren't enough; India needs skilling, investments, a conducive business environment, dispute resolution mechanisms and much more to make it happen

Two essential minerals to manufacture semiconductors and advanced electronics are gallium and germanium. China accounts for 98% of global production of raw gallium and 67% of global production of raw germanium, very cost-efficient in making their products but announced export controls earlier this month, which will come into effect from August 1, 2023. Both minerals are in India's list of 30 "critical minerals." The country produces a little gallium as a byproduct while producing alumina depends entirely on import for germanium – as the Ministry of Mine's June 2023 report "Critical Minerals for India" says.

China's action is retaliation against the US, European Union and Japan which have cut it off from export of chips and chip-making equipment. This trade logjam is likely to have serious repercussions for the semiconductor and electronics sectors worldwide. Given the border-diplomatic-trade tensions between the two, India's direct business with China is already under stress. As scarcity hits global production and supply, India would be at the receiving end from *either side*. A similar fate awaits India in *EV and mobile phone manufacturing* as China dominates the global production and supply of lithium needed for lithium-ion batteries.

How does India navigate the challenges? The India Semiconductor Mission (ISM) would have to spell that out.

ISM: Need to go back to the drawing board

Notwithstanding the brouhaha over the "Semicon India 2023" event at Gandhinagar on July 28 in which some of the world's leading semiconductor producers participated, India needs to go back to the drawing board to make the India Semiconductor Mission (ISM) a success. Two particular recent developments, including the Micron's MoU with the Gujarat government to set up a $2.75 billion facility in Gujarat, explain why.

What exactly is Micron's project?

Its June 22, 2023 announcement needs careful reading as it gives a full picture of what is to be expected. The announcement says three things: (i) Micron would be setting up a new "assembly and test facility" in Gujarat under the Centre's "Modified Assembly, Testing, Marking and Packaging (ATMP) Scheme" (ii) the total project cost is "up to $2.75 billion" of which (iii) "Micron's investment will be up to $825 million" (30%) and the rest will come from India – "50% fiscal support for the total project cost" from the Centre and "20% of the total project cost" as "incentives" from the Gujarat government.

On June 28, 2023, the Gujarat government signed an MoU in presence of Union Minister for MeiTY Ashwini Vaishnaw. The Gujarat Chief Minister's office

(@*CMOGuj*) tweeted that this was for "setting-up ATMP facility at Sanand". 'ATMP' stands for "Assembly, Testing, Marking and Packaging (ATMP)"– the same as the Micron's June 22 declaration – that is, an *assembling facility*. Vaishnaw, however, tweeted to describe this as "India's first manufacturing plant", thereby *creating doubts* about the exact *nature* of the facility.

That is because the MeiTY offers *three distinct and separate schemes* under the "Modified Programme for Semiconductors and Display Fab Ecosystem" for support.

- Two of these are for setting up (i) "semiconductor fabs and display fabs" *(manufacturing)* and (ii) "compound semiconductors/silicon photonics/sensors (including MEMS) fabs/ discrete semiconductor fabs and semiconductor ATMP/OSAT units". Under these two, the MeiTY gives "fiscal support of 50% of project cost".

- The third scheme is for (iii) "semiconductor design companies" *(designing)* for which the MeiTY gives "Design Linked Incentive (DLI) Scheme" of "50% of eligible expenditure" and also "product deployment linked incentive of 6%-4% on net sales for five years".

- The fourth scheme is for the "modernisation and commercialisation" of the Mohali's "Semi-conductor Laboratory (SCL)" for which the MeiTY "will take requisite steps".

Clearly, Micron›s facility falls in the second scheme (ATMP) – which is not "semiconductor fabs and display fab" or *manufacturing* nor the DLI-support for "design companies" or *designing*. Besides, Micron›s June 22 statement makes it very clear that its Sanand facility «will *enable assembly and test manufacturing* for both DRAM and NAND products and address demand from domestic and international markets" in two phases. Phase I "will include 50,0000 square feet of planed cleanroom space" and Phase II "will ramp capacity" and "would include construction of a facility similar in scale to Phase 1."

So, neither phase I, nor phase II of the Micron's facility will either manufacture or design chips.

However, in future, India may sign an MoU for manufacturing or designing chips with Micron or any other manufacturer. But that is for the future, although not unlikely. Remember, India's automobile sector (both cars and bikes) came up first as assembling facilities and then expanded to manufacturing.

Incidentally, the "modified" schemes were issued by the MeiTY on May 31, 2023 *after* the Vedanta-Foxconn's Gujarat project (the MoU had been signed in September 2022) failed to take off – *without explaining* what was modified.

Misdirected priorities

Two *questions* arise from the MoU with Micron.

The first is about the government's *actual mission*. The "India Semiconductor Mission" says it "aims to build a vibrant semiconductor and display ecosystem to enable India's emergence as a global hub for *electronics manufacturing and design*". Micron's facility is *neither*. An ATMP facility comes at the bottom of the semiconductor *value chain*. Nevertheless, it is a welcome development.

The second is about the business model.

Since Micron will invest 30%, and India the rest 70%

(50% by the Centre and 20% by the Gujarat government), will it be a CPSU, controlled and run by the government of India? Will it be a joint venture of Micron-Government of India-Gujarat government? Or will it be a private entity controlled and run by Micron? This needs to be clarified as that will determine how Micron and India share *profits/ dividends* generated from the Sanand facility.

The other recent development (mentioned at the beginning) is about the stillborn Vedanta-Foxconn's Gujarat project, announced in September 2022.

Foxconn pulled out of it a few days ago. But by then the project was dead because (a) neither Vedanta nor Foxconn had the technology to manufacture 28nm chips and (b) neither found *a technology partner* or a manufacturing-grade technology *license* for eight months. This led to MeiTY›s «modified» schemes on May 31, 2023.

Why and how the deal was signed in the first place? Why did the Centre announce 40% "capital subsidy" and the Gujarat government a host of other incentives (subsidised land, power tariff, electricity duty, water supply, stamp duty and registration fee etc.) – as MoS for MeiTY Rajeev Chandrasekhar told in the Lok Sabha on December 7, 2022?

But these are not the only issues with the ISM.

Subsidy-filled drawing board

What policies, plans and strategies have been prepared to achieve the ISM's "aims"?

The ISM website only talks about (i) fiscal incentives of 50% of project cost and (ii) DLI incentive for which Rs 76,000 crore has been kept aside, which includes "product deployment linked incentive of 6%-4% on *net sales* for five years".

There are *two additional incentives* under the Production-Linked Incentive (PLI) schemes, to develop a domestic semiconductors and display manufacturing «ecosystem» (DSDME) by promoting electronics manufacturing with semiconductors as the foundational building block.

These are: (iii) Rs 55,392 crore for large scale electronics manufacturing, IT hardware, SPECS scheme and modified electronics manufacturing clusters (EMC 2.0) and (iv) Rs 98,000 crore for allied sectors comprising of ACC battery, auto components, telecom and networking products, solar PV modules and white goods.

Sure, chips are indispensable in today's world and form essential components of electronic devices, enabling communications, computing, healthcare, military systems, transportation, clean energy and countless other applications (smartphones, radios, TVs, computers, automobiles, medical equipment, video games and much more). India must do whatever it takes to design and manufacture chips and also develop the "ecosystem" (DSDME).

But that calls for more than just subsidies.

Fundamental challenges to chip-making

In March 2023, senior MeiTY scientist Prashant Kumar said India possessed a big talent pool of semiconductor *design* engineers, but *no* skilled manpower to *manufacture*. This is known for long but the problem is, those *design* engineers work for multinationals like Micron, Intel, Samsung Electronics etc., not for any domestic company.

So, the first priority is clear: designing chips. Manufacturing chips should be a long-term goal.

A beginning should ideally be made to acquire and foster designing talents and then graduate to manufacturing talent. What would this take? Developing a semiconductor ecosystem is not *only about technology or talent.*

Assuming that India overcomes the talent and raw material problems, for any industry sector or segment to thrive also needs *skilling* (education and training), *investment* (as distinct from fiscal support/incentives) and *conducive* business environment – level-playing field, open competition, quick administrative and legal clearances, efficient dispute resolution mechanisms etc.

There is a yet another factor to be considered. In the short run, chips assembling may turn out to be another *mobile phone* sector. As Raghuram Rajan and other economists have pointed out by studying the trade data, India is *assembling* mobile phones, rather than manufacturing, and exporting the assembled sets. In the process, India is running up huge bills on importing the components – leading to higher and higher trade deficits in the sector.

The ISM needs to go back to the drawing board.

Jul 31, 2023

***

Dharavi: Challenges of Rebuilding Economically Viable Cities

India urgently needs a national blueprint for urban renewal as urban population booms and is set to rise from 31.8% in 2011 to 38.2% by 2036

The Maharashtra government's formal nod (through a government resolution or GR notified on July 14) to the Adani group for redeveloping Dharavi has rekindled hope that one of the largest urban slums of the world may finally get a makeover – as part of the promise to make Mumbai a Shanghai (or a Singapore) by both central and state governments.

The Adani group would carry out the project through a special purpose vehicle (SPV) with 80% equity, the rest 20% coming from the Maharashtra government. This was set out in the request for proposal (RFP) document issued in 2022 when international bids were invited (same as in 2018). The RFP also said that the Maharashtra government had notified 240 ha (2.4 sq km) of Dharavi for redevelopment. The timeline to complete the project is seven years and involves 59,165 families (46,191 are residential and 12,974 non-residential).

What remains unclear is whether a large number of

small business enterprises run from the area would find a place in the redeveloped Dharavi or shifted elsewhere. For one, the RFP was silent on it, merely saying that "SPV will have to construct *free housing* for the eligible slum dwellers and occupants, including amenities and infrastructure" and "in-lieu of it, the SPV Company will be entitled to construct free sale area to sell in the market" – the business case for a private entity to get into the PPP project and can't be really grudged.

Maharashtra Deputy CM Devendra Fadnavis did assure the Assembly, in December 2022, that an industrial and business zone was part of the plan, all business enterprises would get more space, a common facility centre and tax sops for five years. But there is no blueprint of it in public domain and remains a mere promise. Besides, the SPV's blueprint is also not available in public domain – causing apprehensions in the minds of the residents.

The opacity and promises without a blueprint make it impossible for informed debates and fresh ideas to come in. Hopefully, the picture would be clear soon as work starts on the project.

There are at least five reasons why this situation is not healthy.

- Dharavi is the largest urban slum redevelopment project in India and its execution is likely to set the template for all such future endeavours (Indian mega cities like Mumbai and Delhi are riddled with slums).
- India's urban population is set to *explode* from 31.8% in 2011 to 38.2% by 2036 – that is, an addition of *218 million* urban population by 2036 – as per the Indian government's 2020 Report of the Technical Group

Population Projections. This rapid urbanisation will be fuelled by *migration* from rural areas. Remember, Dharavi was built by migrants on marshy land entirely on their own.

- It is not known what kind of template of *urban renewal*, or *inner-city* development in the case of Dharavi, is Maharashtra trying to set. Is there a vision document, a blueprint? Given that the SPV is led by a private entity with 80% equity, and consequently, 80% voting rights – it isn't really important whether it is the Adani group or any other in this case (given the zero-success rate of all other previous Dharavi projects in the past decades) or in some other case – it might entirely be up to the private player to decide. The absence of an official blueprint or definite guidelines is an open invitation for it.

- Cities (or inner-cities like Dharavi for that matter, which worried urban planners in the US in 1990s because of deep economic distress) are *growth drivers*.

- Across India, cities, including megapolises like Delhi, Mumbai and Bangalore, are infrastructure nightmares. Past few weeks have seen flood ravage scores of such cities – both in plains and hills.

What template Dharavi would set?

For every urban development planner and thinker, the works of Jeb Brugmann, Cambridge University professor instrumental in urban development of 49 cities in 21 countries, is an *essential reading*. Particularly, his 2009 book "Welcome to the Urban Revolution" for telling what made transformations of cities across the world successful. He came to Dharavi too, more than a decade ago, after the PPP mode of development had replaced (in 1990s) the earlier *in situ* redevelopment plans of various Maharashtra agencies had failed.

Expressing his shock after a particular presentation by a private builder on *dismantling and rebuilding* Dharavi as a "world class city", he wrote: "How could anyone who had observed Dharavi for so long miss the most obvious fact about it: that the *residential-industrial citysystem* was proving itself every day in the market place to be world class? It stood as probably the *most successful, scaled poverty-reduction programme* in the history of international development. Within the Indian context, Dharavi's migrant generations had developed an *accessible, replicable citysystem* for the advancement of the country's poor majority."

He added: "It was a *stunning example* of Indian entrepreneurial ability and ambition. With millions of poor households migrating to India's cities each year, it seemed almost obvious that this migrant citysystem just needed to be accompanied with the same *public investment in urban infrastructure* offered to every other Mumbai city model and master-planned suburb, and replicated throughout country."

Brugmann went to explain how the World War II-ravaged Tokyo was rebuilt. Japan's central planners rebuilt the wrecked water, sewerage and road systems (infrastructure) but *left it to the residents* ("citizen city-builders") to rebuild the city's *housing and commercial spaces*. These citizen city-builders "created" a flexible city of villagelike, residential-commercial settlements "in some ways remarkably like the migrant-entrepreneurs of Dharavi".

He also recounted how the world abandoned the

dismantling and rebuilding approach long ago. Rio de Janeiro abandoned its drive of dismantling urban slums and relocating the residents to high-rise buildings in "mid-1990s". Instead, it began redeveloping slums (*in situ*) into more stable, lawful, sanitary, mixed-use neighbourhoods "with minimal clearing and relocation". Europe abandoned its dismantling approach of 1960s-1970s after "planners learned the folly of ghetto clearance and master-planned urban renewal". Similar was the experience of North America.

But Brugmann didn't ask Indian planners to follow anyone (Tokyo or Rio), howsoever tempting that might have been.

He advised: "...the true measure of Mumbai's "world-class" nature and the true test of its ability to tame its chronic crisis (like monsoon flooding, crime and corruption) will not be its success imitating the models of other cities. It will be whether it musters the will and confidence to create a *new urbanism of its own*". (That is because there are new sources of advantage produced by shared economies of density, scale and association of co-located firms or industrial cluster.).

A few years later, Edward Glaeser, Harvard's economics professor and author of "Triumph of the City: How Our Greatest Invention Makes Us Richer, Smarter, Greener, Healthier, and Happier" looked Dharavi from an economist's eye.

In an article in 2011, he started off declaring that "Mumbai's Dharavi slum is the most entrepreneurial place I've ever been." Two of his other observations are particularly interesting for economists: (i) migrants to Dharavi are also learning *new skills*, including developing insights into the grocery demands of urban consumers and (ii) their businesses remain tiny "because raising capital is difficult and because their small scale enables these urban entrepreneurs to slip past the web of regulations". Another one relevant for town planners and sociologists is (iii) "Dharavi is safe – not because Mumbai's police force is so effective but because the community looks after its own".

India's urban mess

Gurgaon is a shining example of what happens when a city is left entirely to a private builder with *no blueprint* to follow – it is a cluster of disparate high-rise office buildings with little else. Not everyone can be expected to be Tatas and build self-sufficient and sustainable cities like Jamshedpur, Mithapur and Hosur. What would stop the redeveloped Dharavi from being another Gurgaon (irrespective of the private partner in the PPP)?

Herein comes the critical role of government. Dharavi is a self-built housing-industrial citysystem which houses about 10 lakh people, a large number of who run their businesses from their homes or find employment there. Their businesses may not be relocated, as Fadnavis has promised, but his government must come out with a clear blueprint for the SPV to build a self-sufficient and sustainable city, not just "construct *free housing* for the eligible slum dwellers and occupants, including amenities and infrastructure" as the RFP mandates. If any evidence of the abject failures of Maharashtra governments in urban renewal is ever needed, the crippling monsoon floods of Mumbai this year and for the past several decades is a grim reminder.

It is, therefore, for the central government to step in. It has the resources and wherewithal to mobilise international institutions to frame a vision for urban renewal. The *piecemeal* Smart City Mission is not enough (again, the recent urban flooding and economic losses they caused prove it). India needs a national vision, plans and strategies to make cities not just liveable but economically self-sufficient and sustainable.

More so since India is also battling chronic and massive livelihood crisis in both urban (unemployed rate spiked to 8.5% in June 2023) and rural areas (the demand for manual and low-paying MGNREGS works touched the pandemic high in June 2023) for long.

Jul 18, 2023

PS: *The Shinde cabinet approved a proposal seeking 283 acre of Mumbai's salt plan land from the Centre for Dharavi revamp project.*

***

Paying for Russian Oil in Yuan Will Hurt Globalisation of Rupee

Indian oil refining firms paying in Yuan for Russian oil may be inevitable but would open a floodgate to weaken INR further; Brazil, B'desh, and Argentina shifting to Yuan trade is a big threat too

On July 5, 2023, the RBI released the "Report of the Inter-Departmental Group (IDG) on Internationalisation of INR", which was submitted to it nine months ago in October 2022. Apparently, the release was strategically timed as two days earlier, on July 3, 2023, it was revealed that Indian refiners had started paying for Russian oil in Chinese Yuan from June 2023 – raising the spectre of India ending up internationalising Yuan, rather than Rupee.

Seemingly, the idea of releasing the report is to convey that the RBI is doing its bit to internationalise Rupee (in trade settlements) but not a word is said about the problems India is facing in paying for Russian oil after the US and Europe sanctions made payment in USD difficult or that Russia is not keen to accept payment in Rupee (the rupee trade with then USSR dates back to 1950s) or in UAE Dirham – in which Indian refiners were forced to pay more than five months ago. More than a year of the India-Russia talks for Rupee settlement was going nowhere and was abandoned in May 2023.

The latest revelation says that the Indian Oil Corp (IOC), India's biggest buyer of Russian oil, became the first public sector entity to pay for Russian oil in Yuan; two of the three private refiners are also doing the same but it is not known since when. The amount of Yuan payment may be small at present but is likely to grow fast as India's reliance on cheap Russian oil is huge – up from 2% of the total import before the Russia-Ukraine war to 46% in May 2023 – and for other reasons which would be clear soon.

Challenges to internationalising Rupee

Indian refiners paying in Yuan is a real tragedy because the IMF had identified and listed Indian Rupee along with Chinese Renminbi (Yuan is the currency unit), Brazilian Real, Russian Ruble, and South African Rand "as the key emerging market currencies with the potential for internationalisation" as the IDG report says.

In 2023, the IMF's forex reserve or SDR (Special Drawing Right) basket has five currencies: USD (43.38%), followed by Euro (29.31%), Renminbi (12.28%), Japanese Yen (7.59%), and British Pound Sterling (7.44%). Indian Rupee is conspicuous by its absence.

What determines SDR (reserve currency) allocations or international trade settlements?

While the two primary determinants are (i) the large size of the economy (GDP) and (ii) the large share of global trade, the IDG identifies four "pre-requisites" for internationalisation of currencies: (iii) deep and liquid financial and forex market (iv) currency convertibility and credible commitment to an open capital account (v) wide use of currency in private sector transactions and (vi) macroeconomic and political stability.

Of the six, India fits the bill in two (fifth largest economic, macroeconomic, and political stability) and needs to work on the rest. Its global trade has remained stuck below 2% (1.6% in 2020) for several decades, Rupee is not fully convertible, its financial and forex market isn't deep or liquid enough, its unstable currency policy (demonetisation of high-value notes in 2016 and withdrawal of Rs 2,000 notes while keeping it a legal tender) and progressive devaluation of Rupee (vis-à-vis USD) in the past few years is unlikely to encourage big private corporate entities and HNIs to rely exclusively on Rupee transactions.

The current situation is ideal for an alternate currency to emerge though because of the new geoeconomic fragmentation resulting from the Russia-Ukraine war (the US and Europe on one side and Russia, and China on the other, along with other countries in their camps) and the economic distress (high inflation, high-interest regimes) in the US and Europe have opened up the field for other currencies to challenge the hegemony of USD and Euro – which Yuan is more likely to mount.

What if Russia and China demand Yuan payment?

Indian refiners paying in Chinese Yuan for Russian oil presents a new setback for Rupee because India's dependence on Russian weapons is also very high – 45% of the total during 2017-2022 – followed by France (29%) and the US (11%).

What if all non-oil trade with Russia is sought to be settled in Yuan?

According to the Ministry of Commerce and Industry, Indian imports from Russia skyrocketed from $9.9 billion in FY22 to $46.2 billion in FY23 (mainly due to oil) while its export fell from $3.3 billion to $3.1 billion during the same time – leading to a sharp jump in the trade deficit from -$6.6 billion to -$43.1 billion in one fiscal. Even if Russia demands payment in Russian Ruble the sharp rise in trade deficit and continued dependence on cheap Russian oil would dent Rupee.

More importantly, what happens if China demands payment in Yuan?

According to the Ministry of Commerce and Industry, import from China has risen by 40% in the past five fiscals (from $70.3 billion in FY19 to $98.5 billion in FY23), export has fallen by 8.6% in the same period – taking the trade deficit higher by 55.3% (from -$53.6 billion to -$83 billion). In FY19, the trade deficit with China was 29% of India's total trade deficit – which has grown to 31.6% in FY23.

Yuan is fast emerging as a serious challenge to the dominance of the US dollar. Many countries, like Brazil, Bangladesh, and Argentina have already started settling trade in Yuan instead of USD; Yuan has replaced USD in China-Russia trade. It has helped China set up global offshore Yuan markets in Singapore, London, Paris, Hong Kong, and Luxembourg. Besides, in April 2023, Yuan overtook USD to become the most-used currency in China's cross-border transactions.

These are troubling signs. China is not just (i) the second largest economy after the US but also (ii) the global leader in manufacturing (28.7% of global manufacturing output in 2019, as against 16.8% of the next in the list, the US) (iii) the global leader in the export of goods (14.3% of the global share in 2020, as against 8.1% of the second leader, the US and (iv) also the global technology leader – leading in 37 of 44 "crucial technology fields spanning defence, space, robotics, energy, environment, biotechnology, artificial intelligence (AI), advanced materials and key quantum technology areas" because it has established "stunning lead in high-impact research".

India may be the fifth largest economy, but its share in global manufacturing output is 3.1% (in 2019), its share in export of goods is 1.6% (in 2020, as per the Economic Survey of 2022-23), and doesn't count in technological innovations – all key factors to make a currency to grow to global significance.

Hence, India's dependence on China will continue to grow in the foreseeable future – for importing manufacturing goods, intermediaries, raw materials, and also technology transfers. Under the circumstances, Rupee isn't able to stand up to the Yuan. Irrespective of how far Rupee and Yuan have devalued vis-à-vis USD in recent times, the fact remains that at current prices one USD is equivalent to 7 Yuan in contrast with 83 Rupee.

India's share of global trade has to rise

There is yet another stumbling block for Rupee.

One of the primary roadblocks for Rupee to grow in international stature is India's poor share in global trade (1.6%). The pie is unlikely to grow because India has (i) erected import barriers that dampen exports and (ii) chasing bilateral FTAs – individual countries with relatively smaller shares of global output and trade – while the rest of the world is converging with mega multilateral FTAs like the RCEP, IPEF, and CPTPP. Members of these mega trade blocs contribute the most to global GDP and trade.

As Fortune India argued earlier, the biggest challenge for India to boost its exports is to integrate with global value chains (GVCs), which is virtually impossible if mega trading blocs are shunned. There is no evidence that bilateral FTAs benefit more than multilateral FTAs or that India's earlier trade regimes failed to expand trade because of unfair practices or discriminations (it was more because of poor products and bad governing standards) and none of the three reports cited to justify renegotiations of bilateral FTAs supported import substitution.

These are some of the fundamental issues that should engage the RBI and FinMin.

Jul 12, 2023

***

Are Top Banks Getting their Economics Wrong?

A mere statement from the RBI assuring that "robust systems" exist isn't enough

India's premier banks are increasingly churning out economic concepts that are difficult to fathom. The latest example is the SBI's June 19, 2023 research paper titled "Withdrawal of 2,000 note: How it could result in a bank deposit boost, repayment of loans boost, consumption boost, RBI CBDC boost and a possible GDP boost". This follows the RBI's decision of May 19, 2023 to withdraw 2,000 notes (worth Rs 3.62 lakh crore) constituting 10.8% of cash-in-circulation in March 2023.

The SBI Research calls this a "precision strike" – a variation of "master stroke" and "surgical strike" with which every government action (including the twin shocks of demonetisation and GST) used to be qualified with – and concludes: "We expect Q1 FY24 GDP growth at ~ 8.1% with an upward bias due to the impact of 2,000 note withdrawal event...this reinforces our projection that FY24 GDP could be higher than 6.5%, basis the RBI estimate".

What logic or evidence SBI gives in support?

It says the withdrawal of the notes would (a) boost

bank deposits (b) boost repayment of loans (c) boost consumption demand and PFCE (d) boost the RBI's CBDC (Central Bank Digital Currency) and (e) boost GDP growth – the title of the paper and the text claim.

It then calculates these gains in money terms: The withdrawal of the notes (i) is likely to increase banks deposits by Rs 1.5 lakh crore (after partial withdrawal by depositors) (ii) lead to 30% of deposits or Rs 92,000 crore might go for loan payment (in cash credit and overdraft) (iii) consumption demand may be "frontloaded" by Rs 55,000 crore which, in turn, would boost PFCE by Rs 1.83 lakh crore through "multiplier effect" and thereby, boosting the GDP growth to 8.1% in Q1 of FY24 – from 6.5% estimated by the RBI.

What is striking here is the proposition that the deposits of Rs 2,000 notes would lead to "frontloaded" consumption demand. Why would that happen? The SBI explanations: "With the bank note remaining a legal tender, unlike demonetisation, consumption could see a boost."

This begs the question: Why didn't the deposits of demonetised notes of 1,000 and 500 boost consumption demand in 2016 and later?

After all, the depositors got equal monetary value in return, in lower denominations of 100, 50, 20 and 10 (later in 2,000 and 500 notes) – all of which continue to be legal tenders – and presumably, also used for consumption (given the cash rationing at the time). Since money supply is a function of the value and transactions, if the demonetisation of 1,000 and 500 notes wouldn't have mattered because those were replenished with notes of equal value – just as it would happen for the 2,000 notes.

Further, going by SBI Research's economic logic, if the withdrawal of 2,000 notes, constituting 10.8% of cash, can boost the GDP by 1.6 percentage points (8.1% minus 6.5%) then the withdrawal of 1,000 and 500 notes, which accounted for 86.9% of cash-in-circulation in November 2016, would surely have boosted the GDP growth by a greater magnitude. Here, all other factors of GDP growth are kept constant (unchanged) – following the SBI logic.

What happened was just the reverse.

The GDP growth fell to 6.8% in FY18, from 8.3% in FY17, and then progressively fell to 3.9% in the pre-pandemic FY20 (revised upward from 3.4% in recently). That the demonetisation began the derailment of economy by wiping out millions of jobs and small businesses (thereby damaging informal economy contributing nearly 50% to the GDP) is no longer disputed.

Bank deposits did go up as people rushed to exchange the demonetised notes in 2016 but a few other things also happened which points to SBI's poor economic logic.

One is write-offs of loan defaults (NPAs). The SCBs had written off Rs 1.08 lakh crore in FY17 (demonetisation fiscal), which progressively increased to Rs 1.63 lakh crore in FY18, Rs 2.37 lakh crore in FY19 and Rs 2.38 lakh crore in FY20 (before the pandemic). The SBI itself wrote off Rs 20,339 crore in FY17, which sharply increased to Rs 1.5 lakh crore in the three next fiscals (FY18-FY20) – averaging Rs 50,000 crore.

These write-offs then required re-monetisation of banks.

Two, the SBI re-introduced "penalty" on the poor for not maintaining minimum monthly balance in 2017 after five years, collecting Rs 1,771 crore during April-November 2017 – which was more than SBI's July-September quarter net profit (Rs 1,581.55 crore) and nearly half of its net profit of April-September 2017 (Rs 3,586 crore). In all, SCBs collected Rs 10,000 crore in such penalty in three fiscals of FY17-FY19.

Three, the SBI also imposed costs on banking transactions beyond four transactions, either through bank branches or ATM, at 15 plus GST for each such transaction.

Why did the banks impose such costs on people? Obviously because banks needed to mobilise more resources to make their balance sheets look healthier.

But this is not the first instance of SBI Research getting its economics wrong.

It had advocated for demonetisation in March 2016 – months ahead of the actual event. It said the RBI would get a "windfall" gain of Rs 3-4 lakh crore from demonetisation. Both turned out to be false. Almost the entire money came back to the system; the "windfall gain" was zero. The failure to get "windfall gain" led to a wild goose chase by the IT department. Then, the Centre demanded higher shares of RBI's reserve money, which eventually materialised with transfer of Rs 1.76 lakh crore in August 2019. Less than a month later, in September 2019, the Centre announced the corporate tax cut of Rs 1.45 lakh crore. The same month, state governments were told they wouldn't get the GST Compensation because of lack of resources.

In essence, public paid for demonetisation – not just with penalty for not maintaining minimum balance, higher NPA write-offs, subsequent bank recapitalisation and 15 plus GST for more than four banking transactions in a month, but also due to overnight loss of millions of jobs and small business (cash was rationed and millions stood outside banks for months to get their own cash).

RBI's confusion over 2,000 note withdrawal

The RBI notification asking people to deposit 2,000 notes by September 30, 2023, is also bizarre.

Its circular of May 19, 2023 gave four reasons for this: (a) it was issued to re-monetise after demonetisation (oxymoronic) (b) printing of these notes stopped in FY19 (c) its life-span was 4-5 years and (d) stock of banknotes in other denominations was adequate. To compound the confusion, it said that the withdrawn notes "will continue to be legal tender".

Indians and Indian economy were paralysed for months following the overnight, unprepared demonetisation – despite warnings from former RBI Governor Raghuram Rajan, followed by a note from the RBI (as he wrote in 2017 book "I do what I do"). If it remains a legal tender why should it be withdrawn?

The big questions are: Legal or not, is the currency note issued by the RBI a safe and reliable tender? If yes, does it come with a pre-determined sell-by-date or is it completely arbitrary?

The poor may not have much of a choice but the rich billionaires do and they may opt for foreign currencies to keep their money safe. People's trust in Indian legal tender has been broken twice in the past seven years (demonetisation of 2016 and now).

Was the RBI's decision political?

Doubts arise because the demonetisation came just ahead of the Uttar Pradesh elections (February 2017) and it starved the opposition of cash; the number of candidates contesting this election fell by 30%. Four states with high stakes, Madhya Pradesh, Rajasthan, Chhattisgarh and Telangana, face elections later this year.

For the record, the RBI circular came five days after the BJP lost the Karnataka elections (counting on May 13, 2023).

RBI's actions have been questionable of late. Here are two more examples.

Free pass to banking fraud and missing notes

On June 8, 2023, 10 days after RBI Governor Shaktikanta Das red flagged governance failures in SCBs and listed five "innovative ways" in which stressed assets (NPAs) were concealed and evergreened, the RBI gave a carte blanche to all banks and financial institutions to go for "compromise settlements" with accounts marked as "fraud and willful defaulter" ("Framework for Compromise Settlements and Technical Write-offs").

It didn't stop there.

It said banks and other financial institutions were free to give fresh loans to those very debtors after 12 months – which was banned earlier. The RBI didn't explain why.

Those supporting the RBI may argue that this gives PSBs a level-playing field since private banks do it or that there should be separation of banks' commercial activities (fresh loans to willful defaulters and fraudsters) from the criminal proceedings (which the RBI's new framework leaves untouched).

But which fraudster and willful defaulter would like to pay back loans after tasting blood – compromise settlement means pay back next to nothing, no repayment (recovery) of the rest, fresh loans after 12 months and too slow judicial proceedings to act as deterrent (ask Vijay Mallya, Mehul Choksi, Nirav Modi and others who have fled the country and declared fugitives). Besides, most loan defaults involve PSBs – which are public depositories and mainstay of Indian banking/finance systems.

The magnitude of public money at stake with willful defaulters is Rs 346,479 crore as on December 2022 – as the Transunion CIBIL, a credit information company registered with the RBI, has revealed. There are 16,044 willful defaulters – borrowers who have the ability to pay but don't pay – with SCBs. This was a straight 41% jump from Rs 245,767 crore in December 2020.

So, banks and financial institutions would now have to take heavy haircuts on 3.46 lakh crore again – after SCBs wrote off Rs 12.3 lakh crore as NPAs in the past eight fiscals of FY15-FY22.

Fortune India explained why such "compromise settlements" is invitation to more banking frauds and willful defaults – which are on the rise in recent years and many such business tycoons have fled the country with bank loans. Many like the Sandesara brothers, fighting banking frauds (involving $1.7 billion) in India, are running flourishing oil business in Nigeria (fled India in 2019) and are also suspected to be doing business with public sector oil PSUs.

The second example is about missing 500 notes.

A national daily recently reported that the

whereabouts of 1,760.65 million of 500 notes (both old and new ones designed post-demonetisation), valued at Rs 88,032 crore, is not known. The report is based on the RTI replies from the three government mints – Bengaluru, Nasik and Dewas – and the RBI reports showing the notes it received during FY16 and FY17.

This mismatch may not actually amount to theft but what has caused disquiet is the RBI's late-night response to it on June 17, 2023, which said: "These reports are based on erroneous interpretation of information collected under the Right to Information Act, 2005 from the printing presses. It may be noted that all banknotes supplied from printing presses to RBI are properly accounted for. It is further informed that there are robust systems in place for reconciliation of banknotes printed at the presses and supplied to RBI which include protocols to monitor production, storage and distribution of banknotes."

This statement doesn't explain (a) why or how the mismatch happened and (b) why is the report which relies on official records was "erroneous".

A mere statement from the RBI assuring that "robust systems" exist isn't enough. It is the credibility which is on the line for long, particularly because RBI's robust systems (i) haven't deterred PSBs to invent "innovative ways" to evergreening loans, as the RBI Governor recently found out (ii) it is giving a free pass or "revdi" to fraudsters and willful defaulters and (iii) its explanation for withdrawal of 2,000 notes lacks conviction.

Jun 28, 2023

***

It's Time to Measure the Impact of PLI, DLI Schemes

Since PLIs and DLIs were introduced, there has been no post facto study on their efficacy on the ground.

The country's push for 'Make in India' has come in the forms of Production Linked Incentive (PLI) schemes and then Design Linked Incentive (DLI) schemes. But are they working? The National Account Statistics shows, the manufacturing *value added* was 17.3% of the GVA in FY15, which has moved up slightly to 17.7% in FY23. *Growth* in manufacturing value added was *1.3% in FY23* when the GVA grew at 7%. In the past nine fiscals since FY15, manufacturing value added grew at average of 6% as against the GVA's 5.6%.

At this rate of contribution and growth in *value added*, manufacturing is not driving economic growth substantially. Besides, manufacturing's *job share* is going down – from 12.1% in 2017-18 to 11.6% in 2021-22 (PLFS data). As against the promise to create 60 lakh new jobs in five years through the PLIs (Budget speech of 2022), there is no data to show how many jobs have indeed been created.

The PLIs and DLI schemes were brought in place

of 'Make in India', introduced in September 2014, which could not boost manufacturing in six fiscals of FY15-FY20.

The PLI was first approved by the Union Cabinet on March 21, 2020 – three days ahead of the pandemic national lockdown (announcement on the night of March 24, 2020). In 2022, Finance Minister Nirmala Sitharaman said the industry demanded it. Initially given to three sectors, the PLIs expanded to 14 sectors and will soon cover three new sectors – toys, leather and new age e-bikes – to take the total to 17 sectors. The allocations have also gone up from the initial Rs 1.97 lakh crore to Rs 2.06 lakh crore with the addition of Rs 9,765 crore for the PLI 2.0 for IT hardware (raised to Rs 17,000 crore from Rs 7,325 crore) announced in May 2023.

Parallelly, the DLI was announced for semiconductor sector in December 2021, under the "Semicon India Programme" with an allocation of Rs 76,000 crore, to develop semiconductors and display manufacturing ecosystem. Under this scheme, Centre subsidises 50% of project cost.

With the addition of DLI, every part of the supply chain for *semiconductor and electronics sectors* are now assisted with subsidies, including electronic components, sub-assemblies, and finished goods.

But there is no *post facto* study to measure their impact or efficacy.

Causal relationship between PLIs and growth

Three years down the line, the PLIs have run into problems as many feared.

The recent review of PLIs by Ministry of Commerce

and Industry shows (i) there were no takers for PLIs in six of 14 sectors – steel, textile, battery, white goods, solar panels and automotive and (ii) in the rest eight sectors – large-scale electronics manufacturing, IT hardware, bulk drugs, medical devices, pharmaceuticals, telecom and networking products, food processing and drones and drone components – only Rs 2,900 crore was disbursed by the end of FY23, out of Rs 1.97 lakh crore of allocations. This works out to just 1.5% of the fund earmarked.

Post the review, the Ministry of Commerce and Industry said (iii) PLIs generated "actual" investment of Rs 62,500 crore, resulting in "incremental production/sales" over Rs 6.75 lakh crore; created 3.25 lakh new jobs and "boosted" exports by Rs 2.56 lakh crore.

The statement also says that (iv) the sectors for which PLI schemes exist saw an "increase in FDI" inflows from FY22 to FY23 – in drugs and pharmaceuticals (46%), food processing industries (26%) and medical appliances (91%) and that (v) the PLI schemes "transformed" India's exports basket from traditional commodities to high value-added products such as electronics and telecommunication goods, processed food products etc.

The "first-ever disbursement" under the PLI came only in September 2022 – as approved by the "Empowered Committee" under the NITI Aayog.

Value added or mere assembling of smart phones?

While the ministry says (iv) the PLIs "led to increased value addition in the electronics sector and in smartphone manufacturing, 23% and 20% respectively", there is no study or data analysis supporting it.

Former RBI Governor Raghuram Rajan coauthored

a paper (along with Rahul Chauhan and Rohit Lamba), "Has India really become a mobile phone manufacturing giant?" published on May 30, 2023, which claims there is no value addition but mere *assembling* of smart phones in India.

Rajan claims he analysed trade data for mobiles phones and noticed *three distinct trade trends*: (a) after the high tariff (20%) barriers were imposed in 2018, imports of mobile phones fell and exports started taking off, turning positive five months after that. They checked import of mobile phone components – semiconductors, PCBAs, displays, cameras and batteries – and found (b) a sudden spurt in imports of these components after the tariff barrier. They also found (c) commensurate rise in net imports when exports of mobile phones took off.

They noted that the "combined net exports" (exports minus imports) of mobile phones and components "fell" from under $12.7 billion in FY17 to $21.3 billion in FY23 and commented: "In other words, it is entirely possible that we have become more dependent on imports during the PLI scheme."

As for value additions, they wrote that from the trade data available "we cannot even tell…whether India is paying out more in subsidies and tax waivers to mobile manufacturers who bring the assembly to India than the value they add in India – since the value added from the assembly is *such a small fraction* of the value of a mobile phone".

They claimed "net exports" was "still hugely negative" and "has not increased substantially since 2018".

Their advice: "The government, which should have

better data on value added, should undertake a detailed assessment on how many PLI jobs have been created, the cost to the country per job, and why the PLI scheme does not appear to have worked so far before extending to new sectors."

An analysis of India's trade data shows exports of *electronic goods* have gone up in recent years but imports grew far more, raising trade deficit on such goods from -$30.6 billion in FY15 to -$53.7 billion in FY23.

After an earlier round of review of PLIs, the NITI Aayog, which is tasked with *appraisal* of public-funded projects and schemes, was supposed to provide real time progress and monitor the PLIs. In its annual report of 2021-22, the Aayog declared that it was "developing a PLI dashboard to monitor all PLI schemes". Since the PLIs are given on increased investment, production, exports and employment generation, this dashboard was to *track changes* in these areas. The dashboard is still to go live though.

Vedanta-Foxconn setback

As for the DLI for semiconductor, it has turned out to be a setback. It was announced on December 15, 2021 with an allocation of Rs 76,000 crore with the promise of 50% subsidy to anyone setting up "semiconductor fabs and display fabs in India". The Gujarat government signed a deal for setting up such a facility with the Vedanta-Foxconn on September 13, 2022 with an investment of Rs 1.54 lakh crore with a promise to create 100,000 jobs.

Had this deal gone through, at 50% subsidy on capital expenditure, the Centre's entire allocation of Rs 76,000 crore would have been exhausted by this single deal. But *nine months later*, on May 31, 2023, the Ministry of Electronics and IT (MeiTY) issued a statement declaring that fresh bids are being sought "under the modified Semicon India Programme" for "semiconductor fabs and display fabs".

The reason was evident on the same day, May 31, 2023, from multiple news reports. The Vedanta-Foxconn project was grounded because it was struggling to *find a technology partner* and a manufacturing-grade technology *license* to make 28 nanometer (28 nm) chips on which the project hinges. The joint venture doesn't have the required technology.

New bids are now open till "December 2024" and given that the Vedanta-Foxconn project had a two-year timeframe India would have to wait for another three-and-half years (from June 2023) before the promised 28nm chips and 100,000 jobs are realised.

Why should the bids be open till December 2024 (one-and-half years later) is another question. Presumably, the Vedanta-Foxconn experience shows that none with the required 28nm chips technology has yet agreed to set up shop in India.

Recall the heartbreak Vedanta-Foxconn caused to Maharashtra when, in September 2022, the deal was signed with Gujarat – just ahead of the Gujarat elections in December 2022 – and after a prolonged negotiation with the Udhav Thackeray government in Maharashtra. By then, the Thackeray government had been replaced with the Shinde-Fadnavis government (sworn in on June 30, 2022). The new government tried to assuage the new opposition stating the Prime Minister had assured a similar or bigger project for Maharashtra.

While seeking the new bids for semiconductor and display fabs, MoS for MeiTY Rajeev Chandrasekhar said the "modified" bid was "sweetened", without specifying with what or how. It would be wrong to assume that the subsidy has been increased; it remains unchanged from December 2021.

On December 7, 2022, IT minister Rajeev Chandrasekhar informed the Lok Sabha in writing that the "incentives offered to Vedanta-Foxconn" included 40% of "capital subsidy" by the Government of India, among a host of other incentives by the Gujarat government (subsidised land, power tariff, electricity duty, water supply, stamp duty and registration fee etc.).

Assuming that a semiconductor project materialises by December 2026, it should ideally be a true 'Make in India', not 'Assembled in India'?

Jun 22, 2023

***

West is Vigilant about Predatory Pricing, India Not

Following the June 2 train accident, prices of flights to Bhubaneswar skyrocketed and kept rising, with no check in sight

Predatory pricing is alive and kicking in India. But developed economies have found ways to check them. The most glaring case is the cost of flights to and fro Bhubaneswar following the June 2 train accident. From a normal price range of Rs 6,000-8,000 for a flight between Delhi and Bhubaneswar, it went up to Rs 56,000 the very next day, on June 3, 2023 (more than what it cost for a Delhi-Paris flight on the day). Despite Civil Aviation Minister Jyotiraditya Scindia appealing to airlines on June 5 to ensure reasonable airfares, it went up even further.

On June 7, 2023 – two days after Scindia's appeal – a search of the MakeMyTrip website yielded shocking results. It showed, the only direct flight for the day was priced at Rs 12,492 (Air Asia, 16.30 hour); one-stop flight at a minimum of Rs 25,691 (Indigo, 22.55 hour) and a maximum of Rs 56,207 (Vistara, 17.50 hour); two-stop flight priced at a minimum of Rs 24,636 (Air Asia, 19.25 hour) and a maximum Rs 87,508 (Vistara, 19.55 hour).

The minister's appeal appeared to be ignored. Why this was so would be clear soon.

Predatory pricing is not limited to flights to Bhubaneswar, nor was Scindia's appeal of June 5. On the same day, June 5, the Delhi-Leh flight ticket touched Rs 52,000. Scindia was at an event later in the evening where he was asked why flight ticket prices were soaring. He replied: "In 1993, my father brought in an open sky policy and we deregulated the civil aviation sector, so there is no regulator for pricing of fares".

For the record, after a price capping review on August 10, 2022, Scindia tweeted: "The decision to remove airfare caps has been taken after careful analysis of daily demand and prices of air turbine fuel. Stabilisation has set in & we are certain that the sector is poised for growth in domestic traffic in the near future." That is, there are no price caps on flight tickets in India.

Scindia is right, and his explanation makes is clear that his appeal was ignored. India did de-regulate airline tariffs in March 1994 by repealing the Air India Act (not in 1993 as Scindia said). However, what he didn't say holds the key to the predatory pricing seen more than 22 years later (after 2016).

Here is a brief background.

Predatory pricing is official

On June 15, 2016, then Civil Aviation Minister P Ashok Gajapathi Raju announced the National Civil Aviation Policy (NCAP) "with a vision to create an eco-system to make flying affordable for the masses" With the NCAP-2016 came the "Ude Desh ka Aam Nagrik", in short, "UDAN" of 2016, "for promoting regional connectivity in the country as envisaged in NCAP-2016".

On the face of it, both NCAP-2016 and UDAN-2016 aimed at enabling the masses (aam nagrik) to fly. This embodies the Prime Minister's dream *"mera sapna hawai chappal pahanne wala hawai jahaaz me bathe"* (my dream is to let people wear slippers to fly in airplanes). But as it turns out, 'the road to hell is paved with good intentions'.

NCAP-2016 essentially fixed a minimum cap on flights at Rs 2,500 but no maximum cap. What this meant was that a Captain Gopinath-type budget airline Air Deccan of the early 2000s was no longer a possibility in India. "Airfare of about Rs 2,500 per passenger for a one-hour flight", says NCAP-2016. There was only one way for the flight tickets to go after 2016 – that is UP.

That was what happened with the Indian Railways in 2016 also. The Indian Railways came out with the "policy of Dynamic Pricing" in 2016, under which "the fares of the railway tickets are to increase by 10% after every 10% of berths or seats being sold". Hence, train tickets keep rising as seats get progressively booked – something which the airlines also do in India. Notice, the phrase "dynamic pricing" was not used in the NCAP or UDAN. Has anyone noticed, the refunds for cancelled train and plane tickets have been reduced to a few hundred rupees even when cancellations are before the last 24 hours?

Two other things: (i) a "Tariff Monitoring Unit (TMU)" working under the DGCA "monitors airfares on certain routes on a monthly basis to ensure that the airlines do not charge airfares outside a range declared by them" and (ii) "fare bands" are revised from time to time "to keep the aviation sector viable while protecting the interests of the passengers".

DGCA has the data to check for violations of declared

"fare bands" by airlines (like charging Rs 50,000-80,000 for New Delhi-Bhubaneswar flights or Rs 52,000 for New Delhi-Leh flights) and take appropriate punitive measures if violations were noticed. Try to locate the TMU on the DGCA website to know what monthly "fare bands" airlines have declared and you will draw a blank.

Aviation expert Praveen Paul explains to *Fortune India* what is happening.

He says DGCA's TMU is "blackhole" because nothing is known about its functioning or the "fare band" it receives every month (not put in the public domain). Hence, the violations are not known to the passengers. The India-type predatory pricing doesn't happen in developed countries because, despite dynamic pricing, (a) their airlines have very strong pricing oversight committees and their passengers' associations are very strong and (b) their regulatory bodies monitor for predatory and mercenary pricing. He gives the example of his students at Bangalore's St Joseph's University who are forced to take buses/trains to their homes outside Karnataka during vacations because Indian airlines know the timing and raise prices so high that students can't afford the air tickets. It is a normal routine.

India, of course, doesn't have aviation and train regulators or passengers' associations. The protests against skyrocketing airfare for Bhubaneswar flights are limited to social media. It must be pointed out that the flights governed by the UDAN policy, flight prices are controlled by the government but those are limited to unviable and unlinked sectors in the northeastern states, hilly states of Uttarakhand and Himachal Pradesh to develop. For that, the government provides viability gap funding (VGF), waives off airport charges, and gives various tax concessions (in excise, VAT, service tax, etc.).

Predatory pricing in fuel and telecom

Predatory pricing is not limited to flight and train tickets. Since April 2022, retail fuel prices have remained unchanged despite India importing huge amounts of cheap Russian oil, at or below $60 a barrel. Oil refining and marketing firms—both from the public and private sectors—are making windfall gains. Domestic consumers get no relief from the cheap oil.

Now, recall how Reliance Jio used predatory pricing in 2016 – free call and data services for mobile phones for 200 days and then at dirt-cheap rates for more years – to eventually kill competition and competitors, and capture a dominant position.

The Competition Commission of India (CCI) junked all objections to Reliance Jio's predatory pricing in June 2017, stating that giving free services couldn't, by itself, "raise competition concerns unless the same is offered by a dominant enterprise," while holding that the Reliance Jio wasn't the dominant player when it offered the free services.

The telecom regulator had earlier allowed Reliance Jio's "free and promotional services" and in February 2018, the Telecom Disputes Settlement and Appellate Tribunal (TDSAT) ruled in its favour by stating that no rules were violated. Now, six years later, the TRAI would be examining tariff plans – both present and past – to check predatory pricing.

West is acting against sellers' inflation

Predatory pricing has two new names these

days in the US and Europe – "sellers' inflation" and "greedflation". *Fortune India* wrote last month about how those countries are waking up to this phenomenon which they didn't suspect to find where they find now and are preparing to act tough (strengthening anti-price gauging measures, among others). The "causal link" between corporate profits and rising inflation would have been considered "heretical" until mid-2022. Economist Isabella Weber of the Amherst, Massachusetts University almost single-handedly demolished the prevalent thinking since the 1970s that inflation could only be caused by excess demand over supply/capacity or too much money chasing too few goods – but not by marking up prices. Costs going up were considered "purely a matter of inflated wages" with "no role for profits or the power of firms to set prices".

On June 6, 2023, Christine Lagarde, president of the European Central Bank, acknowledged that there wasn't "good data" on corporate profits to fully understand "sellers' inflation" although it was "observed" that corporates took "advantage" of cost-push by demand-supply mismatch and/or supply bottlenecks to raise profit and cause inflation thereby either (i) by not cutting down profit margins to accommodate cost-push in some sectors or (ii) by raising profit margins per se in other sectors. She sought competition authorities to look into the "legitimacy" of such practices.

The New Yorker wrote the same day, on June 6, 2023, that Isabella Weber's "heterodox ideas" about government price controls (not by "regulators", which is different as regulators are independent and autonomous entities) are now transforming policy in the US and across Europe.

It said: "Today, in a host of key sectors, that's more

or less happening. The European Union is regulating the price of natural gas, the Biden Administration is regulating the price of oil, and the G-7 is enforcing a global cap on the price of petroleum products produced in Russia." In contrast, nobody talks of sellers' inflation or predatory pricing seen in so many sectors in India.

More than a month after former RBI Deputy Governor Viral Acharya demonstrated with data and analysis that the Big 5 of Indian conglomerates, Reliance, Tata, Birla, Adani, Bharti groups, were profiteering by market dominance and asked for breaking them down ("dismantle or reduce the market power of Indian conglomerates") there is silence from the government and industry.

Jun 16, 2023

***

The Flip-Side of RBI's "Compromise Settlement" Formula For Stressed Asset

Banking system needs more stringent stressed asset management norms and tighter regulatory oversight, rather than 'compromise settlements' with willful defaulters causing the stress

Ten days after Governor Shaktikanta Das red-flagged governance failures in public sector banks, the RBI has allowed all banking and other financial institutions to go for "compromise settlement" with loan defaulters classified as "willful defaulters" or "frauds". In its circular, "Framework for Compromise Settlements and Technical Write-offs", it proposes "to provide further impetus to resolution of stressed assets in the system as well as to rationalise and harmonise the instructions across all REs (regulated entities)" without citing any study or analysis to justify it.

While loan defaulters' account marked as "fraud" need no explanation, those marked "willful defaulters" are ones who have the ability to pay the loans but don't. Both types of loan defaulters are invariably associated with money laundering, diversion of loans for purposes other than the sanctioned ones and other unacceptable or criminal activities. More often than not, these activities involve big corporate entities and their list has grown longer in recent years, as is the amount of write-offs as NPAs. The RBI has zealously guarded their identities in the name of protecting their business interests, rather than transparency and accountability in banking operations.

For better appreciation of what is in store with the "compromise settlement", it is important to recall what the RBI Governor himself recently described as "innovative ways to conceal the real status of stressed loans", while addressing the directors of PSBs on May 29, 2023 in Mumbai.

He listed the following "innovative ways" of concealment of stressed assets:

- "Bringing two lenders together to *evergreen* each other's loans by sale and buyback of loans or debt instruments";
- "Good borrowers being persuaded to enter into *structured deals* with a stressed borrower to conceal the stress";
- "Use of Internal or Office accounts to *adjust* borrower's repayment obligations";
- "*Renewal* of loans or disbursement of new/additional loans to the stressed borrower or related entities *closer to the repayment date* of the earlier loans";
- "One method of evergreening, after being pointed out by the regulator, was *replaced by another* method".

Das then asked: "Such practices beg the question as to whose interest such smart methods serve".

Instead of answering the question and seeking

tighter regulatory oversight and improvement in banking governance, Das merely advised banks and other financial institutions to ensure "conformity" with the policies and strategies laid down by their board and the RBI's "guidelines" – knowing fully well that these had failed and "innovative ways" have been found to "conceal" stressed assets.

The RBI's "compromise settlement", issued on June 8, 2023, is the very anti-thesis of what should have been done. Essentially, the RBI circular says: (i) all regulated banks, NBFCs and financial institutions are now empowered ("delegation of powers for approval/sanction") to "write off" loans marked as willful defaults and fraud and (ii) such debtors can be given "fresh" loans after a "cooling" period of 12 months or more (with the approval of their boards) of such compromise and write-offs.

Such powers are more likely to incentivise further banking frauds and willful defaults. Before explaining that, it may be pointed out that a write-off under a "compromise settlement" is different from normal write-offs of NPAs as in this case, there is no requirement to pay the outstanding amount and consequently, no recovery of the write-offs either. Such write-offs necessarily involve huge haircuts.

To understand why the RBI circular could be counter-productive, attention must be paid to four sets of critical data the RBI provides.

One is the rising write-offs. According to the RBI data, the NPA write-offs in SCBs (including that of willful defaulters) during FY05-FY14 was Rs 63,000 crore – which skyrocketed to Rs 12.3 lakh crore during FY15-FY22 (FY23 data is missing from the RBI's annual report of 2022-23 released recently). This is *19.4 times* higher. The spike during FY15-FY22 has a lot to do with exuberance in loan sanctions and evergreening during the previous UPA years but it also has a lot to do with deteriorating economic growth (which nosedived from 8.3% in FY17 to 3.9% in the pre-pandemic FY20 and -5.8% in FY21 before recovering to 9.1% in FY22). The "recovery" of NPAs written-off (not under 'compromise settlement' which is foregone) has been a mere 16.6% during FY18-FY22 – according to a Rajya Sabha reply of March 28, 2023.

Two, sudden spike in banking frauds, especially in FY18. It went up from Rs 34,993 crore during FY05-FY14 to Rs 5.89 lakh crore during FY15-FY23 – *16.8 times* more. The number of fraud cases also went up by *1.4 times* in comparison.

Three, dramatic rise in willful defaults. According to the Transunion Cibil registered with the RBI, there was a 38.5% or Rs 94,000 crore, rise in willful defaults – from 12,911 accounts for Rs 245,888 crore in December 2020 to 14,206 accounts for 285,583 crore in December 2021 to 15,778 for Rs 340,570 crore in December 2022. This reflects the big "governance gap" – the gap between loan appraisals and risk management.

Four, high haircuts and low recovery through the Insolvency and Bankruptcy Code (IBC) of 2016. According to the regulator IBBI's data up to March 2023, the recovery is mere 17.6% (combined for resolution and liquidation processes) – that is a haircut of 82.4%. Such low recovery points to the IBC's many failures but the ones relevant in the present context are "asset stripping", gaming of the system and diminishing political will (allowing the dilution of IBC and RBI's regulatory powers) which have worked to the disadvantage of lenders (banks and other financial institutions) – as *Fortune India* explained in "Poor run for IBC continues. What ails it?"

All the four sets of data point to huge gaps in the stressed asset management and calls for more stringent norms, rather than more concessions and compromises.

Shifting the blame for banking failures

The blame for the NPA and banking crises of the recent past has been shifted to former RBI Governor Raghuram Rajan – the one who initiated the bank clean-up with his Asset Quality Review (AQR) in 2015. The Economic Survey of 2020-21 held him responsible for worsening the NPAs by stating that his AQR "led to a second round of lending distortions" causing further NPAs and the said AQR "could not bring out all the hidden bad assets in the bank books and led to an under-estimation of the capital requirements". More recently, on June 9, 2023, Union Minister Rajeev Chandrasekhar said Rajan "wrecked the entire banking system and the financial sector".

What such statements reflect is the unwillingness to take responsibility for bad governance in the banking system which led to multiple failures of banks and NBFCs in 2018. Essentially, these banks and NBFCs were hobbled by banking frauds – PMC Bank, Punjab National Bank, ICICI Bank, Yes Bank, Lakshmi Vilas Bank, IL&FS, HDIL, DHFL etc. Besides, many corporate tycoons involved with these banking frauds and others have fled the country and some loan defaulters have been found to have stashed their assets in tax havens while claiming bankruptcy.

True, bank balance sheets are a lot healthier and robust now but this has been achieved through (i) massive write-offs of NPAs (Rs 12.3 lakh crore) (ii) recapitalisation

(Rs 3.12 lakh crore) and (iii) bailouts (Yes Bank and IL&FS, for example) – all with public money. It would be a mistake to consider the healthier and robust bank balance sheets a result of improved banking norms or regulatory oversight.

Add this loss of public money in write-offs, recapitalisation and bailouts to the gains that could have resulted from alternate and prudent deployment of it (economists call it "cost of opportunity lost") and the magnitude of loss due to banking failures would be clear.

Jun 13, 2023

***

Is Protectionism Helping or Harming India's Exports?

The biggest challenge for the country is to integrate with global value chains (GVCs) to boost exports.

India scored a diplomatic victory recently at the India-EU Trade and Technology Council meeting in Brussels, when Foreign Affairs Minister S Jaishankar neutralised the voices calling for action against India for exporting Russian oil to European countries in violation of the sanctions. Jaishankar pointed to the relevant EU Council regulation to assert that if the Russian crude was "substantially transformed" in India then it could no longer be treated as Russian fuel anymore.

This was an easy victory because of the hypocrisy of European countries who knowingly allowed India to export fuel for more than a year because they faced energy crisis.

But India's hypocrisy lies elsewhere.

Public good or private interest?

India's export of cheap Russian oil (after refining) has benefited companies, not the common man, because retail prices of petrol and diesel have remained unchanged. Two companies, Reliance Industries and Nayara Energy, have imported 45% of cheap Russian oil to India in FY23 –

far higher than their 35% share in the domestic refining capacity. Western countries capped the Russian crude at $60 per barrel when the Brent was trading over $110 per barrel and Russia also supplied crude below this ($60) price to India.

These two companies accounted for about 95% fuel exports to Europe in FY23 and India emerged as the largest fuel supplier of Europe in April 2023. India has imposed windfall tax on such exports but every such imposition is followed by a cut – virtually a monthly flip-flop loop. Meanwhile, an unknown Mumbai-based private company Gatik Ship Management, registered as an exporter only on March 31, 2023, has emerged out of nowhere to become a giant international supplier of Russian oil – owning 58 oil tankers from just two in 2021.

The last time India cut excise on petrol, diesel and gas for domestic consumption was in May 2022 and it was meant to control runaway inflation. But this cut didn't lower the retail price of petrol and diesel which has remained unchanged since then. Gas cylinder became costlier the very same May 2022 (when the price was Rs 950 and was raised by Rs 50 in the same month), it is now over Rs 1,100 (Delhi).

Similar is the case of coal import.

In July 2022, Coal and Mines Minister Prahlad Joshi told the Lok Sabha that "there is no shortage" and "production has been going up". But two months earlier, in May 2022, the government had allowed coal import until March 31, 2023 and changed the *coal mix* (30% imported coal) for thermal plants *unilaterally* by invoking *emergency power* (requiring *no consent* of buyer states). Imported coal was *10 times costlier* at the time.

The burden of higher cost of imported coal is on public –either directly or in state subsidies.

In FY23, coal imports jumped 30% in volume and 56.8% in value (USD) – draining out forex reserve. In February 2023, Joshi again told the Lok Sabha that India had no coal shortage and in March 2023 that India would be exporting coal by 2025-26.

Then there are frequent flip-flops on exports.

In 2022, India banned sugar exports for a year (till October 31, 2023), then limited it and is now contemplating further ban in 2023. India has banned wheat, certain types of rice, imposed and relaxed export duty on steel and iron pellets in the past couple of years.

True, India has to act keeping its interest in mind but whimsical changes – sometimes within days as happened in 2022 when wheat export was banned, then made conditional (May 2022) and then it was contemplating import wheat in August 2022. In April 2022, the Prime Minister had offered the US President to feed the world following the supply disruptions from Ukraine after the war broke out.

The guiding principles of good trade policy are its predictability and stability. Frequent flip-flops erode trusts in both domestic and foreign traders.

No data, analysis to support import substitution

There are many myths swirling around Indian trade. One is that protectionism helps or is helping Indian trade.

Even diehard government backer Arvind Panagariya repeatedly opposed resurrecting the failed policy of 1960s and 1970s. In 2020, he wrote that it was "doomed" to flounder again. In 2022, he wrote there was no economic analysis "whatsoever" to support or justify raising customs duty and argued that "a central principle of public finance is that customs duties should not form a revenue-raising instrument". In May 2023, he said India would do "a really big favour" by lowering import barriers, thereby preventing trade diversions (switching from less costly to more costly source).

Fortune India has analysed trade data to show both exports and imports have fallen post-high tariff regime (because both are linked). In FY23, (a) exports of "core" merchandise (excluding petroleum products and gems and jewellery which are import-dependent) fell but imports of "core" merchandise went up – which drains forex reserve, raises trade deficits and disables exports as a growth engine – and (b) imports made a new high in FY23 – 26% of the GDP – pointing to the ineffectiveness of import substitution policy.

More recently, Viral Acharya, former RBI Deputy Governor, listed four negative impacts of higher import tariff: (a) high tariff on agriculture (above 35%) with its low efficiency (employing over 40% workers but generating 15% of the GDP) "prevents a market-based rotation of jobs" from low-skilled to high-skilled (b) makes Indian goods costly and globally uncompetitive (c) makes imported goods costlier in India (such as iPhones), forcing Indians to go for inferior domestic products and keeping inflation higher and (d) disincentivises investments in efficiency and builds up market concentration.

In the meanwhile, India's problems with the EU – with which it is re-negotiating trade – is not over. Last month a WTO panel gave adverse ruling for erecting tariff barriers on ICT products. Two other complainants were Japan and

Taiwan. As against 0% tariff on these items (mandated by the WTO), India imposes 7.5-20%. What India does about it will be known soon.

How will India join global value chains?

More trouble is brewing.

The Indo-Pacific Economic Framework (IPEF) is seeking *advance notices* from members on all tariff changes and exports restrictions. India is not part of its trade pillar but that of other three (supply chains, clean economy and fair economy). How India handles the fallout – restrict India's ability to join their "supply chain".

The biggest challenge for India is to integrate with global value chains (GVCs) to boost exports.

India's share in global exports is miniscule – merchandise exports below 2% and services exports 3-4%. The extraordinary success of Bangladesh and Vietnam (also China) as exporters of apparel and textile products – the three beat India – owes it to "greater integration" with GVCs and *despite* not being top producers of cotton and synthetic fibre. India (along with China) is among the top 10 producers of cotton and synthetic fibre but of no use because it is not part of the GVCs.

Vietnam is a member of all three emerging multilateral trade blocs – RCEP, IPEF and CPTPP – but India has kept out of all three.

In fact, seven countries are members of all the three bloc – Vietnam, Australia, Japan, Malaysia, Singapore, New Zealand, Brunei. Three are part of two blocs – South Korea, Thailand and Philippines. China not only leads RCEP but is seeking membership of the CPTPP (earlier called TPP) too.

Are bilateral FTAs better than multilateral FTAs?

Does becoming part of mega trading blocs help? Yes, it does.

Economist Ashoka Mody recently wrote that most MNCs looking for alternate homes to China (China+1 strategy) are either "friend-shoring" to Vietnam (which is part of all three mega trade treaties) and other Southeast Asian countries "which (along with China) are members" of the RCEP and that most US multinationals are "near-shoring" to Mexico and Central America. India is not a major gainer (except for iPhone plants).

An IMF paper recently warned that "geoeconomic fragmentation" is "intensifying" after the Russia-Ukraine war (it began when US President Trump began de-globalisation) along the two *power blocs* – the US and Europe on one side and Russia-China on the other. It said, this new alignment would *directly impact trade, investment and technology transfers*. By keeping out of mega trade blocs, India is likely to harm its cause.

Is there any advantage of having only bilateral FTAs and by keeping out of multilateral FTAs?

Trade experts vouch there is no study or analysis to prove this.

Logically, multilateral FTAs make more sense because of wider canvas (bigger GDP and trade shares) and ease of doing business. In contrast, bilateral FTAs call for individual negotiating and every time a partner plays truant (like India imposing tariff barriers or flip-flops on exports and imports), all bilateral FTA partners need to take out their *spreadsheets*.

India is opting for bilateral trade because three reports say that India didn't benefit from its earlier trade treaties – which flies in the face of data and reasoned arguments of Arvind Panagariya and Arvind Subramanian (who first warned against it in 2020).

The latest is the Exim Bank report of Mach 2022.

This report recognises India's loss from not joining the RCEP (loss of a huge market and loss of opportunity to join its value chain, "especially for hi-tech goods") but also notes the "potential threat to many domestic industries, primarily from China". It flags concerns about trade in general: (i) "preferential tariffs" offered by India are "significantly lower" than its trade partners and (ii) "technical barriers to trade" (TBT) to widen its access to foreign markets. But then, it also recognises that if India raises its "preferential tariffs" it would lose out on exports and the TBT problems (technical regulations, standards, and testing and certification procedures) can be taken care through the WTO.

The second is the Economic Survey of 2021-22 (of January 2022), which advocates re-negotiating bilateral FTAs, but without talking about multilateral ones and without explaining how protectionism will help. It talks about the need to join global value chains, but *only in the context* of what India is doing to improve its chances of doing so (addressing infrastructure, tardy business processes and labour market reforms and the PLIs "to create the capacity to integrate with the global value chains" etc.).

The NITI Aayog's 2018 report ("A note on free trade agreements and other costs") is on similar lines. It recognised that China moved up in value chain and is more diversified – leaving India far behind. It proposed "a second thought" on joining the China-led RCEP (being negotiated then) because of the looming presence of China.

But not one of these reports said India's exports suffered because partner countries were unfair or despite quality goods from India. On the contrary, they pointed to India's disadvantages because of uncompetitive products.

Not one of these reports even mention protectionism either, let alone suggest it as a solution.

It is often forgotten that India is also a part of a series of smaller regional trading blocs like ASEAN (AIFTA), APTA, TIG, SAFTA, among others.

Export of electronics and automobiles?

Often the rise in exports of electronics and automobile are said to have resulted from protectionism but such claims are questionable.

In the case of 'electronic goods', the trade deficit is consistently rising – from (-) $30.6 billion in FY15 (when import barriers started going up) to (-) $53.7 billion in FY23. That is, exports may be up but imports continue to surpass by higher margin.

In the case of automobiles, India imported all technologies – for the Ambassador cars to Hero Honda bikes. Besides, the SIAM data doesn't prove much. It shows:

- Export of passenger vehicles (passenger cars, UVs and vans) in FY23 was 6.6 lakh units – far lower than FY17 (7.6 lakh), FY18 (7.5 lakh) and FY19 (6.8 lakh).
- Export of two-wheelers have risen but at 36.5 lakh units in FY23, it was lower than 44.4 lakh units in FY22 and closer to 35.2 lakh units in FY20.

- Total auto exports (PVs, two and three wheelers, commercial vehicles etc.) fell from 56.2 lakh unit in FY22 to 47.6 lakh unit in FY23 (marginally ahead of 47.5 lakh units in FY20).

May 30, 2023

***

To Ban or Not to Ban Auditors for Corporate Frauds

It is the multiplicity of authorities, processes and legal battles that defeat the very objective, while punishment is not even a certainty

The Supreme Court's order of May 3, 2023, paving the way for criminal action against the auditors of IL&FS Financial Services Limited (or IFIN) – BSR & Associate, a KPMG affiliate and Deloitte – for alleged abetment and collusion in corporate fraud is a significant step forward as it stops auditors from getting away simply by resigning.

The IFIN auditors had precisely sought such an escape and the Bombay High Court, in its April 22, 2020 order, allowed it by quashing a five-year ban. Three years later, the Supreme Court has quashed the Bombay High Court order and upheld the constitutional validity of Section 104(5) of the Companies Act, 2013 – which allows the National Company Law Tribunal (NCLT) to remove as well as ban auditors found guilty of corporate frauds.

The IL&FS Group had collapsed in 2018, after a series of loan defaults led to its bankruptcy proceedings under the IBC of 2016 the same year. It was found that the group had falsified ("window dressed") account books, hid massive debts and NPAs for *four years* up to FY18. It had a debt of Rs 91,000 crore and 70% of its loans were NPAs. The IFIN, its financial arm giving loans to group companies as well as external entities, was found to have indulged in multiple irregularities for *seven years* between FY12 and FY18 by the Serious Fraud Investigation Office (SFIO) in 2019. The SFIO blamed not just the management and auditors, but also the independent directors and the RBI – which didn't act tough despite its successive inspections finding fraudulent activities in FY16 and FY17.

Another development has taken place that promises stricter oversight of audit and auditors.

On May 3, 2023, the Finance Ministry notified and brought the activities of chartered accountants, company secretaries and cost and works accountants – who engage in accounting, auditing and related works – under the money laundering law, the PMLA of 2002. This change requires that these professionals maintain records of certain financial transactions, identify parties involved, verify these transactions and report "suspicious" ones to authorities. However, given that this has caused unhappiness among these professionals (involved in audit, accounting and other related activities) it remains to be seen how effective this would prove.

Nevertheless, both are steps in the right direction.

Relevance of Supreme Court order

A day before the Supreme Court's May 3, 2023 order came, the Adani Group's auditor Shah Dhandharia – named in the Hindenburg report – resigned as the auditor of Adani Total Gas; its status as the auditor of the flagship group company Adani Enterprises is not known.

When the SEBI's investigations into the Hindenburg allegations are complete and if at all Shah Dhandharia is found guilty of auditing misconduct, it can no longer claim immunity from criminal prosecution by citing its resignation.

The Hindenburg report of January 2023 had called Shah Dhandharia "a tiny" firm with very young hands and "hardly seems capable of complex audit work". It pointed to the enormity of auditing the Adani Group by flagging that (i) Adani Enterprises "alone has 156 subsidiaries and many more joint ventures and affiliates" and (ii) "Adani's 7 key listed entities collectively have 578 subsidiaries and have engaged in a total of 6,025 separate related-party transactions in fiscal year 2022 alone, per BSE disclosures".

One of the Hindenburg's allegations was that the Adani Group violated the SEBI mandated 25% public- float or free-float. The global index services provider MSCI has cut down the Adani Total Gas's free-float from 25% to 14% and that of Adani Transmission from 25% to 10% with effect from May 11, 2023.

Why auditors need strict regulations

Coming back to the Supreme Court's May 3, 2023 order, what it essentially does is to make the second proviso of Section 104(5) applicable to the IFIN – that is, imposing a five-year ban on the KPMG affiliate and Deloitte.

The first proviso provides for removal of auditor from a firm if found to be involved in corporate frauds. Both the provisions, removal and imposition of ban is through the NCLT proceedings, were introduced in the Companies Act of 2013. The exercise to incorporate the first proviso was initiated through the Companies Bill of

2009 and the second proviso in the Companies Bill of 2011. The objectives were to make the oversight of auditing and auditors "more stringent" and but through a fair process (NCLT proceedings).

These changes came primarily because of the Satyam Computers scam of 2009.

Recall the enormity of audit failures in the iconic Satyam Computers.

Satyam Computers collapsed overnight in 2009, after the man behind it, Ramalinga Raju, wrote to the SEBI confessing that he had been cooking up the accounting and financial books for seven long years! His letter mentioned (a) "non-existent" bank deposits and interests accrued (b) "understated liability" and (c) "overstated debtors' position". Even a CA student undergoing "articleship" would have discovered the frauds by doing a very simple and basic task – matching Raju's claims about bank deposits with the actual bank statements in any of those seven years. But its auditor, the famed global giant PricewaterhouseCoopers (PwC), failed to perform this basic task for seven years.

The PwC was banned for two years by the SEBI (along with disgorgement) in 2018 – 10 years later.

The ban was overturned by the Securities Appellate Tribunal (SAT) in 2019. This was stayed by the Supreme Court, which upheld the SEBI's power to punish the auditor. In a parallel exercise, in February 2023, the SAT set aside the SEBI orders (of 2018) barring Raju and others from the securities markets for up to 14 years – 14 years after the scam hit. The CBI case against Raju and others, meanwhile, drags on while they are out on bail.

The PwC is one of the four global Big 4 audit firms – others being KPMG and Deloitte engaged by the IFIN mentioned earlier and Ernst & Yung. The Big 4 was once Big 5. The fifth one, Arthur Andersen, collapsed along with its client Enron in 2000 – for the same work of cooking up accounting books and financial statements to mislead investors and others.

It may sound strange for the KPMG affiliate and Deloitte to seek waiver from criminal prosecution after being found guilty of colluding in corporate fraud by the SFIO. Their basic argument was they had already resigned and hence, Section 104(5) didn't apply to them. The Bombay High Court said it was satisfied with their resignations and the second proviso (ban for five years) of Section 104(5) was not applicable. It said the second proviso "is only attracted" when "despite" the application for ban, an auditor opposes it "frivolously", inviting a final order under the second proviso. It also held that the SFIO investigation was "interim" and hence, can't form the basis for seeking a ban. The Supreme Court, dismissed this by stating that the SFIO report was final insofar as the IFIN was concerned but given the "complex structure" of the IL&FS Group, it might provide supplementary evidence after investigating other group companies).

Notice how tough it is to punish an auditor for patent acts of corporate frauds, especially if it involves one of the Big 4. The long delays in investigation and follow-up action, multiplicity of authorities (the Institute of Chartered Accountants of India (ICAI) is yet another watchdog of accounting and auditing standards) and multiple, long-drawn legal battles. Surprisingly, however, none of these cases flagged an easy remedy: Dismantling an intrinsically flawed, *self-certifying* auditing system in India. India allows a firm to hire its own statutory auditor and pay for its audit work. When that happens, auditing can be a farce. Ask Raju or an IFIN executive.

May 12, 2023

***

Pricing Power Behind High Inflation?

Why central banks such as RBI need to look at high prices charged by dominant firms instead of focusing on higher repo rates only.

Reserve Bank of India (RBI) kept repo rate unchanged at 6.5% in its latest monetary policy despite consumer price inflation (CPI) staying above its 6% target in January and February, even though March CPI came in at 5.6%. RBI's logic: Inflation is expected to moderate in FY24 and monetary policy actions it has already taken are "still working through the system." RBI governor Shaktikanta Das explained: "It›s a pause for now, to assess the progress so far, and MPC wouldn›t hesitate to raise the rate if and when required."

RBI, in fact, stood out among world›s major central banks in announcing a pause in the rate hike cycle. U.S. Fed (despite bank runs) and European central banks increased rates by 25-50 basis points recently to control four-decade-high inflation rates. In India, RBI›s assumptions have gone wrong for years, with January and February inflation (6.5% and 6.4%, respectively) coming in higher than its estimate of 5.8-5.9% for Q4 of FY23.

However, the fight against inflation has taken a twist in U.S. and Europe. More and more economists are calling it a "sellers' inflation" — caused not by rising input costs like wage-price spirals of 1970s but companies using market dominance to increase prices. As this blunts the impact of rate hikes, RBI may have to tweak its strategy of increasing the repo rate to bring inflation under control.

Sellers' Inflation

The development is so unusual that a study by University of Massachusetts Amherst titled "Sellers' Inflation, Profits and Conflict: Why Can Large Firms Hike Prices In An Emergency?" published in February 2023, says that even suggesting a possible link between corporate profits and high inflation would have been considered "heretical" until 2022.

The reasons are simple. Since 1970s, the two dominant inflation triggers have been excess aggregate demand in relation to capacity (Keynesian) and too much money chasing too few goods (monetarist or neoliberal), says the paper. Under these theories, high inflation is purely a matter of inflated wages and there is no role for profits or power of firms to set prices. This is wrong, says the paper, concluding that U.S. is predominantly seeing a sellers' inflation that started in second quarter of 2021 and continued in 2022.

During this period, profit (after tax) of non-financial U.S. corporations broke a new record, surpassing previous highs of the period after World War-II, says the paper. Wages didn't contribute as they "have consistently failed to keep pace with inflation and most workers have faced declining real wages," it adds. Instead, this inflation is driven by "ability of firms with market heft to hike prices." The four sources of this ability are — monopolies or market concentration in hands of a few price makers;

compromised competition; versatile product portfolio and good revenue management; and access to diverse markets for money (making rate hikes ineffective) as well as consumers (finding people to sell at a high price). Since sellers' inflation is not demand-driven, it cannot be brought down by raising interest rates which, in fact, will hit smaller firms. Tackling this requires "price gouging" laws backed by close monitoring, windfall profit taxes and price controls for significant sectors where competitive markets are compromised, says the paper.

Eurozone and U.K.

The first sentence of a research paper by French bank Natixis, "Euro Area: Wages, Profits And Inflation", released on March 27, 2023, reads: "One factor behind stickiness of core inflation in euro area has been ability of companies to sustain high margins."

SELLERS' INFLATION	CAUSES...	... EFFECTS
• "Sellers' inflation" is also referred to as "profit-price spiral". • It is fuelled by excessive increase in prices by companies to make higher profits.	• A highly concentrated economy in which a few firms, called "price makers", set prices of products and services taking advantage of their market dominance. • Versatile portfolios and revenue models designed to make sure customers stick to them even in bad times.	• Persistent inflation, irrespective of fall in input cost and rise in interest rates. • Undermines economic stability. • Causes financial harm to smaller competitors. • Leads to fall in real wages.

It doesn't talk about sellers' inflation but says corporate profits were "excessive" in 2021 and "re-accelerated throughout 2022," driven by mark-up, which continued to grow strongly. Wage share has declined sharply over last two years, it says. The high mark-up was possible because "pent-up demand during pandemic meant people were less price-sensitive as they came out of lockdowns," says Dirk Schumacher, who heads the European research unit of Natixis.

U.K. is also going through a "cost of living crisis." A study by its trade union Unite titled "Profiteering Across The Economy – It's Systemic," published in March 2023, found sellers' inflation at work as many companies pushed up prices through price gouging. It found wages fell sharply in U.K. in 2022 and had no role in keeping inflation high. Now, workers are facing a difficult choice. They risk wage-driven inflation too if they demand higher wages to overcome their cost-of-living crisis.

The surge in price mark-up has come after the unprecedented stock market boom in 2020 and 2021 amid millions losing their lives and livelihoods to the pandemic. The global economy shrunk by 3.1% in 2020 before growing 6% in 2021. A study by Swiss bank UBS and PwC says billionaire wealth went to "a new high" — from $8 trillion at beginning of April 2020 to $10.2 trillion by end-July — in just four months. The trigger was huge fiscal and quantitative easing by governments and central banks, it says.

Central Bank Action

Central banks of U.S. and Europe have been flagging the problem since 2022. For example, vice chair of U.S. Fed, Lael Brainard, pointed out in September 2022 that "reductions in mark-ups could make an important contribution to reduced pricing pressures." Isabel Schnabel, member of European Central Bank's executive board, said in May 2022 that "profits have recently been a key contributor to total domestic inflation."

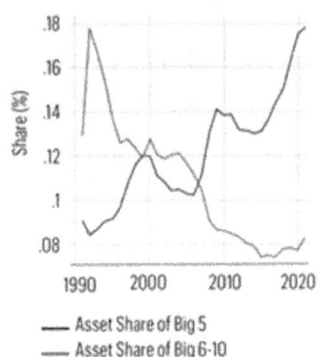

MARK-UP SHOWS RISE IN PRICE FOR EVERY PERCENT RISE IN INPUT COSTS;
SOURCE: PROWESS, CENTRE FOR MONITORING INDIAN ECONOMY (AUTHOR'S CALCULATIONS); VIRAL ACHARYA PAPER

ON MARCH 7, US FED CHAIR JAY POWELL WAS REBUKED FOR IGNORING SELLERS' INFLATION DURING HIS TESTIMONY TO CONGRESS.

Now, pressure to act is mounting. On March 7, US Fed chair Jay Powell was rebuked for ignoring sellers' inflation during his testimony to Congress, with Sherrod Brown, chair of the Senate Banking Committee, telling him: "The Fed can't force corporations to change their ways or rewrite the Wall Street business model on its own. But you could talk about it. High interest rates, falling wages and increasing unemployment are hallmarks of failed policies that end up helping Wall Street, large corporations and the wealthy."

On March 24, Andrew Bailey, governor of Bank of England, urged companies to refrain from price increases with a veiled warning: "And I would say to people who are setting prices, please understand that if we get inflation embedded, interest rates will have to go up further."

India's Big 5

RBI and Central government have not yet acknowledged sellers' inflation in India even though RBI has noticed an unusual phenomenon. Its March 2023 bulletin expressed concern that while CPI remained high, core inflation (excluding food and fuel) "continues to defy the distinct softening of input costs." One would expect RBI to probe further but it did nothing more than mentioning the problem.

Viral Acharya, former RBI deputy governor who teaches at New York University's Stern School, has raised a red flag while explaining this anomaly. "When input prices rise, if market power in an industry is high, wholesale price inflation in that sector rises a lot more. And that feeds into CPI," he says.

He, in fact, blames Big Five – Reliance, Tata, Birla, Adani and Bharti groups – for driving inflation because "the Big Five are able to charge product prices that are substantially higher than other competitors." Helping them are "sky-high tariffs" shielding them from competition by foreign firms. He said these conglomerates wield immense pricing power in retail, resources and telecommunication sectors and should be broken up.

Acharya also questions the "national champions" policy. "Creating national champions, which is considered by many as the industrial policy of new India, appears to be feeding directly into keeping prices at a high level."

In a just published paper, "India at 75: Replete With Contradictions, Brimming With Opportunities, Saddled With Challenges," he writes that post-1991 liberalisation, these Big Five have not only expanded footprint in more and more sectors but also increased their share in assets of non-financial sectors from 10% in 1991 to nearly 18% in 2021. At the same time, the share of the next big five business groups fell from 18% in 1992 to less than 9%. "In other words, Big Five grew not just at the expense of the smallest firms but also of the next largest firms," says the paper.

That wages are not contributing to inflation is evident. In FY21, corporate profits soared to historic high, partly due to job and wage cuts, says CMIE. PLFS (periodic labour force survey) data also confirms that post-pandemic recovery is profit-led rather than wage-led. Acharya says real wages have risen in urban areas but fallen in rural areas, where most of the jobs are.

RBI and finance ministry often blame external factors for inflation, calling it a "spillover from geopolitical shocks." The role of domestic factors such as fuel costs, tariff and non-tariff import barriers, extreme weather conditions causing crop loss and pass-through of input costs are either ignored or soft-peddled. A big reason for this is propensity for "positivity" in public narrations. The finance ministry's Monthly Economic Report of April 2022, released in May 2022, claimed inflation doesn't hit the poor but the rich and thus, when inflation moderates, there is "redistribution of income." It used 2011-12 household consumption expenditure but excluded critical elements that reflect impact of inflation on households: (a) income levels (b) expenditure on luxury goods and (c) savings.

One can hope for a reality check by RBI when it next looks at inflation and interest rates, keeping in mind that disciplining inflation calls for measures other than interest rates, too — like U.S. and Europe are realising now.

May 8, 2023

Future of Indian Trade is in Services Exports

Services exports are booming, significantly reducing trade deficits generated by merchandise trade, but it remains a blind spot for policymakers with little data, analysis or efforts to push

Going by the headlines, India's exports are booming, creating new records and set to scale new highs. The Ministry of Commerce and Industry has embellished the trade data for FY23 with claims such as India's overall exports scaled "new heights"; merchandise registered "highest ever annual exports" with 14% growth in FY23; services exports grew at 27% to "lead the overall exports growth", creating a "new record"; China's share in import basket declined to 13.8% etc.

These are partial truths and lack perspective. A closer look at the trade data released for the full FY23 on April 13, 2023, shows how the new Foreign Trade Policy (FTP) of 2023, released on March 31, ignored product improvements and services sectors' potential to boost exports by focusing entirely on process improvements. Some of the key information revealed by the trade data are:

(i)   Exports of "core" merchandise (excluding petroleum

products and gems and jewellery, which are largely import-dependent) actually fell ($-0.45 billion) but imports of "core" merchandise increased ($62.86 billion). This is a double whammy – indicating a weakening of both external demand and domestic demand.

(ii) Both merchandise exports and imports declined in the second half of FY23 – indicating a progressive weakening of growth globally as well as domestically. Exports decline by $19 billion and imports by $33.6 billion.

(iii) Labour-intensive merchandise exports – apparel and textile, handicraft, carpet, jute etc. – fell in FY23.

(iv) Trade deficit went up from $83.5 billion in FY22 to $122 billion in FY23.

(v) Imports made new highs – 26% of the GDP, taking it back to pre-tariff hike levels and pushing trade deficit – pointing to the failure of the import substitution policy. China's share in India's import basket may have declined in FY23, yet it remains high at 31.2% of the total trade deficit of India and went up in absolute numbers – by $5.7 billion until February 2023.

(vi) Real bright spot is services exports. It generated a trade surplus of $144.78 billion, thereby dramatically reducing deficits generated by merchandise trade. But the ministry provides no details of services exports – as it does assiduously every month and every year for merchandise trade of top 30 "commodities". It only provides three headline numbers for services trade (exports, imports and trade balance). The RBI database does the same.

Internal challenges: Neglect of services, including its exports

It defies logic that the details and analysis of services exports are not provided by the ministry and the RBI.

Services exports are relatively new but are the main driver of Indian trade in recent years and hence, its neglect is a self-inflicted injury India should treat immediately. India's trade generated a *surplus only twice in 73 years* (since 1949-50) – in 1972-73 and 1976-77 (Economic Survey of 2022-23). As per the UNCTAD data available for 2005-2021, services exports are delivering a surplus since 2010.

This skewed approach has consequences for domestic production and job creation. It must be kept in mind that the services sector and services exports have grown with little help from the government while manufacturing – the base for goods exports – and merchandise exports have received maximum support but have failed to deliver. Here is how.

(a) Services contributes maximum to national income (GDP) since 1982-83 – when it overtook agriculture – and contributes 60% or more to the GDP since FY13. Manufacturing is stuck at 17-18% since FY07 and at 9-17% in the other fiscals since 1950-51. Manufacturing gets a wide-ranging, long-standing and excruciatingly long list of tax incentives to boost production and exports – tax holidays, refunds and incentives under GST, SEZs, EOUs, Deemed Export Benefit Scheme, Advance Authorization Scheme, Duty Drawback, DFIA, ECGC, MEIS, RoDTEP, RoSCTL, EPCG, PLIs etc. Services have just two – SEIS, and EPCG.

(b) Services sector has always been the *Number 2 job provider* (since 1950-51); it overtook agriculture only for the year 2018-19, but agriculture has reclaimed its Number 1 position thereafter (EPW, Planning Commission and PLFS).

(c) Services are "more labour intensive than manufacturing or mining" (creating more jobs, even if a big part is informal, low-productive and low-paying), supported by both (i) relatively cheap labour and (ii) English-speaking tertiary-educated workforce. A large body of studies show, the 1991 trade liberalisation "displaced" exports from traditional, labour-intensive sectors to skill and capital-intensive (in manufacturing and to an extent, services). Thus, trade liberalisation has hurt domestic job creation, which neither import substitution nor FTP of 2023 sought to address.

(d) *Advantage of English* for boosting services exports is likely to end soon for two reasons: (a) shift of focus from English in higher education to 22 "Eighth Schedule" languages (which doesn't include English) in the New Education Policy (NEP) of 2020, as a result of which the DU colleges, for example, have drastically cut down English teaching and (b) in 2015, the UPSE ended primacy of English in civil services exams, making English skills at par with those of 22 Indian languages for the purpose of qualifying to take the exams, reversing its earlier role for "evaluation" of the exam (or clearing/passing the exam).

(e) Global share of services exports is 3-4% as against less than 2% for that of merchandise exports during 2015-2020.

In short, India needs to put its house in order first by reversing its thinking and FTP of 2023.

External challenges: Geo-economic fragmentation

The falling exports and imports in the second half of FY23, as mentioned earlier, are in line with global developments.

The UNCTAD's latest report says, global trade "turned negative" in the second half of 2022 with merchandise trade registering a 3% decline in the fourth quarter of 2022 while services trade remained constant. It also says global trade is "set to stagnate in the first half of 2023". The IMF has also revised global growth for 2023 downward, from 2.9% in January 2023 forecast to 2.8% in April 2023 forecast – which is a huge drop from 3.4% in 2022.

Seven of India's top 10 exports destination in 2022 are facing a sharp decline in their growth in 2023 –except China, Hong Kong and Bangladesh – as per the IMF's April 2023 projections. This would mean the worsening of global growth in output and trade would weaken India's growth prospects further. India's growth is already slipping from 7% in FY23 to 6.5% in FY24 (RBI). Going by the latest trends in trade, this would only add to the trade deficit and lower merchandise exports.

The threats from the global re-alignments in trade along the power blocs in the post-Russia-Ukraine war and sanctions are huge.

But to understand this better, here is how India has already hurt its cause.

India unilaterally terminated 68 Bilateral Investment Treaties (BITs) – which are signed between trading partner nations and impact investment flows. This would play up more and more as India engages with a series of bilateral FTA negotiations. India also kept itself out of three mega multilateral trade agreements – (i) CPTPP was signed in 2018, after the US pulled out in 2017 but in April 2023, the UK joined it; it contributes 15% to global GDP (ii) China-led RCEP of 2019 and (iii) the US-led IPEF of 2022. The latter two trade blocs contribute 70% of global GDP and 53% of global trade.

The fallout is obvious, most multinationals leaving China under their China+1 strategy are either shifting to RCEP member countries ("friend-shoring") or going back home to the US and nearby countries ("near-shoring"). India isn't benefitting much from this shifting of global manufacturing because it is not a part of any of these trade treaties. Such re-alignment also threatens India's chances of joining global value chains (GVCs) because not just multinationals but the US, European Commission and China are now increasingly looking at strategies to make GVCs more resilient by moving production home or to trusted countries.

More trouble is waiting.

The IMF's World Economic Outlook of April 2023 describes this phenomenon as "geo-economic fragmentation" and says, the threats from this fragmentation are rising, which would lead to "more trade tensions; less direct investment; and a slower pace of innovation and technology adoption across fragmented 'blocs'".

Not just that, an IMF analysis shows the fragmentation of investment, caused by this "geo-economic fragmentation", may cause "2 percent loss in global output" in the long run. The impact would be more on emerging markets like India which would not only lose out on FDI inflows but also "transfer of better technologies and know-how".

Will G20 leadership help India's trade?

India is now heading the G20 and holding a series of conclaves throughout the country (also once at Washington). But the G20 conclaves are more about global political and economic orders – the war, sanctions, monetary, fiscal, financial and structural policies to promote growth and maintain financial stability are on their plates. Besides, these necessarily require long-drawn deliberations and negotiations, over several years, for changes to happen.

After the two rounds of G20 Finance Ministers and Central Bank Governors (FMCBG) last week in Washington, the areas flagged by Finance Minister Nirmala Sitharaman for possible positive outcomes relate to (a) regulating cryptocurrencies (b) strengthening multilateral development banks and (c) resolution of debt crisis faced by many low and middle-income countries.

But these engagements can be leveraged to India's gains.

Raghuram Rajan and Rohit Lamba have precisely pointed to this recently. They argued, India could persuade G20 leaders to open up to the possibilities of services exports in sectors traditionally considered "non-tradeable", like health, education, legal and accounting services, by lowering barriers to the globalisation of services. This would, they argued, doubly benefit India – by boosting services exports and improving the domestic education and health standards.

Apr 18, 2023

***

Credit Suisse, Yes Bank Legacy: Tense Future for AT1 Bonds

Writing off AT1 bonds of Credit Suisse in Europe and Yes Bank in India pose a threat to this post-2007-08 global financial instrument meant to soar up capital and absorb financial shocks.

After the fall of Credit Suisse, a Global Systemically Important Bank (GSIB), the fate of yet another instrument put in place after the 2007-08 crisis to prevent bank runs now hangs in balance. Called Additional Tier 1 (AT1) bonds, this is a Basel III tool to generate adequate capital for banks to ensure they "absorb shocks" arising from financial and economic stress, reducing the risk of spillover from the financial sector to the real economy. This is meant to prevent the 2007-08-like massive taxpayer-funded bailouts.

But it may soon become irrelevant. In both the Credit Suisse and Yes Bank cases, the first response of their respective regulators and governments was to write it off by inversing the protocol laid down for their treatment in crisis – in which AT1 bond holders are protected (higher in the "order of seniority") ahead of equity holders. The contrarian action, which would be clear soon, is at the heart of current turmoil in AT1 bond markets of Europe and India.

On the one hand, the Credit Suisse's AT1 bond investors are preparing for a lawsuit, on the other, European market regulators (of which Swiss FINMA is not a part) and Bank of England have rushed to assure their AT1 investors that their interest would take precedence over equity holders in case of a similar crisis. In India, those of the Yes Bank, which collapsed and the RBI took over for its "reconstruction" in 2020, are currently challenging the write-off in the Supreme Court.

If the Supreme Court upholds their interest and strikes down the write off – as did Bombay High Court ("quashed and set aside") in January 2023 and put it on hold for six weeks, which the apex court extended further – AT1 bond may survive. If not, it is unlikely that banks would sell AT1 bonds or investors would go for it.

Before going further, here is a brief on AT1 bonds to understand what is happening.

What is AT1 bond?

AT1 bond is meant to shore up Tier 1 capital of banks – paid-up equity capital, disclosed reserves (like NPA provisioning) and surplus etc. which are used for regular banking operations "without triggering bankruptcy" (also called "going-concern capital"). Tier 2 capital (also a regulatory or mandatory requirement like Tier 1 capital) is a bank's supplementary capital to absorb losses "only in a situation of liquidation of the bank" ('gone-concern capital") – as the RBI explains.

AT1 bond is a perpetual (no maturity date) debt instrument, higher-interest yielding (for example, Yes Bank offered 9-9.5% interest on it when FD rate was 6.5%) and higher-ticket size (of Rs 1 crore and above for Yes Bank).

But it is also highly risky because it can be converted to equity (market determined return) or written down (value reduced) and is also not protected by deposit insurance.

Hence, the RBI discourages individual investors (HNIs) and put stiff conditions while permitting it in 2014, and market regulator SEBI completely banned it for individuals in October 2020 and allows only qualified institutional buyers (QIBs) to invest as they are capable of appreciating the high-risk better.

Turmoil over Yes Bank's AT1 write-off

The Yes Bank had collapsed in 2020 after a series of scandals involving questionable investments (including in the IL&FS and DHFL both of which collapsed too), high upfront charges, high and undisclosed NPAs and multiple banking frauds like money laundering.

The RBI announced a moratorium on the Yes Bank (stopping it from making any payment to any depositors or discharge any liabilities to any creditors) on March 5, 2020. The next day, on March 6, 2020, it appointed an "administrator" for the bank. It released a "draft" scheme of the bank's reconstruction on the same day (March 6, 2020). This "draft" provided for writing off the AT1 bonds. But the "final scheme" of reconstruction, notified later on March 13, 2020 with the Central government's approval, "deleted" this provision.

But a day later, on March 14, 2020, the Yes Bank's "administrator" wrote off the AT1 bonds valued at Rs 8,415 crore (issued in 2016 and 2017).

The Bombay High Court "quashed and set aside" this write-off on January 22, 2023. It said (i) the "final scheme" of March 13, 2020 "did not authorise Administrator to write off the AT-1 bonds" and (ii) the administrator "exceeded his powers and authority...after the bank was reconstructed on March 13, 2020".

In fact, the judgement records that at one time the RBI had, in a note to the Central government, "proposed to balance the interests of all stakeholders and in fact proposed conversion of the said AT-1 Bonds and a decision was taken to write-down the same". Note, a "write-down" (value reduced) is different from "write off" (value reduced to zero).

So, why did the RBI not act against the administrator and undo the write-off? This will remain a mystery and the role of the Central government, directly or indirectly, can't be ruled out. Interestingly, the judgement notes that the "administrator" didn't write off the first tranche of Rs 280 crore of AT1 bonds (at 10.5% interest) issued in 2013 and offered "no reason" to explain "this discrimination".

The Yes Bank's misdeeds extended to its AT1 bonds too.

On April 21, 2021, SEBI issued an order holding the bank guilty of (i) "fraudulent acts" in facilitating "down-sale" of AT1 bonds issued in 2016 and 2017, from the institutional investors to its own "hapless and unsuspecting customers" (ii) "lured" the customers through "misrepresentation and fraud", making some of them "to alter their position from FDs to these AT1 bonds" by presenting the AT1 bonds as "super FDs" yielding much higher interests. The SEBI further said this "devious scheme to dump the AT1 bonds" continued till 2019 (iii) despite knowing "that the financial status of YBL had become unviable", leading to "writing down of these AT1 bonds". It imposed heavy penalty, including Rs 25 crore on Yes Bank.

The SEBI found 1,346 individuals had bought the AT1 bonds (Rs 697 crore), of which 1,311 (more than 97%) were "existing customers" of the bank (who invested Rs 663 crore); 277 customers had their FDs "prematurely closed" for this (Rs 80 crore) and many of these customers were "of advanced age of more than 70/80/90 years".

Yes Bank has not challenged this SEBI order (Bombay High Court order said).

Write-off of AT1 violates RBI guidelines and Yes Bank protocol

Coming back to the write-off, the Yes Bank told the NSE and BSE in March 2020 that it went by the Clause 2.15 of the RBI's 2015 "Master Circular – Basel III Capital Regulations". But this Clause says: "If the relevant authorities decide to reconstitute a bank or amalgamate a bank...the AT1 instruments will be fully converted/written-down permanently before amalgamation/reconstitution in accordance with these rules." The RBI also provides the protocol for this "fully converted/written-down" (called the "order of seniority") in Clause 2.10, which says: "If a bank goes into liquidation before the AT1 instruments have been written-down/converted, these instruments will absorb losses in accordance with the order of seniority indicated in the offer document and as per usual legal provisions governing priority of charges."

The "offer document" here is the Yes Bank's "Information Memorandum" for AT1 bond offers – a statutory contract. The Bombay High Court says, Clause 4 of this document lays out that "the claims of the bond holders in the bonds shall be superior to the claims of the investors in equity shares and perpetual non-cumulative prescribes shares issued by the bank".

Thus, the AT1 bond investors should have got protection (conversion to equity or write down), not written off. Now the Yes Bank and RBI have challenged the Bombay High Court order, which is now being heard by the Supreme Court.

In this (SLP), the RBI has justified the write-off (contrary to its own "final scheme" of reconstruction and its 2015 guidelines) by arguing: (a) so that "the capital provided by the public sector is not diluted" (b) the SBI "may not have even agreed to invest the money if the loss absorbent bonds were not to be written off" and (c) there would be "dilution" of SBI's money. In an earlier affidavit to the Madras High Court, the RBI had said (d) the AT1 investors "reaped high financial rewards" earlier and hence, shouldn't "shift the onus of loss upon RBI".

At the time of its takeover by the RBI, the SBI and seven other banks had pumped in Rs 10,000 crore, of which the SBI's share was Rs 6,050 crore. The AT1 bonds written off were worth Rs 8,415 crore.

Turmoil in Europe over AT1 bonds

A similar thing has happened in the Credit Suisse case.

The Swiss authorities turned the protocol upside down, writing off $17.5 billion of AT1 bonds but ensuring that the equity holders get $3.23 billion (UBS's acquisition price), that is 37% of $8.7 billion market value of Credit Suisse at the time.

The Swiss regulator FINMA, in its communication on March 23, 2023 said what was the protocol: "AT1 instruments in Switzerland are designed in such a way that they are written down or converted into Common Equity Tier 1 capital before the equity capital of the bank concerned is completely used up or written down." This is what is the case with Yes Bank too (a global practice).

And then it employed clever wordplay to justify the reversal: "The AT1 instruments issued by Credit Suisse contractually provide that they will be completely written down in a "Viability Event", in particular if extraordinary government support is granted. As Credit Suisse was granted extraordinary liquidity assistance loans secured by a federal default guarantee on 19 March 2023 ("viability event"), these contractual conditions were met for the AT1 instruments issued by the bank."

Seemingly unconvinced by its own argument, it added that the reversal could happen because of the Swiss government's Emergency Ordinance of March 19, 2023: "The Ordinance also authorises FINMA to order the borrower and the financial group to write down Additional Tier 1 capital."

Expectedly, the move spooked the European AT1 bond market (valued at $250-275 billion), forcing the EU banking regulators and Bank of England to immediately distance themselves (although they welcomed the Swiss move to save the bank) and declared unequivocal support for their AT1 investors.

On the very next day, March 20, 2023, the EU regulators, of which the Swiss FNMA is not a part, said: "...common equity instruments are the first ones to absorb losses, and only after their full use would Additional Tier 1 be required to be written down. This approach has been consistently applied in past cases and will continue to guide the actions of the SRB (Single Resolution Board) and ECB (European Central Bank) banking supervision in crisis interventions."

The Bank of England too said the UK "has a clear statutory order" in which shareholders and creditors would bear losses in which AT1 instruments "rank ahead" of equity investments, adding that it had followed this process in the unwinding of SVB's UK unit.

True, neither the status of GSIB (tighter oversight and monitoring) nor the Basel III norms (tighter banking norms and higher capital mobilisation through AT1 bond) could save the Credit Suisse from collapsing. As explained earlier in the Fortune India article "SVB Bank crisis: India's vulnerabilities and the deep malaise in US banking system", the real causes lie in the broader (neoliberal) economic framework governing the world; mere tinkering like GSIB, Basel III, AT1 bond wouldn't help. The turmoil over AT1 bonds is more like a shadow-boxing.

Apr 4, 2023

***

National Champions: Costs and Benefits Of India's New Growth Model

By the very concept, "national champions" are state-backed, too big to fail, too powerful for normal laws, scrutiny, regulatory oversights and too big to compete with

The Hindenburg report has brought a sharper focus to the term "national champions" in public discourses. Economist and political scientists from India and abroad are increasingly using this term to explain India's new growth model driven by a few big private business groups to take the country into the next level of growth.

The term doesn't find a mention in official documents or public pronouncements of officials and hence, the exact concept, its economic logic or goals can't be explained accurately. All that is known is that India wants to build four-five big SBI-like banks to meet growing investment needs and launched PLI to "develop global champions" in manufacturing (including food processing).

But economists and experts are taking note of government policies and actions and cues from similar global experiences to describe what it means. At least five descriptions of "national champions" have emerged in the past one month: (i) "large business groups with plans to invest heavily in line with government plans and incentives" (ii) "large private oligopolistic conglomerates" controlling "significant parts of the old economy" (iii) a "model where the government picks a few large conglomerates to implement its development priorities" and (iv) "essentially family-dominated multi-sector business groups" which flourish "under government patronage" – likening it to the "gilded age" of America (19th century "robber barons"), South Korea ("chaebols" of 20th century) and China (state-owned enterprises or SOEs of 21st century) and describing the current Indian phase of growth as "India's gilded age". Indonesia, under President Suharto (1967-98), also qualifies for championing "national champions".

The more specific one describes it as (v) a growth model that Prime Minister Narendra Modi "honed" first as Gujarat chief minister (2001 to 2014) which "was premised on the state giving a set of corporations concessions on land, on capital, on tax, on environmental and building clearance in exchange for setting up shop". What India is seeing now is "scaling up of that model".

All these narrations involve the Adani group, though not limited to it, but none is to commend India but warn against the dangers of this model. Here is what they are telling.

High cost of incubating "national champions"

Economist Nauriel Roubini, who forewarned the impending US housing market collapse in 2006, which led to the 2007-08 Global Recession, recognizes that "in some ways" such concentration of economic power (with private businesses) has served India well, but then goes on to warn: "…the dark side of this system is that these conglomerates have been able to capture policymaking to benefit themselves. This has had two broad, harmful effects: it is stifling innovation and effectively killing early-stage startups and domestic entrants in key industries; and it is changing the government's Make in India programme into a counterproductive, protectionist scheme."

He also notes that the fallout of the Adani-Hindenburg episode doesn't seem to extend beyond the group but it "does have macro implications for India's institutional robustness and global investors' perceptions of India", reminding that: "The Asian financial crisis of the 1990s demonstrated that, over time, the partial capture of economic policy by crony capitalist conglomerates will hurt productivity growth by hampering competition, inhibiting Schumpeterian "creative destruction" and increasing inequality." His advice: "It is thus in Modi's long-term interest to ensure that India does not go down this path. The country's long-term success ultimately depends on whether it can foster and sustain a growth model that is competitive, dynamic, sustainable, inclusive and fair."

Economist Amartya Lahiri lists four "clear problems" of promoting "national champions": (a) it creates the potential for markets and regulators to treat them as "too big to fail", opening the door to "market hysteria, delayed discovery of problems and spillovers of sectoral problems into systemic shocks" (b) market concentration "often be bad for efficiency and productivity at the economy-wide level" (c) "need" to provide "access to additional cash flows" to one engaged in infrastructure development, given the long gestation period and low returns, but risks turning the country into "an industrial oligarchy" and (d) the "optics" of an "uneven playing field" can become "significant deterrent" for foreign investors.

Economist Pranab Bardhan doesn't use the term "national champions" but flags the "symbiotic relationship" between business and politics at the highest level in India, giving rise to "crony capitalist oligarchy". He points out that this means "extreme inequality and corporate concentration", rules and goalposts changed midgame, predatory pricing and waiver of environmental regulations allowed in an economy already saddled with low accounting and regulatory standards. He warns: "India's crony oligarchy is likely to keep much of the economy trapped in a low-productivity mire for quite some time.

Political scientist Ashutosh Varshney draws parallel with the South Korean "chaebols" (which he considers more appropriate for the "gilded age" phenomenon) who produced global leaders like Samsung, Hyundai and LG. That model worked because they were "heavily international trade-oriented", competed with world best producers, international competition provided a "disciplinary check" on their businesses, generating "huge efficiencies". They produced cell phones, computers, electronics, semiconductors and auto, capturing significant global export markets for their country. In contrast, the Adani group is "mostly in non-tradable sectors" and the efficiency gains that come from international trade are "missing".

A 2013 paper of the London School of Business ("Turning national champions into global brands") says despite their ubiquity "many national champions have historically, from a financial perspective, performed poorly" and that "for every success, there are multiple failures". For "national champions" to succeed, it says, there must be other requirements: consistent and predictable policies with openness, accountability, honesty in decision-making and action-taking; short-term state-support, conditional on market performance and fostering competition etc. The last one is particularly important as 2022 World Bank analysis of China's phenomenal industrial success attributed it to policies ensuring "market "competition".

It is precisely these kinds of undemocratic protections (from parliamentary debate and scrutiny) and lax regulatory oversights (by the government and the SEBI) which causes further doubts in the "national champions" model.

True, India has serious fiscal constraints, particularly to push infrastructure projects which costs more, takes longer time to complete and produce low returns. The GDP growth is slipping from 9.1% in FY22 to 7% in FY23 and 6.4% in FY24 (BE) and private investment (private GFCF) has fallen drastically from 16.8% of the GDP in FY08 to 10.1% in FY22, despite the corporate tax cut of 2019 and the PLI of 2020. But the "dark side" of this model castes a long shadow calling for extreme caution and mindfulness.

Mar 23, 2023

***

Why are Globally Systemically Important Banks Like Credit Suisse Failing?

Current bank runs in the US and Switzerland are the failures of the new global financial order put in place after the 2007-08 financial crisis, ironically, to avoid such eventualities

The financial world is in a tizzy with the collapse of Credit Suisse, a "too big to fail" Global Systemically Important Bank (GSIB), which is least expected to go down. Coming as it did within ten days of the first of four mid-size US bank runs – from Silicon Valley Bank (SVB) to Signature Bank, Silvergate Bank and First Republic Bank – this turn of events is bound to shake public trust in banking and regulatory oversight more than we think, notwithstanding the immediate relief provided by their respective governments, regulating authorities and other banks with a rare joint statement from six central banks (from the US to the UK, Europe, Canada, Japan and Switzerland) to boost the flow of US dollars.

It is all the more shocking because Credit Suisse was being tracked and monitored by multiple regulators and institutions across the world simultaneously and it was supposed to follow stringent banking and disclosure norms of Basel III as a designated global SIB. Its failure actually marks the failure of the new global financial order put in place after the 2007-08 financial crisis to particularly avoid recurrence.

What is a Global Systemically Important Bank?

Following the 2007-08 financial crisis, the G-20 leaders set up the Financial Stability Board (FSB) in 2009 as a successor to the Financial Stability Forum (FSF) with a broadened mandate to ensure international financial stability. Starting with 2011, the FSB designates 29 to 30 banks as GSIBs every single year in consultation with the Basel Committee on Banking Supervision (BCBS) and national authorities.

The FSB is headquartered in Switzerland's Basel city; Credit Suisse is based in another Switzerland city, Zurich – a global hub of banking and finance. Basel III (which takes its name after Switzerland's same Basel city) containing various rules on capital and liquidity also came up in 2010 and is an improvement on the Basel II framed in response to the 2007-08 crisis (improved further in 2017).

The FSB's first list of 2011 made the significance of designating "too big to fail" (TBTF) financial institutions – called Systemically Important Financial Institutions (SIFIs) at the time, intending to separately identify banks, insurers as well as non-bank non-insurers which later metamorphosed into GSIBs. Its report said: "SIFIs are financial institutions whose distress or disorderly failure, because of their size, complexity and systemic interconnectedness, would cause significant disruption to the wider financial system and economic activity. To avoid this outcome, authorities have all too frequently had no choice but to forestall the failure of such institutions through public solvency support.

As underscored by this crisis (2007-08), this (failure) has deleterious consequences for private incentives and for public finances. Addressing the "too-big-to-fail" problem requires a multipronged and integrated set of policies."

Notice how the concept of the bailout was institutionalised ("through public solvency support") in the new global financial order.

Credit Suisse has been on the GSIB list since 2011. Ironically, the last list naming it as a GSIB was published on November 21, 2022 – 119 days before its takeover by UBS was announced (March 19, 2023) – indicating the futility of all the tracking, monitoring and tougher banking and disclosure norms that the status of GSIB entails, like (a) higher capital buffer (b) total loss-absorbing capacity (TLAC) (c) group-wide resolution planning and regular resolvability assessments and (d) higher risk management functions, risk data aggregation capabilities, risk governance and internal controls.

The TBTF was the logic the US government used to nationalise Fannie Mae and Freddie Mac, provide liquidity support and facilitate the takeover of Bear Stearns, AIG, Lehman Brothers etc. during the 2007-08 crisis. But the concept of TBTF goes back to 1984 when another such occasion arose involving another bank, the Continental Illinois National Bank. Literature shows, TBTF arises out of institutions (practices and laws) such as bailouts, limited liability, regulatory forbearance, forgiving resolution procedures, deposit insurance, lenders of last resort, and preferential treatment of large versus small banks.

Also note that a bailout is not a new concept but traces its history to Wall Street's first collapse in 1792 (231 years ago), which entailed a rescue act by the US government.

But the moot question remains unanswered: Why should a bank be allowed to grow to be TBTF or too big to pose systemic risk in the first place?

Duncan Watts, Columbia sociologist and network scientist, had argued in 2009 that instead of going by the regulators' judgment calls about systemic risks – which failed in the case of Lehman Brothers then and Credit Suisse now – a better approach "would be for regulators to routinely review firms and ask: "Is this company too big to fail?" If yes, the firm could be required to downsize or shed business lines until regulators were satisfied that its failure would no longer pose a risk to the whole system." His article was aptly titled "If Too Big to Fail? How About Too Big to Exist?"

Bail-in and bail-out

The US and Switzerland officials object to the use of world "bailout" (given the notoriety it acquired during the 2007-08 crisis for rewarding rather than punishing the bankers and other wrongdoers) but there is no escaping it now.

The US government has appointed the government-run Federal Deposit Insurance Corporation (FDIC) as "receiver", is facilitating mergers and takeovers along with regulators and also providing liquidity along with other banks to save its banks. President Biden has assured that all deposits are safe. Notwithstanding the claims of not bailing out, Amiyatosh Purnanandam, a US corporate economist who studies bank bailouts said: "If it looks like a duck, then probably it is a duck. This is absolutely a bailout, plain and simple."

The case with the Switzerland government is similar.

It has (i) brokered the takeover of Credit Suisse by another Swiss bank UBS at $3.3 billion (at a 60% discount to on $8.7 billion market value of Credit Suisse at the time) (ii) has given a guarantee of $9 billion to the USB against the potential loss from this takeover – more than the acquisition price and market value of the Credit Suisse ($3.3 billion and $8.7 billion, respectively) and also (iii) giving liquidity assistance of $108 billion.

There is another element in it, called "bail-in".

That is, the Credit Suisse bondholders have lost their entire $17 billion. This "bail-in" is the provision of depositors and bondholders forfeiting their money, which the Indian government wanted to bring in through the Financial Resolution and Deposit Insurance (FRDI) Bill of 2017 (proposing that in case a bank fails the depositors' money will be used to bail it out, as one of the resolution tools) but the idea was abandoned due to stiff resistance.

Credit Suisse's failure has been a long-drawn process.

Its market value was rapidly falling for about two years (from over 12 Swiss Franc in 2021 to about 2 in midweek and then to less than 1 now). The trigger was its large shareholder Saudi National Bank publicly refusing to pump in money last week, plunging its market value to a new record low.

Just days before the bank run, Credit Suisse reported (i) "material weakness" in its financial reporting for 2021 and 2022 – issues related to a "failure to design and maintain an effective risk assessment process to identify and analyse the risk of material misstatements" and various flaws in internal control and communication. This escape from detection for two years is strange given its status as a GSIB.

Further, this revelation came after a series of scandals involving investments, banking practices, management and worse in the past two-three years: (ii) in February 2023, it reported net loss of more than 7 billion Swiss francs for 2022 and warned of a substantial loss in 2023 (iii) it was convicted in cocaine-related money laundering which involved a Bulgarian gang (iv) a Bermuda court ordered compensation of $600 million due to fraud committed by its former advisor (v) Panama Papers-like investigations into its secret accounts (leaked data on thousands of customers) (vi) lost $5.5 billion when US family office Archegos Capital Management defaulted in March 2021 (highly leveraged bets on certain technology stocks backfired) (vii) forced to freeze $10 billion of supply chain finance funds in March 2021 when British financier Greensill Capital collapsed and Swiss regulators rebuked it for "serious" failings in handling business (viii) CEO Tidjane Thiam was forced to quit in March 2020 in a spy scandal, after an investigation found the bank hired private detectives to spy on its former head of wealth management Iqbal Kahn after he left for arch rival UBS.

Nouriel Roubini, known for accurately predicting the 2007-08 Great Recession, warned that the SVB's collapse had had a "ripple effect" and that Credit Suisse could prove to be a "Lehman moment" (when one institutional failure spreads to another).

Cost of undoing or lack of banking reforms

The US adopted the Glass-Steagall Act of 1933 following the 1929 Great Depression (sparked by banking failures, stock market crash), effectively separating commercial banking (traditional banking) from investment banking (not traditional banking) to restrict bank credits being used for speculative activities (stock market) and instead direct it to productive use in industry, commerce and agriculture. Essentially, this prevented the use of retail deposits (or bonds) to fund investment banking activities. This was reversed in 1999 by the Clinton administration, and it played up in the 2007-08 crisis again. But the situation remains unchanged yet (although in 2020 the US Congress made a strong case for breaking the monopolies of tech giants Apple, Amazon, Facebook and Google).

In contrast, though equally harmed by the 1929 crisis, Europe did not go the whole hog for such separation. Most of it adopted the "universal banking" model in which both commercial and investment banking went hand-in-hand, which endures. In a 2019 reform ("ring-fencing"), the UK requires banking groups with more than £25 billion of retail deposits to split their retail and investment banking activities into legally separate subsidiaries. Credit Suisse, as well as the USB, are both universal banking entities.

The other is the Dodd-Frank Act in 2010, adopted by the US after the 2007-08 crisis, which applied tougher regulatory oversights to smaller banks (asset threshold of $50 billion). This was weakened (the threshold was raised to $250 billion) in May 2018 by the Trump administration. Ironically, Federal Reserve chair Jerome Powell, who was part of this dilution is now fighting to save the SVB and other banks that escaped scrutiny precisely because their assets were less than the $250 billion threshold.

Food for thought

Now consider a few things going forward.

Why not break banks and companies "too big" too big to pose systemic risk, as the Columbia sociologist suggested, instead of celebrating them as "too big to fail" or GSIBs and then bailing them out "through public solvency support"? Multiple such entities have crashed in the past 15 years – from the Lehman Brothers, Fannie Mae, Freddie Mac, Bear Stearns, AIG to Credit Suisse. Why shift the risks of their failures resulting out of their unethical and illegal acts to the public (banks or individuals through tax)?

As for the other factors for these bank runs, why not revert back to more prudent interest rates, rather than near zero for long periods of time; tighter monetary supply, instead of creating debt-fuelled enterprises through liquidity infusion; higher corporate tax rates than individual tax rates; tighter regulation on stock markets' speculative activities, rather than let them be called 'casino' and 'ponzi' scheme; tighter capital flow, rather than the deregulated or lightly regulated and unhindered global flow of capital; lifting the corporate veil on secret banks, tax havens and shell companies and tighter regulatory oversight, rather than a lax one?

Remember, the *Golden Age of Capitalism was during the 1950s-1970s* when both developed and developing countries registered the highest ever GDP growth (3.8% and 3%, respectively), the average top corporate tax rate was 70-80% in the US and 99.25-80% in the UK and there was tight control on capital flow and banking activities.

Mar 23, 2023

***

Why Hindenburg Report, Short-Selling are a Blessing in Disguise

Global evidence shows short-selling is an efficient tool to discipline financial markets and promote good corporate governance practices

Short-selling is a *legitimate* trading practice all over the world, including India. But the meltdown in the Adani group's stocks following the US-based investment research firm Hindenburg's report (January 24, 2023) has brought it more infamy than appreciation for its role in accelerating price corrections, checking pricing anomalies and facilitating liquidity. The dangers of overvaluations creating bubbles in the stock market is far too well known to the world for nearly a hundred years – from the 1929 Great Depression to the 2007-08 Great Recession – to blindside one to condemn short-selling as either predatory or immoral.

There is no disputing that the Indian stock market is way too overvalued compared to global peers, and for a long time. Overvaluation may reflect excessive exuberance of investors for various reasons but more often than not, it is also a function of weak financial fundamentals, accounting and auditing manipulations and other bad corporate governance practices – which eventually causes the bubbles to burst. This is a live experience.

Here is how overvalued the Indian stock market is.

Overvalued Indian stock market

The Economic Survey of 2022-23 says the Nifty50 with its PE multiple (price to earnings ratio) of 21.8x in 2022 was "expensive" compared to its global peers – the PEs of MSCI World (capturing large and mid-caps of 23 developed economies) was 17.3x and MSCI EM (capturing those of 24 emerging economies) 14.6x in the same year. It also shows how overvalued it was in the previous five years between 2017-2021: PE of Nifty50 averaged 27.4x, against MSCI World's 19.4x and MSCI EM's 14.6x.

In 2023, the trend endures.

As on January 31, 2023, the PEs of MSCI World and MSCI EM stood at 18.18x and 12.83x, respectively. But the Nifty50's PE was 20.73x at the time. Even after the Hindenburg report came, the Nifty50's PE averaged 20.86x at the end of February 2023 – higher, not lower, than it was before January 24, 2023. One may take satisfaction in the fact that the meltdown in Adani group companies didn't dent the broader market and also that the Nifty50 has substantially corrected itself from a PE multiple of 38x during January-April 2021 and the peak of more than 40x during February-March 2021.

If the Adani group companies are considered (Hindenburg report alleged seven of its 10 companies were overvalued by 85%), there has been a sharp decline. The PE multiple of its flagship Adani Enterprises has fallen from 320.8x on January 24 2023 to 75.7x on February 28 (the Adani Gas' PE falling the most, from 844x to 140.8x, during the same period). Some experts do see further downside risks in these stocks because of its high debt and liquidity constraints, for example. Just for comparison, the Ambani group's flagship Reliance Industries' PE was far low at 25x at the end of February 2023.

If you think the Economic Survey of 2022-23 was worried about overvaluation, banish it. It was actually celebrating with phrases like "India outperformed its peers during FY23 (April-December)" and "Indian Benchmark Indices witnessed swift recovery". The reference here is to both Nifty50 and S&P BSE Sensex. The report didn't explain why the overvaluation or what steps should be taken to tame it.

The capital market regulator Stock Exchanges and Securities Board of India (SEBI) is not known to be concerned about overvaluations, not even after the Hindenburg report hit. All it said was that it was looking into the "unusual price movement in the stocks of a business conglomerate". The RBI, the other key regulator, has kept quiet too even though, many times in the past, its Governor Shaktikanta Das warned against the uncalled-for market buoyancy. During the boom amidst all-round economic ruin in FY21 (GDP growth plunged to -6.6%), he reminded that there was (i) "disconnect" between 'real' economy and stock market and that such booms posed "risks to financial stability" and (ii) market was "buoyant" because of "so much liquidity" and the boom was "definitely disconnected with the real economy". Not just in India, stock markets boomed across the world when millions were losing their lives and livelihoods, sending the world into a tailspin (-3.1% fall in global output).

How is short-selling relevant here?

Short-selling as counter to market manipulation

Short-selling of equity is not very well known in India (except in F&O where hedging is intrinsic). The SEBI allowed institutional investors to short-sell for the first time in 2007 – until then only retail investors were allowed. Even then, the Hindenburg-type episode is a first.

The SEBI defines short-selling as "selling a stock which the seller does not own at the time of trade". It involves selling a borrowed stock by an investor who expects the price to fall and when that happens, the investor re-purchases the very stock at the lower price to return it to the original owner – the difference is pocketed as profit. But if the price goes up, the investor books a loss.

There is nothing unethical or immoral about short-selling; profit-making underlines investment in the stock market. Not to forget, many capitalist-liberal economists, like Keynes, Stiglitz and Krugman, have likened the stock market to "casino". Before allowing institutional investors to short-sell, a SEBI discussion paper of 2005 argued why it was needed.

It said: (i) short-selling was allowed "in most countries and in particular, in all developed securities markets" (ii) vibrant market should "necessarily provide" for lending and borrowing of securities, enabling investors to earn returns on "idle securities" (iii) most jurisdictions recognise that it had contributed "significantly to market liquidity" (iv) it provided "safeguards" to "prevent any abusive/manipulative market practices" and (v) there was "no level playing field" between various classes of investors without it.

There have been many misgivings about short-selling, which include its (a) potential to destabilise market (b) exacerbate market falls and (c) lead to manipulative activities etc. Therefore, the SEBI allowed 'regulated' short-selling for institutional investors. It put several checks: (i) ban on "naked" short-selling (selling without first obtaining (verifiably) the borrowed stocks leading to delivery failures) (ii) ban on day-trading (squaring-off transactions intra-day) (iii) "framework" regulating lending and borrowing of securities and (iv) deterrents against brokers for failing to deliver securities at the time of settlement. Market volatility is also checked through (v) circuit breakers.

But bans on short-selling are not unknown.

It happened during the 2007-08 stock market meltdown in the US and elsewhere, but not in India as the SEBI and the government stood their ground. The US did it, regretted it and reversed it. The chairman of its regulator Securities and Exchange Commission (SEC) Christopher Cox declared that they "would not do it again" ("the costs appear to outweigh the benefits") and revealed how corporates pressured him not only to reinstate the ban but shut stock market altogether.

More recently, it happened in 2020 when the pandemic hit. Some European countries and India did so (during March 23 to October 29, 2020) while the market was on the downswing. But soon, stock markets boomed in India and across the world to unprecedented levels (moderation happened in early 2022 because of high inflation, high interest rate and the Russia-Ukraine war).

This time, it provoked immediate and strong reaction from the World Federation of Exchanges (WFE), of which the NSE is also a member.

Banning short-selling hurts market

In a paper circulated in April 2020, the WFE presented

the findings of global studies to conclude that a ban actually does the opposite of what is intended. It argued:

- Evidence "almost unanimously" shows that a ban is "disruptive" and hurts market as it "reduces liquidity, increases price inefficiency and hampers price discovery".
- Bans have "negative spillover effects" on other markets, like option markets.
- During price decline and heightened volatility, short-sellers do not behave differently from any other traders, and contribute less to price declines than regular 'long' sellers.
- Bans are "more deleterious" to markets having high presence of small stocks, low levels of fragmentation and fewer alternatives to short-selling.
- Emerging markets should be "particularly wary" of bans on short-selling.

In 2021, a Yale University study said the same: "... research has consistently shown that banning short selling during stretches of particularly volatile equity market activity intensifies the volatility. Such prohibitions impede investors from determining accurate prices of assets and reduce market liquidity. Moreover, short-selling bans in one market can increase volatility in other markets as some investors try to circumvent the ban."

Why India stands to benefit from Hindenburg-type act

All those arguments are not the only reasons why short-selling should be promoted in India, rather than condemned.

India's market behaviour is one-sided and conducive to over valuations and bubbles: Buy a stock, hold it for long and then sell to make money. Tax policy encourages this too. For years, income from capital gain from stocks was tax-exempt if the stock was sold after 12 months (long-term capital gain) but not if sold before 12 months (short-term capital gain). From FY19, this has changed and long-term capital gains are taxed too but at 10% for gains over Rs 1 lakh, against 15% for short-term capital gains.

Price rigging, financial and accounting frauds and bad corporate governance practices (shell companies, tax havens and a maze of subsidiaries to evade tax, round-trip funds, hide related-party transactions, insider-trading, high debt and masking debts by pledging overvalued stocks and violation of 25% public float etc.) don't get the attention they deserve in spite of the fact that these are illegal and criminal activities.

India has seen a series of big-ticket stock market and corporate frauds in the new millennium – from the Ketan Parekh to Chitra Ramakrishnan episodes; from the Satyam Computers to PNB, PMC, ICICI-Videocon, IL&FS, DHFL, HDIL, ABG Shipyard scams involving corporate and banking frauds and the list of fugitive business tycoons is long: Vijay Mallya, Nirav Modi, Mehul Choksi, Jatin Mehta, Sandesara brothers etc. Barring a few, these events reflect massive systemic failure over a long time.

The current political climate too is against checks and balances or scrutiny and action. Hindenburg sparked a strong backlash: denial and 'nationalist' counter-narratives; refusal to allow parliamentary debate (whatever was heard was during the motion of thanks to the President's address) and parliamentary probe (JPC) and comments from several experts branding its action as "predatory" and inimical to India's nation-builders.

Short-selling is recognised as an efficient tool for accelerating price corrections, checking pricing anomalies and facilitating liquidity. By exposing the underlying fundamental weaknesses in corporate entities, it also promotes good governance and aid regulatory oversight. It may not be the panacea for all the ails afflicting financial markets but useful nonetheless.

Mar 13, 2023

***

Games Shell Companies and Tax Havens Play

They are conduits for money laundering, hiding money and properties and evading tax, thereby making a mockery of corporate governance.

Shell companies and tax havens are back in news. Notwithstanding the merits in charges and counter-charges around the Hindenburg-Adani episode, few will dispute the continued activities of shell companies and tax havens in India and across the world. These two entities merit closer attention because their presence is a threat to most, if not all, oversight mechanisms and good corporate governance. Essentially, they facilitate money laundering, hide financial transactions and properties and assist in tax evasion by exploiting legal and regulatory loopholes and more often than not, work in tandem.

In other words, shell companies (corporate entities with little business on ground) and tax havens (secretive and zero or near-zero tax jurisdictions) are the black holes of financial world – which is well recognised for many years. India is cracking down on shell companies for years and introduced anti-tax evasion General Anti Avoidance Rules (GAAR) in the Income Tax Act of 1961 in 2012, but it became operational a decade later, from April 2022.

India is also a signatory (along with about 135 other countries) to the global anti-tax evasion initiative, OECD-G20's Action Plan on Base Erosion and Profit Shifting (BEPS), which too started in 2012 and a decade later, it remains a work-in-progress. Except, on February 2, 2023, the BEPS released a "technical guidance" to implement 15% minimum corporate tax on "large" corporations. The US passed this (15% minimum tax) in mid-2022, which too comes into effect in 2023. This is the first big bang move, out of many in the BEP's list.

Why such a lackadaisical attitude persists is not difficult to fathom, even when the BEPS says "$240 billion are lost annually due to tax avoidance by multinational companies". A 2019 IMF-University of Copenhagen study found $15 trillion (37% or equal to combined GDP of China and Germany then) of the total $40 trillion global FDIs were "phantom" FDIs, channelled through tax haven-based shell companies just to avoid tax.

Therefore, it is time to re-examine how credible India's efforts have been to deal with the twin menace.

What empty shells and tax havens mean for corporate governance

To understand the impact of shell companies and tax havens in India, recollect that they are conduits to 85% or more FDI inflows and outflows.

This would mean, so far as FDIs goes, (a) little transparency, accountability and regulatory oversight and (b) a litany of bad governance practices like: (i) tax avoidance and evasion (revenue and profit shifting) (ii) unhindered flow of unaccounted (black) money (iii) round-tripping (iv) related-party transactions (v) insider trading

(vi) stock manipulations (vii) maze of subsidiaries and associate companies to avoid detection and (viii) violation of 25% public float the SEBI mandates.

If government support (state capture) is available to a corporate using shell companies and tax havens, this would further mean (ix) crony capitalism and (x) regulatory laxity (in detection and investigation of corporate frauds) or regulatory capture. These are recipe for (xi) bigger economic disasters (stock market bursts and damage to investors and 'real' sectors growth).

Indestructible empty corporate shells

At first glance, the very talk of shell companies sounds surrealistic because India is actively purging them for years.

Three big pushes came since 2016. One, a series of investigative reports of 2016-2021, popularly known as 'Panama Papers', 'Paradise Papers' and 'Pandora Papers', exposed the role of empty corporate shells and tax havens in money laundering, hiding money and properties, tax evasion and other financial frauds and on each occasion, India ordered "multi-agency" probes.

Two, when banks and shadow banks started facing financial frauds and began to collapse one after the other, beginning in 2018 – PMC Bank, Punjab National Bank, ICICI Bank, Yes Bank, Lakshmi Vilas Bank, IL&FS, HDIL, DHFL etc. – hundreds of empty shells tumbled out of the woodwork. Central agencies like the CBI, Income Tax Department (ITD), Enforcement Directorate (ED) and Serious Fraud Investigation Office (SFIO) had a tough time chasing them.

Three, action had begun with the crackdown on

black money with the demonetisation of 2016 (99.3% banned currencies returned to banks, the rest locked in legal cases or with Nepali citizens and financial institutions) but empty shells stayed. The Prime Minister said so in his national address on August 15, 2017: "Post demonetisation, the reports from data mining astonishingly revealed that there are 3 lakh shell companies dealing in Hawala transactions. Can anyone imagine? Out of these 3 lakh shell companies, registration of 1.75 lakh companies were cancelled."

On February 6, 2023, Lok Sabha was told that in three years since 2019, 1,12,509 shell companies were closed. More had been shut in the interim (2017-18). Presumably, none would have survived till 2023 but when taxmen went to the BBC offices in Delhi and Mumbai for "survey" on February 14, 2023, shell companies hit the headlines. The taxmen were looking for them, among others.

Not just that, amidst the crackdown, an investigative report of 2019 revealed that a big corporate house had "at least 122 companies" with "little or no business" located at "the same address" in Mumbai. This was years after the same corporate house was alleged to be linked to shell companies named after animals (Tiger Traders, Zebra Consultants, Parrot Consultants, Swan Telecom) during the 2G spectrum trial of 2013.

Yet, no Indian law defines a shell company.

As late as February 6, 2023, the Centre told so to the Lok Sabha (in the same reply mentioned earlier), explaining that what it "struck off" were domestic companies "which had not filed their Financial Statements and/or Annual Returns for a continuous period of two immediately preceding financial years". It was closer to defining shell companies in its reply of July 18, 2022. It said, it "normally refers to a company without active business operation or significant assets, which in some cases are used for illegal purposes such as tax evasion, money laundering, obscuring ownership, benami properties etc."

The problem with shell companies is that many are registered with tax havens and tax havens are too powerful to be touched. Apart from the CBI, ITD and ED, regulatory bodies like SEBI and RBI also know about them but no tangible effect is visible.

Mighty tax havens

British tax expert Nicholas Shaxson wrote in his book "Treasure Islands: Tax Havens and the Men Who Stole the World": "...tax havens are projects of the world's rich and powerful people. And there's no group richer and powerful than the rich and powerful". He and many other experts have pointed out how tax havens, rich and powerful countries like the US and UK, big banks and big accounting, auditing and consulting firms are actively involved with tax haven activities.

Besides, India's own policies of promoting private business and free capital flows (FDI and FPI/FII) come in the way.

Here are a few examples.

The Department for Promotion of Industry and Internal Trade (DPIIT) data shows, between April 2000 and June 2022 (22 fiscals), more than 86% of FDI came through 20 known tax havens – 49% through Mauritius and Singapore; 9.2% through the US; 5.3% through the UK; 2.4% each through Cayman Islands and the UAE; 2% through Cyprus 2% and 1.5% through Switzerland. Not only this.

On average, 85% of FDI outflows from India is also through ten known tax havens during nine fiscals of FY14-FY22 – the RBI reports show.

Ironically, though tax havens have zero or near-zero tax, yet, India has Double Taxation Avoidance Agreement (DTAA) with those very tax havens for years, turning DTAAs into Double Non-Taxation Agreements (DNTAs) in reality. More than 100 countries are listed on the Income Tax Department's website for DTAA.

India did rework the treaties with Mauritius, Cyprus and Singapore in 2016-2017 but this was half-hearted. Global anti-tax evasion group Tax Justice Network (TJN) analysed the reworked agreements with Mauritius and Singapore in 2019 to point out that while capital gains are taxed, other securities like exchange-traded derivatives, convertible or non-convertible debentures and mutual funds aren't, thus keeping the door partly open. Even then, these revisions had salutary effects, it said, as FDI flows from Mauritius slowed down but that from Singapore increased (due to Singapore's other strengths as a financial hub, such as availability of funds at lower rates, effective dispute resolution system, it said); FDI flows from the UK increased but from the Netherlands decreased though no revision had happened with them.

Mysteriously, no such DTAA revision with other tax havens was heard of thereafter. Given that the TJN listed and ranked 70 tax havens for 2021, it is open for shell companies to shift to other tax havens to pump funds in and out.

The only other tool available to India is the GAAR, which requires companies to disclose "impermissible avoidance arrangement" and give their details in tax audit reports. Since it was operationalised from April 2022 it is too early to know how it works.

Notice how all these issues are in the air in the past few weeks.

Audit failure is kept aside as auditing system comes with in-built conflicts of interest. Companies pay for their own audit ('he who pays the piper calls the tune') and so, audit failures don't need shell companies and tax havens. It was so spectacularly demonstrated by the overnight collapses of Satyam Computers in India and Enron Corporation in the US not very long ago. As banking frauds tumbled out in India since 2018, many such instances tumbled out.

Feb 28, 2023

***

States' Fiscal Space Rapidly Shrinking, Here's Why...

Centre is tightening hold on state finances with 'one-size-fits-all' solutions

The Centre seems to have rediscovered the fiscal prudence of state governments by dramatically raising its 50-year interest-free loans to them under the "Scheme for Special Assistance to States for Capital Expenditure". Finance Minister Nirmala Sitharaman said the scheme was being extended for another year with "a significantly enhanced outlay of Rs 1.3 lakh crore" – up from Rs 1 lakh crore allocated in the Budget 2022.

The jump is dramatic, given that the revised estimate for FY23 brought the budgeted allocation of Rs 1 lakh crore down to Rs 76,000 crore – which jumps 71% to Rs 1.3 lakh crore. It is even more so given that the actual disbursements under the scheme for FY21 and FY22 were Rs 11,830 crore and Rs 14,186 crore, respectively (Economic Survey 2022-23). The higher allocation to states for capex goes hand-in-hand with the Centre's claim of raising its own capex by 33% in FY24 (BE) over FY23 (BE). But budget documents show, the Centre's "total" capex, that of the Centre and its public sector enterprises, for FY24 (BE) is 4.9% of the GDP – the same as the total "actual" capex in FY20.

What is even more impressive is that such faith in states' fiscal abilities comes after several months of severe criticism of their fiscal performance. It began with the RBI's "State Finances: A Risk Analysis" report of June 2022, which accused states of giving "non-merit freebies" and "off-budget" borrowing to cause "rising subsidy burdens" and debts going up to "4.5% of the GDP", even while their "own tax revenue" was on a "slowdown". Both the RBI and Centre pulled up banks for lending money to states with the RBI even asking the SBI and others to stop lending against future revenues – a normal banking practice. A national debate raged over states' fiscal profligacy, arising out of "freebies" and "revdi culture" into which the Supreme Court and the Election Commission were sucked in.

What changed in 2023?

From fiscal profligacy to fiscal prudence

The RBI corrected its assessment of states' fiscal performance in its January 2023 report, "State Finances: A Study of Budgets of 2022-23. This report lavished praise and reversed earlier charges. It commended states for "recognition of off-budget borrowings"; borrowing "within" the ceilings; "improved" fiscal health from "a sharp pandemic-induced deterioration in 2020-21"; "secured" financial positions "in terms lower deficit indicators (viz., gross fiscal deficit/ revenue deficit/primary deficit as a per cent of GDP)"; "increased" fiscal headroom (savings) for undertaking higher capex etc. At the same time, it advised states not to adopt the old pension scheme (OPS), unlike a strong warning against this in June 2022 report, by stating that this would eat into their "annual saving in fiscal resources".

Here are a few more revelations from the January 2023 report:

- States "have budgeted higher capital outlay" in FY23 (BE) than in FY20, FY21 and FY22.
- 19 of 31 states/UTs are revenue surplus in FY23 (BE) – up from 13 in FY22 (RE) and 7 in FY21.
- States' gross fiscal deficit (GFD) is budgeted to decline from 4.1% of the GDP in FY21 (first pandemic fiscal) to 3.4% in FY23 (BE).
- States' debt is budgeted to ease to 29.5% of the GDP in FY23 (BE), as against 31.1% in FY21 (pandemic fiscal), which is "still higher" than 20% recommended by FRBM Review Committee in 2018, warranting "prioritisation of debt consolidation".

Evidently, the RBI's June 2022 report was a rush job. It relied more on data of the pandemic fiscals (FY21 and FY22). In contrast, its January 2023 report looked more closely at the budget documents of FY23 (BE). By then, Finance Ministry think tank National Institute of Public Finance and Policy (NIPFP) had already examined the budget documents of states to produce a comprehensive study of 18 major states in August 2022 and presented a contrasting picture.

The NIPFP report showed only one state, Punjab, overshot the 15th Finance Commission's limits on debts in FY23 (BE) – as against ten states the RBI had named in June 2022, five of which had been called "highly stressed" (Bihar, Kerala, Punjab, Rajasthan, and West Bengal). The NIPFP also found that out of 18 major states, eight were revenue surplus and five had fiscal deficits of 3% or less (of their GSDPs).

The Economic Survey of 2022-23, released on January 31, 2023, echoed the assessments of the NIPFP and the revised RBI report. Besides, it said states' capital outlay was 31.7% more than what was budgeted for FY22 and commended the states' capex performance.

Increasing fiscal restrictions on states

Despite good fiscal performance of states, the Centre continues to impose restrictions on them.

While budgeting Rs 1.3 lakh crore loans for capex, two conditions have been put. One, the entire amount has to be spent by states "within 2023-24". Two, "a part will be conditional" and seven conditions are listed: (i) Scrapping old government vehicles (ii) urban planning reforms and actions (iii) financing reforms in urban local bodies to make them creditworthy for municipal bonds (iv) housing for police personnel above or as part of police stations (v) constructing Unity Malls (vi) children and adolescents' libraries and digital infrastructure and (vii) paying state share of capital expenditure of central schemes.

This is a continuation of recent practices.

While giving the interest-free loans in FY21 and FY22, the Centre made it conditional to (a) "privatisation/disinvestment" of state PSUs and (b) "monetisation/recycling of assets".

During the pandemic fiscal of FY21, the Centre allowed additional borrowing of 1% of GSDP to states (from 3% to 4%) with four "reforms": (a) "one-nation-one-ration" system (b) ease of doing business (c) power sector reforms and (d) urban local body reforms. Govind Rao, a member of the 14th Finance Commission, said such conditionalities was never heard of "in the history of independent India". In 2022, Centre reduced the borrowing limit to 3.5% of GSDP but allowed "extra borrowing" to the extent of contributions by employers and employees to the New Pension Scheme (NPS), implying that this was not for states opting for old pension scheme (OPS). This arrangement continues in FY24. This is aimed at Rajasthan, Punjab, Jharkhand, Chhattisgarh and Himachal Pradesh which have reverted to the OPS.

Strangling states for resources

The conditions reflect how the Centre is insisting on its own "reform" agenda from states and tightly regulating their finances after having discarded the "one-size-fits-all" policy paradigm with the dismantling of Planning Commission in 2014 and thereafter championing "cooperative federalism" while adopting the GST in 2017.

States are finding their fiscal space rapidly shrinking in many ways.

- With the GST, states lost rights to indirect taxes. From July 2022, GST Compensation was stopped. A NIPFP study of 2022 showed that the GST Compensation averaged 34% of the states' GST receipt (SGST) during FY18-FY21. Any talk of a fall in states "own tax" (as the RBI did in June 2022), therefore, is inappropriate.

- States are short-changed in devolving tax awarded by the 14th and 15th Finance Commissions – 42% and 41% of central taxes, respectively. During FY16 to FY24 (BE), the shortfall averages 8.9 percentage points – far higher than 4.6 percentage shortfall during the 12th and 13th Finance Commission periods (FY06 to FY15).

- States are short-changed by imposing more Cess and Surcharges, which are not shared with states. These taxes surged from 9% of Centre's gross tax revenue in FY15 to 13.6% in FY23 (RE) and budgeted at 12.6% for FY24.

- Centre restricts fiscal space of states by increasing central schemes (CS) and centrally sponsored schemes (CSS), reversing the UPA's early 2014 move to cut those and hand over the money to states. CS and CSS as percentage of the Centre's budget spending has risen from 40.5% in FY16 to 44.5% in FY23 (RE), and budgeted at 43.2% in FY24. This is contrary to "one-size-fits-all" approach discarded in 2014.

That is not all.

By converting the "subsidised" ration (PDS) to 62.5% of households under the National Food Security Act of 2013 to "free" from January 1, 2023 and mandating that the Centre alone will pay the entire money, states have been denied their space in this welfare programme. Earlier, states subsidised the "subsidised" PDS further.

All these developments are counter-intuitive, given that state governments have outperformed the Centre in every single fiscal parameter for a long time.

States outperform Centre in fiscal prudence

Here is what the Economic Survey of 2022-23, the RBI and budget documents say about the relative fiscal performances during the ten fiscals of FY14-FY23 (Centre's FY23 (RE) against states' FY23 (BE)).

- **Debts:** Centre and states both have crossed the FRBM's debt limits of 40% and 20% of the GDP, respectively. But Centre's average of 52% is 12 percentage points higher, against states' average of 25.9%, which is 5.9 percentage points higher.

- **Fiscal deficits:** Centre's average is 5% of GDP (above the FRBM limit of 3%) while states' average of 2.9% is below the FRBM limit of 3%.

- **Revenue deficits:** Centre averages 4.9% of GDP against states' 0.4%. 19 states/UTs are revenue surplus in FY23 (BE).

- **Capex:** Centre averages 1.9% of GDP against states' 3.4% (1.8 times higher).

Centre must not lose sight of the fact that constitutionally, India is a "Union of States", that is, it is a federal state rather than a unitary state and states are independent entities. Besides, fiscal independence and decentralisation of power are universally accepted good governance practices which are also essential for the realisation of the Centre's avowed goal of "cooperative federalism" and decentralised growth and development model.

Feb 15, 2023

***

Budget 2023: Why India Needs a Jobs Policy

The country's job crisis is structural and systemic; reliance on high growth and manufacturing has simply not worked.

Officially, India entered into "job-loss" growth period in 2017-18, with the Periodic Labour Force Survey (PLFS) revealing a 45-year high unemployment rate of 6.1% and the study of its unit-level data by the Azim Premji University revealing nine million job losses between 2011-12 and 2017-18 "for the first time in India's history".

Two years later in 2019-20, the country witnessed structural shifts in jobs. PLFS reports revealed agriculture›s share of jobs reversed that year, going up from 42.5% in 2018-19 to 45.6% in 2019-20 and 46.5% in 2020-21. Manufacturing›s share, on the other hand, went down from 12.1% to 11.2% and 10.9%, in corresponding years. Jobs also moved away from formal to informal and high productive, high income to low productive, low income and vulnerable ones. The best-quality jobs, «regular wages/salaried», shrank from 22.8% to 21.1% during 2017-18 and 2020-21, while vulnerable «self-employment» went up from 52.2% to 55.6% – with unpaid workers («helper in household enterprises») within this group going up from 13.6% to 17.3%. Even casual workers fell from 24.9% to 23.3% during the period.

These developments were predictable since India had gone through a long «job-less» growth phase. The 12th Five-Year Plan document made it official in 2013 by saying that five million jobs were lost in manufacturing between 2004-05 and 2009-10, although the total number of jobs went up by 2.76 million.

But, even as the Centre prepares for Budget 2023, little seems to have changed in terms of policies.

PROBLEM AREAS

● The Periodic Labour Force Survey (PLFS) doesn't directly reveal the number of jobs created or lost.	● The past four annual PLFS data (2017-18 to 2020-21) show worker-population rate and labour force participation rate rising and the unemployment rate falling, but doesn't explain how.	● This is important since India was reeling under the twin shocks of demonetisation and GST (GDP growth fell from 8.3% in FY17 to 3.7% in FY20) and the 2020 lockdown (growth fell to -6.6% in FY21).	● The Central government needs to revive SMEs, but there's no data on the number of units that shut shop due to demonetisation, GST and Covid-19.	● The quarterly PLFS reports are restricted to urban areas.	● No comprehensive data is available on the number of vacancies in CPSUs, PSBs, autonomous institutions (central universities, colleges, schools, hospitals etc.) and in non-civilian central armed police forces and defence forces.

Betting On GDP, Manufacturing

India's policy response has always veered towards high GDP growth and manufacturing, but neither worked.

High GDP growth is marked by a shift from job-less growth in earlier years to job-loss growth in recent times. Dependence on manufacturing continues through Make in India and Production-linked Incentive (PLI) schemes. Make in India hasn't made a difference as manufacturing jobs continue to slip. The PLI scheme is largely focused on high-skill, capital-intensive sectors, including semiconductor, drones, telecom, electronics, white goods, solar PV modules, speciality steel, etc., and unlikely to produce too many jobs.

The proposed Development of Enterprises and Services Hub (DESH) Bill of 2022, which seeks to replace the SEZ Act of 2005, provides additional sops to SEZ units by (i) extending 15% tax concession to both greenfield and brownfield ventures for an extended period and (ii) allowing SEZ units to sell domestically (which is not allowed for exports-only units) by paying foregone duties on inputs but not on final goods. The finance ministry is learnt to have shot it down, fearing more tax disputes.

One must recall what the trade liberalisation of 1991 did to jobs. According to a large body of studies, it "displaced" exports from traditional, labour-intensive sectors such as textiles, natural/cultured pearls, vegetable products, animal products, prepared foodstuff, and hides and leather (all of which declined) to skill and capital-intensive ones such as machinery, base metals, chemicals, transport, rubber and plastics etc. (all of which rose).

India surely needs big businesses and exporting units because they provide better quality (high-income) jobs. But it needs more labour-intensive ones for millions of unskilled and semi-skilled workers who dominate the workforce. It needs more jobs in rural areas in particular because urban workers have fled there and refuse to return – causing labour shortage of 68% in Tier-1 cities and 32% in other cities in 2022, according to an industry estimate, swelling the ranks of MGNREGS workers.

The government needs to revive small and medium enterprises (SMEs), but there's no data on the number that shut shop permanently due to demonetisation, GST and Covid-19. A survey by private enterprise Global Alliance for Mass Entrepreneurship recently said 14% MSMEs permanently exited their businesses during the pandemic.

Last heard, the Emergency Credit Line Guarantee Scheme (ECLGS) had extended Rs 3.58 lakh crore to 11.9 million MSME units – 18.8% of all MSMEs (63.4 million)' – by November 30, 2022. How are the rest 81.1% doing? There are no answers.

Why PLFS Is Inadequate

Lack of clear and definite data on jobs is also chronic and needs immediate corrective steps through specific budgetary provisions.

The Centre trots out the Employees Provident Fund Organisation (EPFO) data to claim job creations since 2018, claiming 1.5-1.6 million new jobs every month. Such claims were scotched right at the beginning by the then chief statistician of India, Pravin Srivastava, who said the EPFO data was "not" about job creations but "a proxy for formalisation". A year earlier, the NITI Aayog's report of the Task Force on Improving Employment Data, too, said the same. Nonetheless, the slew of incentives towards formalisation of jobs is a good step.

But the question is: Why does the Centre not cite the right data, the PLFS, for job creation claims?

That is because the PLFS doesn't directly reveal how many jobs are created or lost. The Azim Premji University analysed its unit-level data for 2017-18 to reveal the net loss of nine million jobs. Until 2014, it was done by the Planning Commission, which provided yearly and sector-specific data (from job and other surveys, inputs from states, etc).

That is also because the past four annual PLFS data (2017-18 to 2020-21) give a misleading picture. They show worker-population rate (WPR) and labour force participation rate (LFPR) rising and the unemployment rate

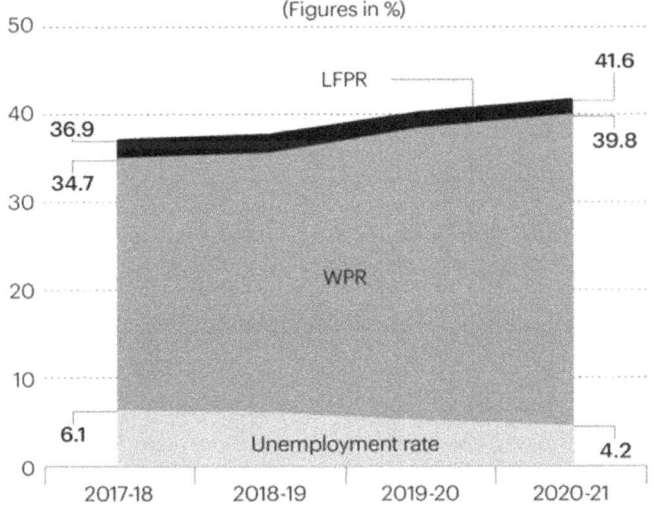

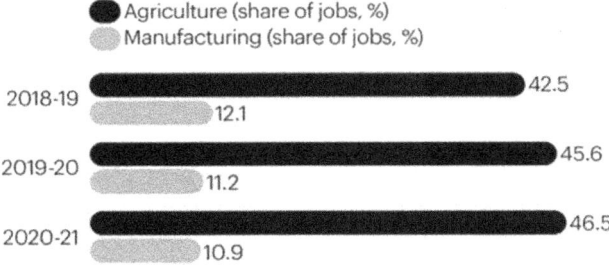

(UR) falling – all positive indicators. But they don't explain how that happened when India was reeling under the twin shocks of demonetisation and GST (GDP growth fell from 8.3% in FY17 to 3.7% in FY20) and the 2020 lockdown, which sparked a massive distress migration (GDP growth fell to -6.6% in FY21).

While no official account exists about job loss from demonetisation and GST, the Rajya Sabha was informed in February 2022 that 2.3 million workers had lost their jobs during the 2020 lockdown. The quarterly PLFS reports are restricted to urban areas.

Government Vacancies

Another good step is to fast-track filling up of government vacancies. After promising to fill 1 million vacancies in Central ministries and departments in June 2022, the Centre has given 0.15 million job certificates in October and November. But there exist very large vacancies in CPSUs, PSBs, autonomous institutions (central universities, colleges, schools, hospitals etc.) and in non-civilian central armed police forces (CAPFs) and defence forces, about which no comprehensive data is available.

For example, on December 12, 2022, the Lok Sabha was informed that 35.3%, or 11,175 posts, of faculty members are vacant in central universities, IITs and IIMs. There were 11.6%, or 0.13 million, vacancies in CAPFs (BSF, CISF, CRPF, ITBP, NDRF etc.) as on January 1, 2021. Another 0.14 million vacancies existed in the Army, Navy and Air Force, as on July 22, 2022; the four-year Agnipath scheme will only fill 46,000 of this, leaving a net vacancy of 90,000 by the end of 2022.

Then, there has been a steady decline in the number and quality of government jobs over the years.

The Railways abolished 72,000 Group C and D posts in six years during FY16-FY21. Hiring temporary and casual workers has been on the rise. A study by the Indian Staffing

India needs to adopt a national employment policy on the lines of neighbours, China (2002), Sri Lanka (2012) and Nepal (2017).

Federation (ISF) revealed in 2014 that (i) 43% government jobs (Central, state, PSUs and local bodies) were temporary (ii) 2/3rd of incremental formal workforce was temporary, with 80% in casual jobs (iii) high incidence of professionals and high-skilled workers, including architects, engineers and teachers, professors were on short-term contracts and (iv) 56% of those working in government schemes like ICDS, NRHM, NRLM (Anganwadi and ASHA workers) were "honorary" workers, getting "honorarium", instead of wages/salaries. ASHA and Anganwadi workers (around 2.5 million) have long agitated for proper remuneration.

It is not as if India has a bloated public workforce. In fact, the truth is far removed. It has a very low count of public servants, *just 6.8% of the total workforce* (PLFS of 2020-21), which is well below the OECD average of 21.1% in 2020 and 17.4% in 2021. In terms of public servants per 1 lakh population, India's 139 was very poor against the U.S.' 668 in 2015 (according to the 7th Pay Commission, 2015).

The challenges are not just the lack of job creation but also structural distortions, which are deeply entrenched and systemic. How does one address such a complex situation? The only way is to develop a vision, expressed through a national policy with strategies, plans and a clear roadmap. India's neighbours adopted their national employment policies (NEPs) long back, such as China (2002), Sri Lanka (2012), and Nepal (2017). Why can't India do so?

Jan 4, 2023

***

Why Demonetisation Verdict Raises More Questions than Answers

By not questioning Centre's contrarian economic wisdom, RBI's acquiescence and its own delay of 6 years to decide the writs, the court has failed to bring checks and balances and prevent recurrence.

The "legality" of the demonetisation policy of November 8, 2016, has been set to rest with the majority decision of the Supreme Court (4-1), but not its economic "wisdom or soundness" (the evidence for the policy) and the "procedural" flaws (the decision-making process) which have been glossed over. These two latter aspects raise questions about accountability and transparency in governance, institutional integrity (also independence) and democratic checks and balances. The implication: It's still hard to prevent such an event in the future.

Contrarian 'wisdom' of demonetisation

By now, there is no doubt that demonetisation caused a derailment of economy (India was the fastest growing major economy in 2015) by wiping out 86.9% of high-value currency notes (of Rs 500 and Rs 1,000) overnight from a cash-based economy. It caused massive and overnight loss of jobs and (small) businesses and none of its objectives were achieved.

The then Chief Economic Advisor Arvind Subramanian called it "a massive, draconian, monetary shock" which he said led to a fall of the GDP growth from 8% in the previous six quarters to 6.8% in subsequent seven quarters. The then IMF chief economist Gita Gopinath warned the world against attempting it. The Finance Ministry's 2012 white paper on black money had specifically rejected the proposal to demonetise Rs 500 and Rs 1,000 currency notes to fight black money. The SIT on black money, set up in 2014, was silent on demonetisation and advocated reducing cash transaction limits.

Moreover, the RBI itself had rejected demonetisation on multiple occasions in 2016, before putting a stamp of approval "as desired by the government", the dissenting judge Justice BV Nagarathna records.

In February 2016, the then RBI Governor Raghuram Rajan had argued against it "verbally", which the RBI "note" later repeated, which Rajan's 2017 book "I Do What I do" made public. In March 2016, the RBI had also rejected this suggestion from a Karnataka committee. The minutes of the RBI's Board of Directors, which met hours (5.30 pm) before the demonetisation announcement (8 pm) of November 8, 2016, revealed that it had rejected the government's arguments for it.

The minutes revealed, the Board of Directors had said (i) the spike in high-value currency notes was in "nominal" terms and "adjusted for inflation, this argument does not adequately support the recommendation" (ii) the presence of counterfeit notes of Rs 400 crore was "not very significant" (0.26%) of Rs 15.4 lakh crore of cash-in-circulation (CiC) and (iii) it was silent on the growth of "shadow economy" (suggesting it found no merit in it).

Why did it then approve demonetisation? The minutes revealed: "The Board was *assured* that the matter has been under discussion between the Central Government and RBI over the last six months during which most of these issues have been considered. Apart from the stated objectives, the proposed step also presents a big opportunity to take the process of *financial inclusion and incentivising use of electronic modes of payment* forward as people see the benefits of bank accounts and electronic means of payment over use of cash".

But none of these facts were told to the apex court in the affidavits of the RBI and the Centre.

The RBI's acquiescence (turning its own wisdom on its head) came after Rajan left and Urjit Patel took over as the RBI Governor in September 2016. The logic for the rejection of demonetisation by the RBI until then and that of the 2012 Finance Ministry's white paper was same: Most black money is not held in cash but in gold and real estate and hence, demonetisation would be futile while imposing high cost on the economy; there are better methods to tackle black money.

'Sealed cover', policy-making and process

While the majority verdict upholds the "legality" of the policy (the dissenting one doesn't), it steers clear of the economic "wisdom" or evidence for the policy decision (also by the dissenting one) and upholds the "procedural" aspect or the policy-making process.

For deciding both the "wisdom" and the "procedural" matters, the court relies on a set of documents which are critical but not in public domain or available to the petitioners. The court sought and received these documents *after completing the hearing*, turning these into "sealed cover" documents.

These documents are: (i) the Central Government's letter of November 7, 2016, which asked the RBI to approve demonetisation (ii) the "agenda note" of the RBI for its Board of Directors on November 8, 2016 (iii) the "recommendations" and the "minutes" of the RBI's Board of Directors meeting on November 8, 2016 (iv) the "Cabinet Note" prepared on November 8, 2016 and (v) the "actual decision" and "minutes" of the Union Cabinet approving it on November 8, 2016.

Since the petitioners had no access to these key documents, it amounts to *denial of natural justice*. The court's role, as also that of the Centre and RBI, is not only questionable for not giving access to the petitioners, but also for turning demonetisation an "academic exercise" and a "fait accompli" for delaying the verdict on 58 writs for *six years*.

Policy and policy-making as 'fait accompli'

Even while turning it into academic and fait accompli, the court verdict could have addressed important governance issues (short for rash policy making and undermining democratic checks and balances) to prevent recurrence: by fixing the Centre's accountability and transparency and the RBI's institutional integrity. As for the Parliament's absence in such a key policy decision, the court found nothing amiss even while finding that the Specified Bank Notes (Cessation of Liabilities) Act of 2017 was a *post facto* development.

The verdict didn't examine the "wisdom" by stating that it is "best left to the wisdom of the experts"; even the dissenting one says the policy was in "the best intentions" and for a "noble objects for the betterment of the Nation".

These observations ignore that this "wisdom" was *contrary* to what domain "experts" had said over a long period of time – (a) the 2012 Finance Ministry's white paper (b) the 2014 SIT (c) Rajan's "verbal" presentation, RBI's subsequent "note" and reply to the Karnataka committee in February-March 2016 and (d) the "minutes" of the RBI's Board of Directors rejecting the Centre's key arguments.

The court also ignored *post facto evidence* that demonetisation hurt the people and the economy. Cash was rationed for months and more than 100 died in the queues (apart from massive and overnight loss of jobs and businesses). The GDP growth fell from 8.3% in FY17 (the demonetisation fiscal) to 3.7% in the pre-pandemic FY20.

Demonetisation failed to achieve any of its stated, and later added, goals.

1. Cash-in-circulation (CiC) has risen sharply from 10.7% of the GDP at the time of demonetisation (FY17) to 14.4% in FY21 and 13.7% in FY22 – thus, outstripping gains from digitisation of transactions and claims of bringing transparency in financial dealings.

2. Tax efficiency has fallen from 11.2% of the GDP in FY17 and FY18 to 9.9% in the pre-pandemic FY20. In FY22, it was 10.8% and in FY23 it is expected to fall to 10.7% – still below the FY17/18 level.

3. Black money didn't extinguish as 99.3% cash came back to the RBI and the rest 0.7% was locked in (a) currencies "confiscated or seized by enforcement agencies or produced before a court on or before December 30, 2016" (b) "exchange" of currencies

held by District Central Cooperative Banks (DCCBs) "pending before the Hon'ble Court" and (c) currencies with Nepali "citizens/financial institutions". The final tally was never disclosed. The "windfall gains" never materialised, despite a witch-hunt by the IT department.

4. Since Rs 2,000 currency notes (not available until then) were issued immediately in 2016, the scope for storing black money in high-currency notes became far easier, not tougher.

5. No claim has been made or evidence provided by the Centre and RBI in their affidavits or argued by their lawyers that terror funding and incidents have stopped.

6. The only evidence of a positive gain the RBI gives in its affidavit is that counterfeit notes have reduced – but the RBI's minutes had said in November 2016 that this was too small and insignificant to begin with (0.26%).

The sum and substance of the demonetisation saga then is, had the Centre acted wisely, taking into consideration the experts' views, that of the RBI's or its own committees (white paper and SIT) or opted for course correction when it became evident that demonetisation was not working, much of the pain to the people and the economy could have been averted. The court, on its part, could have intervened timely, and not waited for six years, it would have helped the people and the economy too. Even now, six years later, it could have fixed accountability, paved a more rational policy making and procedures to prevent recurrence. Worse, the risk of another preventable economic misadventure remains.

Jan 4, 2023

Budget 2023: What Gives China Immunity From Extreme Poverty, But Not India?

A World Bank report of 2022 says China put a premium on human development, income and social security; prepared a rural base and managed urbanisation, infrastructure and competition

China's dizzying rise as an economic superpower has baffled most economists for years because of its authoritarian political structure. Many have tried to decipher how did it sustain high growth for 40 years and lifted close to 800 million – or three-quarters of global poverty ($1.9 USD per day) since 1980. In one of the most influential studies on economic development in recent times, "Why Nations Fail", Daron Acemoglu and James Robinson said China was an exception to their assessment of why some countries are rich and prosperous while others are not, and like many others, dismissed it stating that its concentration of political power ("extractive" political institution) "will not bring sustained growth and is likely to run out of steam". That was in 2012.

Essentially, Acemoglu and Robinson posited that only those nations developed and flourished that adopted "inclusive institutions" – first political and then economic, or from shared political power to shared economic prosperity – after analysing development processes across the world in the past 600-700 years. China became an outlier because it bucked the trend by bringing economic inclusion without political inclusion. India is an outlier too, but in the reverse order (political inclusion but not economic inclusion, and now the first one is changing fast); they didn't pay much attention to India anyway.

In April 2022, the World Bank published a comprehensive study, "Four Decades of Poverty Reduction in China", to explain how this authoritarian political order, contra-intuitive as it may seem, brought shared prosperity to its people. It is essentially China's growth story and holds many lessons for India.

Land reforms and human development

To start from the beginning, the massive transformation of China since 1980, it says, could be possible as it "inherited" equitable distribution of land among its rural peasantry – beginning in 1949 (the year of the communist revolution) when "more than 300 million landless peasants gained access to land"; then in 1953 their land was transferred to "the commune" and "with the 1978 reform, the land was again distributed to each household equally". Commenting on this, agricultural scientists Shenggen Fan and Ashok Gulati wrote in their 2008 paper "The Dragon and the Elephant: Learning from Agricultural and Rural Reforms in China and India", that land reform ensured that in China "landlessness is virtually absent".

In India, the opposite happened. It tried land reforms in the 1950s and 1960s, but it failed as most states, except Jammu and Kashmir, West Bengal and Kerala, "did not implement (it) in the true spirit". Land is a state subject.

Now land reform is absolutely a "no-go" area, neither in politics nor in economics. So, it shouldn't come as a shock that 55% of India's total agricultural workforce is landless (2011 Census, the next decadal Census is to begin only in 2024) and 86% of farmers are small and marginal with less than two hectare (5 acre) of landholdings (Agriculture Census of 2015-16). Nor when told that *45% of rural households* (of 167.9 million, as per the 2011 Census) *worked as menial labour* with less than statutory minimum wages under the MGNREGS in FY21, 43.2% in FY22 and in FY23 (up to December 18, 2022), 32.2% have already done so.

China also began with another advantage: a "relatively high level of human capital". It was better in education, health and relatively (lower) fertility rate than other transitioning and developing countries like India at the time. Even today, it is far ahead of India and many others. The UN's HDI report of 2022 shows China improved its rank from 82 in 2020 to 79 in 2021, while India's slipped from 130 to 132.

Managed urbanisation, incremental industrialisation

The twin advantages ensured that when market-oriented agricultural reforms came, the peasantry directly benefitted from improvements in productivity associated with market incentives. Good and secured income from agriculture meant it was easier to develop the rural non-farm (RNF) sector, strengthening the domestic production base for future industrial growth. It developed low-skilled and labour-tensive industries, which absorbed surplus labour from agriculture.

Urbanisation and industrialisation were incremental and managed and so was migration from rural to urban areas (not something that can work in democracies though). These came with public infrastructure and social security for workers, allowing easy integration of migrants. The cluster-based industrialisation, including export-oriented manufacturing, created more jobs. Its policies supported "market competition". Increased earnings and investments in the "modern sector" in cities generated new demand for consumer goods and services, in turn encouraging additional investment and creating new jobs.

In sharp contrast, India's economic transformation took a different trajectory. It didn't have the twin advantages that China had. India had very poor literacy, low life expectancy and a feudalistic rural social and land structure. India's low-productive and low-income agriculture supported a disproportionately large population without generating enough demand to support high industrial growth. In fact, as the then Chief Economic Advisor (CEA) Arvind Subramanian lamented in his Economic Survey of 2014-15, India was going through "premature de-industrialisation", despite decades of government support by way of tax incentives, cheap land and others. Manufacturing's share remains stagnant for a long, hovering around 17-18% of the GDP, despite 'Make in India', GST and PLIs in recent years. Its employment share is slipping by the day – from 12.1% of the workforce in 2017-18 to 10.9% in 2020-21 (PLFS 2020-21). A 2021 study by the Ashoka University-CMIE found manufacturing jobs halved ("declined by 46%") in five years between FY17 to FY21.

India borrowed the idea of cluster-based industrial pockets and SEZs from China but that didn't make a significant difference to manufacturing, trade or employment as the above facts demonstrate. Instead of market competition, crony capitalism was encouraged. Indian growth remains services-led for decades and 90% of its workforce is in the low-paying informal sector with no job or social security. India spectacularly failed its migrant workers in 2020 too. No other country in the world saw the massive reverse migration that India did when the lockdown was announced. Millions walked on foot, carrying family and luggage along, after losing their jobs, shelter and wages overnight. Such was the trauma that two years later in 2022, an industry estimate says, tier-1 cities faced a 68% labour shortage and a 32% shortage in other cities. Migrants reluctant to return say they prefer the poverty of their villages to the ignominy and low-wage jobs being offered in urban areas without civic and social security.

Decentralisation and cooperation

The World Bank report concludes that China's success in reducing poverty relied mainly on two pillars: (i) "broad-based" economic transformation to open new economic opportunities and raise average income and (ii) targeted support to alleviate persistent poverty. It also concludes that this worked because of "effective governance", governance that brought two critical elements together: (a) ensured coordination among "multiple government agencies" and (b) induced "cooperation from nongovernment stakeholders". India fails in this parameter too with the political and fiscal powers rapidly getting "re-centralised" at the cost of state governments and civil society facing a systemic crackdown via the Foreign Contribution Regulation Act (FCRA).

The report further points out that China's success also hinged on the fact that it encouraged and gave a free hand to area-based poverty alleviation and development models (decentralisation of power) and targeted poor counties and villages as a whole.

The report says China's poverty reduction is "primarily a growth story". It followed an agricultural development-led industrialisation growth model common to the East Asian tigers, as other studies have found earlier. Reforms were incremental and changes were well managed. Once the poverty headcount dropped below 10%, targeted poverty alleviation and social protection systems were brought in and after 2013, the policy efforts are concerted to reach the last mile, involving "substantial government transfers" and mobilisation of resources from "a variety of stakeholders".

Today, China is an economic superpower with relatively more prosperous people.

In 2021, its per capita income (India set to overtake it next year in population), an indicator of the prosperity of its people, was $12,556 (current USD) – 5.5 times more than India's $ $2,777 (World Bank). China started its reforms journey in 1978, and India in mid-198s. Their income inequality level was "at similar levels" in the early 1980s, and it grew at a similar pace until the mid-2000s but thereafter, China's stabilized but India's continued – wrote economists Lucas Chancel and Thomas Piketty in their 2019 book "From British Raj to Billionaire Raj".

In a world where inequality is rapidly growing for the past 40 years in most countries (within the country), India stands out as one "among the most unequal countries in the world" and the rise in its inequality "has no precedent in recent history". Indeed, it is "a poor country with an affluent elite". When the pandemic struck the world in

2020, the World Bank said, India added a whopping 79% of new "extreme poor" to the world population ($2.15 per day, 2017 PPP) – 56 million out of the total 71 million. But China didn't add any. The report casually dismissed it saying "China does not contribute to the global increase in extreme poverty in 2020".

Pray, why so?

Sure, India too has lifted millions out of poverty in the past few decades. But there is no denying that Indians remain very vulnerable to a crisis and the economic fundamentals are not as strong as it is often claimed. And its economic policies are highly questionable. Trying to answer why inequality stopped growing in China in the mid-2000s but continued in India, Chancel and Piketty said in the book quoted earlier: "Differences in national policies, rather than mechanical forces are likely to account…"

Dec 28, 2022

***

US, Europe Lessons for Gig Economy Law

The country needs to revisit the very definition of gig and platform workers similar to those outside the traditional employer-employee relationship, like the U.S. and Europe.

In October, the U.S. Department of Labour circulated a draft rule, making it easier for delivery drivers, truckers, construction workers and janitors to be considered as employees, rather than independent contractors or partners. The objective was to stop "misclassification" of gig workers and provide them benefits granted under the Fair Labour Standards Act, including minimum wage, overtime, social security, and unemployment insurance, among others. The rule proposed to "rescind" the Trump rule (Independent Contractor Status Under the Fair Labour Standards Act or 2021 IC Rule), which made classification of gig workers as independent contractors easier, through "multifactor, totality-of-the-circumstances analysis". The analysis would check "economic reality factors" such as "investment, control and opportunity for profit or loss factors" and an "integral factor" which considers whether the work is integral to the employer's business, to see if a gig worker is an employee or truly independent of it.

The proposed rule would be finalised and notified

once it goes through the mandatory 45-day public consultation process. With over 57 million gig workers (36% of workforce) in the U.S. in 2021, it would mean a significant change, particularly in the ride-hailing and delivery sectors.

Gig Workers In Numbers

U.S.	U.K.	India
57 million (36%) of total workforce (2021)	**4.4 million (14.7%)** of working population (2021)	**7.7 million (1.5%)** of total workforce (2021)

SOURCE: UPWORK'S FREELANCE FORWARD SURVEY 2021, NITI AAYOG 2022

California Law, 2019

California became the first U.S. state to bring such a change in 2019. Its "ABC-test" considers the worker an "employee" unless (i) he/she is "free from the control and direction of the hiring entity" with respect to the performance of the work (ii) performs work classified "outside the usual work" of the hiring entity's business and (iii) is customarily engaged in an "independently established trade, occupation, or business of the same nature".

The move, which has benefitted one million gig workers earlier classified as independent contractors, evoked strong protests from firms, including Uber, Lyft, Instacart and others, who have made fortunes on gig work-based (cheap labour) business models. They fought a pitched battle for a year, bankrolling (spending $200 million on campaign alone) a referendum (voting by rideshare drivers) in 2020 to exempt them from classifying gig workers as employees by mobilising rideshare drivers, and succeeded in getting a "yes". But a year later in 2021, a California court struck down the referendum as "unconstitutional" and "unenforceable" as it had sought to limit the state's legislative power by proposing a seven-eighth legislative majority (87.5%) for amendments to pass.

European Initiatives

In 2021, the European Parliament took a similar initiative to grant rights and benefits to gig workers engaged in the platform economy. The same year, the European Commission proposed five criteria to determine whether the platform is an "employer". These include whether (i) the platform determines the pay, (ii) requires workers to follow rules regarding appearance, conduct toward clients or performance of the work, (iii) uses electronic means to supervise, assess job performance, (iv) restricts work times or the freedom to turn the app off and (e) requires exclusivity or non-competition.

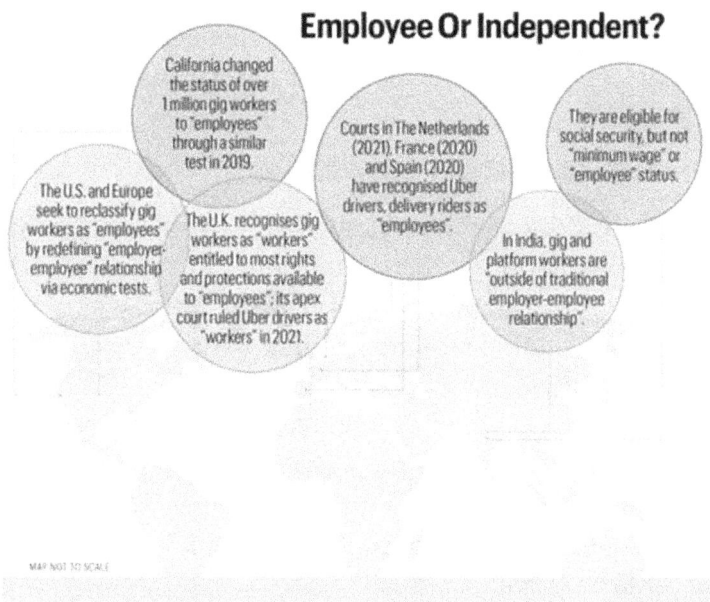

A platform that satisfies any of the two criteria is legally presumed to be an "employer" and those working through it are entitled to the status of "worker", giving them access to labour and social protections.

The U.K., which exited the European Union in 2016, already has a law recognising "worker" as a separate category from "employee" and "self-employed" who are entitled to minimum wage and paid holiday etc., but not full employment rights. In 2021, an apex court ruled Uber drivers as "workers", following which the ride-hailing company classified 70,000 driver-partners as "workers" entitled to minimum wage, paid holiday, pension (contributory) and older benefits like accident and health insurance to worker and family (since 2018).

Courts in the Netherlands (2021), France (2020) and Spain (2020) have also recognised Uber drivers and delivery riders of Deliveroo and UberEats as "employees" and salaried staff. Spain became the first E.U. country to enact such a law in 2021. Indonesia, where close to 90% of workers are informal, treats driver-partners as temporary contractors.

How India Treats Gig Workers

In contrast to the developed economies, India treats "gig" or "platform" workers as informal workers. The Code on Social Security 2020 defines them as those who work "outside of traditional employer-employee relationship". They are entitled to "social security schemes" — in future since the code is yet to be notified. However, they don't find a mention in any of the other three codes relating to minimum wages, industrial disputes and health and safety work environment passed in 2019 and 2020 – which, too, are yet to be operationalised.

Additionally, in 2020, the transport ministry issued a guideline mandating that platform drivers get 80% of the fare from rides, work for not more than 12 hours and are provided insurance. In 2021, the budget promised minimum wages and insurance cover for "all categories of workers". According to gig workers of Uber, Ola, Swiggy, Zomato and Zepto, who spoke on condition of anonymity, apart from insurance the rest are yet to be rolled out.

The labour ministry, meanwhile, continues to consult industry associations and companies engaging gig workers to figure out suitable social security schemes. But there is no forward movement, even after two years.

Industry's Silence

Lack of progress in the labour ministry's efforts is because none of the industry associations and companies engaging gig workers have shared their plans or schemes yet, sources told *Fortune India*. Their reluctance is evident in their lack of response to the Supreme Court directive on a petition filed by the Indian Federation of App-based Transport Workers and Others in November 2021, seeking social security cover for gig drivers. Ironically, the petition before the apex court doesn't even stress on minimum wage for gig workers or redefine the "employer-employee relationship" in line with advanced economies.

According to the Periodic Labour Force Survey (PLFS) of 2020-21, 64.3% of best category workers – regular wage/salaried – had no written contract (legal status) and 53.8% had no social security cover. Also, 89% of India's total workforce was "informal" in 2019-20 (Economic Survey 2021-22) –without legal status, rights and social security protections. Therefore, the idea of a good social security cover for gig workers, who constituted 1.5% of the workforce (7.7 million) in 2021 according to NITI Aayog, appears a little far-fetched.

Debate Over "Moonlighting"

In sharp contrast to the silence over rights of gig workers, the industry is quite vocal when it comes to "moonlighting" – a fallout of the pandemic-induced work-from-home practice.

IT and technology majors, including Wipro and IBM, have declared their strong opposition to moonlighting. Wipro even fired 300 employees for the same. But others such as Infosys, Swiggy and Emeritus have "allowed" moonlighting with prior consent and/or disclosures.

There is, however, a difference between moonlighting and gig work. According to the Oxford dictionary, moonlighting means having a second job that is done secretly, without telling the main employer". It means one indulging in moonlighting is an "employee" of a firm making extra money from a side job with another company.

Gig workers are, however, nobody's employee in India. A survey by the People's Union for Democratic Rights in the Delhi-NCR region in 2021 found that "for most" of the lower-end workers (engaged with deliveries, ridesharing, and wellness), gig work is not something they are doing on the side for extra cash, rather it is their "primary job".

Well-paid workforce is a potent consumer and driver of economic growth. With the number of gig workers set to jump to 23.5 million, or 4.1% of the total workforce, by 2029-30 (NITI Aayog) and not enough quality jobs being produced, Indian lawmakers need to take note of all that is happening in the U.S. and Europe, and follow suit.

Dec 8, 2022

GM Mustard: Where is Data on Biosafety and Higher Yield?

Lack of scientific rigour, opaqueness and conflict of interest in oversight mechanisms continue to cloud the decision-making on GM crops.

Genetically modified (GM) food, which had sparked intense national debate for years during the UPA-II and which had led to an indefinite moratorium on Bt brinjal in 2010, is a cause of concern again after the Centre permitted "environmental release" (one step away from "commercial release") of GM mustard (DMH-11 *hybrid*) on October 18, 2022. The Supreme Court is now hearing the case – a continuation of long-pending litigations relating to GM crops beginning in 2004 (after Bt cotton was released in 2002).

Why does the Centre want GM mustard (DMH-11), which is also *herbicide-resistant* (HT), to be released into the environment without first establishing its need and efficacy? It raises many critical questions but the most basic one is about the *misleading* claims about its objectives.

The Centre's affidavit of November 9, 2022, explaining its position to the court says, it is driven by three *commitments*: (i) increase in farm productivity (edible oil and legume) to make India self-sufficient (ii) increase in farmers' income and (iii) cut in import bill ("55-60% of edible in India is imported").

All three objectives hinge on one single factor: a higher yield of DMH-11. But does DMH-11 give a higher yield than hybrids and traditional varieties widely used in India?

Does GM mustard give a higher yield?

The Centre's affidavit says a *conditional* yes. The sentence reads: "The GM mustard hybrid DMH-11 has shown increased per-hectare yield *by 25-30%* over the *traditional varieties...*", adding, "due to exploitation of *hybrid vigour*". The source of information is not revealed, nor is any other detail.

Note, despite the claim of "hybrid vigour", the comparison is not with hybrids (many hybrids are cultivated in India for decades), but with "traditional varieties". Varuna is a traditional variety of mustard, *not a hybrid*, which happens to be one of the parental varieties used for developing DMH-11 (the other is Early Heera 2).

The Centre's 2016 affidavit was more specific: "*No such claim* has been made in any of the submitted documents that DMH 11 *out-performs non-GMO hybrids*. The comparison has only been made between hybrid DMH 11, NC (national check) *Varuna* and the appropriate ZC (zonal checks) – MSY of 2670 Kg/ha have been recorded over three years of BRL trials which is *28 per cent and 37 per cent* more than the NC & ZC respectively".

Note, here it is against *Varuna* only (in national and zonal checks).

The Centre is apparently relying on the claims of DMH-11's *current promoter*, Prof Deepak Pental of the Centre for Genetic Manipulation of Crop Plants (CGMCP), Delhi University. On August 25, 2022, he told the Genetic Engineering Appraisal Committee (GEAC) – a statutory body which recommended DMH-11's environmental release – that "on average, hybrid DMH-11 showed a 28% yield increase over the mega variety *Varuna*".

On the other hand, the Centre's nodal institute to carry out yield assessment – Indian Council of Agriculture Research (ICAR)'s Directorate of Rapeseed and Mustard Research (DRMR) at Bharatpur – has denied claims of the superior yield of DMH-11.

On November 20, 2022, DRMR director PK Rai told a national daily that GM Mustard (DMH-11) "has not been tested according to ICAR protocol" and that "it has just entered our system. Once trial and studies are over, one will get a clear picture on actual yield of DMH-11".

Rai also said DMH-11 had been sown in *six field trial plots*, before the Supreme Court's injunction not to do so came (on November 3, 2022). Few know that the Centre approved the environmental release on the very day, October 18, 2022, and the GEAC recommended this. The Centre's affidavit of November 9, 2022, disclosed this.

Why this extraordinary hurry when the matter is pending before the court and why is the comparison only with *Varuna*?

What Centre and GEAC missed on yield

The answer to the second part is simple. One, the DMH-11 yield is *lower than at least four hybrids* cultivated in India for decades.

This was revealed by a study of the very same CGMCP (current promoter).

CGMCP scientist Yashpal Singh Sodhi established this at a seminar in New Delhi on February 20, 2015 (organized by the Indian Society of Oilseed Research). His data showed *four non-GM hybrids* had higher yields and a fifth had nearly the same yield as that of DMH-11. His analysis was based on 2013-14 data. He did not include DMH-11 yield in his comparison but compared the yields of 14 mustard hybrids and non-hybrids.

His data showed, as against DMH-11's yield of 2670 kg/ha (as the Centre claims), four *hybrids* had higher yields: *NDDB-DMH-1 (2924 kg/ha), NDDB-DMH-3 (2719 kg/ha), NDDB-DMH-4 (3102 kg/ha), Pioneer-45S42 (2819 kg/ha)* had higher yields. The fifth hybrid, UPL-Advanta-Coral432 (2644 kg/ha), had nearly the same yield.

Two, the DMH-11 yield is lower than *traditional non-hybrid* varieties too, but before that a backgrounder.

The benefits of the system of crop intensification (SCI) are widely known to the world, including India, for decades. Here, existing traditional and hybrid varieties of crops are taken but the management of plants, soil, water and nutrients is altered to give higher yields. Take the case of the system of rice intensification (SRI), practised in India for long. The Cornell University's SRI International Network and Resources Center says about "60 countries" have adopted SRI and paddy yields have gone up by "20-100%". Similar is the case with wheat (WIS) and finger millet, wheat, maize, sugarcane, tef, oilseeds (mustard), legumes (soya and kidney beans) and various vegetables.

For mustard, it is called the system of *mustard* intensification (SMI). Newspaper reports say the use of SMI gives yields 4000-5700 kg/ha – far more than the DMH-11 – in Madhya Pradesh, Bihar, Odisha and West Bengal. Even without SMI, the indigenously developed *Sitara Sringar* of Rajasthan yields 3000-3500 kg/ha.

All the above facts negate the very *raison d'être* of DMH-11: higher yield in mustard would lead to self-sufficiency, raise farmers' income and cut import bills.

Is DMH-11 herbicide-tolerant (HT)?

Another critical concern involves the status of DMH-11 as a herbicide-tolerant (HT) crop.

This classification is important because India (a) doesn't allow any HT crop and (b) doesn't allow farmers to use herbicides in their fields.

In fact, the GEAC's approval for DMH-11 (October 18, 2022) came with a rider: "Usage of any formulation of herbicide is *not permitted for cultivation in the farmer's field* under any situation and such use would require the necessary permission as per the procedures and protocols of safety assessment of insecticides/ herbicides by CIB&RC (Central Insecticides Board and Registration Committee)."

A few days later, on October 21, 2022, the Centre issued a gazette notification restricting the use of *glyphosate* to "any person except pest control operators" because it poses "health hazards and risk to human beings and animals". This came after the action was sought by state governments against the sale and use of glyphosate following a surge in *illegal cultivation of HTBt cotton*. India allows Bt cotton (GMO) but not herbicide-tolerant Bt cotton variety – that is, HTBt cotton.

Now, it is well-known that DMH-11 is transgenic (GMO) as well as herbicide-tolerant (HT). The GEAC (August 25, 2022) clearly spelt out that one of the three foreign genes in it, *bar* "confers *resistance to herbicide phosphinothricin* – commercial name Basta". The other two foreign genes in DMH-11 are *barnase and barstar*.

The Centre's affidavit too admits this but, refuses to call it an HT crop.

The affidavit argues that GM mustard "has not been developed as a Herbicide-tolerant technology" and that its "HT characteristic/trait" is pure because of *the bar* gene used as a marker "for eliminating fertile plants in the hybrid seed production plots". Hence, it argues, it is "not appropriate" to call it HT crop. It further argues that such a label would be warranted only if "this trait is the *sole reason for permitting* GM mustard from the environmental angle". It also tells that Indian farmers are "not permitted" to use herbicides "for the cultivation of GM mustard".

Notwithstanding the wordplay, if an HT crop is permitted for cultivation, farmers would be tempted to use herbicides even if *illegally* as in the case of HTBt cotton. The reason is simple: the sale and import of herbicides are not illegal and the government can barely do more than issue notifications to restrict their use. On the other hand, the advantages of herbicides for farmers are plenty: all weeds are removed with one herbicide, saving labour costs and time. Farmers are unlikely to consider long-term adverse consequences for human lives and soil and water toxicity. Had that not been the case, Punjab wouldn't have known for "cancer trains" or "cancer belt".

The Centre's wordplay is also because of strong opposition to GM food and HT crops *without* first establishing their need, cost-and-benefit analysis, due diligence and scientific rigour in tests for biosafety (human and environment) and removing the conflict of interests in the oversight and regulatory mechanism (GEAC). Besides, the predominance of small landholdings (86% of farmers small and marginal with less than 2 ha or 5-acre land) makes Indian farmers particularly vulnerable to contamination from GM and HT crops (if biosafety is not already established). Agro-climate conditions of India are another critical consideration in this.

Missing due diligence

It is the *unscientific* manner in which the GEAC and the Centre have acted, historically and now, which has sparked protests from scientists, farmers and rights groups. Both have approved GMOs (Bt cotton earlier and now an HT crop to boot) without adequately testing for human and environmental safety, efficacy and socio-economic consequences.

A Supreme Court-appointed technical expert committee (TEC), set up after the Bt brinjal controversy, was categorical in its 2013 report that (i) *GM and HT* crops (ii) crops of *Indian origin* (in which India is "the centre of origin or diversity") "should not be allowed" unless there are "extraordinarily compelling reasons" and (iii) recommended a 10-year moratorium on field trials of *all GM food crops* unless the lax testing, regulatory and review mechanisms, including conflict of interest in regulatory and oversight mechanisms, are fixed first.

A Parliamentary Standing Committee of 2012 very much said the same thing. It "unanimously" recommended that field trials of GM crops "under any garb" should be "discontinued" until "all regulatory, monitoring, oversight, surveillance and other structures" were put in place.

Did anything change in clearance for DMH-11?

The answer is a clear no. Here is why.

One, the biosafety data on DMH-11 is not available in the public domain for scrutiny. The Centre's affidavit says, the dossier on "food and environmental safety (AFES)" was uploaded on the official website for *one month only*, between September 5, 2016, to October 5, 2016, and its scrutiny was allowed *in person* "at the premises of the MoEF&CC" *only*.

Why such secrecy? All such data for Bt brinjal was available in public for years to be verified.

Two, *conflicts of interest* in the testing and clearance process remain unchanged – to which both the TEC and parliamentary panel had particularly objected.

The DMH-11 project (of CGMCP) is (a) funded by the Department of Biotechnology (DBT), along with another public entity NDDB (b) the biosafety risk test data was "generated" by CGMCP (self-certification exercise) and (c) the risk assessment report on the basis of this data was "prepared" by a DBT unit (Review Committee on Genetic Manipulation or RCGM).

Yet, a DBT official co-chairs the GEAC (final recommending authority), carrying a higher weightage (it is a technical post) than the other co-chair, an official of MoEF&CC (generally an IAS officer) – as the 2012 parliamentary panel had commented.

Three, the 2012 parliamentary panel had lamented that long-term environment impact assessment and chronic toxicology studies of GM crops had "not even been attempted till now", nor socio-economic benefits of Bt cotton to farmers studied (it said "no significant socio-economic benefits" of Bt cotton as it is capital intensive, increased investment manifold, exposed farmers to "far greater risks due to massive indebtedness" and after the initial euphoria "only added to the miseries of the small and marginal farmers" constituting the majority). The TEC had shown that the claim of rising milk production by consuming Bt cotton feed was misleading as well.

For the Centre to then claim "transparency" and a "strengthened" regulatory regime" makes no sense.

Finally, whose technology is DMH-11?

To know this, one would have to check the GEAC minutes of November 7, 2002.

It says, M/s *Proagro* Seed Company, Gurgaon, had approached it in 2002 to seek commercial release of its transgenic hybrid mustard and mustard seed carrying *barnase, barstar and bar genes* – same ones that DMH-11 carries but named MT95003 and MT 95005 then. But the GEAC *deferred* a decision because of incomplete studies and tests and unresolved concerns about health and environmental issues involved, it decided to "defer" a decision."

It resurfaced in 2017 as DMH-11, through Prof Pental of CGMCP.

The next big questions that beg answers are: Who owns Proagro Seed Company now? More importantly, who owns the patent for the *barnase-barstar-bar system?* What is the connection between Proagro and CGMCP? Who are the leading producers of the *herbicide* "herbicide phosphinothricin – commercial name Basta" the DMH-11 is tolerant of?

The answer would reveal the secret behind the hurry and lack of transparency in clearing DMH-11 (the decision on Bt brinjal followed several rounds of national dialogue in various parts of the country).

It will also reveal if GM mustard will actually add to the foreign exchange burden by way of royalty outgo for using the technology and buying the herbicide.

Nov 29, 2022

***

COP27: Fighting Climate Crisis Against Carbon Billionaires

The good news is, after the COP15 (2009) commitment to help developing/poor countries with $100 billion a year in adopting green energy, rich countries committed to "loss and damage fund" at COP27

As experts and global leaders began their engagement at Sharm el-Sheikh's COP27 to address the climate crisis in early November 2022, Oxfam International's report "Carbon Billionaires" came with a stunning disclosure: rich individuals contribute the most to global warming. The world already knows that rich countries have contributed the most to push the world into this crisis.

The significance of this report lies in highlighting the key factor that has prevented the 30-year-long engagement (United Nations Framework Convention on Climate Change (UNFCC) was first signed in 1992) from achieving substantial success through multilateral cooperation. Which is, it is an unequal battle of wealth and power in which the most powerful ones are being asked to shoulder the maximum responsibility.

Conflict of interest

Here is how the Oxfam report sums up its findings:

"The world's richest people emit huge and unsustainable amounts of carbon and, unlike ordinary people, 50% to 70% of their emissions result from their investments. A new analysis of the investments of 125 of the world's richest billionaires shows that on average they are emitting 3 million ton a year, more than a million times the average for someone in the bottom 90% of humanity. The study also finds billionaire investments in polluting industries such as fossil fuels and cement are double the average for the Standard & Poor 500 group of companies. Billionaires hold extensive stakes in many of the world's largest and most powerful corporations, which gives them the power to influence the way these companies act."

It doesn't mention India's richest, but the World Inequality Report of 2022 did and showed a similar skewed carbon emission pattern: the top 1% contributed the maximum at 32.4 tCO2/per capita ('t' stands for metric ton), against the national average of 2.2 tCO2/per capita, in 2019. The top 10%, middle 40% and bottom 50% contribute 8.8, 2 and 1 tCO2/per capita, respectively.

Corporates are no different. The same Oxfam report quoted studies to assert that though corporates have, in recent years, made "many high-profile net-zero pledges", most of them are "way off track in terms of setting climate transition plans". Therefore, it proposed a solution that remains virtually unchanged for the past 30 years: "Governments must hold them to account, legislating to compel corporates and investors to reduce carbon emissions, enforcing more stringent reporting requirements and imposing new taxation on wealth and investments in polluting industries."

That precisely is the point economist Mariana

Mazzucato also made in her paper "The entrepreneurial state must lead on climate change" around the same time. It pointed out that several members of the Glasgow Financial Alliance on Net Zero (GFANZ) – a group of 450 financial institutions – had already quit "over concerns about the cost of delivering on their climate commitments". By dropping out, she argued, "they have given the lie to the notion that private financial institutions can lead the transition to a carbon-neutral economy". So, what is needed? More ambitious states to "go beyond market-fixing to become market shapers", she suggested.

In March this year, a research paper pointed out that the world's top banks *provided $742 billion* in finance to the fossil fuel industry – coal, oil and gas, the leading cause of man-made greenhouse gas emissions (carbon dioxide, methane, nitrous oxide, hydrochlorofluorocarbons (HCFCs), ozone etc.) – in the pandemic year 2021. This was higher than $185.5 billion in 2020 and also higher than the 2016 and 2017 levels. This was despite most leading banks pledging to reach net-zero emissions across their financing by 2050 and despite the International Energy Agency (IEA) saying no new oil and gas fields should be developed. The dominant banks are North American ones, including *JPMorgan (JPM.N), Wells Fargo (WFC.N), Scotiabank (BNS.TO) and RBC (RY.TO)*, all of which increased their financing.

The IEA analysis also showed that after a dip in the first pandemic year of 2020, carbon emission went up by 2 billion tons in 2021 – the highest level ever – as the world economy rebounded, "more than offsetting" the previous year's pandemic-induced decline.

European banks are no laggards. Berlin-based nonprofit think tank Finanzwende wrote in its December 2021 paper that "between 2015 and 2020, the *24 largest European banks* have poured almost one trillion dollars into fossil companies and projects".

The current energy crisis in Europe and elsewhere sparked by the Russia-Ukraine war has further shifted the focus back to fossil fuel (as also nuclear fuel).

How are rich countries doing?

How do countries engage in climate negotiations fare in their fight against climate change?

One way of looking at it is their carbon emissions. The World Bank's database shows, the global average per capita carbon emission (or carbon consumption) was 4.5 tCO2 in 2019 – up from 3.8 tCO2) in 1992.

In 1992, developed countries like the US (19 tCO2), UK (9.7 tCO2) and European Union (8.1 tCO2) were way above the global average and emerging/developing countries like India (0.7 tCO2) and China (2.1) far lower. In 2019, the trend continued: the US (14.7 tCO2), the UK (5.2 tCO2), the EU (6.1 tCO2), India (1.8 tCO2) and China (7.6 tCO2).

But there is a significant change. Developed countries are reducing their carbon footprints while developing and underdeveloped countries (like India by a smaller margin and China by a greater margin) are increasing theirs. This is expected since the development process involves higher energy consumption and hence, higher carbon emissions. That is why the burden of climate mitigation should be more on developed rather than developing/poor countries. This would also explain why while the former is committing to net-zero carbon emission by 2050, India and China are reluctant. India has set the goal in 2070 and China in 2060.

What about methane footprints?

Methane, one of the other greenhouse gases, has not received as much attention as it deserves.

A 2021 UN Environment Programme (UNEP) paper said "methane has accounted for roughly *30 per cent of global warming* since pre-industrial times and is *proliferating faster* than at any other time since record-keeping began in the 1980s". It is more dangerous than carbon emissions too. A Stanford University paper from November 2021 said: "While carbon dioxide is more abundant and longer-lived, methane – the main component of natural gas – is *far more effective at trapping heat* while it lasts. Over the first two decades after its release, methane is over *80 times more potent* than carbon dioxide in terms of warming the climate system.

The main sources of methane are agriculture (41%), followed by energy (35%), sanitation and waste sectors (20%) – together contributing 90-95% of global anthropogenic sources. Rice cultivation (flooded paddy fields prevent oxygen from penetrating the soil, creating ideal conditions for methane-emitting bacteria), agriculture waste burning, manure management and gas from *cows and sheep*; oil and gas extraction, pumping, transport and coal mining and from landfills and wastewater treatment are the activities which release methane.

The World Bank data shows total methane emission (CO2 equivalents) is consistently rising – up by 27% in 2019, from the 1992 level. The US, India and China have seen a rise in methane emissions while that of the UK and EU have fallen.

India is so wary of touching agriculture and livestock

that it didn't sign the COP26 (Glasgow) pledge to cut methane (and also stop deforestation) by 2030. Its Long-Term Low Emission Development Strategy report for COP27, submitted on November 14, 2022, is silent on curbing methane and agriculture is not on the list of strategic sectors (such as electricity, transport, urban development, industry and finance) to achieve net-zero by 2070.

Loss and damage funding

This is not to suggest that the UNFCC has not achieved anything. Over the years it has adopted mitigation and adaptive measures. The COP27 added long-term strategies and commitments to achieve net zero to the short-term ones adopted earlier, from 198 participating countries.

At COP15 of 2009 (Copenhagen), developed countries pledged to prove $100 billion a year to help developing/poor countries adopt green energy. Although this commitment remains short on target, reaching $83.3 billion in 2020 – still short by $16.7 billion. Fulfilling this commitment by investing in green energy, R&D and technology transfers will help developing/poor countries keep their end of the bargain. But the overall global scenario is the beak. For example, in 2020, about $5.9 trillion was spent on subsidising the fossil fuel industry, while the global requirement to reach net-zero emissions by 2050 is an investment of about $4 trillion a year in renewable energy until 2030 (including investments in technology and infrastructure), as per a UN climate action report.

The COP27 achieved another milestone when it committed to setting up a "loss and damage fund" – to compensate countries suffering from climate-related loss and damage – which was being demanded for several years. This time, developing countries like India and China, which are big emitters of greenhouse gases, may end up contributing to this fund. But the COP27 failed to add fossil fuels (oil and gas) to coal in the list for phasing out as oil-rich Gulf countries and Russia strongly objected to.

The climate crisis is getting worse by the day and needs stronger commitments, particularly from the rich and powerful. In May this year, the UNFCC warned that the "continued global temperature rise will continue" with "an even chance (50:50) that one of the years between 2022 and 2026 will exceed 1.5 °C above pre-industrial levels" – which COP21 (Paris) committed to preventing.

Recall, in October 2022, while warning the world about recession looming large in 2022 and 2023, IMF Director Kristalina Georgieva listed "climate disaster on all continents" as the third big factor – after the pandemic and Russia-Ukraine war.

Nov 24, 2022

***

What Caused Inequality to Rise in India During Pandemic?

The poorest and most vulnerable were hit the hardest – pushing 70 million people into "extreme poverty" in 2020 alone: World Bank

That the pandemic exacerbated inequality is known. The poorest and most vulnerable were hit the hardest – pushing 70 million people into "extreme poverty" in 2020 alone, as the World Bank report said recently, to which India contributed a whopping 79% – while billionaires' wealth and corporate profits surged to historic highs. The Oxfam-DFI report, released on October 11, analyses government policies and actions of 161 countries to fight inequality during the first two years of the pandemic. Having assessed countries on three key parameters to mitigate inequality – (i) governments' social spending on health, education and social protection (ii) taxation and (iii) labour policies – it pronounced a harsh verdict.

It said "most of the world's governments failed to take major concrete steps to mitigate this dangerous rise in inequality". About India, it is even harsher. India was ranked 123rd among 161 countries and some of the observations are:

- India "reclassified" as having "no minimum wage" in 2020 and is listed among 12 with no minimum wage regime (Bahrain, Oman, Cambodia, Singapore, Ethiopia, South Sudan, St. Lucia, Jordan, Tonga, Lebanon and Tuvalu).

- "India features among the lowest performers on health spending again; it has dropped a further two places in the rankings, to 157th (or 5th lowest in the world) and made small cuts between 2019 and 2021 – at a time of unprecedented health need and crisis."

- India was among five countries which "dismantled" labour rights through "new repressive laws" (others are: Honduras, Indonesia, Slovakia, and Uruguay).

- The only area where India escapes criticism is tax policies where it is ranked 16th but we would soon see why this sounds far too generous.

What is India's national minimum wage?

It may come as a shock to most that India's national minimum wage is still stuck at Rs 176 per day since 2017.

The Oxfam-DFI report reclassifies India as not having a national minimum wage by taking into account two factors: (i) Economic Survey of 2018-19 said "one in every three wage workers (33.3%) in India has fallen through the crack and is not protected by the minimum wage law" and (ii) new Code on Wages 2019 recast the wage regime but hasn't taken off yet.

Thus, the gaping holes and low base in the wage regime endures.

Even this national minimum wage of Rs 176 is not binding. Every state and union territory has its own set of statutory minimum wages – multiple sets actually. Economic Survey of 2018-19 counted "nearly 429 scheduled employments and 1,915 scheduled job categories for unskilled workers" – notified under the Minimum Wage Act by the Central and state/UT governments. Its graph showed five states/UTs had lower than Rs 176 of minimum wage and 32 others higher – going up to Rs 538 for Delhi.

The Centre did set up a committee in 2017 to revise national minimum wage, which recommended Rs 375 per day in January 2019. Months later, in July, the Union Cabinet revised the minimum wage by Rs 2 to take it to Rs 178, but didn't notify or implement even that. Instead, a month later, August 2019, the Code on Wages 2019 was passed, promising equity and welfare of workers by expanding the coverage to include informal workers like gig workers. It promised better social security cover. But the provisions don't guarantee minimum wages to all nor provide for equal-pay-for-equal-work; it removes gender discrimination but not discrimination against ethnic minorities and lower castes (big source of wage inequality).

Until now, the Code on Wages remains on paper (rules haven't been notified). Since it didn't provide a formula to fix minimum wage (or floor rate) and the committee it provided for the job hasn't been set up, there is little hope for a forward movement anytime soon.

Even the pandemic didn't move the Centre. The rural job scheme MGNREGS it runs, which provides low-paying menial jobs but helped millions to beat starvation – saw minimal change in wage rates. The average wage in FY20 (pre-pandemic) was Rs 182, which went up to Rs 200.7 in FY21 and to Rs 208.8 in FY22. In FY23, it is Rs 215.4. This is when minimum wages (agriculture) of states/UTs ranges from Rs 210 (Uttar Pradesh) to Rs 441 (Karnataka).

Why minimum wage is important?

Among the countries that have achieved remarkable success in fighting against income inequality, one is Brazil which took to wage route in a big way (in addition to education, skilling and social welfare). Between 1997 and 2009, it hiked minimum wages by 70%. Several studies across the world, including those by the World Bank (2012) and IMF (2015), and even Indian ones (Mahendra Dev, 2018) have found higher minimum wage and wage growth are one of the critical factors to reduce income inequality.

In India, wages have stagnated for a long time. Last month, India Ratings said "nominal" wages (without taking inflation into account) of households declined to 5.7% during FY17-FY21 from 8.2% during FY12-FY16. Given the high inflation, real growth in wages is negligible. The PLFS of 2020-21 had shown "real" growth in wages for regular/salaried jobs fell by -8.9% and that of self-employed by -4.89%; wages for casual work (lowly paid daily wagers), however, saw a rise of 3.6%.

Dismantling workers' rights

All inequality studies list protection of labour rights, strengthening of trade unions and collective bargains as other labour market factors to reduce income inequality. India fares badly here too.

During the pandemic lockdown of 2020, India passed three labour codes (in addition to the Code on Wages 2019): (a) Industrial Relations Code (IR Code) 2020 (b) Code on Social Security (SS) 2020 and (c) Occupational Safety, Health and Working Conditions (OSHW Code) 2020. Together, these codes amalgamated 44 central laws but made them manifestly pro-business and anti-workers. These laws hurt workers by expanding thresholds for protection against arbitrary hire-and-fire, safety norms, promote temporary and contract jobs, ban strikes and dilute trade unions.

As for expanding minimum wages and social security, which these codes do, such provisions are for the future committees to work out and fix – unlike concrete and definitive ones that dilutes workers' rights and interests mentioned above. Given that about 90% of Indian workforce are informal, without job or social security, the new labour laws worsened workers' precarity.

Agriculture has been at the target of pro-corporate/business policies during the pandemic. Three new farm laws were passed in 2020 to govern trade in far produce, (contract) farming and hoarding food grain stocks, which had to be withdrawn after a year of fierce protest from farmers. Like the new labour laws, the new farm laws too were introduced during the pandemic lockdown in 2020 – first as ordinances and then rammed through the Parliament without consultation, scrutiny or due deliberations.

Why are farm laws relevant here?

For one, agriculture provides far more jobs than industry and services and second, more workers fled to agriculture when the pandemic struck as India witnessed an unprecedented reverse migration like no other country in the world. A study by Ashoka University-CMIE showed the first pandemic year of FY21 saw an unprecedented rise of 4.1% in agricultural workforce. The PLFS of 2020-21 showed the employment share of agriculture jumped to 46.5% in FY21, from 45.6% in FY20.

This development has led to the rise in informal workers, mainly self-employed – low productive, low-income and uncertain jobs/incomes. Another cause of rising inequality is massive job loss that the pandemic caused. A study by Azim Premji University says 15 million jobs were lost permanently during April-December 2020. As against this, the OECD countries claimed to have saved 50 million jobs during the time.

India could have done much to protect jobs and wages but it did nothing. Its half-hearted directive to factory owners and other private industrial establishments to provide wages to workers during the lockdown period was not only challenged but the apex court quashed it.

Regressive taxation

India may have escaped lightly from the Oxfam-DFI's ranking in taxation but its tax policies have become more regressive. It cut corporate tax in 2019 – months before the pandemic hit – as a result of which peak base rate for corporate sector is reduced to 22%, much less than 30%, the peak base rate for personal income tax paid by lesser mortals. It had abolished wealth tax earlier in 2016.

A parliamentary panel found the corporate tax cut of 2019 led to a direct loss of Rs 1.84 lakh crore in the pandemic fiscals of FY20 and FY21. It also led to an unprecedented development – for the first time in the 2011-12 GDP series, corporate tax collections fell below personal income tax in FY21.

The pandemic didn't stop oil tax from rising, despite fall in international crude prices – which hurts the poor as fuel used by two-wheelers and three-wheelers, in agriculture and transport far outstrip fuel used by cars.

Revenues from central taxes (cess, surcharge, customs, excise, CGST, IGST etc.) on oil went up from Rs 3.34 lakh crore in FY20 to Rs 4.6 lakh crore in FY21 and Rs 4.9 lakh crore in FY22. The average crude price was $60.47 in FY20, $44.82 in FY21 and $79.18 in FY22. States did their bit too, though to lesser extent, and their collection went up from Rs 2.2 lakh crore in FY20 to Rs 2.17 lakh crore in FY21 and Rs 2.8 lakh crore in FY22 (all from PPCA).

Then came another shock. In July 2022, the Centre imposed 5% GST on food items – which were exempted earlier – on pre-packaged unbranded food items like wheat, rice, curd, lassi, puffed rice, mutton and fish. These directly hit the poor.

All such tax policies are regressive and cause inequality to rise – which India should be reversing, rather than piling up.

Inequality ignored

India actually ignores addressing inequality, it said. The Economic Survey of 2020-21 (after the first year of the pandemic) acknowledged growing income inequality but refused to act on it, saying instead, "economic growth has a far greater impact on poverty alleviation than inequality. Therefore, given India's stage of development, it must continue to focus on economic growth to lift the poor out of poverty by expanding the overall pie".

As Finance Minister Nirmala Sitharaman said recently, the focus of her next budget would be growth and inflation (touched 7.4% in September). But it is precisely the growth model India has been following since the economic reforms initiated since mid-1980s that inequality has risen sharply – reversing the earlier growth model in which the bottom 50% and the middle 40% improved their share of national income. The current growth model benefits only the top 10% – as studies by Lucas Chancel and Thomas Piketty have shown.

No wonder, India's response to the pandemic crisis has been characterised more by the "free" ration to those very people who are entitled to "subsidised" ration under the National Food Security Act of 2013 (to 62.5% of households). This was launched immediately after the lockdown was announced in 2020.

It may fetch votes for the ruling establishment – which it did during the elections to five states earlier this year and may do the same in Gujarat and Himachal Pradesh too which are going to elections later this year – but it does nothing to pull them out of poverty. It merely prevents starvation deaths and once withdrawn (runs till December 31, 2022), the situation will be very bleak for those 62.6% households with little prospects to get jobs or good wages.

Oct 18, 2022

***

Dolo-650 Bribery Allegation: Why Pharma Cos Need Tight Monitoring

Dolo-650 manufacturer struck gold during the pandemic; was raided by IT in July, accusing it of bribing doctors through Rs 1,000 crore "freebies" to push drug sale during the pandemic

Unethical marketing practices by pharmaceutical companies have always been a big concern, not just in India but globally. In a bid to curb this, the Centre brought the Uniform Code of Pharmaceutical Marketing Practices (UCPMP) in 2015, a voluntary code, which was initially meant to run for six months on an experimental basis but has now become a permanent one.

It is the apparent failure of this code which is at the heart of current litigation in the Supreme Court. When first notified on December 12, 2014 (operationalised from Jan 2015), the Centre had said if the UCPMP was found "not been implemented effectively" by pharma companies it would "consider making it mandatory". Now the Centre has told the court that it is working "adequately" and there is no need to make it mandatory by giving it a legal status.

This stand is questionable for many reasons, but primarily because of (i) the manner in which Micro Labs was given a clean chit in the alleged "freebies" of Rs 1,000 crore given to doctors to push its drugs, including Dolo-650 – anti-pyretic (fever reducing) and analgesic (pain reducing) tablet which rose to fame during the pandemic-induced national health crisis and (ii) then using this clean chit to assert that the UCPMP is working just fine.

IT raids, CBDT alleges Rs 1,000 crore 'freebies' by Dolo-650 maker

An old PIL on marketing malpractices by drug makers was taken up this August by the Supreme Court after a fresh affidavit was filed by the Federation of Medical and Sales Representatives Associations of India (FMRAI) – a national trade union and the original petitioner. This followed nation-wide raids on the Micro Labs in July 2022.

After the raids (at Micro Labs' "36 premises spread across 9 states"), the Central Board of Direct Taxes (CBDT), under which the IT department works, issued a statement, on July 13, stating: "The evidence indicates that the group has adopted unethical practices to promote its products/brands. The quantum of such freebies detected is estimated to be around Rs 1,000 crore."

It explained the "unethical practices" (giving "freebies") as "unallowable expenses" which included "travel expenses, perquisites and gifts etc. to doctors and medical professionals for promoting the group's products under the heads 'promotion and propaganda', 'seminars and symposiums', 'medical advisories' etc.". The CBDT also alleged a tax evasion of Rs 300 crore by the company and declared seizures of unaccounted cash, gold and diamond jewellery worth Rs 2.6 crore.

Months before the IT raids, Dolo-650 was in news for the dramatic rise in sales. This drug was widely recommended by medical professionals after the pandemic struck in 2020, more so at the time of vaccination in 2021 – earning it the sobriquet "COVID-pandemic's favourite snack". When the Supreme Court was told (in August, post IT raids) that bribes had allegedly been paid to doctors through "freebies" to push its sales (reiteration of the CBDT's charge) during the national health crisis, Justice DY Chandrachud, heading a two-judge bench, reacted: "What you are saying is not music to my ears. This is exactly what I had when I had Covid. This is a serious issue."

Micro Labs takes particular pride in the rise of Dolo-650. The first article showcased on its official website reads, "How Micro Labs struck gold with Dolo-650 during Covid-19". This article (of February 2022) says, the company "sold 350 crore tablets since the Covid-19 outbreak in 2020, and earned revenues of Rs 400 crore in a year". It further says, the sales went up dramatically from about 7.5 crore strips annually in 2019 (before the pandemic) to 14.5 crore strips by the end of 2021 – almost doubled. A national daily reported the drug saw its highest sales in April and May 2021 – during the second pandemic wave – when it witnessed sales of Rs 48.9 crore and Rs 44.2 crore, respectively.

Centre relies on 'self-certification' for clean chit

In its affidavit to the Supreme Court on October 4, 2022 – Fortune India has a copy of it – the Centre absolves Micro Labs of the allegations on the basis of a clean chit from the Indian Pharmaceutical Alliance (IPA), an industry body. This is in keeping with the mechanism provided by the very voluntary code (UCPMP).

The Centre goes exclusively by the IPA's findings and completely ignores the CBDT's allegations (of "unethical practices" and Rs 1,000 crore of "freebies"). What does the IPA rely on to give a clean chit to Micro Labs? It relies solely on data provided by the accused. As per this (quoted extensively in the Centre's affidavit), Micro Labs' (a) total turnover was Rs 4,500 crore, of which Rs 2,500 crore was from domestic sales (the year is not mentioned) and (b) the overall expenses on domestic sales in the last four years (FY18 to FY22) was Rs 200 crore; on Dolo-650 alone, it spent average of Rs 9.7 crore during the same period.

On the basis of these data, the IPA concludes that the allegation of Rs 1,000 crore "freebies" was misleading and that the UCPMP "works adequately". The Centre endorsed it without checking facts or consulting the CBDT. Its clean chit read: "In view of interaction with the management of the company and the detailed reply, it is clear that Rs 1,000 crore expenditure on single brand Dolo-650 on freebies in one year is not correct."

Here comes another shocker.

The IPA is a group of 24 pharma companies, including the Micro Labs. This is no secret though. The IPA's website reveals it and so does the Centre's affidavit and yet, none flags the apparent conflict of interest in the IPA's clean chit. Moreover, the Centre upholds the UCPMP which provides for this mechanism.

Flip-flop on UCPMP

A legal backing to the UCPMP is important because that would enable the Centre to regulate marketing malpractices and prevent "freebies" as well as prescription of branded medicines (like Dolo-650) by doctors – which is what the marketing malpractice is all about – instead of prescribing generic names (like, paracetamol, instead of Dolo-650). Prescription of generic drugs is mandatory under the Indian Medical Council (Professional Conduct, Etiquette and Ethics) Regulations of 2002 (framed under the Indian Medical Council Act of 1956). Generic drugs are way cheaper than branded ones but more about it later.

The UCPMP's ineffectiveness was obvious soon enough.

The Department of Pharmaceuticals (DoP), which issued the UCPMP, recommended that it should be made "mandatory" in its 2017-18 annual report, following a review of its working. It said: "The implementation of the UCPMP has been reviewed in consultation of all the stakeholders including NGOs/Civil Societies and it was felt that in order to implement it more effectively, it would be desirable to make it mandatory."

It also added: "With the above intention, the Department has prepared a draft order under the Essential Commodities Act, 1955 and is in the process of finalisation of the same in consultation with Legislative Department/ Legal Affairs." That never materialised and is still stuck with the Law Ministry.

From three years between 2016 and 2018, the Centre was open to making the UCPMP mandatory but changed track in 2019 in a reply to the Rajya. Then in 2020 (September 18) Minister for Chemical and Fertilizers Sadananda Gowda reiterated the same in the Rajya Sabha even while admitting how toothless it was. He said: "The Uniform Code for Pharmaceutical Marketing Practices (UCPMP) is voluntary in nature and under UCPMP, there is *no provision for Department of Pharmaceuticals to directly deal* with complaints received regarding unethical practices."

What was the new discovery that led to the change in stand?

That is not known. What is known is that several new facts came to public domain showing that marketing malpractices continues, pointing to the code's ineffectiveness.

For example, in February 2019, the DoP had revealed in a response to a RTI query that it had received complaints of "bribing doctors, medical shopkeepers and unauthorized medical practitioners to sell their pharmaceutical products" in 2016 against 20 pharma companies (names identified) – which included some of the big and famous ones. What action did the DoP take? The reply said the DoP had forwarded the complaints to the Ministry of Health and Family Welfare (MoHFW), the Medical Council of India (MCI) and a pharma association (not named). What action did the MoHFW or MCI took? The DoP didn't reveal.

In December 2019, more dirt flew. An NGO, Support for Advocacy and Training to Health (SATHI), alleged that medical representatives had paid for "purchase of cars, international conferences, online shopping vouchers and even female companionship for doctors". Following this, three drug makers' associations, including the IPA, were pulled up by the government.

In January 2020, the Prime Minister reportedly met top drugmakers and warned them about bringing in a law to control malpractices and indicated that the Ministry of Chemicals and Fertilizers (under which the DoP works) had been asked work on the law.

Following this, the Indian Medical Association (IMA), the largest body of medical doctors, wrote to the Prime Minister seeking an explanation as to why pharma companies were invited to the PMO for talk, instead of initiating criminal proceedings if it had details of the bribery by the companies.

In the meanwhile, revealing more contradictions, the Centre's affidavit of October 4, 2022 to the Supreme Court made two more disclosures: (i) It had initiated a study in October 2021 "to evaluate the necessity and measure of making the code statutory", but this study couldn't take off and (ii) it set up a High-Level Committee (HCL) on September 12, 2022, under NITI Aayog member V K Paul, to examine the entire issue of marketing malpractices and to find "legally enforceable mechanism". The HCL has been given 90 days to submit its report and one of its members happens to be CBDT chairman Nitin Gupta.

So, why did the Centre rule out a legal status in its affidavit and cite several other mechanisms –Indian Medical Council (Professional Conduct & Ethics) Regulations of 2002 (under the Indian Medical Council Act of 1956), Drugs and Cosmetics Act of 1940 and Prevention of Corruption Act of 1988 – to claim that the existing mechanisms are "robust and effective"?

That is not clear.

Here is another shocking revelation, from the US, which is pertinent to the Dolo-650 matter.

Drugs aren't costlier due to R&D or curative values

On September 26, 2020, a first known study of its kind was published about the US pharma world. An international team of researchers from top universities evaluated if high R&D explained high drug prices in the U.S. – since drug companies often claim so to charge high prices. They studied 60 new drugs approved by the US Food and Drug Administration between 2009 to 2018, and found no such association between R&D expenses and high prices.

This study also found that even curative value of

drugs had nothing to do with high pricing. It said it found "no association between the clinical benefit of a new product and prices" – that is, the pricing of drugs is not determined by their corresponding curative or therapeutic value (clinical benefit as proxy for therapeutical value).

It also added that this finding (disconnect between curative value and pricing) "is in line with results from a previous study of cancer therapies".

The University of California highlighted this study in a paper published three days later (September 29, 2022), which provided some easily relatable facts regarding high drug pricing and R&D. This paper said: "The pharmaceutical industry spent *$83 billion on R&D in 2019*, according to the Congressional Budget Office. Companies are estimated to spend somewhere between *$1 billion and $3 billion* on average to bring a single new product to market. In 2019, the US drug market generated *more than $490 billion* in revenue…"

That is, a revenue of over $490 billion in 2019, from an R&D spend of $83 billion!

The paper went to add: "Americans spend more on prescription drugs per capita than citizens in any other country. In 2019, that worked out to more than $1,200 per person. A 2021 Rand Corporation study found U.S. drug prices were 2.56 times higher than those in 32 comparable countries."

Now you know why pharma companies need a tight leash.

Oct 18, 2022

***

Did Corporate Tax Cut of 2019 Lead to Tax, GDP Boom?

A parliamentary panel estimates a loss of Rs 1.84 lakh crore due to the 2019 corporate tax cut in the first two fiscals of FY20 and FY21 alone

According to IMF's executive director Surjit S Bhalla, the corporate tax cut of September 2019 – from a base rate of 30% to 22% for existing firms without exemptions/incentives and from 18% to 15% for new manufacturing units – has led to extraordinary gains in the economy.

On August 8, 2022, he wrote in a column that a sharp 30% rise in corporate tax collection during April-June 2022 (Q1 of FY23) was because of this corporate tax cut. Had the pandemic not intervened, he rued, the "efficiency" of "this bold experiment in Modi 2.0" would have been visible sooner.

He further claims that this "one of the largest corporate tax cuts in world history" brought about dramatic changes in the overall economic fortunes of India. Using FY20 as the base, he argued, the corporate tax collections increased by 66%, the average tax buoyancy by 2% (highest since FY07) and the GDP by 33%.

There are several claims in these statements. As for

the surge in corporate tax collection, the Finance Ministry had made similar claims earlier, in April this year. In its statement of April 8, 2022, the ministry said: "The gross corporate taxes during 2021-22 was Rs 8.6 lakh crore against Rs 6.5 lakh crore last year, which shows that the new simplified tax regime with low rates and no exemptions has lived up to its promise."

However, the ministry had a different take on the overall growth in revenue collections in FY22 though. The same statement said the total revenue collection had jumped by almost Rs 5 lakh crore in FY22 (from a budget estimate of Rs 22.17 lakh crore to Rs 27.07 crore) – a 34% year-on-year growth, led by growth of 49% in direct taxes and 20% in indirect taxes. It attributed such growth to "rapid economic recovery after successive waves of COVID".

What is apparent in these claims is an obvious attempt to justify the corporate tax cut of Rs 1.45 crore in September 2019. This cut came amidst fiscal distress as the very same month Finance Minister Nirmala Sitharaman had told states at Goa's GST Council meeting that the Centre had no money and hence, wouldn't be paying the GST Compensation anymore. She followed it up with formal letters in November 2019. For the subsequent two fiscals, FY21 and FY22, the Centre borrowed money from the RBI to pay GST Compensation (Rs 1.59 lakh crore in FY21 and Rs 1.1 lakh crore in FY22).

Straight loss of Rs 1.84 lakh cr in first 2 years

Unbeknown to Bhalla and Finance Ministry, the parliamentary Committee on Estimates put out different claims in its report submitted on August 8, 2022.

The panel said the corporate tax cut of 2019 had

resulted in a negative "revenue impact" of Rs 1.84 lakh crore in FY20 and FY21 alone – Rs 87,835.75 crore in FY20 and Rs 96,399.74 crore in FY21. It didn't provide its estimate for FY22, apparently due to a lack of data (more of it later). The panel used the "effective tax rate" in the post-corporate tax cut regime to compute the tax (for those who had opted for the new regime) and then compared it with the tax payable by those very companies under the old regime to calculate the "revenue impact". It sourced its data from the Directorate of Income Tax System).

Corporate tax and profits

Interestingly, corporate tax is paid on corporate profits (after accounting for all expenses) and that may or may not have anything to do with tax rates. It is by now well known that corporates made historic high net profits (after paying tax) in FY21 and FY22 – amidst the pandemic-induced economic ruins all around. CMIE's Mahesh Vyas says that 30,000 companies (5,000 listed and 25,000 unlisted) made "a massive 138% increase in net profits" in FY21 over FY20. In FY22, listed companies alone (excluding unlisted ones) made "extraordinary profits" which grew by 66.2% over FY21. When net profits of listed companies started soaring in Q2 of FY21 (July-September 2020), he had described it as "their highest ever profits in the midst of a severe lockdown" – which kept rising in subsequent quarters.

Why did corporates make historic profits amidst the pandemic ruins?

An SBI research paper of July 2021 explains it for FY21. It quantified the impact of various policy measures that helped. It said (i) corporate tax cut "contributed 19% to the top line" (ii) "extended period of low-interest rate" contributed "on an average 5% to the overall top line" (iii) expenditure reduction (through various ways) contributed "as much as 31%" on top line and (iv) "employee costs have been cut" on an average by 3% in FY21.

It is, therefore, clear that the 2019 corporate tax cut contributed to the soaring corporate profits but didn't raise corporate tax collections. Budget documents show, in FY21 corporate tax collections fell – from Rs 5,56,876 crore in FY20 (actual) to Rs 4,57,719 crore in FY21 (actual). A dubious history was also made when corporate tax collection in FY21 (Rs 4,57,719) fell below income tax (Rs 4,87,144 crore) paid by lesser mortals.

The fall in corporate tax happened in the very fiscal (FY21) in which both listed and unlisted companies recorded 138% net profits (CMIE data). That was also the fiscal when the GDP growth plunged to a historic low of -6.6% – far more than the global average of -3.1%. For IMF's Bhalla to then claim a 66% rise in tax revenue and 33% rise in GDP, over FY20, because of the corporate tax is not only tenuous but grossly misleading.

This brings a question: How many corporates actually adopted the "new simplified tax regime" (22% tax for existing and 15% tax for new manufacturing units) at the centre of the debate?

According to the budget document for 2022-23, only 15.85% of companies opted for 22% tax without exemptions/incentives and only 0.14 % of companies for 15% tax meant for new manufacturing units in FY20. The Finance Ministry has not updated the numbers. And the parliamentary panel mentioned earlier also quotes these figures.

There is more to the subject of tax cuts to corporates

and the rich for that matter. It is a widely prevalent policy which is sought to be justified by the dubious "trickle-down" theory. The theory posits that tax cut for the rich and wealthy benefits the non-rich or that the benefits trickle down. First started by US President Ronald Reagan in the 1980s, it was continued by Donald Trump in 2017. Joe Biden reversed it in March 2022.

The Indian government used the same logic in 2019.

Corporate tax and economy

What did corporates do with the tax cuts in the US in 2017 and India in 2019? There are plenty of lessons to be learnt and hence, need to be recollected. The US Congress studied the impact of Trump's corporate tax cut in 2017 and found:

1) Corporates used the tax cuts to invest in stock markets and stock buybacks reached a historic high of $1 trillion in 2018. A stock buyback is a tool to manipulate stock prices, benefit a few at the cost of employees and existing shareholders and causes financial fragility by sucking out cash surpluses.

2) Corporate tax collection fell by $40 billion in 2018, which was offset by a $45 billion increase in income tax collections due to the (simultaneous) cut in income tax and payroll tax, which led to an increase in private consumption by 0.4% in the GDP.

3) There was "no indication of a surge in wages" and although investment increased "the growth patterns for different types of assets do not appear to be consistent with the direction and size of the supply-side incentive effects one would expect from the tax changes".

What saved the US economy was the simultaneous cut in income and payroll tax that led to higher consumption expenditure and higher indirect tax collections. Corporates made no positive contribution to economic growth.

The Parliament never bothered, except for calculating the corporate tax loss in August 2022 (mentioned earlier).

The RBI did. Its 2019-20 annual report said how the tax cut was used: "The corporate tax cut of September 2019 has been utilised in debt servicing, build-up of cash balances and other current assets rather than restarting the CAPEX cycle." Corporate tax collection fell from Rs 5,56,876 crore in FY20 (actual) to Rs 4,57,719 crore in FY21 (actual). Unlike the US, India didn't go for a simultaneous tax cut in income and payroll tax in September 2019.

So, there was no investment or job creation due to the corporate tax cut in India. In fact, analysis of corporate accounts showed, that the "stellar rise" in corporate earnings/profits in FY22 (over 60%) didn't even lead to a corresponding boom in capital expenditure, rather it grew by a mere 2.3%, a six-year low!

As for job creation, no such claims can be made in any case. Job loss in industries continues. Workers are fleeing industry to informal, low-paying and low-productive agriculture for survival. Apart from other studies, the latest PLFS of 2020-21 confirms it. It shows that agriculture's share in employment went up from 45.6% (of the total employment) in 2019-20 to 46.5% in 2020-21. Employment in manufacturing went down from 11.2% to 10.9% and the share of industry (including manufacturing) fell from 12.1% to 11.8% during the same period. The services sector, which has a large segment of informal work, also fell from 30.7% to 29.6%.

Did Indian corporates put the money in stock markets?

That is not known in absence of any definitive study. All that is known is that Indian stock markets created multiple historic highs during the pandemic fiscals of FY21 and FY22.

Historic trends of tax cuts

The corporate tax cut is part of neoliberal economics for the past five decades. It has fallen worldwide, from more than 38% in 1990 to about 22% in 2018 – as per a 2019 internal IMF paper. This paper warned against the trend saying that such sharp falls in corporate tax undermined both tax revenue and faith in the fairness of the overall tax system and that it was especially harmful to low-income countries by depriving revenue needed to achieve higher growth and reduce poverty.

There are two recent studies which are relevant in the current context.

One is titled "Do corporate tax cuts boost economic growth?", in which a German and an Austrian economist examine 441 estimates from 42 primary studies on the impact of corporate taxes on economic growth. What they find is an eyeopener.

They say "there is evidence for publication selectivity in favour of reporting growth-enhancing effects of corporate tax cuts". That is, there is a pronounced bias toward claiming that corporate tax cut improves economic growth. Such biased studies or claims are conjured up by factors "including researcher choices concerning the measurement of growth and corporate taxes, and controlling for other budgetary components". They also aver that "correcting for this bias, we cannot reject the hypothesis of a zero effect of corporate taxes on growth".

Another one looks at it from a broader perspective by taking into account tax cuts for corporates as well as the wealthy. The latter (tax cut for the wealthy) is also a global phenomenon. Trump did it. India did it in 2016 when it abolished the wealth tax.

This study, "The economic consequences of major tax cuts for the rich", by economists from the King's College London, identifies all instances of major tax reductions on the rich (including corporates) in 18 OECD countries between 1965 and 2015 and estimates the average effects of these major tax reforms on key macroeconomic aggregate.

Their conclusion: "We find tax cuts for the rich lead to higher income inequality in both the short- and medium-term. In contrast, such reforms do not have any significant effect on economic growth or unemployment. Our results, therefore, provide strong evidence against the influential political-economic idea that tax cuts for the rich 'trickle down' to boost the wider economy."

Aug 12, 2022

PS: *In February and August 2023, the Parliament was told (in response to questions) that the corporate tax cut losses had been re-estimated to be Rs 2.28 lakh crore – Rs 1.28 lakh crore in FY20 and Rs 1 lakh crore in FY21.*

***

The Wheels-Within-Wheels in Central Govt Vacancies

Conflicting numbers on sanctioned posts, and progressive growth in vacancies since 2018 pose a unique challenge

When the Centre announced on June 14, 2022, that 10 lakh vacancies in the central ministries and departments would be filled in the next one-and-half years, it came through a one-line tweet from the Prime Minister's Office (PMO). The tweet said: "PM@narendramodi reviewed the status of Human Resources in all departments and ministries and instructed that recruitment of 10 lakh people be done by the government in mission mode in next 1.5 years."

The 10-lakh number sparked speculations about whether these were purely regular civilian jobs in central ministries and departments or included central armed police forces (CAPFs) and other autonomous bodies under the central government.

Muddled sanctioned posts and vacancies in central ministries/depts

That is because until then, the Rajya Sabha had been told, on February 3, 2022, that there were 8.72 lakh vacancies in central ministries and departments as on March 1, 2020

– far lower than 10 lakh the PMO tweeted. The reply didn't reveal the source of information.

On July 20, 2022, the Lok Sabha was told that there were 9.79 lakh vacancies of "civilian regular" posts in central ministries and departments as on March 1, 2021. This time the source was revealed: Annual Report of Pay Research Unit of Department of Expenditure.

A look at the Annual Report of Pay Research Unit of Department of Expenditure (DoE), Finance Ministry, reveals many discrepancies.

When the Centre claimed 8.72 lakh vacancies as on March 1, 2020, the DoE's annual report of 2019-20 said this was higher at 8.86 lakh on the very same date – which works out to be 21.75% of the sanctioned posts. These vacancies were "including UTs".

When the Centre claimed 9.79 lakh vacancies (or 24.27%) as on March 1, 2021, the DoE's annual report of 2020-21 said this was true but if UTs are excluded. If UTs were included, then the vacancies went up to 9.96 lakh – that is, 24.20% of sanctioned posts. This (9.96 lakh) is closer to the PMO's tweet (10 lakh).

Now, if the vacancies "including UTs" went up from 9.79 lakh to 9.96 lakh, why did the percentage fall (from 24.27% to 24.20%)?

That is because the DoE's annual report said the sanctioned posts "excluding UTs" were 40.35 lakh but "including UTs" 41.11 lakh – as on March 1, 2021. Going by the DoE's annual report of 2019-20, the sanctioned posts were 40.78 lakh as on March 1, 2020.

This would mean, the sanctioned posts went up in 2021 (41.1 lakh), compared to 2020 (40.78 lakh).

How did the sanctioned post go up during the pandemic of March 2020 to March 2021? India went into a complete lockdown, there was a massive distress migration from urban areas to rural. The Centre never announced creating new posts, before or after the lockdown. How did this happen?

In fact, something opposite has been happening for a long time:

1) The 7th Pay Commission report of 2015 says, sanctioned posts ("regular civilian") were cut down from a peak of 41.76 lakh in 1994 to 38.90 lakh in 2014 (both "excluding UTs") and 40.49 lakh ("including UTs") in 2014. It doesn't provide the sanctioned posts of 1994 "including UTs". Further, on March 5, 2020, the Centre told the Rajya Sabha that the sanctioned strength was 38 lakh as on March 1, 2018. The trend was a secular decline.

2) Indian Railways abolished 72,000 Group C and D jobs in six years during 2015-16 to 2020-21.

3) The Public Sector Enterprises Survey (PSES) of 2020-21, released on July 21, 2022, by the Department of Public Enterprises said, CPSUs shed jobs – not part of the job data mentioned until now. Regular jobs fell by -5.4% (from 9.1 lakh to 8.5 lakh), casual jobs by -44% and contract jobs by -.6.8% in FY21 (pandemic) over FY20 (pre-pandemic). This is also a long-term trend.

These facts point to a cut down in sanctioned post, rather than increase.

Other central govt vacancies

The above data on sanctioned posts and vacancies are

limited to central ministries and departments. What about vacancies in other central agencies?

CPSUs, mentioned earlier, are a big source of jobs. According to the PSES of 2020-21, the total employees in CPSUs were 13.72 lakh in FY21 – falling from 14.79 lakh in FY20. There is no information on the sanctioned posts or vacancies. Even a 10% vacancy, for example, would mean more than a lakh of jobs go abegging.

Public sector banks (PSBs) also provide plenty of jobs? As per the Centre's reply to the Lok Sabha on July 18, 2022, 5% posts (38,147) were vacant as on July 1, 2022. This would mean the sanctioned posts were 7.63 lakh as on that date (July 1, 2022). Given that the RBI database shows 7.7 lakh were employed in PSBs in FY20 (more than 7.63 in 2022), the Centre's reply would mean the sanctioned posts in PSBs have fallen – reinforcing the assertion that the sanctioned posts are going down, rather than up, as argued earlier.

As for institutions of higher educations, the Centre told the Lok Sabha on March 21, 2022, that faculty positions in Central Universities, IITs and IIMs are vacant. Central Universities had 6,558, IITs 4,370 and IIMs 422 vacant posts. The reply didn't reveal the sanctioned faculty posts or the date of vacancies.

Then there are a large number of autonomous institutions under various central ministries and departments. For example, the Education Ministry runs central schools (Navodaya Vidyalayas and Kendriya Vidayalays) and other institutions like the CBSE, NCERT and UGC; Defence Ministry runs Sainik Schools; Ministry of Health and Family Welfare runs hospitals and medical colleges (AIIMS, Safdarjung), etc.

There are bound to be vacancies in these institutions too – given the evident lackadaisical attitude to filling sanctioned posts.

Vacancies in non-civilian posts

Then there are non-civilian posts under the Centre's control. One is central armed police forces (CAPFs) like the Assam Rifles, BSF, CISF, CRPF, ITBP, NDRF, NSG, PF and SSB. The 2022 report of Bureau of Police Research and Development (BPRD), Data on Police Organisations, shows as against the sanctioned strength of 11.09 lakh, 1.29 lakh posts were vacant (11.6%) as on January 1, 2021.

Among the three defence services, as per the Centre's reply to Lok Sabha on July 22, 2022, the total number of vacancies in the three defence forces – Army, Navy and Air Force – were 1.36 lakh. Except for the Navy (May 31, 2022), the date of vacancies was not mentioned for the army or air force, nor the sanctioned posts for the services were revealed.

On July 25, 2020, defence minister Rajnath Singh told Lok Sabha the three services could recruit 37,301 personnel in the last two years, as against the average annual vacancy of 60,000. That was because of the pandemic. He said the three services had started recruitment under the "Agnipath" scheme and would induct 46,000 in 2022.

This leaves 96,699 (1,80,000 minus 37,301 plus 46,000) unfilled positions in the three services by the end of 2022. There is a buzz the Army intends to cut down its strength to below 11 lakh, from the current strength of more than 13 lakh.

If all these are added, the total vacancies in all central government entities under its control would far exceed 10 lakh, the PMO mentioned. There is no reason why those wouldn't be filled in a time-bound manner.

These vacancies are jarring not only because there is a job crisis but also because high vacancies mean low service delivery to the people for which they have elected the government in the first place.

In fact, the vacancies worsen the grossly inadequate public service in India.

Are there enough public servants in India?

Going by the PLFS of 2020-21, the share of public sector employment (centre plus states) works out to a mere 6.8% of the total workforce. In comparison, the OECD average was 21.1% in 2020 and 17.4% in 2021. This huge gap should burst the myth, if any, about India having a bloated bureaucracy or that India needs to shed its public sector workforce.

There is yet another yardstick to know the adequacy of public servants. The 7th Pay Commission report of 2015 says, going by the size of central sector employment (excluding states), India had 139 public servants per one lakh population in 2014. In comparison, the US had 668. Again, India's score is very poor.

Economists often use such data (public sector workers as percentage of total workforce and population) to argue that India must increase employment in government, rather than reduce it as India has done for years (by reducing sanctioned posts and keeping vacancies unfilled).

It was the PLFS of 2017-18 which delivered the devastating news that the unemployment rate had reached 45-year high of 6.1%. Analysis of its data by the Azim Premji

University said, India lost 9 million jobs between 2011-12 and 2017-18 "for the first time in India's history".

How has the Centre responded to it?

The annual reports of Pay Research Unit of Department of Expenditure (DoE) show, the vacancies in central government "civilian regular" jobs have progressively grown from 17.8% in 2018 to 22.7% in 2019 to 21.7% in 2020 and to 24.2% in 2021. That's sad in the midst of a job crisis.

Aug 4, 2022

***

A House of Cards that is EWS Quota

The income threshold of 8 lakh per annum for EWS quota is under question given that 95-99% of families would qualify, defeating the very purpose of providing quotas for SCs, STs and OBCs

For many, the Economic Advisory Council to the Prime Minister (EAC-PM)'s "Report on State of Inequality in India" would have come as a surprise for stating that an Indian earning Rs 3 lakh a year, or Rs 25,000 a month, would fall in "top 10%" of wage earners in the country. The basis for this claim is the PLFS of 2019-20 — which is meant for tracking the state of employment rather than family income.

Nevertheless, that is the harsh reality of the wannabe economic superpower and the fastest growing major economy in FY22.

Now consider this.

To qualify for the 10% quota (in higher education and jobs) for economically weaker sections (EWS) among upper castes, the cut-off "family income" is Rs 8 lakh per annum. That is, a monthly income of Rs 66,666. Going by the EAC-PM data, this would mean far more than 90% Indian families would automatically qualify for the EWS quota, since Rs 66,666 is 2.6 times of Rs 25,000. The number could very well be 95-99% families, as we will soon find out, in which cases several questions about the rationality of this quota and the quota system in general arise.

But before looking at those questions here is another cause of concern.

The Centre and some states have already started implementing the EWS quota even though both its constitutionality and the rationale of high-income cut-off are sub-judice and pending before the Supreme Court.

10% EWS quota in operation

The Centre began implementing the EWS quota immediately after the Constitution was amended in January 2019 to provide for it — ahead of the 2019 general elections. The qualifying income threshold (there are asset criteria too but those are not contentious) was notified later that month by the Department of Personnel and Training (DoPT).

For example, the Railway Recruitment Board (RRB) set aside 10% EWS quota in February 2019, while notifying recruitments for over 35,000 non-technical posts. This recruitment process was a long drawn and contentious one, eventually provoking job seekers to attack the Railways' properties in Uttar Pradesh and Bihar in January 2022. Following this the recruitment process was put on hold.

In April 2022, the RRB re-notified the recruitment to these posts. It again set aside 10% EWS quota.

More recently, on May 17, 2022, the DoPT issued a notification earmarking the EWS quota for recruitment of head constables in the Delhi Police. Of the 559 vacancies, 56 have been marked for EWS categories. The recruitment will be carried out by the Staff Selection Commission (SSC).

There are no comprehensive data on the actual recruitments made under the EWS quota. In December 2021, the Centre told the Lok Sabha that it had recruited 84 people under this head.

Last year, Telangana issued guidelines for the EWS quota in government jobs and higher education. The Andhra Pradesh Public Service Commission (APPSC) soon thereafter declared that it would be providing the EWS quota for all appointments in the state government.

None seems to care about the pending adjudication before the Supreme Court, which, in turn, raises questions about the legal validity of such a move.

The constitutional validity petitions were referred to a five-member bench of the court in August 2020 but nothing more has been heard of it. The income criterion is being heard by another bench for a long time; the next hearing is scheduled for July 2022.

How many families qualify for EWS quota?

When the EWS quota was brought in 2019, the PLFS of 2019-20 — on the basis of which the EAC-PM report said a monthly income of Rs 25,000 qualifies one to the top 10% wage earners — wasn't available. It came in 2021. The only authentic information about the income levels was available in the NSSO's 2011-12 monthly per capita consumption expenditure (MPCE) survey of households.

This was the same report on the basis of which the finance ministry's Monthly Economic Report (MER) of April 2022 (released in May) made two *absurd claims*: (i) "evidence on consumption patterns" suggests that "inflation in India has a lesser impact on low-income strata than on high-income groups"; and (ii) moderation of CPI inflation from 6.2% in FY21 to 5.5% in FY22 led to "redistribution of income".

Since India doesn't have household income estimates, MPCE is used as a proxy for it.

According to this report (2011-12 NSSO survey), top 5% of households reported MPCE of Rs 4,481 in rural and Rs 10,281 in urban areas.

If 5 members of each family in top 5% were earning, the monthly "family" income would be Rs 22,405 in rural and Rs 51,405 in urban areas — much less than Rs 66,666 that was set as the cut-off in early 2019. This would mean the number of families qualifying for the EWS quota would be far more than 95%.

The finance ministry had to rely on this decade-old NSSO data because the Centre junked the 2017-18 one for showing that "real" MPCE had fallen from 2011-12 level — for the first time in 40 years. This indicated poverty was growing. Thus, the Centre didn't attempt another MPCE even though it did carry out other surveys, like the NHFS-5 of 2019-21, Civil Registration System (CRS) for excess deaths in 2020 and Medical Certification of Cause of Deaths (MCCD) of 2020 — all of which were released earlier this month.

The other data available then was the NABARD's 2018 All India Rural Financial Inclusion Survey of 2016-17. It showed top 1% of rural households earn Rs 48,833 a month — again much less than Rs 66,666 and would mean, 99% rural households qualified for the EWS quota.

Several questions arise from all this.

What is the point of the EWS quota when almost the entire country qualifies for it? Does it not defeat the very purpose of quota for SCs, STs and OBCs (positive discrimination) — which is aimed at correcting the "structural inequality" and historical injustices that deprived them of higher education and jobs?

Educational quota allowed by SC

In the meanwhile, the Supreme Court has allowed the EWS quota in higher education.

In January 2022, it vacated a stay imposed on the EWS quota in the NEET PG counselling by the Madras High Court. The latter had pointed at the pending cases before the former to impose a stay. But the former overturned it, saying that the income criterion (Rs 8 lakh per annum) would be subject to final outcome of the pending petitions.

This begs more questions.

What happens if the income level is found to be irrationally high, without factual basis and then lowered? What would be the fate of candidates who qualify and take admissions by then?

Such possibilities are very real because the apex court has been asking the Centre to provide the rationale for the cut-off of Rs 8 lakh income, which the Centre has failed to do until now.

Incidentally, there are assets criteria to qualify for the EWS quota too: (a) 5 acres of agricultural land and above; (b) residential flat of 1,000 square feet and above; (c) residential plot of 100 square yards and above in notified municipalities and; (d) residential plot of 200 square yards and above in non-notified municipalities.

But these are not at the core of the legal challenges to the EWS quota.

Then there is a question of the constitutionality of the EWS for upper castes.

Prima facie, two constitutional issues arise from the EWS quota. One, it violates the 50% capping on reservations that the Supreme Court had put in the famous Indra Sawhney vs Union of India case in 1993 and two, the basis of reservations for SCs, STs and OBCs are not their low income but socio-economic injustices thy suffered which isn't the case for upper castes.

May 30, 2022

***

Global Talk of Taxing the Rich has Little Appeal in India

EAC-PM's recommendations for a universal basic income and urban employment schemes to address inequality have also failed to generate a buzz inside and outside the government.

Ahead of Amazon's AGM of May 25, 2022, the UK-based tax transparency campaign group Fair Tax Foundation (FTF) revealed shocking details of tax evasion and misleading tax disclosures by the world's largest retailer during the past decade of 2012-2021.

The FTF's investigations show that Amazon actually paid 9.8% tax during 2012-2021 when the US headline tax was 35% during 2012-2017 and 21% in later years (post 2017 corporate tax cut by the Trump administration). The 'tax gap' between the tax Amazon's financial statements declared and the actual cash tax paid is also huge. The gap "has grown to $6.1 billion" in the decade under scrutiny (2012-2021). Amazon reported cumulative tax of $15.7 billion while actually paying $9.6 billion during this period.

A year earlier, the Fair Tax Foundation's investigations had shown that the top six US multinationals, Google, Amazon, Facebook, Apple, Microsoft and Netflix, described as the Silicon Six, avoided paying $100 billion tax between

2010 and 2019 through aggressive tax planning and profit and revenue shifting to tax havens (low tax or zero tax jurisdictions).

In spite of the known history of tax avoidance and evasions by US multinationals, Amazon's AGM is billed to be the first event in which shareholders would be giving their opinion on tax transparency resolution that has been tabled by some of the investors.

Billionaires' call for more tax at Davos

As wealth and income inequalities rise, more so after the US tax cut tax of 2017 and the pandemic struck, many billionaires and millionaires have come forward to call for more tax on themselves.

Even at Davos, where the global super-rich have gathered for annual conclave organised under the aegis of World Economic Forum (WEF), many asked world leaders to tackle the cost-of-living crisis by pushing up taxes on people like them. They even took to the streets demanding fairer tax systems worldwide.

This has come with the realisation that they expect more scrutiny (from media, political and activist groups) on corporate taxation, particularly after the pandemic heightened the inequalities. Deloitte's 2021 annual global tax survey found 79% of multinationals expect more scrutiny and 33% are willing to increase voluntary tax disclosure.

In July 2021, 130 countries, including India, had agreed to US President Joe Biden's proposal to impose 15% global minimum tax for companies. But there is little progress on that front. In such a situation, and in the face of growing tax evasion and avoidance by multinationals like

Amazon, the voluntary call by the super-rich to tax them seems aimed at blunting public ire at them, rather than a genuine desire.

New billionaire every 30 hours, million new poor every 33 hours

The pandemic has demonstrated how billionaires' wealth has surged amidst all-round economic ruin. At Davos, the Oxfam International presented its report "Profiting from Pain" on May 23, 2022, painting a distressing picture.

Among others, it said:

- The combined crises of COVID-19, rising inequality, and rising food prices could push as many as 263 million people into extreme poverty in 2022, reversing decades of progress. This is the equivalent of one million people every 33 hours.

- At the same time a new (dollar) billionaire has been minted on average every 30 hours during the pandemic – 573 more billionaires now than in 2020 when the pandemic began (total of 2,668).

- This means that in the same time it took to create a new billionaire during the pandemic, one million people could be pushed into extreme poverty this year.

- Billionaires have seen their fortunes increase as much in 24 months as they did in 23 years.

- Billionaires in the food and energy sectors have seen their fortunes increase by a billion dollars every two days – the highest levels in decades.

In other words, the Oxfam report says, the total billionaire wealth is now equivalent of 13.9% of global

GDP, up from 4.4% in 2000, with the richest 10 men having more wealth than the poorest 40% of global population. As for income, 99% of global population has been hit by the pandemic with 125 million full-time jobs lost in 2021; while incomes of the richest have already recovered from the pandemic hit, that of the poorest haven't.

The case of India is no different. In fact, wealth and income inequalities have risen more sharply in India than other countries, as the World Inequality Reports of 2019 and 2022 have shown. Multiple wealth and income tracking agencies (Forbes, Hurun, Bloomberg) have shown the Indian billionaires' wealth rose spectacularly during the pandemic while the economy is still struggling and millions have lost their lives and livelihoods.

An analysis shows the dollar billionaires' number in India jumped to 126 at the end of December 2021, from 85 a year ago and their wealth share went up from 9.3% of the GDP in FY16 to about 25% in FY22. A 2% wealth tax on them is likely to generate more than Rs 1 lakh crore to fund welfare schemes to help the poor, this analysis said.

Not only there is little resonance to the global debate on wealth tax on the super-rich In India, the tax burden here has shifted to the poor. After the corporate tax cut of 2019, total corporate tax collections fell below income tax collection in FY21 for the first time in the 2011-12 GDP series – as Fortune India detailed in "Why high GST collection is bad taxation and bad economics".

There is no sign of either a rise in corporate tax or wealth tax on the super-rich in India. In fact, India abolished wealth tax in 2017 even as the world was hotly debating the growing wealth and income inequalities. And unlike in the rest of the world, Indian billionaires have not called for higher tax on them despite India taking a far bigger hit than other major economies.

UBI for the poor in India?

It is in these contexts that the Economic Advisory Council to the Prime Minister (EAC-PM)'s "Report on State of Inequality in India", commissioned to the Institute for Competitiveness and released earlier this month, must be seen.

Taking into consideration the growing income and wealth inequalities and job crisis, the report recommended the following six measures:

- Mapping multidimensional poverty and defining middle class (income level);
- Raising minimum income by introducing Universal Basic Income (UBI);
- Introducing MGNREGS-like scheme to tackle urban unemployment;
- Higher social sector spending;
- Ensuring equitable education, skilling and more job creation and
- Mapping vulnerable households to promote their wellbeing.

While the report flags the right issues and prescribes the solutions long suggested by economists, it falls short on formulations and specifics. For example, it talks about UBI and urban MGNERGS but doesn't spell out their designs, how much fund they would require and how such fund can be mobilised. It doesn't talk of taxing the super-rich at all.

The report may have attracted some attention because it was from the EAC-PM to the government but a complete silence from the latter and lack of material to work with suggest that it may not be of much use.

A formal suggestion for UBI had first came from former chief economic advisor (CEA) Arvind Subramanian in his Economic Survey of 2016-17. It proposed income transfer of Rs 7,620 a year to 75% of population (excluding the top 25% in income). It gathered dust until the Congress picked up the idea in the run-up to the general elections of 2019, called it Nyuntam Aay Yojana (NYAY) in which income transfer of Rs 72,000 a year to the poorest 20% of households was proposed. It was vigorously contested by the ruling establishment (for feasibility), although weeks later the PM-Kisan was launched with retrospective effect in the budget for 2019-20, under which farmers got Rs 6,000 a year in direct cash transfers.

The Rajasthan government's announcement of an urban MGNREGS in this year's budget has also not generated much enthusiasm with unanswered questions about its feasibility and even desirability. It is yet to be tested on the ground. Besides, like the MGNREGS, an urban version of it would be an emergency relief, rather than creation of high-productive, regular jobs with social security for all workers.

The most disappointing part of policy making in the past few years is marked absence of public debates, due deliberations and scrutiny in the Parliament and lack of relevant and reliable data on critical areas like growing poverty (no household consumption expenditure survey after 2011-12, for example) and chronic job crisis (the last one being the pre-pandemic PLFS of 2019-20).

Nevertheless, rub-off of Amazon's AGM would be keenly awaited even in India.

May 24, 2022

Welcome to 'Stressed' PPP Projects, the 2nd Time Round

Despite policy incentives and new PPP contract model to protect private partners from external and unforeseen factors, Ministry of Ports, Shipping and Waterways is saddled with many abandoned projects

India has been battling with stressed banking assets (NPAs) for years. The historic "reform" for resolution of such stressed assets, called Insolvency and Bankruptcy Code (IBC) of 2016, is flailing as recoveries are nosediving. At the end of March 31, 2022, total recoveries from the "resolution" and "liquidation" outcomes under the IBC dropped to 16.6% of the "admitted claims" or debts. This is lower than 25% recovery under the Bureau of Industrial and Financial Reconstruction (BIFR) mechanism.

Now a new category of stressed asset has emerged in May 2022, called "stressed Public Private Partnership (PPP) projects at the major ports".

This is exactly how the Ministry of Ports, Shipping and Waterways described the challenge it is facing, while issuing new "guidelines for early Resolution of Stuck Public Private Partnership (PPP) projects at Major Ports" on May 11, 2022.

PPP port projects abandoned

The ministry's guidelines were occasioned by abandonment of sanctioned PPP projects by private partners, either at the execution stage or after commercial operations. The ministry offered two reasons for this: (i) projects abandoned during the execution phase because of various reasons like aggressive bidding, optimistic projections and unforeseen changes in business; and (ii) abandoned during the execution or after becoming operational as private partners defaulted on their loans, forcing creditors to declare their loans non-performing assets (NPAs) and go for IBC proceedings.

The new guidelines provide "mechanism for resolution" of these stressed PPP projects.

According to this, the concessioning authority (in this case public ports) would take over the abandoned projects after paying for the work done or by taking over 90% of loans of its private partner if the projects were abandoned at the execution stage. For those cases already undergoing IBC proceedings, the concessioning authority (public ports) will be allowed to participate in it, take over the PPP projects and then put it to "re-bidding".

The resolution mechanism is, thus, nothing but nationalisation of PPP projects abandoned by private players. Given that the IBC is yielding only 16.6% (a haircut of 83%), this means the Indian public will end up paying for the failures of private PPP players ("socialisation" of private sector loss).

Besides, the haircut would show up as NPAs of public sector banks (PSBs), which will then be written off as a matter of routine. The NPA write-offs have skyrocketed since 2015. RBI data shows the write-offs jumped from Rs 1.2 lakh crore during the 10 years of UPA (FY06-FY15) to Rs 10.1 lakh crore in the six years of NDA-II (FY16-FY21) — a quantum jump of more than 8 times!

Through this resolution mechanism, the ministry hopes "unlocking the blocked cargo handling capacity of approximately 27 MTPA (million tonnes per annum)". It particularly hopes for early resolution of five "long standing disputes on stressed assets at various major ports" — two PPP projects at the Deendayal Port (earlier called Kandla port) and one each at Mumbai, Thoothukudi and Visakhapatnam ports.

Not a surprising development

The ministry acknowledged that despite several policy initiatives, incentives and due diligence, the survival of several PPP projects is at risk. One of this was an elaborate (234 pages) "New Model Concession Agreement — 2021 for Public-Private-Partnership (PPP) Projects at Major Ports" unveiled in November 2021, which was to benefit (i) 80 "on-going projects with investment of over Rs 56,000 crore"; and (ii) "31 projects of over Rs 14,600 crore to be awarded on PPP till FY25".

A significant provision of this was flagged by the minister, Sarbananda Sonowal, on the occasion, called "Change in Cargo due to Change in Law or Unforeseen Events". This is specifically meant to protect private partners in PPP projects from "external and unforeseen factors" that has forced it to bring the new resolution mechanism.

Dubious history of PPPs in highway sector

This is not the first time PPP projects have landed India in trouble.

During the UPA regime (2004-14), when the PPP was taken up in a big way in building national highways, many projects were abandoned, leading to a build-up of the NPA crisis in the early years of the NDA-II government. Former chief economic advisor (CEA) Arvind Subramanian famously called it the "twin balance sheet problem" — over-leveraged private companies and bad loan-saddled PSBs.

The UPA had virtually abandoned PPP projects towards the end of its tenure. It would be instructive to revisit the PPP fiasco of that era, more so for the role viability gap funding (VGF) played in those PPP projects.

VGF is an upfront payment to private players in the PPP projects by governments (Centre and states) to incentivise building infrastructure. As per the VGF policy spelt out in November 2022 for social and economic projects, the central and state governments would provide (i) VGF of up to 80% of the total project costs (each contributing 40%); and (ii) VGF of 50% of the operational cost (each sharing 25%) for the first five years of operations.

What this means is that the governments will fund 80% of PPP projects and then also fund 50% of operational cost of these projects for the first five years. The rest is to be paid by private partner of the PPP projects. This is why the PPP projects are very lucrative.

During the UPA era, the Planning Commission helmed PPPs, including writing the model contracts and granting of a VGF of 40% by the central government. An "internal paper" of the Planning Commission and RTI replies revealed the murky goings on in PPPs in 2010.

These documents showed that for 20 highway projects under scanner, PSBs had given a loan of Rs 25,940 crore without collaterals to the private partners while the sanctioned cost of these projects was just Rs 13,646 crore. That is, the loans given were nearly double the cost of the projects. Many PPP projects were abandoned and saddled PBSs with huge NPAs. Why did PSBs give 200% loans without collaterals and then landed themselves with NPAs remains an abiding mystery.

There is more.

In all highway projects a VGF of 40% had also been given to private partners by the central government. Taken together, the bank loan and VGF were far excess than the project costs.

For easy understanding, let us say a PPP project of Rs 100 crore was sanctioned. The central government paid Rs 40 crore of VGF upfront. The private partner went to a PSB and took a loan of Rs 200 crore (double the project cost). In all, it received Rs 240 crore for a Rs 100-crore project. This means the private partner didn't need to bring a penny of its own (the reason why it is being owed) and got an excess amount of Rs 140 crore (Rs 240 crore minus Rs 100 crore) to divert to its other projects. When the project is abandoned, or the loan is defaulted banks are holding up to Rs 200 crore of NPAs.

This was not the only cause of worry.

The Gurgaon Expressway toll booths were dismantled in 2012. One of the main reasons was excessive profiteering by under-reporting number of vehicles that passed through the toll booths maintained by the private partner. The other irritant was the huge traffic jams at either side of toll booths. The same was the case with the DND flyway in Noida, which was dismantled in 2016.

NDA revives PPP and VGF

Instead of being wary, the NDA-II government revived both PPPs and VGF in a big way. In 2014, it announced Rs 1 crore of VGF for each 1 MW of solar energy plants. In 2015, it gave "one time fund infusion" to many of the highway projects that were stuck — over and above the 40% VGF the private partners had already received.

Before and after the pandemic hit, the central government aggressively pushed for VGF for private medical colleges (not private hospitals), in the budget and in official communications. It asked states to give unencumbered land, tax concessions and other financial help, which it could reclaim from the Ayushman Bharat (PM-JAY). It also asked states to hand over (public) district hospitals to those private medical colleges for running and maintenance.

Now VGFs for PPP projects are climbing up.

In FY15, the VGF was Rs 596 crore — the Parliament was informed by the government. The Union Cabinet approved VGF outlays of Rs 1,400 crore for FY21, Rs 1,500 crore for FY22, Rs 1,600 for FY23, Rs 1,700 crore for FY24 and Rs 1,900 crore for FY25 at its meeting in November 2020.

But there is no comprehensive study in India of how many projects have been built under the PPP model, how much funds the central and state governments have paid for it and how much NPAs have been built up by these projects.

These are the key to know the efficiency of PPP model. Until then, one can expect more about "stressed" PPP projects.

May 16, 2022

Apex Court's FCRA Order a Big Blow to NGOs, Grassroot Development Work

The crackdown on NGOs using the FCRA wasn't started by the BJP government in 2014. It started much earlier (record of cancellation of FCRA licenses available from 2011) during the previous UPA govt.

On April 8, 2022, a three-member bench of the Supreme Court delivered its judgement on the 2020 amendment to the Foreign Contribution Regulation Act (FCRA) of 2010, upholding the tight regulations brought in on foreign fund flows to NGOs.

This judgement has far-reaching consequences because the 2020 amendment puts several restrictions on entities working in a wide range of human development: health, education, climate change mitigation, civil rights etc.

First things first.

The key elements introduced in the 2020 amendment include:

- Expanding the list of entities prohibited from receiving foreign funding beyond the FCRA Act of

2010 to include the whole universe of "public servant" defined in Section 21 of the Indian Penal Code.

- Disallowing a recipient to "transfer such foreign contribution to any other person" – which denies aid to small and grassroot level NGOs and individuals working among the poorest.
- Making it mandatory to open FCRA account only in the designated SBI branch in New Delhi to receive foreign contributions, for which Aadhaar card is mandatory.
- Stopping the use of foreign funds and suspending the FCRA license on mere suspicion ("reason to believe") and "pending any further inquiry" – without giving on opportunity to be heard or producing evidence upfront (Section 11).
- The period of suspension of license extended from 180 days to 360 days.

It is the arbitrary provision of suspending FCRA license without giving a chance to be heard or providing evidence upfront (Section 11), which came handy when the Delhi High Court, in its February 2022 judgement, ruled in the favour of the government and upheld the suspension of FCRA license of human rights group, Commonwealth Human Rights Initiative (CHRI).

SC upholds 2020 FCRA amendments

The apex court's judgement upholding the 2020 amendment in the FCRA of 2010 is a setback for the NGOs, many of which work in critical areas of development at the grassroot level.

Before talking about the judgement, here is a brief

background for better appreciation of how the amendment hurts the economy and people.

On December 2021, the FCRA licenses of 5,933 NGOs lapsed, either due to their failures to apply for renewal within a stipulated timeframe or rejection of their renewal applications by the Ministry of Home Affairs (MHA) – the regulatory ministry.

The last few years have seen 12,580 NGOs losing licenses, which include IIT-Delhi, Jamia Millia Islamia, Indian Medical Association (the largest body of medical practitioners in India), Nehru Memorial Museum & Library (NMM&L), Press Institute of India (PII), JNU's Nuclear Science Centre, Lady Shri Ram College for Women; Delhi College of Engineering (Government of NCT of Delhi) and Oxfam India.

It came to notice in March 2022 that the MHA had put the US-based Hewlett Foundation on watchlist after finding that it was funding climate awareness campaigns in India, which a government official revealed, was not permissible under the FCRA. From November 2021, no fund has been given to any NGO or association in India.

Even the license of Mother Teresa's Missionaries of Charity, which works for destitute, was suspended on the Christmas of 2021 (December 25), under circumstances which is not clear yet. After a country-wide hue and cry, the license was renewed till 2026 a few days later on January 9, 2022.

The above examples indicate that the FCRA is not only being used to prevent misuse but also as a tool to control NGOs on the ground.

Coming back to the apex court's order upholding

the 2020 FCRA amendment, here are some of the key observations the court made to justify its action:

- "In short, no one can be heard to claim a vested right to accept foreign donation, much less an absolute right"; "By its very expression, it is a reflection on the constitutional morality of the nation as a whole being incapable of looking after its own needs and problems".

- "…the presence/inflow of foreign contribution in the country ought to be at the minimum level…The influence may manifest in different ways, including in destabilising the social order within the country. The charitable associations may instead focus on donors within the country…"

- "It must be borne in mind that the legislation under consideration must be understood in the context of the underlying intent of insulating the democratic polity from the adverse influence of foreign contribution…"

- "The third world countries may welcome foreign donation, but it is open to a nation, which is committed and enduring to be self-reliant and variously capable of shouldering its own needs, to opt for a policy of complete prohibition of inflow/acceptance of foreign contribution (donation) from foreign source."

- Indian passport "needs to be construed" as identification document, instead of the Aadhaar card (the only relief granted).

Foreign donations to political parties pending

Going by the Supreme Court's logic in upholding the FCRA amendment, a few questions arise.

First, if foreign contributions to NGOs can destabilise social order and endanger democratic policy ("insulating the democratic polity from the adverse influence of foreign contribution") and India needs to be "self-reliant", why should foreign funding be restricted only to the NGOs but not to political parties?

Sounds odd?

Actually, the FCRA of 2010, and the FCRA of 1976 that it replaced, both expressly banned foreign contributions/donations to political parties to insulate Indian democracy and government from foreign influence. Section 4 of the FCRA 1976 and Section 3 of the FCRA 2010 say: "No foreign contribution shall be accepted by any political party or office bearer thereof." Section 29-B of the Representation of the People (RP) Act of 1951 also prohibits political parties from receiving funds from foreign and domestic government-run companies.

Political parties are critical to democracy. They fight elections, form governments and make laws to govern the country. Hence, they need to be insulated from influence far more than any NGO.

The *first* to go was the FCRA prohibition (Section 4 of the FCRA 1976 and Section 3 of the FCRA 2010) under an interesting development.

The two leading political parties – the BJP and Congress – were found violating the two laws (FCRA an RP Act) by accepting funding from both foreign companies as well as government-owned companies (19 instances for the BJP and 15 instances from the Congress during FY04 and FY12). This was challenged before the Delhi High Court and in 2014, the court held both the political parties guilty. It asked for punitive action (within six months).

Instead of that, the Centre legalised the violations.

It amended the FCRA of 2010 to permit foreign donations by changing the definition of "foreign source" through the Finance Bill of 2016 and then extended it to the FCRA of 1976, through the Finance Bill of 2018, to give it retrospective effect from 1976 (giving complete immunity from punitive action).

Several petitions challenging these amendments are pending before the Delhi High Court and the Supreme Court.

Second, the Centre brought Electoral Bond in 2017 – an opaque instrument (bearer bond) that allows *anonymous, unlimited and unaccounted money* to be donated to political parties from both domestic and foreign sources. The Electoral Bond is also out of legal scrutiny and disclosure norms. The RP Act of 1951 was amended to keep it out of the scrutiny of Election Commission of India (ECI) and The Companies Act of 2013 was amended to (i) remove limits on such corporate donations and (ii) disclosing the name of the political party to which such donations are being made.

Electoral Bonds make it impossible for anyone, other than the central government, to know which domestic and foreign individual/company is donating to which political parties because these (bearer) bonds are issued by the government-run State Bank of India alone.

This makes the prohibition under the RP Act of 1951 (Section 29B) meaningless and hence, has not been changed yet. The ECI can't scrutinise funding through the Electoral Bond and the Companies Act of 2013 has been disabled from disclosure norms about political funding or amount. Simple!

Now, if a "foreign source" is funding the ruling party now or in future (which wouldn't be known to outsiders), who knows how it compromises India's policies and governance (both at the central and state)?

Several petitions challenging the constitutional validity of the Electoral Bond are pending before the Supreme Court since 2018. Instead, the apex court has allowed the bonds to be freely traded and the three-member bench that upheld the legality of the 2020 FCRA amendment, didn't talk about it at all – or the real "destabilising" and "corrupt" impact it has on governance.

To his credit, Chief Justice of India Justice NV Ramana assured one of the petitioners earlier this month that he would soon take it up for examining its constitutionality.

Crackdown on NGOs

The crackdown on NGOs using the FCRA wasn't started by the BJP government in 2014. It started much earlier (record of cancellation of FCRA licenses available from 2011) during the previous UPA government.

The Ministry of Home Affairs (MHA) records show, the licenses of 20,675 entities have been "cancelled" by 2021. The bulk of these cancellations have come after 2015 (16,745).

There is no record of licenses suspended.

Records show the spate of cancellations began in 2012 when the protest against the Kudankulam (Tamil Nadu) nuclear plant peaked. From 4 cases in 2011, cancellation of FCRA licenses mounted to 3,922 in 2012. It was reduced to 4 in 2013; then went up to 59 in 2014; then hit a high of 10,003 in 2015. After a lull in 2018 (1), the list went up to 1,808 in

2019 and then plunged to 0 in 2020. In 2021, only 3 licenses were cancelled and none so far in 2022.

But these numbers exclude suspended FCRA licenses – which is now permitted for 360 days under the FCRA Amendment Act of 2020 – and that has its own crippling impact.

How crackdown on NGOs hurt economy and people

Recall Prime Minister Narendra Modi's call to NGOs for help during the devastating second wave of the pandemic in May 2021 when scores of people were dropping dead due to the lack of oxygen and hospital beds?

By that time, the NGOs had already been crippled because the tightening of the FCRA norms had started earlier (no amendment is needed to do that as the UPA had demonstrated it too). They were in no position to help the people desperately seeking help. The government appealed to the world community following which at least 40 countries provided oxygen and essential medicines.

By then, the 2020 FCRA amendment had further hurt the NGOs. Ironically, the 2020 amendment was notified on September 28, 2020 – amidst the first wave of the pandemic).

An investigating report of 2022 revealed that foreign funds to NGOs had fallen by 87% in one single year – from Rs 16,490 crore in FY19 to Rs 2,190 crore in FY20 (up to which data is available). By May 2021, when the Prime Minister sought help from NGOs, their foreign funding would have dwindled even further.

Human rights activist Venkatesh Nayak of CHRI says the 2020 FCRA amendment extended the period of suspension of FCRA license to 360 days but kept the limit of foreign funds that can be used during the suspension period at 25% (of the fund received).

This has delivered another blow to the NGOs because the suspension period has been doubled but they would have to do with the same 25% of the funds.

This then is why the Supreme Court's order needs to be challenged through review petitions.

Apr 19, 2022

***

Fewer Rafale Jets Leave Gaps in National Security

90 fewer Rafale jets (36 bought against 126 required) would have added 5 squadrons, taking the total to 37 – 5 short of IAF's need for 42.

The Parliamentary Standing Committee on Defence, which recently reviewed the Air Force's fighting capabilities, was alarmed at the shortage of its fighter squadrons, sought immediate acquisition of new jets but kept silent on the Rafale deal. Had the new deal not truncated the Rafale jets, the Air Force would have been better equipped to face the challenges of two-pronged threats. The Centre ordered 83 LCAs to bridge the gap arising out of order for 36 ready Rafale jets instead of 126 that were planned by the UPA government.

"During evidence, the representatives of Air Force submitted that the present authorised strength of squadron is 42. It was further stated that the total technical life of most of the existing squadron is expiring and consequently the squadron strength is progressively depleting...The committee emphasises for a time bound procurement of these aircraft, so as to replenish the Air Force squadron. The committee also urge(s) that Air Force should ensure that the new aircraft are procured in the near future so as to enhance the combat capabilities of the Force," the committee says in its "Demand for Grants (2022-23)" report, tabled in Parliament on March 16, 2022.

An Air Force representative revealed more shocking details to the panel. The panel quotes the representative saying: "There is an interesting aspect that a very large number of Sukhoi-30 and other fighters are on ground and we are hopeful that when those spares start coming from this year onwards, we are hopeful that will be able to actually add some squadrons."

What those sentences said needs to be re-emphasised to realise how alarming and scary the national security scenario is: (a) IAF's strength of fighting squadrons is "progressive depleting" (b) because the technical life of "most" of the existing squadrons is "expiring" (c) "a very large number" of Sukhoi-30 and other fighters are grounded due to lack of spares and (d) the ministry/government is being urged to buy more fighter jets in the "near future" and in "time bound" manner to fill the gaps.

In short, the security of Indian skies is in danger. The parliamentary panel duly reminded of the risks: "The committee are of the considered opinion that Air Force should have two front deterrence capabilities which is of utmost priority, as the threat on both sides of Indian neighborhood is a reality which cannot be ignored".

Ironically, these warnings come after repeat display of bravado by armed force chiefs.

On October 5, 2021, just ahead of the Air Force Day (October 8), Air Chief Marshal VR Chaudhari declared at a press conference that India was fully prepared ready to deal with a "two-front" war involving China and Pakistan and that the focus has been to enhance the IAF's overall combat capabilities.

His predecessor Air Chief Marshal BS Dhanoa had said the same thing in 2017, naming Pakistan and China. Again in 2017 (the relevance of it will become clear soon), the then Army chief who became the first Chief of Defence Staff (CDS), General Bipin Rawat, had said the Indian Army was fully ready for a "two-and-a-half-front" war.

Huge Gap in IAF's Fighter Squadrons

If the panel's words were scary and alarming its silences were deafening.

For one, it said the "authorised strength" of fighting squadrons was 42 but didn't say what was the gap from the actual requirement – the risk assessment gap. Air Chief Marshal Chaudhari (mentioned earlier) had also said in October 2021 that the IAF's existing strength was 30 squadrons. More ominously, he had added: "Our count will remain around 35 till the next decade, currently it is unlikely it will go up any further." He did explain why but that is understandable.

The parliamentary panel, thus, didn't focus where its focus should have been: the gap in the fighter squadrons which potentially jeopardises national security. Had it done so, it would have raised questions about the new Rafale deal of 2016 which cut the fighter jets being acquired from 126 to just 36.

Had the 126 jets been purchased – original plan had 18 in flyaway condition and 108 to be manufactured locally in India by the Hindustan Aeronautics Limited (HAL) under a technology transfer clause then--this would have enhanced India's domestic capability (all the more needed after the Russian-Ukraine war broke) and justified the 'Make in India' mission. The HAL has a stellar record of making fighter jets in India – Sukhoi-30 and LCAs that the parliamentary panel mentions.

The number of fighter jets to be purchased is decided after proper assessment of the security threat. By arbitrarily cutting down the number to 36 – that is a reduction of 90 jets – the IAF has lost 5 squadrons, going by the norm of 18 fighter jets in a squadron – taking the total to 37 (existing 30 plus 5 additions plus 2 that 36 flyaway jets add).

Thirty-seven squadrons are closer to 42 "authorised" or required by the Air Force and also 2 squadrons more than what Air Chief Marshal Chaudhari estimates (35) said could be added over the next decade!

That is the significance of the new Rafale deal of 2016.

Silence on Rafale deal

The only reference to the Rafale jets/deal by parliamentary panel is half a sentence in the statement of the Defence Secretary: "We have acquired 36 Rafale fighter planes; we have issued order for 83 LCAs."

For the record, none of the serving armed force chiefs (land, air, sea), defence ministry officials, ministers or government's security and defence advisors expressed worries or raised questions about the risks to the national security because of the renegotiated Rafale deal – at least not in public.

All outsiders – defence and strategic experts, investigating journalists and others – have done it. They keep raising multiple questions: risks to national security; suspected kickback; cutting out technology transfer; making Anil Ambani's firm with no experience and no expertise (it was incorporated weeks before the deal) as offset partner for a fighter jet project while the most credible and experienced HAL was kept out.

Role of CAG and SC in Rafale case

The French anti-corruption agency, Agence Française Anticorruption (AFA), found evidence of bribery in the Rafale deal and the French government appointed a judge in 2021 to begin prosecution. No investigation was ordered in India.

In fact, the Supreme Court disallowed pleas for FIR and investigation in 2018 even after a stink was raised by investigating journalists and others. Former ministers Yashwant Sinha and Arun Shourie in the Vajpayee government and activist-lawyer Prashant Bhushan went to the court raising doubts about abut several things, including a higher cost for 36 jets over 126 jets being negotiated by the UPA (95% negotiations were complete a French official had revealed then).

A national news channel revealed in 2021 that India's premier investigating agencies, including the Central Bureau of Investigation (CBI), were aware of the bribery allegations but ignored the evidence. The news channel dug out this evidence in the documents enclosed with the CBI's chargesheet in the AgustaWestland helicopters deal.

But by then, the Comptroller Auditor General of India (CAG), the government's top auditor, too had given a clean chit to the government by producing a "redacted" report in February 2019 – which withheld critical information on "commercial details" like pricing of the fighter jets that would have nailed corruption. A redacted report from the top government auditor, the CAG? The CAG had exposed the corruption in the Bofors deal, the 2G spectrum and coal block allocations and Commonwealth Games.

This was unprecedent and a new low for the CAG.

Even curiouser is the case with the Supreme Court.

It had, in December 2018, given a clean chit to the government by citing the CAG report which came two months later in February 2019. One of its prime arguments (apart from hand-off approach in "national security" matters) was: "The pricing details have, however, been shared with the Comptroller and Auditor General, and the report of the CAG has been examined by the Public Accounts Committee. Only a redacted portion of the report was placed before the Parliament, and is in public domain."

This argument was a reproduction of what the government had given in "sealed cover" affidavit – not open to the appellant or public and hence against all tenets of natural justice. When the order was out, the obvious lies were nailed: (a) the CAG had not yet produced its findings and made it public and (b) there was no question of the PAC examining a non-existent CAG report. The government ran to the court seeking modification in the argument taking plea that the court had misinterpreted its facts.

The court not only obliged but later when its order giving a clean chit to the government without probe or trial were challenged, it rejected all such review petitions. In normal times, misleading the court would have attracted immediate criminal contempt proceedings against the government or a severe censure; the hearings would have started afresh and more likely than not, filing of FIR and probe would have been ordered. In normal times, the CAG would have faced public humiliation.

But that wasn't the normal time. None of it happened. None dared to speak.

Apr 4, 2022

***

Why MGNREGS Wages are Below the Statutory Minimum

Not only have its wages been delinked from the statutory minimum after 2014, a parliamentary panel flags a general lackadaisical attitude in ensuring a fair treatment.

Ever wondered why the centrally sponsored rural job guarantee scheme MGNREGS work pays below the statutory minimum wages and continues to violate the Supreme Court order of 1983 (Sanjit Roy vs Rajasthan case) which said "the State cannot be permitted to take advantage of the helpless condition of the affected persons and extract labour or service from them on payment of less than the minimum wage"?

Enough insight has been provided in latest parliamentary standing committee report, which did a "critical evaluation" of the scheme and was tabled just after the budget in February this year.

Indexing MGNREGS against inflation

The panel's report devotes pages after pages to discusses why the Consumer Price Index-Rural (CPI-R) has not been used in place of Consumer Price Index-Agricultural Labour (CPI-AL) for indexation of wages under the MGNREGS for the past seven years. At least two government appointed committees, starting with 2015, have recommended this.

But this a relatively minor issue; the major one is about denying the statutory minimum wages to the MGNREGS workers, which violates the letter and spirit the MGNREG Act of 2005 and also violates the Supreme Court order of 1983. However, before getting there, here is a brief background and what the parliament panel's report tells.

In 2009, the MGNREGS wage was first indexed against the CPI-AL. The Mahendra Dev committee set up in 2013 to look at the wages afresh, recommended in its 2015 report that the wages should be indexed against CPI-R instead, since CPI-AL and CPI-RL (Consumer Price Index-Rural Labour) were outdated, based as they are on the 1983 household consumption expenditure survey of the NSSO.

The Nagesh Singh committee, which was set up in 2017 to take another fresh look at the MGNREGS wages, endorsed it, explaining why. It said: "In CPI-AL and CPI-RL, food beverages and tobacco account for over 70% of the consumption basket. In CPI-Rural, they account for only 59%. CPI-Rural also provided for higher expenditure on education, medical care, and transport and communication."

That is, CPI-AL/CPI-RL is heavy on food while CPI-R takes into consideration other expenditures, such as on education, health, transport and communication, etc. At the time (in 2017), the ministry of rural development (MoRD) estimated that such a shift from CPI-AL to CPI-R would cost Rs 624 crore.

That (Rs 624 crore) would have been a gain for the MGNREGS workers.

The parliamentary panel says Ministry of Rural

Development (MoRD), the administrative ministry for MGNREGS, accepted the Nagesh Singh committee recommendation and wrote to the Ministry of Finance (MoF) for approval. The MoF took nearly two years to approve it in February 2019.

The MoRD then started the process of revising the MGNREGS wages accordingly (for each state) and sent letters and reminders (a) to the Ministry of Statistics and Program Implementation (MoSPI) "to provide the information whether the base year revision of Consumer Price Index-Rural is under consideration" and (b) to the Ministry of Labour and Employment (MoL&E) "to confirm the status on revision of base year Consumer Price Index-Agricultural Labour". Apparently, no response was received from either until the next two years.

Then in October 2021, a "deliberation" was held between the MoRD, MoSPI and MoL&E, following which it was decided that no change will be made and the indexation against CPI-AL would continue. No explanation was offered for this to the parliamentary panel, nor did the panel ask any.

What did the parliament panel finally recommend at the end of these deliberations?

It expressed concern about "low wage rates" of MGNREGS, pointed out that it had been telling the MoRD to index the wages against CPI-R for years, and then "strongly" recommended the same again. All this without demanding, strong or weak, explanations.

The panel's second key recommendation was to bring uniformity in the wage rates among states, which vary widely.

As pointed out earlier, the panel maintains silence on the payment of minimum wages to the MGNREGS workers, although the issue figured briefly and the MoRD dismissed it — the reason for which will become clear soon.

Why no minimum wage for MGNREGS work?

It is often misunderstood that the UPA government, which brought in the MGNREG Act of 2005 and under which the scheme is run, had deliberately delinked the MGNREGS wages (unskilled manual labour) from the statutory minimum wages of states (agricultural wage for unskilled labour).

Section 6 of the MGNREG Act of 2005 spells out the wage rates. It says (1) the central government can notify its own rates, notwithstanding what contains in the Minimum Wages Act of 1948 that states follow and (2) that until the central government fixes separate rates for the MGNREGS workers, the minimum statutory rates fixed by states under the Minimum Wages Act of 1948 "shall be considered as the wage rate applicable to that area".

From 2006 to 2009, the central government followed section 6(2) of the law and the statutory minimum wages of states were taken as the official MGNREGS wage rates. In 2009, section 6(1) was invoked and separate MGNREGS wages were prescribed at Rs 100 or more for all states.

Here is a catch.

In 2009, most states had statutory minimum wages below Rs 100. Only four states had more than Rs 100 – Goa (Rs 110), Haryana (Rs 141), Mizoram (Rs 110) and Kerala (Rs 125). Thus, the 2009 notification of new wage rates allowed these states to retain their higher rates of more than Rs 100 and allowed other states to give Rs 100 to the

MGNREGS workers (their own statutory rates were less than Rs 100), except three states – Arunachal Pradesh (Rs 80), Odisha (Rs 90) and Jharkhand (Rs 99). In 2011, the fresh notification took into consideration the wage differences in states, particularly those with higher than Rs 100, while indexing with CPI-AL.

So, both the 2009 and 2011 notifications were in good faith and ensured the statutory minimum wages for the MGNREGS workers.

Then in 2013, the Mahendra Dev committee was set up by the UPA government to take a fresh look at the wages. Its first recommendation was: "The baseline for MGNREGA wage indexation from 2014 may be the current minimum wage rate for unskilled agricultural labourers fixed by the States under the Minimum Wages Act or the current MGNREGA wage rate, whichever is higher."

That is, the base wage rates of the MGNREGS works would be higher one of the two – the centrally notified ones and the statutory minimum rates of states – for indexation (inflation proofing) purpose. Its second recommendation was for indexing the wages with CPI-R.

The MoRD accepted the committee's recommendations but the MoF rejected citing the fiscal burden involved. Then the government set up the Nagesh Singh committee of 2017 which rejected statutory minimum wages (for agricultural labour) for the MGNREGS workers on three grounds:

(i) There is a major difference in the work done by the agricultural labour and that of the MGNREGS workers. The wage rate for agricultural labour is "basically a time rate", while that under MGNREGS is "piece rate".

(ii) It is extremely difficult to align the two rates because of wide variations in the schedule of rates (SORs) across states.

(iii) No discrimination exists between male and female worker wage rates under the MGNREGS, while it does in the case of minimum wages for agricultural workers (women get less than men).

The committee concluded that in view of the above three it felt "there is no compelling argument for convergence of minimum wages for agricultural labour and wages notified for NREGA workers in view of the differences in activities performed by these two sets of workers".

Of the three reasons, the third one is truly bizarre. Why should the MGNREGS workers be penalised for not discriminating between men and women in payment of wages?

As mentioned earlier, the central government was too happy to endorse the Nagesh Singh committee report (it delinked from the statutory minimum wages) but hasn't implemented its other recommendations regarding indexing the MGNREGS wages to CPI-R and bringing uniformity to wages across states for the past five years or has offered any explanation for not doing this to the parliamentary panel.

Short-changing MGNREGS workers

As a result of denying the statutory minimum wages, the MGNREGS workers have lost a great deal. A national daily estimated that in the pandemic years of 2020 and 2021 alone, the MGNREGS workers were short-changed by Rs 42,000 crore (the difference between their wages and that of the minimum agricultural wages of corresponding states).

The daily estimated this by using the official data provided by the MGNREGS' website and the notified minimum statutory wages of states – something the MoRD hasn't been able to do. The MoRD told the parliamentary panel that "the details of minimum wage currently applicable within the states is being collected and will be furnished as soon as available".

In addition to not giving the statutory minimum wages, the central government short-changes the MGNREGS workers by giving negligible hike in wages (by way of indexing it against CPI-AL) – from Rs 0-3 for most states to Rs 8-10 in very rare cases. About the 2021-22 MGNREGS wage rates notified by the central government, civil rights group NREGA Sangharsh Morcha commented: "There is no increase in Kerala's NREGA wage rate. Rajasthan's wage rate has increased by just Rs 1. In fact, for 24 states, the increase in the NREGA wage rate is less than 5%." Similar has been the case in previous years after 2014.

Because of this discriminatory approach, the difference in the MGREGS wages rates for states has widened sharply. For example, the wage rates for FY22 varies from Rs 193 for Chhattisgarh and Madhya Pradesh and Rs 198 for Bihar and Jharkhand to Rs 269 for Punjab, Rs 291 for Kerala, Rs 315 in Haryana and Rs 318 in three-gram panchayats of Sikkim. Rest all states/UTs fall between Rs 200 to Rs 300 bracket (majority remaining below Rs 250, the parliamentary panel tells.

The MGNREGS web site shows the average all-India wage rate is Rs 209 for FY22, rising slowly from Rs 200.7 in FY21, Rs 182 in FY20, Rs 179 in FY19, Rs 169 in FY18, Rs 161.7 in FY17, Rs 154 in FY16 and Rs 143.9 in FY15.

The gap between the MGNREGS and statutory

minimum rates has widened too.

For example, in Kerala, the statutory minimum (agricultural) wage is Rs 410, against its MGNREGS rate of Rs 315; for Punjab it is Rs 369 against the MGNREGS rate of Rs 291 and for Haryana it is Rs 377 against the MGNREGS rate of Rs 315. As pointed out earlier, the MGNREGS rates for states are fixed by the central government every year.

This difference worked out to Rs 42,000 crore in the pandemic year of 2020 and 2021 — as a national daily estimated (mentioned earlier).

No unemployment allowance either

There is yet another key issue which is seldom discussed or highlighted: payment of unemployment allowance to those seeking MGNREGS work but finding no job within 15 days — a statutory requirement.

The parliamentary panel reports that in FY22, not a pie has been given as unemployment allowance (until November 15, 2021). In FY21, the unemployment allowance paid was Rs 3,000; in FY20 it was Rs 12,000; for FY19 it was Rs 63,000 and for FY18 it was Rs 2.82 lakh — progressively less and less is paid.

This is when the gap between the demand and supply of MGNREGS work remains very high year after year. For example, in FY22 (as on March 24, 2022), the unmet demand is 11% for households and 23% for individuals.

While discussing this at the parliamentary panel's meetings, the MoRD passed the buck to states. To this, the panel used strong words to pan.

It said: "...the Committee cannot decipher the role of the nodal agency, the Department of Rural Development in this regard merely 'passing the buck' and moving one's face in the opposite direction. This approach can not at all justify the inaction and callous methods of the Central Ministry regarding such a key provision.

"The Scheme is a Centrally Sponsored Scheme with all its modalities being supervised by the Department of Rural Development. In such scenario, the role of nodal agency is definitely of paramount importance and any inaction shows it in very poor light. Therefore, the Committee, while taking very strong notice of the dire situation firmly call upon the Department of Rural Development to shed its lackadaisical manner and ensure that the provision of MGNREG Act, 2005 do not remain unheeded but are implemented in true 'letter and spirit' on the ground level."

One can safely assume that the situation wouldn't be different the next time the parliamentary panel takes up the MGNREGS.

Mar 24, 2022

***

Why Do Employed Youth Hanker after Government Jobs?

Private sector jobs are now more insecure with liberal contractual appointments and hire-and-fire provisions, job and wage cuts and ever growing abysmally low-paying gig work.

Last week, BJP president JP Nadda made a statement while talking about high unemployment in Uttar Pradesh. It attracted less attention than it deserves and hence, needs to be recalled: "Even if one is earning Rs 50,000, one considers oneself unemployed as people want a government job... They get registered at the employment exchange. So, the number (of unemployed) goes up, but the person is earning."

This is unlike that of Rajiv Kumar, Niti Aayog vice chairman, who said about the job crisis in March 2021: "The government's approach has been to focus on the drivers of employment rather than generating some part-time employment in the public sector, except the MGNREGA."

Or that of central minister Piyush Goyal who, in response to businessman Sunil Mittal's comment at a conclave in 2017 that India's top 200 companies had made "significant" reduction in their workforce: "What Sunil just spoke about companies bringing down their employment is a very good sign, in fact. The fact (is) that today, the youth of tomorrow is not looking to be a job seeker alone. He wants to be a job creator. The country today is seeing more and more young people wanting to be entrepreneurs."

Or even that of Prime Minister Narendra Modi who answered job crisis during a TV interview in 2018 thus: "If a person selling pakodas earns 200 at the end of the day, will it be considered employment or not?"

Why are youth hankering after government job?

On the face of it Nadda's answer may seem hyperbolic but actually it isn't. He is closer to truth. Consider what CMIE's Mahesh Vyas, who alone tracks the state of employment on monthly basis, wrote in a column on March 1, 2022. Talking about the state of unemployment in the quarter ended December 2021: "Interestingly, about 1 per cent of the unemployed said that their nature of occupation was that of a salaried employee. More interestingly, in the critical lockdown quarter of April-June 2020, nearly 8 per cent of the unemployed said that their nature of occupation was salaried employees."

Vyas didn't explain why the unemployed were saying they were "salaried employees". He didn't have to; it is known and it is what Nadda was pointing to.

For the record, salaried or regular wage jobs are the best kind of jobs available in India. They are the best paying, regular and some (though not most) get social security too. All the rest kinds of jobs are precarious: self-employed and casual labour. When the pandemic hit, the worst hit were the self-employed and casual workers, not the salaried or regular wage workers. But salaried/regular wage workers are very few. They constituted only 23-24% of all workers between 2017-18 and 2019-20, as per the PLFS reports.

So, why should a salaried employee report as unemployed?

Nadda gave the answer: They are looking for government jobs.

Why should they look for government job when they are earning good money (as Nadda said)? Until and unless this question is understood and addressed the hankering after government jobs will continue. Here is why.

High precarity of private sector jobs

Private sector jobs pay better than government jobs, although the gap has reduced after several Pay Commission awards were implemented in recent decades, and provides social security too (though not assured pension like government jobs did until 2004). And private sector jobs can be highly satisfying too. So, what has gone wrong?

The answers are known for a long too but not admitted in public or addressed through policy interventions: no job security; falling jobs and salaries/wages and in most cases, missing social security cover. The delivery and logistics unicorns are the new toasts of the town but how much do gig workers (delivery boys and girls) they employ earn? Even the multinational ones pay as little as Rs 10,000 a month, sparking multiple protests in recent time. This is less than the minimum wages (per day rate multiplied with 30 since casual workers don't get paid weekly non-working day) in the states of Kerala (Rs 410), Haryana (Rs 377) and Punjab (Rs 369). Fortune India reported how the income of gig workers is on a long-term decline due to decrease in rate cards and incentives.

High priority to flexibility in hiring people on contracts and liberal use of hire-and-fire have also turned private sector jobs highly precarious. The best kind of contract jobs are for a period of three years but a contract employee can be fired at any time within this period with one to three months of notice and the job ends, if the contract is not renewed, at the end of the contract period.

Besides, the pandemic crisis has seen corporate India record historic profits while cutting jobs and wages, as CMIE reported last year. That private sector has been shedding jobs for long is clear from Mittal›s 2017 assertion mentioned earlier. Even before that, the UPA era of 2004-2014 was infamous for job-less growth while India witnessed all-time high growth – annual average GDP growth of 6.8% (2011-12 series, constant prices). It turned into job-loss growth between 2011-12 and 2017-18, as the PLFS of 2017-18 had shown (net loss of 9 million jobs) 9 million jobs. This massive job loss, the study said, «happened for the first time in India›s history».

Liberalised contract jobs and hire-and-fire laws

At 176, the national minimum wage remains unchanged for years and is less than half of Kerala (410), Haryana (377) and Punjab (369). Instead of addressing the precarity of private sector workers, the new labour codes worsened it.

To facilitate contract work, the Industrial Relation Code of 2020 (IR Code) introduced Fixed Term Employment (FTE), ostensibly to ensure social security for such employees, but it (a) took away the possibility of such employment turning permanent after three months – which the Industrial Employment (Standing Orders) Act of 1946 had provided and (b) undid the gazette notification of

March 2018, which introduced the FTE in India for the first time and ruled out the possibility of permanent jobs being converted to contract jobs.

India borrowed the idea of FTE from Europe, which used it as a stepping stone for young and raw hands to establish their suitability for permanent employment but has already found that the transition to permanent job has fallen, a duality has been created in labour market with high wage difference and the duration of contract has dramatically shortened, in some cases like Spain to less than a week.

The new IR Code also makes arbitrary hire-and-fire easier by increasing the threshold for protections. This has been done by increasing the threshold of applicability of Standing Orders from industrial establishments with 100 workers or more to 300 workers or more. Standing Orders provide for employer to "define" the conditions of employment, explain every transgression and grievance redressal mechanism in cases of violation of the defined conditions.

The expansion of threshold means more workers become vulnerable to arbitrary hire and fire because Indian labour laws don't have "written contract" as legal requirement, which could provide some protection or possibility of seeking redressal, except for the FTE introduced in the new IR Code. Contract work is widely prevalent, has existed for decades and forms a big chunk of job markets – both private and government sectors even without FTE. The PLFS of 2019-20 says, even among the best category of jobs, that is salaried/regular wage employment, 67.3% don't have written contracts. They have little legal protection.

All these factors have made private jobs highly precarious. No wonder, youth employed in salaried/regular wage employment in private sector desperately seek government jobs – which Nadda left unsaid.

'Temporisation' of government jobs

What should dishearten those youth (employed but hankering after government jobs) more is that the Centre is not only cutting down the sanctioned posts, it is also increasingly relying on contract and temporary jobs (not permanent, regular or secure jobs). For this, it is emphasising on rehiring retired employees, for a period of 1-5 years.

The Centre stopped publishing data on organised sector workers after 2012. The only study that provides some idea of the hiring trends in the government sector is of 2014 and by Indian Staffing Federation (ISF), apex body representing the staffing industry.

It listed three key devastating findings:

(i) 43% government sector jobs (Central, state, PSUs and local bodies) were temporary by the end of 2013.

(ii) 2/3rd of the incremental formal workforce was temporary, with 80% of them in casual jobs.

(iii) Professionals and high-skilled workers form a substantial chunk of casual and short-term contract employment.

It concluded: "Overall hiring is in the decline in the government sector, along with increasing temporisation."

All the above three developments would have worsened by now, going by the increasing tilt towards temporary hiring and growing vacancies.

Coming back to Nadda's statement, it should be taken more seriously by the governments at the Centre and states and prepare appropriate policy responses, rather than use it to mask the obvious failures of successive governments.

Mar 2, 2022

***

Why High GST Collection is Bad Taxation and Bad Economics

The hype over high GST collection hides the falling corporate tax and rising oil tax, both of which put higher burden on the poor, keep consumption demand low and drag growth down

Amidst the looming threat of Omicron, December 2021 brought cheers as the GST collections crossed the magic mark of Rs 1 lakh crore (at Rs 1.3 lakh crore) for the sixth time in November, out of eight months of the current fiscal (FY22), and raised hopes for faster economic recovery.

This was indeed a welcome development for the government short of fiscal resources, except it perpetuates a regressive tax regime in which indirect tax, like the GST, plays a dominant role in total tax revenue. In contrast, developed nations collect most tax revenues from direct tax. As per the latest data, the OECD average for direct tax collection in 2018 (close to India's FY19) was 67.3% of the total tax collection, while for India, it was 38.3% (for FY19).

Here is a comparative picture of India's tax revenue collections in FY22.

The total GST collection (Centre and states combined) for April-October 2021 was Rs 8 lakh crore (if the November collection is added, the total goes up to Rs 9.4 lakh crore). The

Controller General of Accounts (CGA) data shows, during the same period (April-October 2021) direct tax – corporate and income tax from non-corporate entities – amounted to Rs 6.4 lakh crore. This calculation ignores other indirect taxes like customs, excise, service tax and others and hence, the difference between direct and indirect tax collection is much wider.

Here is another way of presenting the regressive tax system.

Taking all direct and indirect taxes together, the long-term trend (Centre and states combined) shows the annual average of direct tax revenue was 6.6% of the GDP during the past decade of FY12-FY21. In the same period, the annual average of indirect tax was far higher at 10.6% of the GDP.

High indirect tax collection is regressive because indirect tax doesn't distinguish between the rich and poor (capacity to pay) as everyone pays the same tax rates. On the contrary, direct tax is on the income levels/profits and is thus based on the ability-to-pay principle of taxation. When direct taxes fall, tax burden shifts to the poor – as we will see later.

Corporate tax falls below income tax

FY21 will not only be remembered for historic high corporate profits but also for falling behind income tax from non-corporate entities for the first time in the 2011-12 GDP series.

The Budget documents show, in FY21 (RE), corporate tax collection fell to Rs 4.5 lakh crore (23.5% of the gross tax revenue), while that of 'tax on income other than corporate tax' went up to Rs 4.6 lakh crore (24.2% of the gross tax revenue).

The drastic fall in corporate tax had begun with the corporate tax cut of Rs 1.45 lakh crore of September 2019. In FY20, corporate tax collection went down by 16% from FY19 (from Rs 6.6 lakh crore to Rs 5.6 lakh crore). The trend will continue in FY22 (BE) as corporate tax is budgeted to yield Rs 5.5 lakh crore (24.7% of the gross tax) as against Rs 5.6 lakh crore from tax on income other than corporate tax.

This is problematic because it has pulled down the total tax revenue the government needs for higher fiscal spending. Besides, lower corporate tax is regressive for the reason explained earlier. Corporate entities are financially bigger entities with more capacity to pay, while tax on income other than corporate tax is paid by relatively lesser mortals, like individuals (salaried or self-employed), partnership firms, trusts etc.

Tax burden shifts to poor

What happens when direct tax, like corporate tax, go down?

Indirect taxes go up.

Apart from the high GST collections, there is yet another indicator of it: high oil tax. The Petroleum Planning and Analysis Cell (PPAC) data shows, the central government has collected Rs 19.6 lakh crore from oil taxes from FY15 to Q1 of FY22. Of this, Excise and Cess alone amount to Rs 17.4 lakh crore. During this period, the crude price (Brent) has fallen drastically. From over $100/barrel before FY15 (in FY12, FY13 and FY14), the crude price fell to annual average of $58.5 during FY15-FY21. In April and May 2021 (FY22), it has gone over $60/barrel.

How does the government justify high oil tax?

Finance Minister Nirmala Sitharaman said it was because of the "trickery" of the UPA government, which cut taxes but left huge oil bonds for the Modi government to pay. Truth is completely different and is linked to the massive corporate tax cut of Rs 1.45 lakh crore that her government announced amidst fiscal resource crunch.

The UPA government had kept the oil prices low and balanced it by issuing oil bonds when the crude price was skyrocketing (the previous Vajpayee government also followed the same policy). Budget documents reveal that when the Modi government took over in May 2014 (FY15), the total outstanding on oil bonds stood at Rs 1.3 lakh crore.

How much has the government paid off? It paid Rs 3,500 crore in FY15 and Rs 10,000 crore in FY22 towards the principal amount. Plus, it has paid interests of 9,989.86 crore every year, which amounts to Rs 79,918.9 crore between FY15 and FY22. The total comes to Rs 93,418.9 crore.

So, as against oil bond outgo of Rs 93,418.9 crore until FY22, the government has already collected Rs 19.6 lakh crore in oil tax until Q1 of FY22 – that is an excess of Rs 18.6 lakh crore or 20 times more!

Why high oil tax is a burden on the poor?

The poor not only use more petrol and diesel, they are also burdened with inflation that high oil prices bring. This was revealed by a study conducted by the PPAC (through Nielsen) in 2014. The study showed (a) 99.6% of petrol is used by the transport sector, of which 61.4% petrol is consumed by two-wheelers and 2.3% by three-wheelers, as against 34.3% by cars (b) 13% diesel is consumed by agriculture and (c) 70% of diesel is consumed by the transport sector.

While the first is a direct burden on the poor, the second (agriculture) and third (transport sector) add to their cost of food and other essential items (transported) and travel (by bus and train).

To sum up, low corporate tax and low direct tax means the tax burden shifts to the poor as the government needs more resources for its fiscal spending. The pandemic has disproportionately hurt the poor by way of higher loss of lives, jobs and businesses and the impact is visible in low consumption demand in the economy. Going forward, a sluggish demand will continue to drag down growth. Therefore, it makes immense economic sense to reverse the regressive taxation regime in India, apart from other measures to tackle the systemic slowdown.

Dec 28, 2021

***

Index

Amrit Kaal, *54-60*
Auditors *148, 278-83*
AT1 bond *298-05*
Banking frauds *147-8, 204-5, 215-20, 246-7, 265-7, 325*
Big 5 *68, 289, 262*
CAG *82, 90*
Caste *22, 415, 420*
China *15, 50, 58-9, 76-7, 104, 123, 179, 206, 221-2, 235-40, 274-6, 307, 354-60, 444*
Chandrayaan *184-90*
Compromise settlement *205, 217-8, 246-7, 263-8*
COP27 and COP28 *125-34, 377-83*
Command-and-control *200-6*
Data privacy *35-6, 207-14*
Demonetisation *241-45, 247, 330, 348-53*
Dharavi *228-34*
Dolo-650 *392-9*
Drugs *32, 392-9*
Electoral Bond *28-36, 438-9*
EWS quota *415-20*
FCRA *433-41*
Gig economy *361-366, 458, 460*
Global Systemically Important Bank *311-8*
GM Mustard *367-76*
GST *465-9*
Hindenburg *112-7, 319-26*
Job crisis *109, 187, 341-7, 408-14, 415-420, 458-64*
Hunger *16, 98, 198*
Inequality *16, 45, 57-9, 359, 384-91, 378, 421-6*

Israel *15, 72, 108-9, 208, 214*
Kartavya Kaal *11, 60*
MGNREGS *74-5, 386, 426, 449-57*
MSP *62-70*
NGO-FCRA *433-41*
NPA *205, 215-20, 246-7, 263-8*
NYAY/UBI *170, 425-6*
Privatisation *82, 93, 337*
PPP *426-32*
Predatory pricing *256-62, 284-90, 309*
Poverty *37-45, 192-99, 354-60*
Rafale jets *442-8*
RBI *118-24, 215-20, 241-8, 263-8*
Revdi, revdi culture *135-42, 169-76*
SBI *30-5, 39-44, 163-65, 218, 241-8*
SEBI *112-7, 278-83, 301-2, 319-26*
Seller's inflation *256-62, 284-90*
Semiconductor *221-7*
Shell companies/Tax havens *29-30, 70, 86, 143, 151, 327-33*
Short-selling *112-7, 319-26*
Stock market *112-7, 152, 311-33,*
Trade *182, 291-97*
VGF *259, 427, 430-2*
Viksit Bharat @2047 *54-61*
Willful defaulters *205, 215-20, 246-7, 263-8*

Black Eagle Books

www.blackeaglebooks.org
info@blackeaglebooks.org

Black Eagle Books, an independent publisher, was founded as a nonprofit organization in April, 2019. It is our mission to connect and engage the Indian diaspora and the world at large with the best of works of world literature published on a collaborative platform, with special emphasis on foregrounding Contemporary Classics and New Writing.

www.ingramcontent.com/pod-product-compliance
Lightning Source LLC
Chambersburg PA
CBHW020405040426
42333CB00055B/405